FREUD AND NIETZSCHE

FREUD AND NIETZSCHE

PAUL-LAURENT ASSOUN

Translated by
RICHARD L. COLLIER, JR

continuum
LONDON • NEW YORK
www.continuumbooks.com

CONTINUUM

The Tower Building, 11 York Road, London SE1 7NX
370 Lexington Avenue, New York, NY 10017-6503
www.continuumbooks.com

This English translation first published in 2000
by The Athlone Press
This paperback edition first published in 2002 by Continuum

Publisher's Note
The publishers wish to record their thanks to the French Ministry of Culture
for a grant towards the cost of translation.

British Library Cataloguing in Publication Data
A catalogue record for this book is available from the British Library
ISBN 0-8264-6316-9

Library of Congress Cataloging-in-Publication Data
Assoun, Paul-Laurent, 1948-
[Freud et Nietzsche. English]
Freud and Nietzsche / Paul-Laurent Assoun; translated by Richard L. Collier, Jr.
p. cm.
Includes bibliographical references (p.) and index.
ISBN 0-8264-6316-9 (pbk)
1. Nietzsche, Friedrich Wilhelm, 1844-1900. 2. Freud, Sigmund, 1856-1939. 3. Psychoanalysis and philosophy–History. I. Title.

B3317.A7813 2000
193–dc21 00-038946

Printed and bound in Great Britain by
Biddles Ltd, Guildford and King's Lynn

CONTENTS

TRANSLATOR'S PREFACE

> this art does not so easily get anything done, it teaches us to read well, that is to say, to read slowly, deeply, looking cautiously before and aft, with reservations, with doors left open, with delicate eyes and fingers
>
> Nietzsche, *Daybreak*[1]

It is always a treat to see a master artisan at work, carefully fashioning the products of her labour. We come away with an appreciation not only of the product, but also of the processes involved in its production. As the recipient of the Bordin Prize in 1981 from the French Academy, the present text is no exception, equally valuable for what it says as for how it says it. A few points will highlight the processes of production demonstrated here, and hopefully will provide the reader with an informed base that enriches the reading experience.

For the reader of the English language, an understanding of the present study is complicated by the fact that, when originally published, this was the third work in a trilogy that began with *Freud, la philosophie et les philosophes*, followed by *Marx et la répétition historique*. This note will also try to set out some of the themes that subtend the trilogy, and to aid in understanding the status of the analysis presented here, in the context of Paul-Laurent Assoun's multi-volume *paleontology* of contemporary thought.

For Assoun, there are really three figures that constitute the universe of contemporary Western thought, Marx, Freud and Nietzsche, rough contemporaries who, beginning from more or less the *same* epistemological base, mark out three distinct fields, and provide us with a sort of menu of three basic theoretical 'choices', or rather starting points, that raise impressive, if deceptive, analogies, which in turn have spawned entire industries of synthetic work probing the points of contact between any pair. There, we can find combinations of Freud and Nietzsche, or Freud and Marx, alongside Nietzsche-inspired Marxians and Marx-inspired Nietzscheans. And some of us stand in the middle of this cloverleaf of interchanges and entry ramps, fascinated and bewildered by the circulation of traffic between and through the loops, by the complexity of the various *topoi* extending to the horizon, unable or unwilling to choose one or the other yet drawn to and wanting to explore all three directions at once.

Assoun is acutely aware of this difficult position, and so we first see him, in the context of his trilogy, standing in the Marx loop pondering 'Freud and Nietzsche.' At that distance, the analogies are suggestive, even seductive, in their resonance. To examine those analogies closely, though, means standing in the Freud loop and analysing Nietzsche, and then reversing the perspective, at successively complex conceptual levels (principle, theme, stake), all the while keeping in mind the point of origin.

Briefly speaking, the first book, *Freud, la philosophie et les philosophes*, constructs the philosophical topography from which Freud drew insight and/or inspiration. The importance of the project lies not only in terms of mapping an epistemological field regarding the founder of psychoanalysis, but also in demystifying Freud's self-declared aversion to philosophy and, generally, to those who philosophize. *Marx et la répétition historique* analyses Marx's historical dialectic, in particular the idea of repetition as a phenomenon, or a condition. The present study sets the work of Freud and Nietzsche in a complex and nuanced dialectic that shuttles not only back and forth between the two proper names, but also back and forth through each author's work, professional and personal experiences, and even reading habits. Since its original publication, however, Assoun has been busy extending his study of Freud. The important Preface to the 1998 reissue of *Freud and Nietzsche*, included here, highlights the results of that ongoing study, although it may be useful to the reader to re-visit that 'preface' as an 'afterword' upon reading the complete text.

In the present study, Assoun's preliminary perspective challenges the very idea of conjoining two names, or two bodies of theory, on the basis of apparent analogies or 'rhetorical similitudes.'

> Our project will set out from the principle that we can legitimately suspect of being 'bad alloys' every conjunction of proper names which is satisfied by a seductive resonance without relating it to the less timely expression of problematics that at once make the resonance possible and permit the distribution of such honors and equivocations.

With this declaration, Assoun sets out on an amazing intellectual adventure, an impressive example of the type of 'compare and contrast' writing we were taught, and not very well, in grade school.

What does it mean to say 'Freud and Nietzsche'? Furthermore, what does it mean that for almost all of the twentieth century, we have in fact been saying 'Freud and Nietzsche'? These questions frame the present study, but the responses to the questions follow a complicated path, for Assoun quickly reveals that to say 'Freud and Nietzsche' is not at all the same thing as saying 'Nietzsche and Freud.' The conjunction itself constitutes a problem that needs to be understood and analysed, *as a problem*. In fact, in the 1998 preface, Assoun goes so far as to suggest that the stakes underlying the conjunction 'Freud and Nietzsche' extend to another, seemingly impossible conjunction, 'psychoanalysis and philosophy.'

It is, then, not a matter of an inclusive 'and', whereby the two names are set in a sort of orbit around a common terrain, like apples and oranges around the global construct of 'fruit'. What resonates, Assoun tells us, may still differ in tone. The 'and' in fact marks two conjunctions; two kinds of modality, and historicity, are involved. The first equation sets Freud and Nietzsche in a mode of linear time, amid allegations of Nietzsche as Freud's precursor; in the second, however, Freud and Nietzsche are set in parallel universes which, in the context of the history of ideas, begin from a more or less common base of knowledge but yield two widely disparate fields that seem to encroach upon each other at several points, but with different stakes and therapeutic aims. In a way, the second equation treats Nietzsche as Freud's *contemporary* or, in the words of the 1998 preface, his *colleague*. In the first section of the study, 'Freud and Nietzsche,' Assoun composes the history of Freud's encounters with Nietzsche, both via Freud's own personal reading and interpretation, and through an astonishing array of mediators and champions of Nietzsche. In the second section, 'Nietzsche and Freud,' Assoun demystifies an extensive set of analogies and homologies whose surface readings suggest remarkable affinities between the two theorists.

Having done that, though, Assoun's surprising conclusion displaces the stakes of the whole study in two directions. In the direction of methodology, the question all along has been one of the status of knowledge, and the contributions that a dialectical study of non-dialectical theoretical fields (for Freud and Nietzsche both strongly reject closure and the construction of systems) can make. In the second, theoretical direction, the issue subtending the entire study has been that of the material status of drives and desire, in other words, the status of the *subject*. How do these ostensibly unconscious regimes figure in our material reality? Here, we should bear in mind that the present study is the third work in a trilogy. The last part of the conclusion to this study, then, really addresses all three works, and closes the series. The notation providing continuity throughout the series is the gentle appearance of a handful of reference notes and, even gentler, the spectre of Karl Marx.

It is important to recognize that Marx is always present in this text, though in remarkably subtle ways. Marx's name only appears in the notes in two places, in connection with the names of Heine and Reich. His name appears only once in the text, at the very end, though in a manner that is quite provocative. Assoun is summarizing his study; he says that Freud and Nietzsche have given two very different readings of the material nature of the drives, *whose traces Marx has pointed to in his own way*. At the end of this study, Assoun reminds us of where we were at the beginning of it, and in a way where we have been all along.

We have constantly kept close to the problem, perhaps an impossible one, with which the theory of the subject must be explained; it is the question of materiality itself and of the status of the drives and desire as a posture of materiality. As originally published, the problem was one *with which materialist theory must be explained*. 'Materialist theory' was a nod to Marx, a debt owed to Marx. Yet it turns out that neither Freud nor Nietzsche can be used to 'complete' Marx, nor can either be 'completed' by Marx. None of these three proper names identifies the figure of the Law. In the passage between the two publications of this text, materialism came to be displaced/renamed by the eminently anthropological category of subjectivity. Nihilism, neurosis and false consciousness comprise three distinct diagnostic readings, three bodies of thought, of *bodies*. Who, or what, is this *subject* thus referenced?

In Marx it is not always clear how a non-false consciousness arises in the proletariat, how unconscious drives and/or desire can manifest themselves in positive social change. With Freud and Nietzsche, on the other hand, it is not at all clear what would happen if, along either of these two paths, a collective consciousness were to result. What would happen if society consisted exclusively of cured beings, or of *Übermenschen*? An impossible question, perhaps, but no less valid for being so. Does not one of Freud's last writings include in its title the words *analysis interminable*, indicating the impossibility of a total cure, and does not Nietzsche expect Overman *in the future*, an arrival interminably deferred? Marx's proletariat also rises in the future, *at the end of history*. A common set of questions confronts us. How will we *know* when we get there? How do we *know* where 'there' is? Who is this 'we', anyhow? For Marx, Nietzsche and Freud, wherever one starts, one ends up in anthropology!

Assoun declares that the real stake, arching over the study like a parabola, has been a question of the status of knowledge. The apparent convergences and divergences between Freud and Nietzsche reveal two distinct treatments of drives, desire and also of knowledge (as an eminently social construction), for there are two visions of what constitutes human society or 'civilization' and each individual's relation to that aggregate. Both having considered society as 'the' problem, the two theorists pose radically different therapeutics that mark distinct positions of the individual with regard to the social unity. Where Freud seeks to reintegrate the individual in the social, thus in a way making her free *in* society, Nietzsche poses a struggle to be free *of* society. Where the former seeks to come to terms with the moral order, and so validate it, the latter would destroy the present moral order, if only to replace it with another morality.

So it cannot be a question of taking the Freudian cure at first, to create a necessary space from which to engage in a Nietzschean therapeutic, nor can it be one of following Nietzsche in the construction of a new morality, only to require a Freud to integrate individuals into *that* moral order. To make matters worse, from Marx's perspective it could be said that, paradoxically, Freud correctly formulated the therapeutic while botching the diagnosis, whereas Nietzsche identified the real problem but applied an untenable cure. Or just the reverse. It is a puzzle of contradictions and complications that cannot be resolved in the type of dialectic taught to us by Hegel.

Freud and Nietzsche *sketch the contradictory modality by which a theory of drives can make a contribution as a non-dialectical theory, and which merits being fully considered, and understood, from a dialectical point of view*. We know that, where Marx tried to rescue the dialectic from a Hegelian perversion, both Freud and Nietzsche were highly critical of any philosophical system constructed through the dialectical method. But did they themselves manage to outline a non-dialectical theory? Yes, for where Marx argues that the becoming-conscious of living labour power, a rough analogue to desire, will result in a change to civilization through the dictatorship of the proletariat, neither Freud nor Nietzsche posit such an alteration to the basic social fabric. Freud never stops asking whether *any* society's benefits are worth the sacrifices required of the individual by it (his patients learn to live *within* society), while Nietzsche's Overman is the aristocrat who will transcend society without reconstituting it, learning to live in a way *without* society. For Marx's part, in his dialectic the proletarian wants to be neither an obedient subject nor an aristocrat; she looks to a *new* society. But the question remains: can non-dialectical theories be analysed from a dialectical point of view?

Assoun's demonstration is a remarkably clear example of the dialectical method at work, as he shuttles back and forth, pausing as often as necessary (and he has an infinite patience for such interruptions) to examine the many contexts, both textual and historical, that further inform us as to the content and status of each concept or principle in question. It is not enough merely to read the conjunction in two directions and synthesize the analogies, constructing a Venn diagram that gives content to the operator, which would have the effect of raising the 'and' to the status of 'Freud' or 'Nietzsche'. For Assoun, the conjunction retains its status as a logical operator, its Boolean functionality, and the dialectic runs like a knitting machine in reverse, separating the threads and winding them back on to their skeins. Two fields are displayed in the end. What kind of dialectic is this? Assuredly, one without a synthetic terminus, without the comforting promise of resolution, and it only gets more complicated. A third figure stands in the wings.

Part of the challenge of reading this text lies in trying to recognize where that third figure is lurking, for at every key point the text is seemingly engaged in an ongoing dialectic, behind the scenes, with Marx. In the penultimate note, Assoun remarks that *we set out to compare the materialist status of repetition and its drive-related figures*, but we might have missed that point if we were not paying attention. And Assoun delivers several quiet admonitions and built-in tests throughout the text, to see if the reader really is paying attention. *We will leave to future research*; *we are not interested in external analogies here*; he marks the points where he refuses to be side-tracked. In the introduction to Part Two, Assoun warns us about jumping to conclusions and thinking that a simple comparison among analogies will suffice. Right away, we are told to slow down and accept nothing on face value. Then, in the chapter 'Instinct and Drive', after telling us a lot about both Freud's and Nietzsche's concepts of drives, Assoun states that *now that we have defined the phenomenological origins, we should be able to compare their natures and functions, but this still supposes that we have grasped their historical origins*. And so we begin again, reminded that phenomenology and historical materialism both need to be engaged in this study, and we need to be ready for that. Our being in the world is intimately affected by that world having a particular, material history.

Two other concepts which over-arch this text deserve mention. Assoun describes the work of Freud and Nietzsche as complementary psychological heuristics *under perpetual construction*; in other words, they are the products of *a process of permanent constitution*. In a late note, he refers to his own three-volume work as *the history of a field under construction*. Marx never finished his grand theoretical project, and since both Freud and Nietzsche resist systematization, closure is not possible, and subsequent contributors can build on or tear down these bodies of theory from any number of perspectives. There is, as Nietzsche said, much to be done. In Assoun's thought-universe, having read the present text, we are subtly directed back to Marx, to study the latter from the perspective of the former, and then to examine those results. In a way, Assoun is teaching us dialectical reading habits, or more generally, in the spirit of the Nietzschean epigraph above, *to read well.*

The second term is one that we began with. Assoun calls his analytic method a *paleontology*. He describes paleontology as *the progressive reconstitution of two skeletons beginning with partially similar bones, of which we know that in a certain respect they belong to the same genre, but which remain under specific principles of organization*. This is a good definition to carry around while reading this book; it is a useful aid in recognizing what Assoun is trying to do, for there are points in this text where it does seem like he is literally sorting out bones. Set alongside the detailed analysis of genealogy and archaeology in the conclusion, 'paleontology' emerges as a label for a viable alternative mode of investigation, an inquiry into specific principles of organization.

SOURCES

Some technical issues need to be addressed as well. The main reference sources used by Paul-Laurent Assoun in this book are: Friedrich Nietzsche, *Sämtliche Werke in zwölf Bänden* (Stuttgart: Alfred Kröner Verlag, 1964) (abbreviated as *SW* in the Notes); and Sigmund Freud, *Gesammelte Werke* (London: Imago Publishing Co., Ltd, 1948) (abbreviated as *GW* in the Notes).

In general, Assoun has himself translated passages of both Nietzsche and Freud from the original German. I have translated Assoun's French versions of these texts in order to maintain the flow of Assoun's rhetoric; in some cases, I have checked these translations against the original German texts, as well as against the standard, or most readily available and widely used English translations of Freud and Nietzsche. My main interest in consulting available English translations has been to verify the technical vocabulary used, and thus to provide a common intellectual background for the reader, since Assoun is analysing a commonly held perception of affinities between Freud and Nietzsche. For Nietzsche I have consulted the translations of Walter Kaufmann and R.J. Hollingdale; for Freud, *The Standard Edition of the Complete Psychological Works of Sigmund Freud*, James Strachey, general editor (24 volumes; London: Hogarth Press, 1953–66) (Abbreviated as *SE* in the Notes). For the most part, I have rendered the titles of Freud's and Nietzsche's works as they appear in these translations.

DIFFÉREND

In the 1998 preface, a new word appears, *différend.* It can be translated as 'dispute' or 'quarrel', but also as 'disagreement' or even 'difference'; in common English use, as fortune would have it, each of these words carries a particular emotional connotation. In the context of Assoun's use of the word, *différend* seems to me to mean all of these things and something else besides, and to choose one or the other would prejudice the tone of the text. Thus, I have left it as it appears in the French, which is, I suppose, another form of prejudice, but the reader should take it in its general sense of marking a less-than-perfect fit or agreement.

ACKNOWLEDGEMENTS

I hope that, in the translation presented here, I have done justice to this important and timely work. As solitary as the labour seemed at times, it could not have been accomplished without the advice, assistance and inspiration of several people. I wish to thank Daniel W. Smith for his patience and wisdom concerning points of Nietzsche's work, as well as for his guidance through the difficulties of translation, which provided an invaluable learning experience. Still, all remaining errors are mine alone. Thanks also to the staff at The Athlone Press for their faith and support in bringing this project to fruition. Mostly, though, I would like to thank someone who believes everything always returns, who truly lives at the intersection of the two thematics analysed here.

PREFACE TO THE 1998 EDITION

Freud and Nietzsche: how can we pronounce this conjunction, between two proper names that do not seem to 'rhyme' with any others? Where do we situate the 'and' in order to demonstrate the affinity between the founder of psychoanalysis and the 'transvaluator' of morals?

The question that we posed when we first published the results of our inquiry,[1] we must ask ourselves again, at the moment when our work reappears; once more we must confront, here in this strategic place, our exegesis–critique which interrogates the interface between philosophy and psychoanalysis. In this inquiry, we sought to approach the insistent, even persistent murmur associating Nietzsche with Freud, as a *question* in the most radical sense of the word. How can we shake ourselves out of a certain associative indolence – Nietzsche will go with Freud, insofar as we sense 'resemblances' among 'poles of interest' – in order to recognize the necessity of a confrontation (in the literal, 'confronting' violence of a face-to-face encounter) between the subversive affinities of two bodies of thought?

The present re-reading is, for us, in a way, a test of its truth. It is a matter, beyond any 'comparative anatomy' between two modes of thought, of remaining at the level of this 'Nietzscheo-Freudian' syntagm, which implies that we need to deconstruct it, in view of the various theoretical (and thus *ideological*) amalgams which have been produced in its name. That is the challenge: put in Nietzschean terms, to make resonate, with good 'hammer blows' – the hammer of textual and conceptual exegesis – the 'materials' of this 'alloy'. What is the point of consistency (that indicates the density) – and what are the silences that we need to refrain from artificially filling in? As far as the 'hammer' of commentary goes, it is necessary, at the risk of crushing one's object, to make it fit the 'mold' to the extent of those moments of plenitude when the texts correspond with one another.

That is why we have begun with Freud as we re-evaluate this conjunction, which is read first off *from* Freud *to* Nietzsche. It was, in fact, within the framework of an inquiry established on Freud's general attitude toward philosophy and philosophers[2] that we encountered, in the Freudian 'philosophical landscape,' a certain Nietzschean *site*.

On the one hand, Nietzsche is solidly placed among the philosophers cited by Freud as the poles of an *anticipatory reference* to his own discoveries. On the other hand, he is one of those rare, privileged characters who escapes the suspicion of illegitimacy that the creator of psychoanalysis generically casts upon philosophers, as those enamored of 'conscientiousness', who denigrate the Unconscious and belittle, by the same logic, the 'science' of 'unconscious processes,' all while fashioning their various 'world visions.'

The Nietzschean *topos* at the heart of Freud's discourse thus had to be archived in his behalf. And that – beyond the avatars that elaborate our own construction of the conjunction 'psychoanalysis and philosophy'[3] – created a symptom. The presence of Nietzsche *in* Freud exceeds that of a mere 'chapter', however rich, in a larger treatise on the 'philosophemes' in Freudian use. There is indeed a 'case of Nietzsche,' an exceptional status which gives rise to the present inquiry and upon which it has imposed its full enormity.

In this archaeology of the conjunction 'Freud, philosophy and philosophers,' it was in fact quickly apparent that the figure 'Freud and Nietzsche' merited a separate destiny. It is true, in a sense, that Nietzsche is only one among other elements in Freud's philosophical galaxy. He certainly appears at the central nucleus, the fourth 'term' of the quadrilateral Plato–Kant/Schopenhauer–*Nietzsche* that we saw outlined when we probed the 'philosophemes' referenced in the Freudian text. It is not even certain that Nietzsche is the one who 'counted' the most for the creator of psychoanalysis, as the link to Schopenhauer seems in a way more appropriate to Freud's immediate 'mode of use.'[4]

If we reconsider Nietzsche's appearance in the ensemble of the history of Freud's use of philosophy, on which we have previously written,[5] Nietzsche would seem to be neither more nor less than a significant episode in this general confrontation. But there is a wholly other thing that is in question here. Nietzsche – it is, in some way, his intention *and* his ambition – *is* a philosophy unto himself and for this reason he imposes upon the attention of the one who set out to forge a new 'psychology' – thus a totally different thing than *just another* psychology (a 'psycho-analysis') – which gives value *mutatis mutandis* to another link, from Freud to Wittgenstein.[6]

The inquiry which follows reflects a movement that starts from an intensive examination of Nietzsche's presence in Freud's speech and writings, and a reconstruction of the context of their encounter ('Freud and Nietzsche,' Part One of the present work). From there, however, the inquiry leads to a thematic and critical *dia-logue* ('Nietzsche and Freud,' Part Two of the present work) which is not simply a matter of 'communication' and a pacific exchange of ideas, but entails an active engagement of dual *logoi*.

There are indeed two ways of approaching the relation Freud-Nietzsche. First, there is the genesis of the encounter, which puts the *event* of this meeting in context; second, there is the thing itself, the bond that the founder of psychoanalysis himself forges, first with the Basel professor, and then with the thinker of Sils-Maria, and the effects of the latter on the thought and *text* of the former.

That is what we have placed as the first element in the present inquiry. We need to be able to judge in what context, and with what sort of *relays* Freud undertakes to comprehend Nietzsche (Part One, Chapter 1, the section 'The First Intermediary: Josef Paneth'), and without which Freud's reading of Nietzsche would remain indecipherable, or would be doomed either to distortion or to a retrospective 'optical illusion.' The essential thing lies rather in the 'vis-à-vis' that is here somehow forged between these two major bodies of thought, which invites philosophical discourse both to relinquish and reconsider its modes of 'authority'.

It is important, in this regard, to assume a certain 'decontextualization' here; let us agree that Freud adopts a very particular 'attitude' regarding Nietzsche, which is useful to put in relief. Interpellating Nietzsche, he must, in the name of his 'science', psychoanalysis, tear away from certain stereotypes that the contemporary reception of Nietzsche was already quick to establish. That sets the limit of every attempt to decipher this bond in terms of 'reception' and of the history of ideas; the *encounter* here comes to destabilize all models of 'reception'.

We can verify this, because it is not as a simple philosopher–reader (of other philosophers) that Freud produces some quite original philosophical effects that 'ricochet' and touch the very heart of philosophical *logos*.[7] Freud is decidedly not a reader (of Nietzsche) like any other, and on this point these two 'monstrous originals' are joined. Also, it is in this sense that the present inquiry, organized in conformity with the legitimate requirements of academic analyses – an efficacious antidote to the scatter-shot variations on content comparisons between the two works – has taken on the style, in a way imposed by its object, of a *genealogy*.

Moreover, we must become aware, while undertaking this comparison in its fullest breadth, of how Freud's position relative to Nietzsche is 'existentially' transformed. Freud, born in 1856, first encounters Nietzsche (1844–1900) with the energy and attitude of a young bachelor who has just begun his university studies, at the very moment when a university professor in Basel – himself a young man precociously employed as an academic, before abruptly abandoning his career – begins to make himself heard, hurling his first volleys of invectives (aimed precisely at the academic world and its mediocrities, among other things). The dialogue will be completed three quarters of a century later, by the creator of psychoanalysis, in an apparent soliloquy – Nietzsche having died in the meanwhile, exactly at the moment of the birth of psychoanalysis. Henceforth, then, Freud will reapproach Nietzsche *from his own foundation*. His attitude toward Nietzsche follows from the considerable internal metamorphosis that his own 'thinking' undergoes. Freud's beginnings coincide with the birth of Nietzscheism, just as the birth of psychoanalysis coincides with the death of Nietzsche.

Nietzsche was the object of Freud's youthful admiration, whose effects can be felt right through to the end of Freud's career; however, when the time came to undertake his own *conquista*, Freud reapproached the thinker of Sils-Maria, if not as an equal, at least as a 'colleague' in the field of enigmas, and reinterrogated him, in private, if not publicly, with the resources forged in the meantime from 'metapsychology', psychoanalysis' *ad hoc* knowledge.[8]

The best way to re-read this movement and reintroduce ourselves to it seems to us to consist in interrogating here these two aims of the trajectory and the two questions that they signify:

- On the plane of genesis, it is important to grasp how the bond between Freud and Nietzsche is formed, and renegotiated.
- On the plane of content, we need to show evidence of what led to this confrontation, the 'thing itself' which subtends the collision and gives significance to this 'encounter'.

I THE SPECTROSCOPY OF AN ENCOUNTER

The Figures of a 'Linkage': From 'Encounter' to 'Dialogue'

We can suggest an 'outline' of this Freud–Nietzsche link, whose stages and aspects are detailed in the present work, in order to perceive straight away the dynamic in its blueprint form, over the course of some three quarters of a century.

1 The moment of the sudden collision–encounter, matched by 'reservations' whose tenor and significance are plainly visible, occurs during Freud's formative years. He is informed, at the source, so to speak, in the context of the 'Viennese reception,' of the existence and importance of the author of the *Untimely Meditations*.
2 Thus 'integrated', at a respectful distance as well as with a sort of reasoned defiance, combined with the intelligence of a shared secret, Nietzsche seems to be rediscovered by Freud, precisely in the years of the first formulations of psychoanalysis. It is no accident if at this exact moment, when the creator of psychoanalysis begins to see himself as a 'conquistador', he (re)turns to Nietzsche, as in quest of an obscure but necessary 'alliance'. Here, the ambivalence is repeated, an aporia between the affinity of their enterprises (that of giving names to things which had not been named before)[9] and the heterogeneity of their 'codes' (for, here and there, they do not use the same words, and certainly not about the same 'things'). So it comes to pass, in any case, that Nietzsche begins to be cited in the *Freudian Oeuvre*,[10] on such decisive points as the conception of dreams, sexuality and the Unconscious.
3 In a third period, Nietzsche inhabits the Freudian text; he has become one of the chosen hosts. Not only is he hailed specifically as 'anticipating' some such 'article' evoked by the 'psychoanalytic doctrine,' which are designated as *Ahnungen und Einsichten*,[11] an ensemble of 'intuitions' and 'apperceptions' that constitute a Nietzschean 'pre-science' of the analytic 'thing' (examined in Part One, Chapter 2, 'Nietzsche in Freudian Discourse'), but in two major works dating from 1914 and 1925, Nietzsche is found, recognized, and even in a way 'enthroned' as a 'precursor' of psychoanalysis (but we must determine in what such a status can consist).
4 There is yet a final phase, more 'cryptic', which seems to us to strengthen and intensify the confrontation between Nietzsche and Freud in a more intimate sense. The enormous metapsychological recasting of the years 1920–30 will put the Nietzschean comet back in the metapsychological sky. This time, Nietzscheism is 'over-present', even though, paradoxically, Freud shows no need to cite explicitly the author of *The Will to Power*. It is here that the critical reading must be at its sharpest.

After having been an admirer – as reticent as sincere – of Nietzsche (around 1875), after having felt in the latter a 'colleague' in 'discoveries' (around 1900), then becoming a user of Nietzschean pre-metapsychological intuitions (around

1914), Freud turns out to be a reader of *The Will to Power*, this touchstone of Nietzscheism, as revealed in his concept of the death wish (around 1920).

This subterranean debate may contain the most capital stakes for the interface between philosophy and metapsychology. In addition, it is useful, to lend its weight to the present re-introduction, to highlight this moment of truth which in a way gives 'pause' to this inquiry.

Nietzsche's 'Viennese Reception': The 'Originary Scene' of the Encounter

There is indeed an originary scene of the 'encounter' between Freud and Nietzsche. It has a place – Vienna – and a time – around the 1870s. The 'Viennese connection' of a nascent 'Nietzscheism' furnished the context for the young Freud's discovery of Nietzsche, which revealed the promises and stakes of a link that, already, takes on an eminently personal cast, insofar as Freud manifests (somewhat precociously) his vocation as a *Selbstdenker*, a 'Self-thinker.'

It is symbolic that the *Neue Freie Presse*, the journal which would publish commentaries favorable to Freud from 1895 on, as well as to Stefan Zweig's works on psychoanalysis, and to which Freud gave one of his extremely rare interviews at the end of his life,[12] was also the journal that extended a warm reception to Nietzsche's Second *Untimely Meditation* in 1874.[13] At this point, Freud had just begun his medical studies and was in search of some philosophical benchmarks (1873–5). The 'Reading Society of German Students in Vienna' (*Leseverein der deutschen Studenten Wiens*), created in 1871, played an important role in Nietzscheism's *in statu nascendi*. Josef Paneth, whom Freud recognized as his first 'intercessor' with Nietzsche, in a well-known letter to Arnold Zweig (Part One, Chapter 1, 'Arnold Zweig and the Impossible Discourse'), organized around 1875, in concert with Victor Adler, a discussion of the *Untimely Meditations*.

We know that Freud was a member of the *Leseverein* between 1873–8.[14] He was thus implicated in this group of early interest in and of a certain adherence, even, to Nietzsche's thought. Given the ignorance in which Nietzsche was held by the German academic world that he so reviled, it is interesting to note this quasi-'exotic' infatuation of the 'Viennese group.' The most patent manifestation comes in 1877, with the profession of faith contained in a collective letter to Nietzsche, still at Basel,[15] in which we recognize the names of men with whom Freud was well acquainted, such as Victor Adler, Heinrich Braun and, the most fervent emulator of Nietzsche, Siegfried Lipiner.

But there is more. A number of Jewish students also participated in this enthusiastic Nietzschean movement,[16] in order to shore up their own position, in the framework of an interrogation of their cultural and intellectual identity, and within a debate concerning German culture and pagan mythology. Thus it is not by accident that Vienna figures at the 'head of the list' in the enumeration that Nietzsche makes, toward the end of his life, of the places who had recognized his work since 'the first hour.' 'In Vienna, in St. Petersburg, Stockholm,

Copenhagen, in Paris and New York, everywhere that I have been discovered,' in marked contrast to the attitude of indifference toward his thought that he felt in his native 'Germany, Europe's dull country.'[17] Everything happens as if Nietzsche, in 1888, remembered the warm Viennese reception of some 15 years earlier, and the demonstration of love from these 'lofty characters,' these 'elite intelligences' who had given him a such a sign that in 1877, he even considered returning to Vienna to meet these admirers and disciples. At that time, Vienna could have been called the capital of a small Nietzschean 'republic', though, it is true, a sparsely populated one! And among these adherents to Nietzscheism, would we not have to count a certain student named Sigmund Freud?

We will note, in any case, this very concrete conjuncture of a possible, physical encounter between Nietzsche and Freud, in 1877–8. How can we not re-read, without some retrospective regret, Nietzsche's letter to Paul Rée describing, in November 1877, a trip to Salzburg that was postponed until the following year?

> I would, perhaps, like to combine this trip with a visit to Vienna, for there may be found there a cluster of persons who have the dubious taste to appreciate my writings (you know that I have myself moved past this point of view), but it does seem to me that there are some capable minds among them, including one genius.'[18]

The genius to whom Nietzsche alludes is none other than Siegfried Lipiner (1856–1911), Freud's classmate and author of a *Prometheus* which Nietzsche had praised in the most vivid terms (before cooling off seriously toward its author). But had Nietzsche responded to the appeal of his imitators, he probably would have counted among his hosts a medical student, also enamoured of philosophy, named Sigmund Freud (no doubt curious to meet the author of the texts that he had read and admired). At the very least, this visit had a decisive resonance for the future creator of psychoanalysis, an 'historic' opportunity to see, 'in flesh and bone,' the author whose thoughts Freud would readily qualify as being in some way out of his reach.

In this concrete conjuncture, the notion of a 'missed encounter' between Nietzsche and Freud takes its most literal signification. Nietzsche will thus not make his planned trip to Vienna, where Freud would go on to hatch, some 20 years later (with Breuer), his own 'cuckoo's egg,' the *Studies on Hysteria.* And Nietzsche could not have suspected that, among this cenacle of sympathizers, would be found one who will use his own personal 'genius' to create a certain 'science of the Unconscious,' which in its own way will call into question his posterity. In a way, we remain the sole witnesses of this rendezvous, dated and missed! Indeed, Nietzsche finds himself at a turning point in his own destiny, which will lead him to resign from the University at Basel and set out on the route to Sils-Maria. At this point, the two destinies are disjoined, but how can we not be taken by this real, historical blink of an eye, at the moment of reconstructing in some way, via the text of their works, this encounter, as impossible as it is necessary? The present work could well be conceived from the standpoint of supplementing the facts of this 'countermanded meeting.'

Freud in the Discovery of Nietzsche

Such is the context that favoured an encounter; but, we should recall, Freud is a strange sort of Viennese who, even though marked by his membership and implicated in the movements of ideas, never reacts purely and simply 'in the Viennese manner' according to the tempo of the *Zeitgeist*. It is important to grasp how he approaches Nietzsche, at the source as well as via mirror effects.

To this end, we can observe the appearance of Nietzsche's name in Freud's *Letters from Youth*, a magnificent testimony to his precocious intellectual autonomy. There, we see mentioned a certain 'shame' at citing David-Friedrich Strauss' formula 'Thus we live, happily.' Using this phrase to conclude a letter to his friend Silberstein in March, 1875, Freud adds that 'although in 1873, Fred. Nietzsche had reproached this phrase of David Strauss as an indication of philistinism.'[19]

This allusion to a first, sibyllic approach is interesting for several reasons. In the first place, we sense that Freud is well aware of the Nietzschean polemics of the moment and what is implicated in their stakes, which confirms that he had at least heard about the *Untimely Meditations*, presumably through the intermediary of the Viennese reception mentioned above (although he confuses Basel with Strasbourg!). Second, he cites Strauss, in all conscience, and in spite of Nietzsche's sarcasm (for whom Strauss was, we know, one of his 'bugbears'), as if the young Freud gallantly assumes the risk of indignity and 'opprobrium' on the scale of a Nietzschean evaluation, by making this 'philistine' adage his own. A certain 'eudemonism' may be involved, though trivial in view of the demands of Nietzsche's 'nobility', in the sense defined below. Finally, this allusion figures in the letter which preceded the great missive (of 15 March 1875) wherein Freud gives an account of his talks with Franz Brentano, his first 'master' in philosophy, and where we can gauge Freud's philosophical filiations. This letter contains a summary of Brentano's directives for the constitution of an authentic philosophical culture (*philosophische Bildung*), as we have detailed elsewhere,[20] and it is worth asking if Nietzsche had his place there.

In fact, we can search in vain for Nietzsche among the philosophers whom Brentano (whose influence on the young Freud was considerable) recommended his students, like Freud and Paneth, to read and become acquainted with. After Descartes, Locke and Hume, there is hardly any place for contemporary thought, according to Brentano's views, except for Auguste Comte and 'the Englishman,' John Stuart Mill.[21] We understand that, on the one hand, Nietzsche is only at the very edge of his own work in 1875; on the other hand, Brentano's 'philosophical universe' seems impervious to the 'instinctualist' vein in which he would have spontaneously ranked the author of *The Birth of Tragedy*. At best, Nietzsche would have represented the 'mystical' phase which, in the cyclical conception of history that subtends Brentano's perception of the philosophical present, merely completes the 'movement'. So it is not certain from what side Freud might receive any encouragement for his nascent Nietzschean appetence . . .

Indeed, around 1875 Freud is more sensitive to the thought of Ludwig Feuerbach, who had just died (1872), and whom Freud presents as 'of all the philosophers, the one that I venerate and admire the most,'[22] the hero of 'free thought' and of the struggle against religious prejudice. We also understand that, from this perspective, the struggle with D.-F. Strauss cannot be as antipathetic for Freud as it was for the author of the *Untimely Meditations*.

But precisely, if Freud adheres overall to the 'philosophical line' of his master Brentano, the respect that the latter inspires in him does not prevent him from being sensitive to a renewal that he perceives, with the nascent 'Nietzscheophilic' group, from the side of this 'untimely' thought. Furthermore, the author of the *Untimely Meditations*, through his critique of the educational system, could well appear as a support in this battle for a new *Aufklärung*, which is felt at least until the time of *Human, All Too Human* (1878), when a sort of 'Voltaireanism' arises, compatible with that of Freud.[23] A syncretism of the *Freie Denkers*, paradoxically, served as the crucible for a form of 'neo-liberalism', although Nietzsche, the philosopher of the tragic, would seem to be incompatible with 'rationalist' sobriety.

From this synthesis, a revealing action is taken. At the instigation of Freud himself, a small periodical is created, whose distribution, it seems, was ultra-confidential. Announcing its demise in January, 1875, Freud writes that 'the journal that we have founded, the three of us, then the four – myself, Paneth, Emmanuel Löwy, and Lipiner – died down in the peace of the Lord.'[24] Among these 'founders' and editors of this first Freudian review, we can recognize two notable mediators of Nietzscheism: Josef Paneth, the 'friend Josef' of the *Traumdeutung*, whom Freud presents as the one who more that anyone else initiated him to Nietzsche, and Siegfried Lipiner, the one most engaged in the Nietzschean 'apostolate', who could even boast of his status as a recognized disciple of Nietzsche.[25]

Freud seems resolved to assume parentage of this 'journal.' 'It is I who have delivered it the *coup de grâce*; I called it to life, and I called it back from life.'[26] Now, the review of which he was the animator in this decisive sense confronted metaphysical problems in which the Nietzschean component was very well represented, indicative of the Nietzschean *Gesinnung* – a sensitivity, if it does fall short of outright 'obedience' to things Nietzschean – of the principal editors.

The 'Case of Strauss'

We can appreciate, in this context, the meaning of the allusion to Nietzsche interposed by Strauss. David-Friedrich Strauss (1808–74) had been 'elected' by Nietzsche to play the part of the incarnation of an all-too 'timely' philistinism. This fierce diatribe, comprising the first *Untimely Meditation* (1873), paints the portrait of the 'cultivated philistine.' The term *Bildungsphilister* delightfully sets side-by-side the most injurious and pejorative term in the academic vocabulary which, since the beginning of the nineteenth century,[27] had designated the self-satisfied and uncultivated (lacking culture) bourgeoisie – with the striking *Bildung*, which returns to the lofty notion of 'culture' or of an internal education, an ideal of cultivated individuality. What Nietzsche is aiming at, by way of Strauss (the author of the *Life of Jesus* (1835) and especially *Ancient and Modern Faith* (1872)) as a 'person-target', is precisely this form of profound un-culture disguised as knowledge, a 'philistinism' masquerading as 'science'.

The subtitle of Strauss' work especially targeted by Nietzsche, a 'confession', reveals its true subject, a new 'profession of faith' which, having abjured Christianity and the religious ideal, blissfully dedicates itself to a 'new faith' (*der neue Glaube*) that takes over from the old one (*der alte Glaube*). It replaces the suffering of the Cross with a sort of cult of happiness – a type of sentiment of joyously accepted dependence regarding creation, under the tutelary sign of 'science'. The theories of evolution and of Darwinism are called to the rescue of this *Weltanschauung*, in order to legitimize its rational harmony.

Nietzsche's 'tragic sense', combined with a kind of 'Voltairean' will to lucidity, would not know how to accommodate this cult of scientific determinism and its smug ideal of harmonious Reason. In addition, the author of the *Untimely Meditations* does not mince his words.

Thus, for Freud, Strauss' little phrase, which Nietzsche had cited, pops up: *So leben wir, so wandeln wir beglückt* (So we live, so we carry on, filled with happiness). The phrase, in fact, concludes a sort of profession of a eudemonist faith that the author of the first *Untimely Meditation* presents, in the fourth section of his anti-philistine assault, as 'the paradisiacal page' of this 'book of confessions.'[28] The whole force of Nietzsche's contemptuous sarcasm is contained in this act of citation, intended to illustrate the epitome of mediocrity in Strauss' *Weltanschauung*. '"Here is our man," applauds the philistine reader, "because that is how we have always lived; it is how we live each and every day."' The author of *Ancient and Modern Faith* only manages, in Nietzsche's eyes, to establish a 'philistine' ideal that is the furthest from any authentic 'culture', by dressing up with a vaguely lyrical pathos a scientific legitimation of common knowledge and the most trivial eudemonism, a type of intellectual 'comfort'.

What did Strauss want to signify by this maxim? It is an elegy to the universality of modernism, a type of cultural democracy that permits the citizen to gather all the fruits of 'historical studies,' of 'natural sciences' and of 'the works of our great poets.' At the moment when he evokes an intense enjoyment 'of reading great writers and performing the works of our great musicians,' while speaking of 'a stimulation of mind and sentiment, of imagination and humour which leaves nothing to be desired,' Strauss makes his declaration of the beatitude of the modern condition of culture, a kind of sentiment of the 'affluence' of material and cultural progress.

It is there that we can grasp the difference in attitude between Nietzsche and Freud, in their encounter with the same evocation. Where Nietzsche sees only a journalistic culture, an enjoyment of the cafes and popular distractions, which finds its legitimation in what he calls a 'heinous theory of well-being,' dully animated by a 'hatred of genius,' Freud, for his part, could more easily give his approval to this programme of 'a happy life,' so derogatory to the Nietzschean ideal – or at least he could recognize a more magnanimous indulgence. After all, the young Freud is really a Feuerbachian, and subscribes to a certain confidence in the possibilities of a being reconciled with its sensible immanence, finding a legitimate happiness in its adherence to its own 'matter'.

It is no accident that a long time afterwards, in the anecdote narrated by Lou Salomé (see below, 'Lou Salomé, The Mercurial Feminine'), it is against the intoxication by torment, extolled by the Nietzschean poem, that Freud reacts by evoking the first 'head cold' that comes as sufficient to 'cure' him of such inclinations. This care of the self and the legitimation of the requirement for happiness, which amounts to a 'lack of taste' and the most severe and impardonable concession to the 'philistinism' for which Nietzsche cannot find harsh enough words, are not really shameful for Freud – no more so in 1875 than in 1913 – although the movement of his own thought would be in the direction of a strong relativization of the possibilities for happiness. Through an irony of the history of ideas, it is under the Nietzschean reference that Freud will return, in the years around 1920 when he introduces the death wish, to the theoretical and therapeutic revisions which will take as their slogan the 'will to happiness' (*Wille zum Glück*), after Otto Rank.[29] We can point here to a symbolic event of an impossible encounter; in 1926, after their last conversation and before their definitive estrangement, Rank offers Freud a gift of the complete works of Nietzsche![30]

This defence of the legitimacy of the pleasure principle and of a tempered eudemonism in no way prevents setting to rights, in an affinity with Nietzsche, a wholly other aspiration, that of the 'nocturnal aspects' that scientific lucidity neglects and, at base, denies.

The Différend of the Ideal: Vornehmheit

From the very beginning, Freud's attitude toward Nietzsche is fixed, and will remain so to the end of his life, as stated in his letter to Arnold Zweig. 'He represents a nobility inaccessible to me' (*eine mir unzugängliche Vornehmheit*).[31] Such is the original 'stopping point', a kind of non-encounter which constitutes the other side of this otherwise intense 'encounter'. The question, we will see, clarifies their differences (*différend*) over happiness.

How can we understand this *Vornehmheit*, alluded here as the limit-point of Freud's own access to an 'enjoyment' of Nietzsche? In its contemporary denotation, *Vornehmheit* designates the formal quality of what is 'noble' (*edel*) and refined (*fein*), with a nuance of elegance and of 'distinction' (even 'snobbery'). In a familiar connotation, *vornehm* is perhaps best rendered in French by 'huppé' (and in English by 'upper-crust'). The notion of 'superiority' (in a certain sense of 'class') returns to the sentiment of an 'aristocracy' of spirit. In brief, Freud says that he is 'out-classed' by the Nietzschean ideal.

We would be wrong to interpret this remark as referring only to Nietzsche's idiosyncrasies; it is not the 'distinction' of the personality which is at stake here, but rather something that constitutes one of the main operators of Nietzsche's mode of thought. The recurrence of the term *Vornehmheit* in Nietzsche's work, from *The Birth of Tragedy* to *The Will to Power*, from the Greek tragic ethos to the quest for the Superhuman, attests that Nietzsche's thought is engaged in drawing out the conditions of possibility of this 'nobility', and even to promote it as an ethico-philosophical category.

Was ist vornehm? – it is a question that Nietzsche never ceases asking. It even appears as the title to the ninth chapter of *Beyond Good and Evil.*[32] At the other end of this trajectory, the question is literally taken up again in a long section in *The Will to Power.*[33] The term evokes the notion of 'elevation' or 'height' (*Höhe, Erhöhung*). The noble soul 'is marked' in that it 'always lives at a radiant height' (*in einer durchleuchtenden Höhe*), literally 'in a height shot through with light.'[34] The characteristics are 'an aptitude for recognition,' the absence of fear of oneself,[35] which goes together with a form of 'obedience'.[36] It is distinguished by a placid acceptance of 'the fact of its own selfishness'[37] at the same time as a certain depth of suffering (*das tiefe Leiden*) that isolates it.[38] In brief, the 'noble soul' thus defined is lofty, generous, courageous, mindful of and respectful of the self and suited for suffering.

It is certainly no accident if this vivid metaphor of *Vornehmheit* runs, like a 'thin red line,' through Nietzsche's thematic work. But it does reflect an evolution; taken at first in a Greek 'tragicist' aestheticism, it tends to be presented as a kind of wisdom. Freud, impressed by the portrait of the 'noble soul,' is quite capable of accommodating a remark from *Human, All Too Human*: 'A noble soul (*eine vornehme Seele*) is not that which is capable of the highest jumps (*Aufschwünge*), but that which rises a bit and falls a bit, always inhabiting a freely radiant air and height.'[39] 'Nobility' is here clearly demarcated from a kind of ethereal 'levitation', as far as its being a predilection for contortions. (*Aufschwünge*, in the vocabulary of sports, designates 'leaps that hang in the air'). The aptitude to maintain oneself constantly at the same height, in a sort of *tranquillitas animi*, is not unrelated to the disposition of the mind in 'free-floating attention' (*gleichschwebende Aufmerksamkeit*), which would be that ... *of the analyst in the position of listener.*

It is not that the notion of *Vornehmheit* will always take more 'flight' for Nietzsche than for Freud, before being in a way 'instituted' by the notion of the 'superhuman' (*Ubermenschliches*). Freud confirms that his 'constitution' cannot support such 'takeoffs'. He has well understood what the idea implies and for his part rejects himself as a candidate to scale such peaks. His words seem to echo those of Nietzsche in *Ecce Homo*: 'He who knows how to breathe in the atmosphere that fills my work knows that it is an atmosphere of the heights, that the air is crisp. One must be made for this atmosphere ...'[40] 'Ah, well,' Freud seems to reply, 'I am not made for that.' We know that Freud's whole profession of faith goes to call forth the necessity of working in the sub-soil.[41] Freud breathes rather poorly at the altitudes that Nietzsche requires; this is a theme that regularly returns, for example in the correspondence with Rée[42] (and recalls, with a Heine-inspired humour, the banal gravity of 'immanence'). To the sun-drenched, snow-covered heights symbolized by the Dolomites, Nietzsche's site of preference, Freud opposes a more temperate climate propitious to the legitimate requirements of happiness; it not the same vision of the 'land where the oranges bloom' in the words of Goethe (who was equally dear to one and the other).

It is again no accident if, to the question hammered out: 'What is noble?', Nietzsche answers: 'That one should disregard the happiness of the greatest number: the happiness of the peace of the soul, of the virtue of comfort (*sic*), of the Anglo-English haberdashery of a Spencer.'[43]

If we think about it, one question illustrates well the *différend*, that of the evaluation of labor. Nietzsche, sensitive to the grandeur of creative labour ('All the great ones were great workers'), puts a symmetrical emphasis on the mortal threat of labour as a social ideal, denouncing the 'praisers of labour' (*Lobredner der Arbeit*). In a well-known aphorism in *Daybreak*, we find this 'glorification (*Verherrlichung*) of labour' reviled for its celebration of 'actions useful to all', its impersonal nature, in short for its 'fear of everything that is individual.'[44] Freud appears to respond to Nietzsche in a note in *Civilization and Its Discontents*, half a century later. 'If no particular disposition prescribes as necessary a certain direction to one's interests in life, common professional labour can intervene in that place, as accessible to anyone.' What is evoked here is the counsel given by Voltaire's *Candide*, to 'cultivate one's garden.'[45] Freud and Nietzsche, great labourers who are gripped by a 'destiny' that demands an *œuvre*, concur at base on the diagnosis of the anonymizing effect of 'common' labour. But therein lies the difference, for where Nietzsche battles against this denaturalization of individuality by a laborious triviality functioning as the repressive 'police force' of unicity, Freud soberly declares that all in all, labour serves as an acceptable and accessible regulatory dynamic that can 'guide life' (*Lebensführung*) and allows 'the individual to be firmly anchored to reality, to the extent that he is integrated securely in a sphere of reality within the human community.' Without adding his voice to those of the *Lobredners*, the praisers of Labour, Freud links this 'activity' back to the libidinal economy. Indeed, it is the same stake as the question of happiness.

Once subjected to a retrospective appraisal, Freud's remark in the crucial letter to Arnold Zweig takes on its full meaning; whereas many of his friends and classmates became fascinated by Nietzsche's *Vornehmheit*, something, from this moment on, arrests the philosophy student named Sigmund Freud. He is not content to suggest that Nietzsche is 'too great for him' or that he 'places the bar too high' for his tastes and means, as one might be tempted to interpret him. He submits to a critique the demand for *Vornehmheit* that, lending its colour to Nietzscheism, even to its *Weltanschauung*, continues to gain density in his text and thought.

However, Freud does not profess to carry 'second-rate' ideals. What we hear within his reach, in his 1918 declaration, at the same moment where he claims hardly 'to worry about good and evil' (whereas that was *the* worry for Nietzsche), is that 'if it is necessary to speak of an ethic, I profess for my part a lofty ideal, of which I am aware of generally falling short in the most appalling ways.'[46] Freud, we know, presents himself as a Jewish atheist who refuses to make the least profession of moral faith, such that his ethics come from the Self (*selbstverständlich*). His claim for an ideal takes its meaning as a response to Nietzsche's affirmation that 'Israel triumphed with its vengeance over all of the most noble ideals.'[47] Indeed, there is for Freud a sort of *Vornehmheit* of the Law. Moreover, it is the creator of psychoanalysis, the supposed 'enemy of ideals,' who claims that his ideas are incompatible with the points of view of 'the solid majority' (Ibsen's phrase), little inclined toward 'free thought.' In a sense, then, there is a Freudian version of *Vornehmheit*, but precisely one relieved from the narcissistic elation of 'ideals'.

Freud and Nietzsche are defined by a somehow 'organically' recalcitrant character from the point of view of the 'great number,' but they do not place the principles of their 'dissidence' at the same point from the norm.

II GENESIS OF AN ALLIANCE: FREUD WITH NIETZSCHE

However, past the time of the encounter, we see an evolution, as 'logical' as it is 'historical', of the exchange between Nietzsche and Freud: the time of the 'alliance'. It is the passage from the conjunction of affinities to the conjugation of their foundational projects.

'Sources of the Nile': The Freudian 'Conquista'

This *Aufklärer* named Freud, defiant toward the 'vertigo of heights,' has sensed all the same in advance an exceptional ally in Nietzsche, a community of 'free spirits' (*Freie Geister*) in the sense of *Human, All Too Human*.

We now move on to a point a quarter of a century after Freud's encounter with Nietzsche, at the moment when the latter has just ended his life and the former is just beginning to undertake his 'creation' (*Schöpfung*). Nietzsche seems to Freud to be a pioneer of the *terra incognita* of the Unconscious; better put, Freud perceives in Nietzsche a *Tiefenpsycholog* 'before the fact' (*avant la lettre*), a true 'conquistador'. We can grasp the moment of Freud's realization of this affinity in his letter, dated 1 July 1900,[48] where Freud confides to his friend Fliess (in the final period of their impassioned intellectual 'liaison') that he finds himself on the verge of his own discovery, and confesses his 'return to Nietzsche' or at least to *his thoughts about* Nietzsche.

The missive begins on a somber note, associated with the emergence of a sense of a 'personal destiny,' a moment of 'difficult times for myself and my cure,' Freud says, by way of self-definition. What kind of man, then, is the inventor of 'psychoanalysis', in his own eyes, at this critical moment? 'I am not... not at all a man of science, nor an observer, nor an experimenter, nor a thinker' (*kein Mann der Wissenschaft, kein Beobachter, kein Experimentator, kein Denker*). What else is there? 'I have only the temperament of a conquistador (*Conquistadortemperament*), an adventurer, if you will, with all the curiosity, audacity and tenacity of such a man.'

The consequence is a 'practical' matter. 'Of such men, we are accustomed to appreciate them when they succeed, if they have truly discovered something, but otherwise they are tossed to the side. And that is not at all an unjust fate.' The creator of psychoanalysis thus places the axis of his originality in the necessity of being a 'conquistador', exactly at the moment when he is confronted with the most acute reality of his own experience. Although having to found a 'science of the unconscious,' he must not be simply a 'man of science,' but a 'discoverer'. This is the moment when he undertakes the search for the 'sources of the Nile' of the Unconscious. So it is – and it is, it seems to us, anything but an accident – that his thoughts (re)turn to Nietzsche.

'I have at present taken Nietzsche (*ich habe mir ... jetzt den Nietzsche beigelegt*, literally, 'I have set Nietzsche at my side'), in the hope of finding words for the many things that remain mute within me.' Only to add: 'too lazy (*träge*) for the moment.' At the least, this 'viscosity' (*Trägheit*) merits examining.

Here, grasped in all its immediacy, is the moment of truly inaugural truth for Freud regarding Nietzsche. It is in the after-effects of the first encounter – in a way striking and blind, according to the described modalities – that Freud realizes that henceforth he himself can and must take a decisive step toward this body of thought that, a quarter of a century earlier, he had 'stepped aboard,' and in a small way 'stumbled over.'

Thus confronted with the most intimate identity of his project, and proceeding toward his discovery, Freud is spontaneously reconciled with the Nietzschean text, as his own testimony shows. His is the solitude of the 'conquistador' who searches, if not with a compass, then at least with 'a travelling companion.' The formula given is dense and significant: to seek in 'Nietzsche', the Text which bears the Nietzschean signature, 'many (*vieles*) things that remain mute within me.' So, Nietzsche would be supposed, by Freud, to hold these words that carry the expressions that respond, for Freud, to a sort of 'mutism'. The 'Nietzschean oracle' will thus be consulted, only to send back, like its Delphic model, its own demand to the consultant.

It is a way of acting on this affinity, but also on the same (albeit displaced) effect of sideration that seized him at the moment of encounter. But Freud is 'too inert' to return to the text, in order to make the famous 'ascent'. At least 'Nietzsche' is there, set alongside the Freudian foundation, as some kind of 'touchstone'.

Nietzsche, *Tiefenpsycholog* Before the Fact

Freud has meanwhile overcome his inertia to read Nietzsche, since his work attests that Nietzsche is enthroned there as a *Vorgänger*, he who 'came before,' in such essential areas as the Unconscious, dreams and sexuality.

A decisive, as much as symbolic, moment occurs on 28 October 1908, during a meeting of the Vienna Psychoanalytic Society, where Freud evokes Nietzsche; the creator of psychoanalysis addresses the circle of his first disciples on the topic of the philosopher of Sils-Maria. Freud has already discovered among his disciples (from Hitschmann to Rank) an interest in Nietzsche. During a previous meeting of the Society (on 1 April 1908), Freud mentioned his vain attempts to read Nietzsche (an echo of his *Trägheit*, the 'inertia' mentioned in his 1900 letter to Fliess), but this time, it is *Nietzschean knowledge* which is in question. Freud does not speak about Nietzsche as merely one philosopher among others, nor as a simple object of a diagnostic; rather, the 'diagnosis' itself leads to an astonishing homage. To say that 'the degree of introspection attained by Nietzsche had never been attained by anyone before him, and doubtless will never be again,'[49] is to declare that 'the Case of Nietzsche' demonstrates, if not the success of self-analysis, otherwise held to be impossible, then at the very least a sort of 'monstrous lucidity' about the Self. It is an exceptional case of access to an exceptional knowledge, under the effect of dissolution linked to a morbid process. 'Nietzsche, projecting toward the external world this series of brilliant discoveries about his own self,' permits him to 'hit the nail on the head.' It is necessary to recall that Freud began *his own* experiments in self-analysis at around the same time that Nietzsche's project finally ended its course in an impasse.

Thus Nietzsche is confirmed as something other than a lover of high peaks, but rather as one who also knew how to 'dig' in the deepest strata of the *Trieblehre* (the doctrine of the drives) and who knew how to extract its precious 'gems'. These 'pre-metapsychological' intuitions, which we will examine in detail (in Part One, Chapter 2, 'Nietzsche in Freudian Discourse'), testify to Nietzsche's contribution to an anthropological knowledge of the Unconscious, a potent antidote to the vain speculation constituting the sterile regime of philosophy, as seen by Freud.[50]

While anticipating the detailed study of these junctures, the only solid material in this rapprochement, we need to raise a capital point. Where the apostles of a Nietzscheo-Freudian ecumenism had exalted the affinities in order to base their arguments for a common *Weltanschauung* – a tendency attested, though with important nuances, from Otto Gross to Otto Rank, and passing through Thomas Mann – the creator of psychoanalysis, through his strategy of marking 'little points' of encounter (which nonetheless open, discreetly, on to larger perspectives) acts on Nietzsche's contributions to anthropological knowledge in a somehow 'positive' way, in terms of unconscious processes. This precise and syncopated strategy of citation and reference, which has the disadvantage of allusivity, has at the same time the advantage of *not* accrediting the 'mixture' with the flattering status that would link psychoanalysis with some *Weltanschauung* – something Freud rejects in principle[51] – while blunting the 'point' of Nietzsche's *Witz.*

That goes back to a reading of Nietzsche, not as a *Weltanschauer*, a forger of 'world visions' – a widespread tendency whose damage is well known, insofar as the first vision of the world to appear can slip across the horizon and be validated *as a world-vision* – but as an 'ally', in terms of a conquest of a new and not 'conventional' knowledge. Subsequently, such a reading as we propose permits setting aside the nostalgia for a *Weltanschauung* that haunted Nietzscheism (as in the eyes of Freud, it does all 'philosophizing'), to extract the 'essence' of 'positivity', moreover against the grain of any doctrinal 'positivism'.

Lou Salomé, the Mercurial Feminine

All the same, Freud does not remain alone together with the Nietzschean text; he will also see it come to him, via Lou Andreas-Salomé, the woman who had been close to Nietzsche. It is not a matter of indifference that Nietzsche should return to Freud, in a way, through a 'messenger'.

In 1911, at the moment of their encounter, Lou brought to Freud a sort of renewal of direct contact with the person of Nietzsche and the spirit of his work. It is true that Nietzsche's presence remained between them discreet and in a way demure; it is hardly the case that, in the moment when the *Hymn to Life* confronts him with the prospects of an inaccessible enjoyment, Freud revives a bygone complicity, forged in the trio of Nietzsche, Lou and Paul Rée, which Lou had evoked in veiled words. For once, Freud is reading Nietzsche in someone's presence, and moreover that someone had physically been in Nietzsche's company, even his 'lyricist' . . .

We should bear in mind that, in the amiable person of Lou, Freud sees come back to him a secret nostalgia for an encounter that did not take place – in 1875. On the other hand, Lou, who herself knew Nietzsche a little later on (around 1882), brings something of his 'person' to Freud. Freud, in the meantime, has become a user of Nietzsche's texts. The woman, as messenger, thus gives flesh to the conjunction; where Freud, a decade earlier, had sought the words for the many silent things within him, Lou communicates, quasi-silently, something of that 'Nietzschean thing,' through her proximity to Freud. But precisely, in the presence of this Nietzschean spirit, Freud responds to it with a dash of irony.

The story of the *Hymn to Life*, set in 1912, found yet a new development that Lou's diaries have since made known. Freud and Lou met again in 1928, and the earlier episode was brought back onto the carpet, at the same time as Nietzsche's presence. 'I had just asked him,' Lou recalls, 'if he remembered our conversation from several years before. In fact, he did remember it . . .'[52] If the 'mnemonic trace' of the episode thus rose up again, it was because he who had joked about it long ago had since been submitted to his own torments, more severe than a mere 'head cold.' In 1923, Freud had been diagnosed with cancer of the jaw, beginning a period of 'terrible, tiresome and painful years' that defied the limits of 'human resistance.' With that in mind, Lou ceded to an impulse that she herself later described (in 1936) as 'inexplicable'. 'Revolted at the idea of his fate and his agony, I said to him, my lips trembling: "What I babbled in the heat of enthusiasm, you have proved!" ' On an autumn day in 1928,

Lou Salomé thus makes *a posteriori* the *Hymn* written with Nietzsche into a prophecy of Freud's torments; she readdresses it to Freud himself, as a confirmation of its youthful 'suffering', from the time when she was the 'lyricist' of the Nietzschean hymn.

This dénouement takes on a symbolic meaning, which only better expresses the *différend.* Freud has never denied the extent of suffering in human reality; what he does reject, though, is the masochistic exaltation and the pathos of this suffering. Lou, sobbing, intensely sincere regarding Freud's physical ordeal, affects to take up again her *Hymn*, enjoining him in a way to 'give' himself over to his suffering in the spirit of the hymn; Freud, for his part, while touched by this act of affection, responds with the sober Stoicism of *Ananké.*[53] That is how we must understand his reaction. 'Freud does not answer. I only feel his arm around my shoulder.' No point in dwelling on the suffering, nor on weaving verbal ornaments; such is his ethic on the matter.

III THE STAKES OF A DIFFÉREND: METAPSYCHOLOGY AND GENEALOGY

We have returned to the very centre of the Nietzsche–Freud 'différend' (a term to be understood in its most radical sense) that we can demonstrate via the difference between their respective 'attitudes', subjective and otherwise. It is here, at the heart of this divergence, between genealogy and metapsychology, that we must place the inquiry.

The 'Crux' of the Différend: The Drive Between Eros and Power

If we re-examine the schematic of our narrative of confrontation between Nietzsche and Freud, in its thematic and its problematic aspects, we see that we could strengthen it around two extremities, which demarcate the space of tension.

- The point of departure, or *terminus a quo*, is constituted by the notion of 'drive' (*Trieb*), but therein a divergence of models of deciphering 'instinct' (Part Two, Book I, Chapter 1, 'Instinct and Drive') is revealed.
- The point of arrival, or *terminus ad quem*, reveals the main bifurcation to be between a genealogy of 'will to power' (*Wille zur Macht*) (Nietzsche) and a metapsychology of the 'death wish' (*Todestrieb*) (Freud).

All the drama of the rapprochements and divergences is played out between these two poles and is focused on *this final aporic point, 'Will to power' versus 'death wish,' whose stake is none other than a reading of the subject in its setting within the symbolic order, where the question of the father is a symptom.*

In our re-reading of this long confrontation, we would like to highlight this nodal point. It seems to us to be the best means, consequently, of reintroducing the 'aporic relationship' between these two formidable (and formative) powers of contemporary thought, less in order to 'orient' the reading of the ensemble than to carry to a certain point of exacerbation what is profiled in our own conclusion, and so to suggest the dynamic.

The 'Will to Power' in Metapsychology

Metapsychology's precise ambition is to recast philosophical problems in the register of Unconscious signification.[54] Freud does not intervene at this level in order to produce a philosophical evaluation of Will to Power, but to bring to expression what it – marked by Nietzschean philosophy – signifies in view of the 'science of the Unconscious.' In other words, Freud has to speak here, not in the interiority of philosophical discourse, but with the sole, and firm, authority of clinico-metapsychological knowledge. 'Here there is a place, as a metapsychologist, to situate what is called "Will to Power".' Now, the label *Wille zur Macht*, wherein Nietzsche undeniably engages the *ultimum verbum* of his thought, also designates a sort of 'enigma', Nietzsche's philosophical thing-in-itself; it is the metapsychological evaluation, the *Beurteilung* of the concept which Freud brings into play.

We should emphasize that Nietzsche, who previously was explicitly solicited to support certain articles of theory (see above, 'Nietzsche, *Tiefenpsycholog* Before the Fact'), is never cited by name here, in the decisive passages in Freud's texts of the 1920s, where the notion of 'Will to Power' appears. The contrast, paradoxically, argues for a privileged importance of this 'coded' exchange on the latter terrain. It is this point, which calls into question the legitimacy of the Nietzschean project, that will be 'proved' by metapsychology, which is summoned at a decisive moment in the evolution – and which comes to stress the introduction of the death wish, to be proved in the manner of *Wille zur Macht*.

What is this 'willing' whose 'object' is 'power'? In particular, what do we place under the 'to' (*zu*) that will 'catapult' the Will toward power, if power (*Macht*) does not demand a 'will' at its level? To this question, encountered by every (philosophical) commentary on the Nietzschean project, Freud suggests an original clarification, which comes to designate its other side.

The question intersects the metapsychological elaboration of a 'doctrine of power' (*Machtlehre*). We know that Freud has always been one of the most reticent theorists with regard to an overestimation of the drive-related potency of 'power'; that was the central stake in his controversy with Adler. In addition, he never ceases, when he sees the claims of this 'mobile drive' that is power rise, to reaffirm the primacy of the 'libido.'[55] It is not the case that he denies a problematic of power – there is indeed a 'drive for power' (*Machttrieb*) – but all this is for Freud assigned a place in the overall economy of the drives, as far as the insistent reference has had for its effect, if not for its finality, to redirect the denial of Eros in its unconscious power, with a paradoxical secondary effect of 'sexualizing power', for want of recognizing the power of the sexual.

On the other hand, if Freud is in a position, in a first moment, to remember not to overestimate the role of 'power' to the detriment of the libido (thus localizing the 'drives for power' on the side of the 'Ego drives' and opposed to the 'sexual drives'), he is led, in a second fundamental moment, to recognize 'power' itself, in its place, in the economy of drives, between Eros and Thanatos. At the moment when Freud lets the term *Wille zur Macht* slip into his text, this 'disengagement' is revealed.

The passage can be recognized by the displacement, in Freud's text,[56] of a reference to *Willen zur Macht* – which again goes back to the anthropological version of Nietzsche accredited by Adler – by a problematic of *Wille zur Macht*, imposing in a way a face-to-face comparison with Nietzsche (although, to be precise, Nietzsche is no longer named as the 'proprietor' of this category.)

The wish-for-power (*Willen zur Macht*) is a drive for appropriation sustained by self-preservation, which Adler fashioned as a mobile determinant, that is organized in 'complexes' (inferiority/ superiority). Will to Power (*Wille zur Macht*) is quite another thing; introducing the concept in the mid-1920s, the years of *Beyond the Pleasure Principle* and the essay on masochism, Freud makes it the equivalent of the 'drive for destruction' (*Destruktionstrieb*). There is, we know, a terminological ethic in Freud, who is aware that there is only a single step, from having 'ceded the words' (*in Wörtern*), to 'ceding the things' (*in Sachen*). To what end, then, are the metapsychological use and redefinition of *Wille zur Macht* engaged?

Here is the decisive moment, when 'the metapsychological sorceress' finds herself solicited for what she can tell, and do, concerning Will to Power. What 'unconscious reality' does she recover, via this 'philosophical signifier' that she designates – knowing precisely that a philosophical category comes along with the expression – all while veiling, under the sublimation effect of the *Begriff* (Concept), the unconscious Real that psychoanalysis unveils?

Will to Power versus Death Wish

To say that 'Will to Power' may be defined as a drive for destruction and/or expropriation is not to turn power into a principle unto itself, a type of *princeps* mobile drive. The libido remains at work, in this context, in order to accomplish its function as 'liaison'; in fact, it is a matter of 'rendering inoffensive this destructive drive (*diesen destruierenden Trieb*) that is the 'death wish' properly speaking.[57] The libidinal task is effectuated by the turning away toward the exterior of this endogenous destructive drive, which energetically claims its 'part' in the drive-related dimension of life. It takes place by means of the active 'organic system' of the musculature, directed toward 'the objects of the external world.' Thus, it is the drive for destruction and/or expropriation, depending on where one puts the accent, at the moment of annihilation (*Destruktion*) or appropriation (*Bemächtigung*), which merits – a metaphysical promotion, in a way – the label of 'Will to Power.'

Wille zur Macht, thus 'read' by Freud, is not a manifestation of aggressive selfishness pure and simple, nor is it the exalted form of domination – he avoids the most widely pronounced misinterpretations of Nietzsche's concept. But it is no longer a principle in itself, a type of *ne plus ultra* that would confront us in a naked display of power; still, it is a libidinal strategy, *but in the limit-point where Eros is found situated in the extreme potentiality of 'de-liaison' or 'dis-intrication' from the death wish (properly internal).*

Will to Power is not a simple 'wishing' for power, nor a drive for self-preservation, nor of 'valorizing' (*Erhaltungstrieb* or *Geltungstrieb*), as in the psychologized version put forth by Adler, a 'humanist' version of Nietzschean metaphysics. It is, if we give Freud's interpretation its most developed expression, the movement of exteriorization, in the most radical sense of 'externalization', of the mortifying potentiality, coming to expression according to a scansion of destruction and domination, of annihilation and mastery.

We are a long ways from an 'axiological' reading of Will to Power; metapsychology has the sole aim of locating the function of *Wille zur Macht* in the dynamic of drives in some way *in materia.* But from here it is a question – an essential point for our purposes – of registering the consequences of this reading for the Nietzschean conception. This metapsychological diagnostic, which simultaneously avoids a reductive psychologization and the denial of philosophical signification, brings us closer to an understanding of what is in play for the 'final Nietzsche,' as far as the intelligence of the Freud–Nietzsche *différend* is concerned.

Let us try to represent for ourselves what seems to be the (unconscious) subject of 'Will to Power.' It would not know how to be an 'actor', since 'power' is, even more than the object of 'willing', its 'motor'; whoever would 'wish' for power would strongly resemble an 'impotent', an impardonable fault of 'reactivity' in Nietzsche's ethic. *Wille zur Macht* confirms that there is no 'object' of volition named 'power'.

All the same, this subject is not the simple plaything of an anonymous force; Will to Power, thus subjectivated – finding its subject in some way in order 'to act' – visibly alludes to a particular enjoyment, so 'particular' truly speaking, that every ultimate effort (in the Promethean sense) of the author of *The Will to Power* is to characterize this enjoyment, to produce a knowledge of it . . . as impossible. The poignant efforts of the 'final Nietzsche' attests that he must be made the plaything of this enjoyment and 'to pay with his person' in order to attempt to carry it, in a final experience, from lived experience and writing to expression.

This subject is thus not that of the libido, yet it is 'libidinal'; we understand that the task which comes to expression in and by 'Will to Power' remains arrayed to a libidinal logic, one of 'liaison' and 'investment', but its 'object' is by nature heterogeneous to the 'erotic'. The finality originates in the libidinal economy, but the means at work 'plug' this strategy into the economy of the drives of death and de-liaison which furnish it, paradoxically, with its 'energy source'. In this we see the constituent paradox of 'Will to Power' that the metapsychological decoding manages to 'pin down.'

The question of crime permits us to show *in concerto* how Eros and Thanatos are negotiated; the 'pale criminal' comes to incarnate this narcissistic effigy and its eroticized destructiveness.[58] This exceptional position must be deciphered for Freud in terms of the position of the act with respect to guilt, in the 'negative' sense of neurotic guilt, whereas Nietzsche turns it into a symbol of the reversal of the Law.

The 'Originary Scene' of Will to Power: The Subject of the Eternal Return

We understand the 'vertigo' of the subject in question here; the subject realizes, via 'destruction', a libidinal aim. At the precise moment when this 'deviation' of the potential for de-liaison toward the 'outside' is realized, what happens 'in' the subject? There is indeed a (sexual) enjoyment, since it is the libido which brings it into action, but it is only possible to 'bail out' by expelling (outside oneself) the 'death wish' then set in motion, a veritable 'counter-libidinal' force. The subject is in this way activated, in a strange 'eroticism', by the *Todestrieb*, the death wish.

We understand that the subject 'disappears' in this movement, since it is precisely at the moment when it is expelled to the outside – the centrifugal movement of destructivity – that the subject realizes the libidinal 'gain' that returns to its 'Ego' in an indescribable sentiment of 'elation'. We have in this a point of confusion, or of 'short-circuit', between Eros and Thanatos, which could instruct us on the status of the subject of Nietzsche's *princeps* experience, his so-called revelation at Sils-Maria, in the summer of 1881, where the truth of the eternal return and the postulate of the Superhuman was signified to him, while the Will to Power found, in this 'zero hour' of 'high noon', its Real and its subject.

We could see how this was accomplished in an explosive cocktail of 'world-destruction' and 'omnipotence', since the subject is found confronted with the naked figure of the Real, at this point of 'short-circuit' between the 'inside' and the 'outside'. Pleasure and anguish are indissolubly linked in a lived experience of enjoyment, an accomplishment of *amor fati* and the confrontation with *Tuchè*, absolute Accident.

But by that we also grasp the same stake of the Nietzsche–Freud *différend*. On the one hand, 'The Will to Power' informs us specifically about the economy of the 'death wish' in its 'magical' activation; but, on the other hand, where Nietzsche sees the epitome of affirmation, the 'great Yes' bestowing sense right up to the point of non-sense, Freud radically resists any imaginary construction of 'Power'.

To say that *Wille zur Macht* finds it signification in the libidinized expression of the death wish is to reject its 'glorification'. Power is in no case the 'last word' of desire; it only occludes the object of a lack – that of 'castration' and/or the 'death wish'. The subject would not know how to find its being in power; it can only experiment with its 'division' (*Spaltung*). It is thus a phrase – Will to

Power – with which it is fundamentally tempting to 'treat oneself', if we do not evaluate it in terms of its weight in the drive-related economy and alterity. It is a morbid figure of enjoyment, which produces unconscious truth in its metaphysical disguise.

The 'feeling of power', while effective, takes its signification from the subjective effect of narcissistic and phallic potency. To think in terms of power, is to redirect a certain imaginary of castration and an illusion of its beyond, while psychoanalysis brings back desire to the proof of its structural lack.

Power and Grief: The Question of the Father

What psychoanalysis never ceases articulating is that the subject is taken in a constituent relation to prohibition, which is personified in the (unconscious) function of the father.[59] The subject is structured around the 'murder of the father,' in relation to its desire (properly speaking), and it is there that it negotiates its attitude regarding power. The accent that Freud places on the anguish of castration confirms that power is a (massive) metaphor for castration. What does this mean, except that the subject only defines its 'will to power' as an expression of the relation to this proof of castration, which returns it to the father?

Under the modalities of the castrating father – made imaginary – the one who notably rises in the 'decline of the Oedipus complex', POWER (in a way, in unconscious capital letters) is found to be made symbolic. This generic question, and its multiple and complex repercussions, must be situated here in order to understand what will be in play in this *crossed relation between power and death, via the father* – through the contrasting evaluations of Nietzsche and Freud.

Nietzsche's thought is deployed across the horizon of the problematic of the 'death of God' – a balance of the effects of the phrase 'God is dead.' Now, it is necessary to begin on this path, whose very breadth must not frighten us, except to keep us from any reductionism. Psychoanalysis situates the idea of God on the side of the transfiguration of the image of the father. 'Psychoanalysis teaches us the intimate coherence between the father complex (*Vaterkkomplex*) and the belief in God and shows that the personal god is psychologically nothing but a glorified father (*ein erhöhter Vater*) . . .'[60] It is thus that we encounter Nietzsche's declaration of the death of his father, in his earliest autobiographies, as the major event that destined his being and the trajectory of his life.

Far from any 'psycho-biographical' temptation, let us re-read in this perspective the words with which the young Nietzsche recorded, in a way, this originary grief in his 'proto-historical' writings.

The precocious autobiography never ceases to state, and repeat, the shock of this moment – in July 1849 – which signified to him, in his fifth year, his abandonment by his father. 'Such was the first crucial moment beginning from which my whole life took a different direction.'[61] Nietzsche never ceases coming back to the event. 'Misfortune in fact struck – my father died.'[62] The autobiography is finalized by the recollection of this primitive strike of the tocsin. 'And this misfortune struck: my father died.'[63] There, in Nietzsche's words, is the first of the 'ruptures which have marked (his) life': 'The death of my father, pastor of Röcken.'[64] Evoked in the simple past, that of lived experience, the moment comes back to a dated thought (26 July 1849). 'The thought of seeing myself forever separated from my father took hold of me and I cried bitterly.'[65] Such is the germinal point of suffering – a type of gap in the (parental) Other – that Nietzsche formulates, in 1864, as an acute regret that, 'beginning from that moment, my development did not take place under the watchful eyes of a man.'[66] A life henceforth lost from the view of an absent father, which introduces there a moral 'lesion'.

If there is a 'diagnosis' in this, it is from Nietzsche himself that it originally rises, as a 'self-writing' in the grip of an originary grief for the father. 'The pain and grief overtakes everything.'[67] The disturbing thing is that he who would become the discounter of a dead God, in his vocation as a thinker, is engendered from this primitive catastrophe that he retells even up to his final autobiography, which opens with the formidable declaration that 'I am, to express myself in an enigmatic way, already dead, insofar as I am an extension of my father.'[68]

This declaration is all the more striking, in that it had already been made by Nietzsche over the course of some 40 years of autobiographical writing, as a veritable self-diagnosis; 'I am,' he recognizes, 'his extension after a too-precocious death.'[69] We would be wrong to see this as a matter of hyperbole or of a stylistic convention; it is the clearest expression of Nietzsche's identification with his dead father, a melancholic anchorage which Freud will activate in a generic manner by making melancholy 'the identification with the dead father' (of the primitive horde).[70] The great scene of Nietzsche's final collapse, in Turin, in January 1889, engulfed, in a way, by an intense pity at the sight of a mistreated animal, may well carry the mark of this melancholy.

Nietzsche literally declares that, having himself reached the age at which his own father had died, he did nothing more than survive. 'So I *truly* became a shadow.' That puts into perspective the sequence that follows: somatic ailments, self-destitution (resignation from the University at Basel), taking up a wandering life.

Are we engaged in the search for a psychoanalytic key to a way of thinking about ethics and power, which Freud has otherwise himself outlined?[71] It is, rather, a question of a wholly other thing; that is, to draw out, with all the tact and decisive spirit that is necessary, this point of *vacillation of the symbolic* which decides the genealogical project.

Conclusion: Freud or Nietzsche, the 'Moral Symptom'

The reconstruction of the affinities and the deepening of the *différend* lead to a strange sight, where the conjunction 'Freud and Nietzsche' is deployed as … a disjunction, 'Freud *or* Nietzsche.' This is certainly not to signify that there would be a choice (this 'or' is not *ad libitum*, for each to choose, which would return very precisely to the dilettantism of ideologies or of *Weltanschauungen*). What is designated in this 'or' is the double reading of the position of the subject with respect to life and death, via the Law and desire. That may provide us with a viewpoint on the question of the destinies of morality for Nietzsche and Freud, as two destinies of 'guilt' – two versions of the genealogy.

The other name for 'Will to Power' is 'innocence of becoming' – which founds a metaphysics of perversion – let us say of the constitution of a pure Law of the challenge and of the Superhuman, whose postulate is the affirmation of the 'circle' of Will to Power, the eternal return and Overman, supporting the truth of the eternal present of the 'willing'. The Real, here, takes the form of the *Tuchè*, the sovereign Accident. But that permits us to understand the disconcerting phrase that 'the father is always only an accident.'[72] There is the support of the Law placed at the side of this radical contingency, a confluence of the 'Father' (*Vater*) and Chance (*Zufall*). Another way of saying the same thing is that 'the father' (written by Nietzsche in quotation marks, a paternal 'citation') 'is always a comic character' (*eine komische Person*).[73] Perhaps the secret to the (genealogical) quest for an origin of morals lies in this identification of the father and of the originary object of the loss, which marks the world with a seal of ontological contingency.

The 'genealogy of morals,' in its Freudian version, stumbles on the originary event of the murder of the father (*Vatermord*) which marks the 'beginnings of morality and of law.' It is a major sequel to primitive guilt, which runs from the murder of the father to the 'reconciliation with the father' (*Vaterversöhnung*),[74] a kind of *post mortem* pact with the father which assures the posthumous life of the originary Deed for every 'child of man.' From totemic liturgy to Superego cruelty ('moral masochism'),[75] psychoanalysis establishes in its own way the Nietzschean description of the 'moral symptom.'

It is the point of abutment, which we can understand as the point of arrival of this formidable confrontation, which questions *in fine* the very being of the Law. While Nietzsche engineers the modalities of 'overcoming', the quest for the source of the Nile of morality, in hopes of reversing this destiny, psychoanalysis makes of the 'renunciation of the drives' (*Triebverzicht*) the point of no return for the unconscious subject articulated in desire by guilt, since it is there where the subject feels guilt that it desires. The *Vatersehnsucht* – longing for the father – is precisely this unconscious tropism. The contrasted reading of the Promethean myth carries this divergence to expression. Where Nietzsche sees, even beyond the transgression, the acknowledgment of the creation of gods by heroes,[76] Freud makes the most startling unconscious apologue for the 'renunciation of the drives.'[77]

The experience of the Unconscious gives us a perspective on its strange relation to morality. No one is better placed than the analyst to measure the fragility of the sentiment of goodness in the human subject. The morbid effects of 'goodness' are confirmed there, and Freud firmly bars the way to a conception of psychoanalysis as a sort of re-education in moral identity, an 'amelioration of the moral personality,' as in James Putnam's formula.[78] But there it is; what is demonstrated in the Unconscious is not some radical 'immorality,' a sort of 'immoralism' no more suited to psychoanalysis than the least moral *Weltanschauung*. What *is* demonstrated in the trials and tribulations of the symptom is a relation to prohibition, as obstinate as it is contradictory.

If we think about it a bit, we find that Freud shows a genealogical acuity, which renders acute precisely one of the major consequences of the introduction of the 'death wish' and of the 'Beyond of the pleasure principle': the notion of 'moral masochism.' Thus we must understand the formidable genealogical potentiality of the conclusion of his essay on masochism:

> We habitually represent things as if the moral requirement (*die sittliche Anforderung*) was the primary thing (*das Primäre*) and the renunciation of the drives (*Triebverzicht*) was its consequence. But the origin of morality (*die Herkunft der Sittlichkeit*), in that way, remains unexplained. In reality, the reverse (*umgekehrt*) seems to happen; the first renunciation of the drives is extorted by external powers and it begins by creating morality (*die Sittlichkeit*) which is expressed in the Conscious (*Gewissen*) and demands a new renunciation of the drives.[79]

The sentiment of guilt requisitioned by the Superego allows it to be brought to life, while interrogating its radical duplicity. The feeling of guilt would not be able to cause a renunciation of drives; there is first off a renunciation of drives that constitutes moral renunciation. In a way, it is the Freudian version of *Umwertung*. Moral illusion is based on the generative 'paralogism' that it is in the name of the Conscious that the struggle against the drives is undertaken, while in truth the Conscious itself *originates out of this primary renunciation*, which then demands another renunciation, and so on, *ad infinitum*. For each new renunciation, aggressivity is internalized, 'nourishing' the Superego, deriving from this insatiable Molochian logic the resources of its ferocity. It is in this prodigious reversal that Freud responds to the 'problem of Nietzsche,' but, doing this, he formally challenges the response that the *Genealogy of Morals* delivers, or rather that which the radical response claims.

For Nietzsche, the quest for an outside to the Law appears as the temptation to return to the point where the question of the father is suspended in a way; the 'body' of Will to Power comes to incarnate something like a subversion, or even a perversion – by way of the metaphysics of innocence – while psychoanalysis obstinately summons back the condition of desire from the side of the Law. Moreover, Will to Power is proposed not only as a diagnostic operator, but as an antidote to the illness of morality, by replacing a repressive Superego with a Superego 'drunk with innocence.' It is, if we think about it, what drives every 'return to Nietzsche' of yesterday as well as of today.

Psychoanalysis returns us for its part to a relation, in a sense unsurpassable, to desire and the Law, but which requires us to renegotiate the relation between desire and its mortifying deviations – on condition of recognizing the price paid to the death wish, as toward human desire. It is a point of access to the Law which is not by way of desire, and not a possible economy of the Law from the moment that the subject is taken up in the order of desire; of this declaration, which bears all its experience, Freudianism would not know how to 'let go.'

That is how we should understand Freud's 'paradoxical phrase,' that 'the normal man is not only more immoral than he believes himself to be, but also much more moral than he knows.'[80] It is perhaps in the irony of this tension that the conjunction Nietzsche–Freud comes into play, between the 'moral symptom' and 'man'-as-the-symptom …

INTRODUCTION

FREUD 'AND' NIETZSCHE: THE STAKES OF A CONJUNCTION

'Freud *and* Nietzsche'. This conjunction has been recognized and accredited for a long time, indeed from the very beginnings of psychoanalysis, ever since resonances were perceived between the work of the former and the words of the latter.[1] How could we not recognize it, at least intuitively, when such-and-such a declaration by Nietzsche 'sounds Freudian' to our ears? Beyond this intuitive perception, however, the threads of an analogy have been persistently woven together, to the point where a common ground has been constructed between the two theorists. The temptation to see such an analogy in itself *already* links the founder of psychoanalysis (in defiance of his own protests) to Nietzsche as his great 'precursor'.

But the threads of that analogy, though obstinately woven together, are at most only tenuous, and like Penelope's labour the analogy is forever undone and started anew. It is necessary to move away from the analogy and on to the basic comparison that it indicates, but which has too often eluded us. The Nietzscheo-Freudian theme is imposed upon us, as an already-existing preliminary requirement, but we have hesitated to make it explicit, and so the analogy has come to appear sufficient unto itself, by way of suggestion, as vast as it is vague. Thus an eclectic discourse came to accommodate the haziness of this rapprochement, by weaving an analogy from rhetorical similitudes.

We propose to make explicit both the content and the meaning of this conjunction that, far from sufficing unto itself, produces a host of problems, and even constitutes a problem in itself. What should we think of the seductive, yet impressionistic syntagm 'Freud *and* Nietzsche'? How can we rigorously interpret the conjunction? It is all the more timely a question, given that Nietzsche, in one of his final aphorisms, had suggested a hermeneutic of this very conjunction, by interpreting certain 'ands' of 'bad alloys': those who, for example, say 'Goethe *and* Schiller' or 'Schopenhauer *and* von Hartmann'.[2] What would he think about the fact that, just shortly after his death, people would be forging the alloy 'Nietzsche *and* Freud'?

Our project will set out from the principle that we can legitimately suspect of being 'bad alloys' every conjunction of proper names which are satisfied by a seductive resonance without relating it to the less timely expression of problematics that at once make the resonance possible and permit the distribution of such honours and equivocations. The implication is that, in the first place, we should relate the comparison 'Nietzsche–Freud', naturally made possible in retrospect by the second term, to the overall context of the relation of the founder of psychoanalysis to philosophy and to the philosophers from which he draws meaning. From this first perspective, we would straight away falsify the question of Nietzsche–Freud relations by isolating them from the general relation of Freud to philosophers and to philosophy in general. A reminder is never more necessary than here, that the prestige of the precursor produces the illusory effect of a *tête-à-tête*. Against this prejudice, we should recall that Freud approaches Nietzsche the philosopher with the *habitus* and posture that defines him in the context of philosophical reality. For this reason, our present inquiry is necessarily detached from our preceding study, where we presented this posture in its complex unity and ambivalent coherence.[3]

But our previous work, if it furnishes us with a basically indispensable canvas, in no way exhausts the specific question approached here. It is necessary to undertake a second perspective, to restore Nietzsche to a privileged place, without however anticipating the result of our inquiry. When Freud encounters the figure of Friedrich Nietzsche, he feels, despite his impulse to apply to him the general policy he reserves for the philosophizing breed, that he has to deal with something other than some non-privileged actualization of thought. And had he been tempted to avoid this privilege, others are poised to induce him toward such an engagement,[4] as mediators have seldom been as zealous as those between Freud and Nietzsche.

Nothing is more revealing, from this point of view, than the confrontation of Freud with the two figures of Schopenhauer and Nietzsche. In what we have previously called the 'Freudian philosophical topography',[5] Schopenhauer occupies the centre. At the heart of this 'galaxy', Nietzsche occupies merely the position of first satellite, and moreover who would not think of contesting Schopenhauer for the function of a solar centre, for profound historical and ideological reasons that we have already placed in evidence.[6]

Such is without a doubt Nietzsche's first *place*, if we approach the Freudian philosophical choice of object positively. He would always appear near Schopenhauer, benefitting from the latter's effluvia and virtues. In Freud's eyes, Nietzsche would in a way be a brilliant double of Schopenhauer. That is, from the point of view of Freud's personal use of philosophers, Nietzsche would come just after Schopenhauer. Freud encountered Nietzsche with a jovial sense of fraternity, in a common lineage from the master of Frankfurt. Freud's use of Nietzsche thus seems to be mediated by Schopenhauer, who really lends himself better to Freud's immediate needs. That is why, in a sense, the relation specific to Nietzsche does not carry a substantial modification from the regimen of Freud's general relation to philosophy, and so Nietzsche is found inserted into that regimen, submitted to the general statute without derogating or subverting it.

However, if Freud's relation to Schopenhauer is valued at first as a document of Freud's philosophical investment, his relation to Nietzsche is valuable in itself, beyond even what Freud himself specifies, seen from the dimension that later stakes have assigned to these 'partners'.[7] Independently of Freud's own views, and much to his chagrin, a sort of complicity was forged between psychoanalysis and Nietzsche, that forces us, without prejudging the analogy, to investigate the two in synchrony. That is why, if Freud's relation to Schopenhauer is primary with regard to the positive relation between Freud and philosophers generally, and thus *de facto* secondarizing his relation with Nietzsche, all this acquires an import of another order. The Freudian project came to be defined by its position and opposition, and thus 'by parentage', with respect to this privileged *philosophical* project which, not fortuitously, seems constantly to encroach upon the borders of psychoanalysis.

Thus *for us*, again, Freud's relation to Nietzsche appears privileged and in the last instance the richest in meaning. Again, it is useful to approach this relation in its historical particularity, in order to forestall any confusion between our interest and that of Freud, which would effectively, and at once, falsify our comparison. In order to conduct an exhaustive and objective comparison between these problematics, it is useful to view it as disengaged from the stakes visible to Freud and to historical consciousness, leaving us free to appeal to the texts in order to carry our explication to its term.

The conjunction 'Freud and Nietzsche' is, in effect, an immediately historical artefact. We understand that it was forged as a product of a particular elaboration. Before posing the theoretical question of foundations, we must examine the question of a problem which is objectified in a historical context. The best introduction to the problem will be thus to describe the genesis that made possible and imposed the conjunction and the parallelism between these two proper names. We will first examine the encounter between two precise realities, the psychoanalytic movement and those who had made themselves Nietzsche's testamental executors.

A STRANGE CONTEMPORANEITY

It is striking to measure the gap that historical consciousness has excavated between Nietzsche and Freud, who after all are rough contemporaries. Some benchmarks help express this contemporaneity.

Nietzsche is a dozen years older than Freud.[8] When Nietzsche is named professor of philology at Basel, Freud had not yet started his medical studies. The first *Untimely Meditations*, after *The Birth of Tragedy*, appears in the same year that the young Freud enters the Faculty of Medicine in Vienna (1873). Freud becomes a physician at the very moment when Nietzsche experiences the essential event – the revelation of the eternal return – that will decide his philosophy (1881–2).

When Nietzsche's philosophy enters its decisive period of production, during the 1880s, Freud is struggling for direction in his career. His voyage to Paris, to Charcot, is contemporary with Nietzsche's gospel, *Zarathustra* (1885–6). Nietzsche reaches his final crisis at the moment when Freud begins to turn his full attention to psychoanalysis, via his correspondence with Fliess (1887–8). When Nietzsche experiences his mental collapse, Freud, aged 33, is just discovering his identity.

In this period of Nietzsche's waning life, psychoanalysis is born. At the time of Nietzsche's death, *The Interpretation of Dreams* has just appeared, while the correspondence with Fliess, that would confirm Freud's thoughts and establish the path to his future identity, reaches its zenith (1901). A few years after Nietzsche's death, the first psychoanalytic group is formed (1902): Freud is 46.

These few benchmarks suffice to show that, chronologically, Nietzsche and Freud are indeed contemporaries, but while the first had expressed himself since his thirtieth year, Freud would not find himself until his fortieth year, by which time Nietzsche had put the final touches to his own work. Freud will continue to unfold his work for nearly four decades after Nietzsche's death, which in a way obscures the fact of their contemporaneity. Nietzsche's work, if long ignored, is only discovered toward the end of the 1880s, at the moment of the birth of psychoanalysis. It is thus an objective accident of history that at the beginning of the new century, we discover both psychoanalysis and the phenomenon of Nietzsche. That is, in fact, the first historical given we must take into account in order to prepare ourselves to understand how Freud came to know about Nietzsche and how a rapprochement would become possible between Nietzsche and Freud.

Beginning with a few preliminary signs,[9] it is only between the beginning of the 1890s and the turn of the century that a movement takes shape around the rediscovery of Nietzsche's work, even in Germany. But as with Schopenhauer, a long silence is followed by an infatuation that introduces Nietzsche's name to debates throughout the intellectual world.[10] This is the wave that would carry Nietzsche's name to Freud. Thus it is no accident if Nietzschean terms appear during this time, in Freud's correspondence with Fliess,[11] without this first trace (of Nietzsche *in* Freud) implying any real information. Nietzsche's terminology had found its way into the vocabulary of the intelligentsia of this period, and had even earned a certain salon affectation.

This great wave of discovery occurs between 1894, the date that Lou Salomé's biography of Nietzsche appeared,[12] soon followed by that of (his sister) Elisabeth Förster-Nietzsche (1896–1904),[13] and 1913, with the appearance of the nineteenth and final volume of *Gesammelte Werke*, begun in 1899.[14] It is a symbolic fact that at the same moment that Sigmund Freud makes his entry into the scientific field, through the formulation of his *Traumdeutung* (published in Vienna), the first stone in the literary monument to Nietzsche's work is laid, the well-known *Gesammelte Werke*, thus tieing Freud's *terminus a quo* to Nietzsche's *terminus ad quem*.

But if Nietzsche thus gains his *monument*, it appears above all as a stake in a quarrel that, under the influence of his own sister, takes on a scholastic sheen. In order to pose in terms of an origin the context of the 'encounter' between Nietzsche and Freud, it is useful to recall that this collected edition of Nietzsche's work, offered to readers, was made the object of a conflict over *property*, even before its author was dead. At the beginning of the century, all contact with Nietzsche's work had to submit, for good or ill, to a detour through Elisabeth Förster-Nietzsche,[15] founder of the Nietzsche-Archiv foundation. Elisabeth actively patronized the appearance of the Complete Works as well as a pocket edition (*Taschenausgabe*), and in the years before the war (1910–13) assured the text a substantial distribution. The Nietzsche-Archiv, whose history Elisabeth wrote in 1907, significantly titled *The Nietzsche-Archive: Its Friends and Enemies,*[16] plays the ambiguous role of a general staff, and deliberately controversial.

In contrast, a current issuing from Basel and Franz Overbeck sketched an opposing vision of Nietzsche, which would find an important formulation in a 1908 work by Carl-Albrecht Bernoulli.[17] Indeed, if someone had wanted, in the period of the birth of psychoanalysis, to become familiar with the life and work of Nietzsche, they could turn to the works of Raoul Richter,[18] Richard M. Meyer[19] or even Ernst Bertram.[20] But these contributions are important to our own project only as a backdrop of general knowledge about Nietzsche, the soil on which the relations between Freud and Nietzsche will flourish, but which Freud himself refused to exploit.

And *that* is precisely what we will have to take into account, as a negative complement to the explosive diffusion of Nietzsche's work contemporary with Freud's establishment of psychoanalysis. Freud himself never lost an occasion to curse 'his' great gods *whom he had not read.* We will simply point out here the declarations that we will analyse later.[21]

In 1908, Freud declares in no uncertain terms that 'he does not know the work of Nietzsche'.[22] Given that by this date it was impossible not to know Nietzsche's *name,* whose prominence was at an apogee, it is necessary to understand that in any case Freud neither read nor studied Nietzsche's *work,* which confirms a contemporary attestation, where Freud 'made the remark that he had never been able to study Nietzsche'. Not that he had never taken up a volume of Nietzsche in his hands, but, according to his own words, he was not able 'to go beyond a half-page in his attempts to read Nietzsche'.[23]

Freud makes the same declaration in 1914: 'I have denied myself the great pleasure that reading Nietzsche brings'.[24] This time, the refusal to engage Nietzsche's work takes the form of a voluntary penitence that results in the same privation. A final confirmation occurs in 1925 where Freud says that he had 'for a long time avoided'[25] Nietzsche. Fortuitous or voluntary, we will need to inquire into the motivations for this abstinence or penitence, but it is, at the very least, a fact which sets a strict limit to Freud's role as a reader of Nietzsche.

Moreover, it is also a fact that a durable relation ties the two together, that there exists a Freudian discourse on Nietzsche and a commerce between the two thinkers that Freud does not deny. Thus if the relation is only incompletely linked to a direct knowledge of the philosophical work, it must come from other channels, of which it is all the more important to examine, as they constitute the historically determined relation from Nietzsche to Freud, and as such must be integrated at least as positive preliminaries to any examination of the question of their relationship.

Before speculating on the relation between the works in themselves[26] *in abstracto,* it is necessary to define those threads that have woven between Freud and Nietzsche a relation at once denied and insistent. There, the signs of a 'Freudo-Nietzschean chronicle' take on a considerable importance, given that the *events*, in their anodyne, anecdotal appearance, weave the figure of these relations by sketching their historical particularity.

In the period that we have defined as inaugurating the relationship, two major, discrete events at once establish the chronology. We need to investigate them in order to begin to write this chronicle and to discover the deep meaning, at once manifested and occluded by the singularity of events.

'NIETZSCHE' IN THE WEDNESDAY SEMINARS (1)

That Nietzsche was regularly implicated in the reflections of the first analytic circle is demonstrated by his appearance as the topic for two meetings of the famous Wednesday seminars of the Vienna Psychoanalytic Society during 1908. The purpose of these meetings was to present a lecture followed by a general discussion, in the course of which Freud naturally had occasion to take a position. The minutes of these meetings constitute important documents of the weekly poles of interest of these first analysts, in this period of the enthusiastic clearing of a new field[27] – and, for what concerns us, of the apprehension of the phenomenon of Nietzsche by the psychoanalytic movement at the moment of its origin.

On 1 April, 1908, Eduard Hitschmann proposed a lecture commenting on the third essay of *On the Genealogy of Morals* dedicated to the theme, 'On the Ascetic Ideal'. From the minutes kept by Otto Rank,[28] we know the ideas developed regarding Nietzsche on this occasion. Hitschmann denies that Nietzsche is a philosopher, but rather 'a moralist, although distinguished, it is true, by an uncommon acuity'.[29] On the other hand, the minutes point out 'the contrast between his behaviour in daily life and the principle theme of his works',[30] that is, the opposition between the sadness of his character and the Dionysian intoxication that permeates his writing. The setting in relief of this contrast aimed at inducing an psychological interpretation of the case of Nietzsche – we understand by that a clarification of the content of the *work* through the drive-related experiences of the *author*.

This interpretation comes back, on the one hand, to consider Nietzsche the psychologist of morality, and on the other to cause a reflection on Nietzsche the man himself, as an objection to his enterprise, in terms of a psychoanalytic diagnostic. 'It is interesting to note that Nietzsche has discerned the essential elements of the psychology of others, but has not succeeded in seeing that his own ideas corresponded to unrealized desires.' Hitschmann comes in this way to reconcile Nietzsche's theory of the ascetic ideal with the sexual asceticism of Nietzsche the man. 'In submitting the ascetic ideal to a critique and to a psychological interpretation, by advocating a life without restraint and without regard, he rejects the circumstances in which he is forced to live. Nietzsche's life itself is none other than ascetic; his tendency toward asceticism is linked to his admiration for Schopenhauer.'[31]

The result is a philosophically reductionist interpretation. 'Nietzsche rejected the ascetic ideal when he recognized that he had cheated life as well as himself. So, the subjective ideas of a philosopher can be explained by his personal traits and experiences, which are clearly illustrated in *On the Genealogy of Morals*.'[32] Curiously, Hitschmann thus makes a literal, and a bit mechanical, use of an idea dear to Nietzsche himself, according to which 'every great philosophy up to our day has been the confession of its author, and (whether he willed it so or not) constitutes his *Memoires*'.[33]

Thus we have, not a philosophical reading of Nietzsche, but an exercise in *pathology*, to which the philosophical text serves to support as a document. In addition, if Hitschmann's contribution to the understanding of Nietzsche's ideas is deceptive, it expresses well that the relation to Nietzsche is mediated for psychoanalysis, from this moment on, by pathology, that is to say that the study of the pathological structure subtends any philosophical or artistic production.

It is moreover interesting that the ensuing discussion gives way to a controversy. For Isidor Sadger, 'Nietzsche is a model of hereditary stigmata', and he finds symptoms of hysteria in his precocious (beginning in childhood) 'epileptoid states without loss of consciousness'.[34] Others, on the contrary, protested against this reductionist approach, and placed Nietzsche's value in the debt psychoanalysis owed regarding certain of his ideas. Alfred Adler, first and foremost, declared resolutely that 'of all the important philosophers who have bequeathed to us something, Nietzsche is the closest to our way of thinking.'[35] On the other hand, 'he evokes arguments that speak against the linking of a preoccupation with philosophy to a single neurosis. The philosopher is much too complex a being, and the philosophical technique is by nature linked to something completely different.'[36] It is not fortuitous that Nietzsche as a philosopher finds an apologist in Adler. We know the role that Nietzsche plays in Adler's own thought, but here he is supposed to speak in the name of the analytic movement and places Nietzsche 'in a line running from Schopenhauer to Freud'. Moreover, like Max Graf,[37] he bestows upon Nietzsche a particular gift of self-analysis. 'Nietzsche's *work* contains observations that recall those that we make of a patient when therapy has progressed well and that is a measure of analysing the undercurrents of his own mind'. Even Paul Federn maintains that 'Nietzsche is so close to our ideas that it only remains for us to ask ourselves what has escaped him. He has intuitively anticipated certain of Freud's ideas'.[38]

Such is the double figure of Nietzsche in the analytic movement: on the one hand, as a distinguished precursor; on the other, as an eminent pathological case,[39] at once a theoretical referent and an object of diagnosis. That permits us the better to situate Freud's own, personal position on these two points that define the stakes of the psychoanalytic discourse on Nietzsche.

When his turn comes to speak, Freud begins by taking the occasion to emit one of his stereotypical statements on philosophy in general. 'Professor Freud', the minutes read, 'insists above all on his particular relation with philosophy, to whose abstract nature he is so antipathetic that he has in the end renounced its study.'[40] Right away, Freud announces that there would be no discourse – on Nietzsche in this case – other than an analytic one.

For who Nietzsche is in particular, Freud's declaration is clear. 'He does not know Nietzsche's work'. But it is not through a fault of interest; on the contrary, 'his occasional attempts to read him have been stifled through an excess of interest'.[41] Freud informs us here that he has tried several times to glance through Nietzsche, without ever succeeding in possessing an overall knowledge. According to a peculiar strategy, but one whose mechanisms we have demonstrated elsewhere,[42] an excess of interest triggers in Freud a reaction against speculation. But it informs us that Freud's particular relation to Nietzsche is only the echo of his personal relation to philosophy in general.

As for the anticipations, Freud tends to take them on trust, and even takes account of his indirect contact with Nietzsche's work, but he denies any influence. 'Despite the similitudes that many have raised between Nietzsche and himself, Freud can assert that Nietzsche's ideas have no influence on his work'.[43] A natural consequence, given that he has assured us that he has never read Nietzsche! But we know that, for Freud (and we cannot insist too much on this point), every engagement with philosophers is dialectic.[44] As if to confirm his own independence of thought, Freud reminds us that 'Nietzsche failed to recognize infantilism as well as the mechanism of displacement'.[45]

On the second point, Freud shows himself to be remarkably more prudent than the other participants. The abundance of diagnostic elements put forth by Sadger, Graf, Adler, Federn and Stekel contrast with Freud's sobriety. Freud merely congratulates Hitschmann for having 'raised some interesting problems' bearing on 'the psychology of Nietzsche the man', on the 'factors of a psychosexual constitution' that 'made a philosopher' and on 'the subjective determination of philosophical systems, apparently so objective', and would welcome a study of the influence of 'infantile impressions' on 'great realizations', and to remark on the precocity of the young Nietzsche's investigations into evil. That is Freud's position, which expresses the prudence of his discourse on Nietzsche, as much on a philosophical level as on a psychographic one.

'NIETZSCHE' IN THE WEDNESDAY SEMINARS (2)

But Nietzsche's spectre was decidedly in the air, since a few months later, on 28 October 1908, he was the object of a new lecture during a Wednesday session of the Vienna Society. This time, pathography clearly came to forefront, since Häutler spoke on *Ecce Homo*, treating the autobiography as a document,[46] by practically paraphrasing the work and punctuating it with psychoanalytic remarks.

This new exposition on Nietzsche generated analogous reactions among the attendees. Friedmann and Frey again took up the precursor *leitmotif*. 'Without knowing Freud's work, Nietzsche has sensed and anticipated many things.'[47] The two then offer their own psychoanalytic diagnosis of Nietzsche's neurosis.

Freud, this time, seems more willing to discuss matters, but he centres himself on psychography and the question of diagnosing Nietzsche's illness. In order to understand the importance of this approach, it is necessary to recall that 'the case of Nietzsche' had become the object of an important and sensational literature in this period, as a specimen totally indicative of the great question that psychopathology had posed, that of the relation between genius and madness.[48] In Germany, Paul Möbius had presented, in the same year as Nietzsche's death, an important synthesis on the relations between 'psychiatry and literary history',[49] before applying it in his monographs, such as that on Nietzsche,[50] in which he systematized the hypothesis of progressive general paralysis.

We should not ignore that it is in this precise context that Nietzsche came to be discussed during the Wednesday meetings (only eight years after Nietzsche's physical death). It is no accident that Hitschmann had quoted from Möbius during his lecture.[51] As for Freud, it is said that, not without some indelicacy for Häutler, he began his talk by declaring that he 'would welcome hearing from a psychiatrist today'.[52] 'The discussion', he remarked, 'would have been simple: Nietzsche was paralytic.' We recognize here the thesis to which Möbius had given his titles of legitimacy.

This curious remark, which gives the impression of reporting the diagnosis of Nietzsche's illness on the level of psychiatry, must be understood in two senses. On the one hand, the case of Nietzsche must be treated *first of all* on the psychiatric level, if we adopt the thesis of paralysis, before speculating in every direction;[53] but otherwise the psychiatrists, by this diagnosis, rid themselves by a simple word of what constitutes the real problem of Nietzsche the man. So Freud concedes that 'euphoria is very nicely developed, etc.',[54] but adds that 'this would be oversimplifying the problem'. Notably, 'it is very questionable to discern the responsible paralysis from the content of *Ecce Homo*'. Freud, against the efforts to find traces of madness in Nietzsche's work of the year 1888 which preceded his collapse, takes a very clear position. 'In the case where paralysis has struck great spirits, extraordinary things have been accomplished shortly before the illness (as in the case of Maupassant). The sign that this work of Nietzsche is plainly legitimate and must be taken seriously is the maintenance of a mastery over form'.[55]

The relativization of the psychiatric diagnostic is followed by what we might consider an outline of *Nietzschean psychography*.[56] Despite the concision of this text, a product of a rapid (and summary) intervention, we can see in it the important embryo of what would be contained in a Freudian monograph on the case of Nietzsche. We recall that Freud defines 'a psychography of personality' as an analysis that makes it possible to define the identity of a subject who produces works by means of 'affective elements', of 'complexes dependent on the instincts' and of 'the study of transformations and final results proceeding from instinctual forces'.[57] Now, Freud never produced a psychography of a philosophical personality, and this short account is a very rare outline.

In it, there are only elements, to the extent that Freud states that 'it is a question of a person whose premises are unknown (on the subject of which we lack preliminary information),[58] thus he remains irreducibly 'an enigmatic personality'. But Freud accentuates the maternal fixation and Nietzsche's paternal complex,[59] and on the role of Christ as an adolescent fantasy, and so on his basic narcissism, in relation to his homosexual tendencies.[60]

But the essential element of Nietzsche's particularity resides in the parallel and inverse development of illness and lucidity. Freud considers illness as 'the cause of all the disruptive elements in the tableau (of the personality)'. However, thanks to his narcissism, Nietzsche is able to 'explore the recesses of his self' 'with a great perspicacity' and to make 'a series of brilliant discoveries about his self'. What is at stake here is the famous 'endopsychic perception' that Freud puts at the base of mytho-philosophical knowledge.[61] The drives basic to Nietzsche's 'psychology' would be in the development of endo-psychic perception feeding on narcissism under the reactionary effect of illness. In this way, Freud recognizes in Nietzsche the title that he claims for himself as the 'first psychologist',[62] to the extent that, *via* the diagnosis, the homage is made vivid. 'The degree of introspection attained by Nietzsche had not been attained by anyone before him and doubtless will never be again'. Jones, attentive to the modulations of Freudian speech, comments that 'this is certainly a beautiful compliment, coming from the mouth of the first explorer of the Unconscious',[63] and moreover one notably stingy with his compliments. Nietzsche's sagacity is thus played out within the confines of introspection and projection, to the extent that, as his illness progressed, 'Nietzsche is not content to discern the exact connections; he projects toward the exterior as an exigency of life (*Lebensforderung*) what he has discovered in his own self', thus universalizing his own experience. Whence the genesis of his *work*; 'thus are born the baffling, but fundamentally correct, products of Nietzsche's vision'.

Just before foundering, Nietzsche had launched opprobria against the tendency of critics, who had just begun to discover him, to centre themselves on his personal problems to the detriment of his *work*. 'What interests them, is not *what I say*, it is the fact that *it is I who say it*, and the reason for which it is exactly I who have come to say it . . . they judge me in order not to have to deal with my work; by explaining the genesis – and they think they have sufficiently – *refuted it*'.[64] It is an interesting testimony for two reasons.

On the one hand, we see that the tendency to take Nietzsche the man into account in order to explain the work is a constant, from the beginning, of the discourse on Nietzsche, such that the psychoanalytic discourse extends it in its own way. It is a tendency naturally aggravated by the *man's* mental collapse which links the question of the *work* to that of the 'case'.

On the other hand, we catch a glimpse of how analytic discourse, above all that of Freud, allows the discourse centred on personality to be transcended, given that the recourse does not serve to 'refute' the work, but rather to clarify the drive-related conditions of it. In this sense the analytic discourse on Nietzsche, though in an embryonic stage, permits a materialization of the need that the discourse of 'critics' anticipate even while it leads them astray, by clarifying the work by its genesis without insidiously discrediting the one by the other. Perhaps only Freud was in a position to explain the link without falling into the reductionism of a 'key' that, while permitting the work to be opened, kills the text.

Moreover, we should note that Freud's diagnosis is not pronounced in favour of neurosis. 'There is no proof at all of a neurotic illness', he states. On the other hand, he always has recourse to a psychiatric diagnosis, not at all minimizing 'the role that paralysis plays in Nietzsche's life', to the point where he outlines, in order to conclude his diagnosis, a bond between paralysis and an aptitude for self-analysis. 'It is the process of relaxation due to paralysis which has rendered him capable – an extraordinary realization – of passing through all the recesses and recognizing the drives which are at the base (of everything). So, he placed his paralytic disposition in the service of science'.[65] It is an astonishing suggestion that would link Nietzsche's genealogical voyage to the path of dissolution, sealing the temporality of the *work* with that of the illness, to the point where the origin as a quest is born of a pathological remission, generating an intelligibility of *Trieb*.

But there is not only a clinical diagnosis in this dense text. Freud also affirms, in even more expressive terms than the preceding ones, his relation as a reader of Nietzsche:

> Freud would like to say that he has never been able to study Nietzsche: in part because of the resemblance that these intuitive discoveries have with our own difficult research, and in part because of the richness of his ideas, which have always prevented Freud from going further than a half-page in his attempts to read Nietzsche.[66]

A double reason, strangely cumulative, proceeds on the one hand from the dread of reading Nietzsche, out of fear of short-circuiting the delivery of analytical truth, as is explained elsewhere,[67] and on the other from the fear of being submerged in a speculative inflation. It is a double excuse for not accompanying Nietzsche in this voyage of which Freud still comes to show, with a development that implies some familiarity, its importance and interest. But there remains what was said, if we take Freud at his word, that he has never read more than a half-page of Nietzsche. That is perhaps the space of some striking and unforgettable aphorism; no more than that is needed to encounter Nietzsche![68]

THE WEIMAR ENCOUNTER: NIETZSCHEO-FREUDIAN CHRONICLE

In 1911, when the Congress of Psychoanalysis was held in Weimar, there occurred an important event in the relations between Nietzsche and psychoanalysis.

On 21 and 22 September 1911, the Congress met in Weimar, which had become the capital of Nietzsche studies. There, in fact, Elisabeth Förster-Nietzsche held court. Eleven years after the death of her brother, whom she had tended to during his last years,[69] she guarded his work with a conscience marked by a sense of property rights.

Thus it passed, by an accident of history and geography, that the Freudian court came to sit in the Nietzschean citadel, in the same place where Nietzsche had spent his last years, in a place that, symbolically, held the vestiges of the great Goethe.[70] As we have seen, there had been questions regarding Nietzsche in the Wednesday symposia in the preceding years. The idea was broached to visit the Nietzschean camp. Two 'deputies' were thus chosen and went before Nietzsche's sister to pay homage to the great thinker of Weimar. Ernest Jones summarily describes this episode, which was a notable date in the Freudo-Nietzschean annals:

> (Hanns) Sachs and I made the most of our stay in Weimar by going to see Madame Förster-Nietzsche, sister and biographer of the great writer. Sachs spoke to her of our Congress and the similarities that existed between certain of Freud's ideas and those of her illustrious brother'.[71]

He could not pass up the occasion to mark for this established and recognized 'precursor' a sort of confirmation of recognition, before his appointed and official (if not the most authorized) interpreter, whom Jones described as invested in the function 'sister and biographer'!

In what, then, could the conversation have consisted? Jones describes it in a very short phrase. There was a question of the Congress and 'some similarities . . . between certain of Freud's ideas' and those of Nietzsche. Since the time that the famous similarities had been evoked, it had been deemed necessary to inform the party involved. The terms Jones used are significant, for they correspond to Freud's strict formulation for philosophical affinities, and denote nothing other than a declaration of analogy. Jones does not tell us what the interested party's response was, which seems to indicate that the conversation was cut short. How could it be otherwise?

First of all, psychoanalysis as a theoretical content must have been little known to Elisabeth and suspect by its origins. Her appreciation of Freud may have been somewhat obscured by the antisemitic context. Her late husband, Bernard Förster,[72] had played an active role in the 1881 campaign, during which 250,000 signatures were collected demanding that Bismarck stop the immigration of Jews to Germany, and she herself shared these ideas before becoming a fervent follower of Hitler. Thus was the message that the two deputies of this 'Jewish science' carried to her, that it recognized in itself a parentage with the cherished philosophy of her noble brother, an announcement that had to leave her, at the least, with some reservations.

That is not all; the visit of the two emissaries coincided with the news that Lou Andreas-Salomé was in Weimar. It was, in fact, on the occasion of the Congress that she effectively made contact with Freud.[73] Now, between the two women reigned an old and bitter rivalry over Friedrich Nietzsche, a rivalry of nearly 30 years, since the year 1882, where there occurred the curious idyll between Nietzsche and Lou. It was a visibly affective stake; Elisabeth had seen this stranger penetrate the restrained intimacy of her brother whom she jealously kept watch over, to arouse one of his rare passions, then to install herself in Tautenbourg;[74] she had attended to the injurious effects on her brother of the deterioration of their relationship, and then encouraged Nietzsche's resentment toward Lou. But after her brother's mental death, and before his physical demise, the stakes of the rivalry had been redoubled on a philosophical plane, when Lou published her biography in 1894, disputing from that moment on the claim of Nietzsche's sister and hagiographer to the property rights to Nietzsche's work.

The arrival of the enemy had to raise, as we can guess, her animosity, and a troublesome association was thus knotted at the time between the dreaded image of Lou and the analytic movement, by a negative transfer effect from one representation to another! H.F. Peters describes exactly this context:

> Lou, well aware, carefully avoided her great adversary. She had to have been amused when she learned that two of the collaborators closest to Freud had paid Elisabeth a visit and had told her that her celebrated brother had anticipated a number of Freud's findings. Knowing of Elisabeth's virulent antisemitism, Lou could see the torment it caused her, to think that the name of her brother was associated with that of Freud.[75]

That was assuredly not a recommendation susceptible to facilitating contact. Elisabeth could even suspect a misdeed stemming from the rivalry. 'Was she (Lou) going to drag the name of her brother into the psychoanalytic mire'?[76] The two messengers must thus be very coldly received, as manifesting the double demon of the Jewish science and the scheming Lou, joined in a mysterious and unsettling complicity! We see that the context, at the turn of the century, hardly played in favour of an official rapprochement, and the conversation was not followed up.

But on the Freudian side, what did this approach signify? Is it necessary to see in this well-marked homage a notable exception to the general policy of defiance toward philosophical systems? In fact, it is useful to put the episode in its place. If it is important to raise it for a Freudo-Nietzschean chronicle, it is just as important not to overstate its significance, but above all to grasp in this occasion the elements of comprehension regarding Freud's attitude toward Nietzsche.

We point out, first of all, the conjunctural aspect. Taking account of the environment that Elisabeth had created in Weimar, it would have been quite difficult to avoid some kind of approach, however traditional.

> The Silberblick villa (seat of the Nietzsche Archives where Nietzsche had lived his last years) rapidly had become the meeting-place of all that Germany counted among artists, writers, and poets of some renown ... The pilgrimage to Weimar was *de rigueur* for every fervent German Nietzschean, and a number of passing cultivated strangers clambered up the hill in order to pay their respects to the sister of Zarathustra.[77]

This 'was designed to promote a Nietzschean movement'. Also, 'she held open house every Saturday afternoon and granted audiences to the fervent visiting Nietzscheans'.[78] Did she not receive visits from Persian dignitaries who emulated Zarathustra, American professors, Hindu students and erudite Japanese? The deputies of this new science which christened itself 'psychoanalysis' only assumed their place among the heteroclite rondo that danced around Nietzsche.

This infatuation in fact attained its zenith in the years that preceded the First World War, which would see the development of a veritable 'cult of Nietzsche'.[79] To pay a visit to the Archives or to sign the guest register moreover did not imply a Nietzschean obedience; it was, at its limit, the expression of a ritual by which the intelligentsia recognized the value of 'Nietzsche' in the place where he was revered.

Peters recalls the objective context. 'Nietzsche's name was often cited in the official discussions during the Weimar Congress. It was generally known that Nietzsche's sister, Elisabeth, lived in the city and energetically directed the Nietzsche Archives, which she had founded'.[80] It was thus a matter of a small official prestation that was nothing more than an officious allusion; but, precisely, the official aspect of the delegation limited the meaning to a simple diplomatic contact with the official sanctuary, which is far from expressing, despite its claim to exclusivity, the bubbling up of the first Nietzsche-ism that exploded during this period. The brevity of Jones' final 'communiqué' is thus in the end justified for what is only a formality, something like an exchange of information.

Everything thus permits us to believe that there was no deception, because that would have hardly been invested in such an approach, a simple extension of the *Acts* of the Congress. The conversation, in its cold objectivity, suffices unto itself. There is no point of departure for some pact between Freudians and Nietzscheans, but simply a point of contact, a report of similarities, moreover one not countersigned by the other party.

Let us then not see some allegiance, nor even a lapse in the great Freudian principle of abstinence from philosophy. It was in precisely this same Weimar Congress that Freud manifested his coolness toward Putnam's attempt at a Hegelian interpretation of psychoanalysis. It is significant that Jones, who held the office of a delegate, declared that 'most of us did not see the necessity of adopting a particular philosophical doctrine, whatever it was'.[81] Especially not Hegel, we might say, but not Nietzsche either.

There remains the significance of the event, limited but precise. Nietzsche is the only contemporary philosopher who had been made the object of such a manifestation of respectful sympathy from a faction of the official analytic movement, at the very moment of its institutionalization.

The approach, by its character at once unusual and natural, symbolizes the official relation, at once exterior and a little obsequious, which Freud had tolerated with the Nietzschean School. Despite his scant attraction to the master's sister at whom, in private, he let fly some invectives,[83] Freud addresses himself as to a somehow administrative authority on Nietzscheology, as if finally this relation to Nietzsche was better accommodated politically than by a more intimate contract – and even permitting an economy. It is indeed through this façade that it is useful to approach their relations.

But behind this façade, that leads back to the question of a diplomatic exchange between two institutions, there is nevertheless the reality of a living Nietzscheism which causes, for Freud, intimately, and under the influence of certain members of his immediate circle, the idea of certain affinities between the two men and the two bodies of thought, to fructify. There is, on the other hand, what Freud says about Nietzsche, he who affirms not having read the latter. Thus it is now towards Freud's personal encounter with Nietzsche that we will turn,[83] preliminary to approaching the systematic comparison of the themes and the thoughts.[84]

PART ONE: FREUD AND NIETZSCHE

1

THE GENESIS OF AN ENCOUNTER

I merely take Nietzsche where I would, I hope, find words for many things that remain mute inside me — Freud.

FROM ONE TRANSVALUATION TO ANOTHER

Near the end of his productive life, Nietzsche writes, as if to express both a meaning and a term: 'Turin, 30 September, 1888, the day when the first book of *The Transvaluation of All Values* was completed'.[1]

Reaching a critical point, where the discovery that fabrication in seduction narratives reveals an impasse in his theory of neurosis, Freud writes to Fliess (on 21 September 1897): 'I no longer believe in my *neurotica* .... In this *general collapse of all values* only psychology remains intact. Dreams certainly preserve their value and I attach increasing value to my efforts in meta-psychology'.[2]

Thus, less than a decade later, expressing a decisive crisis rising from psychoanalysis, with his 'ideal child/problem child' called meta-psychology, and at the moment when he finds himself on the track of the foundational theory of desire, Freud spontaneously resorts to the expression with which Nietzsche had named his own project. That Nietzsche's mode of expression, though by virtue of a metaphor, would be imposed to name this theoretical cataclysm out of which would emerge a new discourse, symbolizes an affinity of approaches. It indicates the interest in examining the convergences and divergences between the transmutation of values in the psychology to which Sigmund Freud attached his name, with what Friedrich Nietzsche had undertaken through his critique of morality.

But that implies that we go back, beyond the objective rapprochement of psychoanalysis with Nietzschean psychology (evoked in the Introduction), to the origins of the personal relationship between Freud the man and Nietzsche, that materializes where these two modes of expression cross.

Freud approves of Nietzsche's axiological metaphor, and uses it in the framework of his theory of dreams. By examining the 'work of dreams' as 'procedures of figuration',[3] he comes to consider the relationship between the thought of the dream and its content. Having done that, Freud notes a remarkable contrast between the 'sensible intensity' or 'vividness' of dream-images and the 'psychic intensity of the corresponding elements in the thought of the dream' or their 'psychic value' (*psychische Wertigkeit*).[4] He thus affirms that 'the intensity of the elements of the one has nothing to do with the intensity of the elements of the other; between the oneiric materials (*Traummaterial*) and the dream, there is a complete "transvaluation of (all) psychic values"' (*Umwertung der psychischen Wertigkeiten*).

In other words, 'while the work of the dream is being accomplished, the psychic intensity of ideas and representations which make up the object is transported to other ideas and representations which, in my view, have no claim (*Anspruch*) to such an emphasis' (*Betonung*).[5] In that, there is a question of a displacement (*Traumverschiebung*) that Freud alternatively calls a 'reversal of psychic values'. The same characterization is made of the whole work of deformation and occlusion that defines the dream's mode of expression. Thus Freud can find no better expression than Nietzsche's to characterize the major process of the work of the oneiric Unconscious.

But this is only a metaphor; what Freud calls 'psychic value' (*Wertigkeit* and not *Wert*) is the intensity linked to the 'interest' that a representation creates. It is thus the accentuation of an affect which displacement produces via transference, overthrowing the intensities that would determine the overall change of the physiognomy of dreams, and which Freud had marked as 'arbitrary' in the preceding formula.

At any rate, we should take notice that the master expression of Nietzsche's axiology serves spontaneously to express for Freud his own essential mutations, those of 'theoretical values' and of 'psychic values'. So how does this borrowing of modes of expression come about?

A BORROWED EXPRESSION

By the end of the nineteenth century, Nietzschean study circles had formed in Germany, such as the one in Berlin (where Fliess taught) centred around Koegel, who was director of the Nietzsche Archives from 1894–7.[6] We know, from a letter to Fliess at the beginning of the century, that Freud was one of those interested in Nietzsche. On the first of February, 1900, Freud in a long letter to Fliess, confided that

> I have merely come to take Nietzsche where I might find, I hope, the words for many things which remain mute within me (*die Worte für vieles, was in mir stumm bleibt*), but I have not yet opened his books. Too lazy for the moment'.[7]

This letter is an important document, understood as a spontaneous testimony, in the stream of a familiar correspondence. There we find this remarkable formula whereby Freud turns to Nietzsche in the hope of *finding the words for the many things that remain mute within him*. It expresses, more suggestively than any of the later official declarations,[8] the sense of Freud's initial personal investment in Nietzsche. Freud seeks a mode of expression (*langage*) that profoundly *concerns* him, but paradoxically Nietzsche is reputed to be able to express what remains obstinately mute within Freud. Here is summarized all the strangeness of the relation between Freud and Nietzsche.

Freud is drawn to Nietzsche in search of a mode of expression (*langage*) for his own inexpressible thoughts, which explains why he will always remain at the threshold (of Nietzsche's work). We understand this better when Freud declares a little later that he has not been able to read Nietzsche, more than a half-page.[9] Undoubtedly, Freud is thinking about the episode evoked in his letter to Fliess, but the 'laziness', invoked here to defer the approach, dissimulates the complexity of his inhibition. It expresses a recoiling before an approach as contradictory as that of the mute who seeks to read in order to learn how to speak! Surely, Nietzsche could not have filled the role of a monitor for Freud.

We have a better understanding, from this perspective, of the mixture of admiration, attraction, and anxiety Freud felt toward Nietzsche, and his determination not to read him 'out of an excess of interest'.[10] The reading is forever deferred, for the day when those numerous important things that remain mute will find a voice. But therein lies a vicious circle, given that in order to read Nietzsche, Freud must change his mode of expression!

THE FIRST INTERMEDIARY: JOSEF PANETH

In a letter to Arnold Zweig[11] dated 11 May, 1934, we find some crucial information on Freud's youthful attraction to Nietzsche. 'During my youth,' said Freud of Nietzsche, 'he represented for me a nobility that was out of my reach. One of my friends, Dr. Paneth, had come to make his acquaintance in the Engadine (in the Italian Alps) and wrote me many things about Nietzsche. Even later, my attitude towards him remains fairly much the same.'[12] Thus is revealed the outline of an indirect, yet strong link between Freud, who was just beginning his career – Jones puts it at around 1885[13] – and Nietzsche, the itinerant philosopher who was ending his own in the Engadine, surrounded by nature. It is a living link, personalized in a way, emanating from a man who had experienced Nietzsche in flesh and bone.

Josef Paneth, one of Freud's closest friends, died prematurely in 1890,[14] at the very moment when Nietzsche foundered. Paneth thus recalled the echoes of Nietzsche's final period, that of the transvaluation of values. It is likely that through this channel Freud came to be invested in a Nietzsche-inspired vocabulary, transmitted through his correspondence with Fliess. From this point, what seems like a simple borrowing expresses, if we believe the resonance of Freud's belated admission to Zweig, a veritable *idealization* which paradoxically compromises *identification*. 'He represents for me a nobility, which' adds Freud in 1934, 'was out of my reach.' The temptation is overcome from this moment on, as with philosophy in general; but the admission nonetheless expresses a precocious, *personalized* interest in Friedrich Nietzsche. Still, it is remarkable;

the evoked image of Nietzsche captures in this period the image of an Italy which attracted Freud as well, who invested it with the same ambivalent prestige, that of a 'nobility out of reach'.[15]

The expression seems like a response, via a denial, to Zarathustra's gospel. 'That is why, my brothers, we need *a new nobility*, because for many noble things there needs to be a *nobility*'![16] Freud does not deem himself a good recruit for such an enterprise, and gives his reasons.

We must now clarify Freud's indications, whose memory is useful here only for an approximation. In Nice, at the end of December 1883, Paneth first makes Nietzsche's acquaintance. We can establish this from Paneth's correspondence. On 15 December 1883, Paneth writes his wife that Nietzsche had requested him to send his card, after having learned that Paneth had sought a meeting, and Paneth wrote that we was 'impatient to make his acquaintance', adding that 'he is not as unapproachable as they say'. On 17 December, he tried in vain to present himself to Nietzsche. Finally, on 26 December, 'I returned to Nice and was finally able to see Nietzsche'. It seems that a real friendship was formed between Nietzsche and Paneth, for Paneth immediately confided that

> he was extremely amiable; he bore no trace of pomposity or prophetic bearing, such as I had feared after his last letter. On the contrary, he is very simple and natural ... yet he recounted to me, without the least affectation and without any vanity, that he had always felt himself invested in a mission and that he always wanted ... to explain the work that he carried inside him ... He told me his life.

On 3 January, 1884, after another walk with Nietzsche, Paneth writes of having 'had six hours of very animated conversation', adding that 'everything that he said was expressed with the utmost simplicity'. There follows a phrase that introduces the word 'nobility'. 'His bearing is simple and unpretentious, full of nobility and dignity'.[17] We can judge from these excerpts the tone of Paneth's letters, which must have at the same time made the person of Nietzsche known to Paneth's friend Freud. This is the Nietzsche who had written the first two parts of *Zarathustra* and had begun to start on the third (see the letter from 3 January 1884, cited above).

ARNOLD ZWEIG AND THE IMPOSSIBLE DISCOURSE

Towards the end of his life, Freud again had occasion to take a position on Nietzsche. Arnold Zweig[18] furnished the occasion. 'In April, 1934' recounts Jones, 'Arnold Zweig made known to Freud that he intended to write a book on Nietzsche's mental collapse, and had completed a first draft. Freud had advised him to renounce his project, although he admitted that he could not say precisely for what reasons'.[19] This episode is all the more interesting, given that, in order to satisfy Zweig's request, Freud comes to explain the reasons why he, himself, had never written a psychography of Nietzsche.

In a letter dated 11 May 1934, where Freud formulates the conditions to which he must respond to such an enterprise, he is led to insist above all on the requirement for veracity.

> When it is a question of a person of our time whose influence is still as vibrant as that of Friedrich Nietzsche, a portraitist of his person and his fate must follow the same rules as for a portrait; that is to say that, however elaborate the conceptual tableau, the resemblance cannot stray in the least essential point.[20]

Thus, starting from 'historical reality', Freud seems to mistrust a 'historical novel', asking 'what would we do with an imaginary Friedrich Nietzsche'?[21] The first requirement is thus of a positive order; it is necessary to record the facts. 'Since the subject cannot pose for the artist, it falls to the latter to amass such givens that it will only be a matter of completing them to give proof of a penetrating understanding.' In the case of insufficient information, circumspection is imposed. No one is more suspicious of an arbitrary reconstruction than Freud, however brilliant and seductive it may be, and all the more so since Nietzsche's illness remains such a complex matter. 'You must try to know' he counsels Zweig, 'if there exist sufficient information for such a portrait. . . . But with Friedrich Nietzsche, there is something there that goes beyond the ordinary. There is also the matter of an illness which is most difficult to explain and to reconstruct; that is to say, there are doubtless psychic processes which bind one in a given way, but they do not always have psychic motivations at their base; and to attempt to unravel such would be to run the risk of falling into serious error'.[22] Thus Freud confirms here his distrust of any purely psychogenetic interpretation of Nietzsche's illness.

As Zweig persisted in his project and 'asked for suggestions pertaining to Nietzsche's life', Freud responded on 15 July, 1934: 'You overestimate my knowledge of Nietzsche, as I cannot teach you what would be useful for you'.[23] Moreover, this time Freud formulates it as a veritable denial of a Nietzsche psychography:

> In my opinion, two facts block the approach to the problem of Nietzsche. In the first place, one cannot see, whoever he is, whether one has in hand some elements concerning his sexual constitution, and with Nietzsche this domain is a complete enigma.[24] In the second place, he suffered from a serious illness, and after a long period of preliminary symptoms a general paralysis set in.'

This traditional diagnosis is a second motif of hesitation. 'With a general paralysis, conflicts vanish into the etiological background.' Thus the psychoorganic illness itself literally bars access to Nietzsche's conflicts.[25] Freud's last position on Nietzsche's case is thus resolutely agnostic. Nietzsche the man remains irreducibly dissimulated to analysis by the double rampart of his hidden secrets and his psycho-organic illness.

Those are the avowed reasons why we cannot have a complete monograph by Freud on the case of Nietzsche, of which we might have dreamed. But there is another, affective reason, that Freud declared in a preceding letter to Zweig. After having enumerated the etiological obstacles, Freud adds with an honesty that for him accommodates a lucid misrecognition. 'I would not know how to say if those are the true reasons for my opposition to your project. Perhaps the way you compare me to him is another.'[26] Freud refuses to be identified with Nietzsche, whom Freud associated once more with his youth. 'During my youth, he represented for me a nobility that was out of my reach'. Freud suggests that, at the threshold of a psychography of Nietzsche the philosopher, something other than the technical difficulties stop him, something which enters into play from the side of the ideal of the Ego and of knowledge.[27]

We should add that Freud postulates a continuity of his attitude toward Nietzsche. 'Later as well,' he affirms, 'my attitude toward him remained fairly much the same'. We can nevertheless infer that this attitude, systematized afterwards, has followed the vicissitudes of Freud's position on philosophy[28] (in general), and has been influenced as well by the stakes involved in the use of Nietzsche at the core of the analytic movement.

It is thus that Freud would see Nietzsche launched in an assault against his grand theory of sexual etiology, in Adler's hands.

NIETZSCHE AND THE ATTACK ON THE LIBIDO

In its own way, Adler's defection affected Freud's relation to Nietzsche; in fact, Adler's 'individual and comparative psychology' makes privileged references to Nietzschean terminology. The theory of the Unconscious as a *Kunstgriff* (artifice) of organic inferiority lent a sort of credibility to Nietzschean analysis. During the great debate of February, 1911 which resulted in the rupture, Nietzsche's 'will to power' was opposed to Freud's libido as a polemic alternative, at the very moment when the analytic movement was in its most intensive confrontation with Nietzsche.[29]

It is only too clear that a profound divergence separates Adler's universe from Nietzsche's, and that what Adler borrows from Nietzsche does not mortgage Nietzsche's own theories, as far as a theory of overcompensation is made to extend from the nature of Nietzsche's Will to Power. It is a long way from the anodyne astuteness of Adler's neurosis to an expression of Nietzschean willing. At most, the convergence is made possible by a common thematic, that of the psychology of unmasking (*Entlarvungspsychologie*). It is no less than the paradoxical strategy whereby Adler resorts to categories of obedience (or of Nietzschean tonality) in order to break with the drive-based foundation of Freudian psychoanalysis. Nietzsche serves objectively, in the decisive conflict of the early 1910s where disagreements with Freud emerged, to dismiss the claims of

Freud's Libido to the profit of another principle, by reactivating the axis of aggressivity. In that respect, when Freud announces that he is prepared 'to execute against him (Adler) the vengeance of the offended goddess Libido',[30] he can not fail to recognize that Nietzsche's mode of expression has been used in the offense against him![31] This circumstance could only confirm Freud's defiance in the face of the reference (to Nietzsche), as plastic as any other philosophical reference, which serves, like it or not, to allay the shock of the analytic message and to pare down the etiology of sex.

Turning to the other great schismatic, C.-G. Jung, Freud again discovers Nietzsche's name as the stake in the conflict. We can vividly gauge this by following the manifestations of Nietzsche in the important correspondance between these two men before their rupture.

Between 1907 and 1912, Jung evokes Nietzsche to mention the therapeutic that associates Freudian theory with Nietzsche's philosophy,[32] to associate Dionysus with sexuality,[33] and to recommend Lou Salomé to Freud.[34] Each time, Freud lets the allusion pass without pursuing it. It is a symbolic act; at a decisive moment in the crisis, in 1912, Jung cites Zarathustra in order to claim the autonomy of the disciple by saying that 'one pays back poorly the debt to one's master by always remaining a student'.[35] Nietzsche will thus furnish the dissident disciple the mode of expression for his emancipation! Indeed the master interprets it as a mortal danger for $\Psi\alpha$. It is also the only occasion where Freud pronounces Nietzsche's name in this exchange of letters, in order to make his 'approbation' to 'necessary intellectual independence' and to 'the citation of Nietzsche' that supports him, but also to deny ever having made any 'attempts at intellectual repression'.[36] Thus Freud only accepts an identification with Zarathustra in order to deny his function as a master.

We note here simply that Nietzsche intervenes between Freud and Jung to mark the assertion of the disciple, which is met by the master's silence, as the gospel of the revolt of the disciple against the master, and finally as a reference to his own dissident work – as an indication of Nietzschean ideas in Jung's work.

LOU SALOMÉ, A NATURAL LINK

Our inquiry would not be complete if we did not take into consideration, in order to account for Freud's relation to Nietzsche, the support of those who were able to articulate in positive terms Freud's affinities with Nietzsche, and who contributed to the creation of the image that is Nietzsche's destiny – those who, during the time that Freud refused to read him, read Nietzsche for him and kept alive his old flame for an inaccessible nobility.

We know the importance of intercessors in Freud's relation to other philosophers, but without a doubt there have never been mediators as diligent as those between Nietzsche and Freud. Freud is literally bombarded with Nietzschean solicitations; everywhere around him, he discovers Nietzsche, and he has constantly to reiterate his act of avoidance.Without counting those analysts impressed by Nietzsche that we have seen to constitute nearly a Nietzschean culture in the Wednesday seminars, there remain three types of mediators who have played the most active roles in the work of treatment and information:

- Those with a *personal* affiliation between Nietzsche *the man* and Freud *the man*. That is the role played by Lou Salomé.
- Those with a *literary* affiliation, artistically and subtly weaving an analogy between the two *œuvres*. This function fell to Thomas Mann.
- Those with a *philosophical* affiliation, those philosophers admitted to the Freudian circle, among whom we can distinguish the philosophical analyst who has achieved the most systematic rapprochement between the two *problematics*, Otto Rank.

Thus it remains to evaluate, by following these three degrees of rapprochement, the respective part that each of these great mediators played in the rapprochement between Freud and Nietzsche, and to estimate their impact, immediate or subtle, on Freud, and the usage that makes it possible to carry this comparison, as outlined, to term.

In the eyes of observers, Lou-Andreas Salomé was the natural link between Freud and Nietzsche. Jones recites this opinion well. 'It is said of her that she was linked to the great men of the nineteenth and twentieth centuries, Nietzsche and Freud'.[37] Freud himself accredits this idea, since 'he spoke of her as the single real link between Nietzsche and himself', as indicated by the homage that he pays her at her death, in a letter dated 11 February 1937, to Arnold Zweig, a connoisseur of things Nietzschean and a zealot of the rapprochement between the two thinkers.[38] As a living link, she knew the two men, (though) 30 years apart.[39]

But, in contrast to this version, everything proceeds as if Nietzsche did not intervene actively in the relation between Lou and Freud, such that Freud seems hardly to have gained any knowledge of Nietzsche out of it. Nietzsche seems to be the hidden god, without a doubt tacitly present in their relationship, if we should believe Freud's final word on it, but rarely and in some way soberly mentioned. So, when Nietzsche is cited by name, it is always a little like an external stake, in correspondence – Freud, in a 1932 letter, exploits one of Lou's references in order to declare that 'I am often irritated when I hear mention of your relationship with Nietzsche in a sense in which you were clearly hostile and which could not absolutely correspond to reality'.[40] In 1934, Freud proposed to her to become a 'counsellor' to Arnold Zweig, who had a study of Nietzsche underway, and moreover provoked a horrified refusal by Lou.[41] So, if Lou was 'the only real link' between Nietzsche and Freud, their tacit contract seems to require that they evoke Nietzsche as little as possible.

The real gain from this link regarding Nietzsche–Freud relations is shown in the most vivid manner in a familiar episode, where Lou witnesses Freud's reaction towards the man that she knew. She notes in her *Journal of a Year*, in the well-known discussion of her defence of Freud against philosophy, dating 23 February 1913,[42] Freud's 'dread of the *Lebensgedicht* that he had to read in Nietzsche's compositions'. This anecdote, related in the biography by Lou-Andreas Salomé, expresses vividly, through its spontaneity, what in a way characteristically separates Freud from Nietzsche in their respective understandings of life.

> One day, he had received, a little before my visit, a copy of Nietzsche's *Hymn to Life*. It was my *Prayer to Life*, which I wrote in Zurich, and which Nietzsche had put to music with slight modifications. It was scarcely pleasing to Freud, who always expressed himself with so much sobriety. He could not approve of the extreme enthusiasm that we use and abuse when we are young and lack experience. In a playful manner, gay and cordial, he read the last verse to me in a high voice:
>
> *To think, to live a millennium*
> *Sink all that you have!*
> *If you have no more happiness to give me,*
> *Alas – your torments remain ...*
>
> He closed the book and struck the arm of his chair. 'No, you know! I do not agree! A good, chronic head cold suffices amply to cure me of such desires!'[43]

The *Hymn to Life* comprises a history that seals the bygone idyll between Nietzsche and Lou Salomé – and doubtless for that it is symbolic that it should be an occasion for sarcasm from Freud. But this poem that Lou, as if to justify Freud's derision, presented as a sin of youth, had truly captivated Nietzsche. There is no doubt that he considered himself its co-author, according to the exchanges he made with Lou.[44] This effusion of vital sentiment, mixed with *amor fati*, yields an existential glorification of suffering, as a form of an adherence to life, on the model of the amorous relation. And it is in this sense that, in *Ecce Homo*, Nietzsche emotionally evokes the last verse that Freud scoffed at.[45]

Freud's reaction may seem elementary and, all in all, facile; he refuses to enter into the play of enthusiasm and opposes it with, somewhat cynically, a totally prosaic conception of sorrow – as if it were true that metaphysical suffering is opposed *toto caelo* to the consecutive suffering of a head cold! On this point, he is inspired by Wilhelm Busch's caricature, of a poet whose toothache is sufficient to suspend the most sublime reveries.[46]

Without overstating this momentary reaction when Freud's heart is full of the pleasantries of the world, it reveals an indication of Freud's resistance toward every excess of *Schwärmerei* (exaltation), which pushes him to adopt, as a spontaneous antidote, the materialist scepticism of a dash of *Aufklärer* (enlightened awareness). It is the refusal to be the dupe of an exaltation, and a materialist reminder of physiological immanence against the temptations of intoxication. This is what stops Freud at the gates of the temple of Dionysus!

But it is necessary to go further. Is there not for Freud, notwithstanding his prosaic admission, a veritable theory of suffering? Do we not encounter, in neurosis and in his reflections on civilization, an absolute limit that makes him say that it is not part of the plan of 'Creation' that humans be 'happy'?[47] How does a theory of instinct misrecognize this ultimate question of suffering, the *nexus* of life and death? Yet never would Freud's speculations on these matters imply, if we are to believe him, a valorization of sorrow – rather it is the negative limit of the pleasure principle. From this point of view, Freud would not know how to experience *amor doloris*, especially in an epoch such as that of the text (of *Hymn to Life*), where there is not yet a question of a beyond to the pleasure principle that implies a death wish.[48]

That is why the *Hymn to Life* is not of a poetic genre appreciated by Freud. He clearly prefers the intimacy of Heine or Goethe's sober lyricism. It is a difference of sensibility that already traces a line of divergence between Nietzsche and Freud, which distinguishes the cry from the murmur, the dithyramb from the elegy, tragedy from witticism. In vain would we seek to find a hymn in Freud, be it to Life, or to Death, or to the Unconscious. This is an idiosyncratic difference that is expressed as well by the contrast between the cult of music inseparable from Nietzsche and Freud's personal 'aversion' to music.[49]

Without a doubt, we can temper the opposition of sensibilities by revealing that Romantic exaltation exasperated Nietzsche just as much, who let fly invectives against Romanticism. He sees in it, from one end of his work to the other, the symptom of a 'modern barbarism', of an epoch of 'nervous exhaustion' at the same time as one of 'nervous overstimulation', and conceives his work as 'a struggle against Romanticism'. To be precise, Nietzsche sees in Romanticism a caricature of the true expression of instinct that he calls 'Dionysism'.

Freud, for his part, does not distinguish one from the other; in such a Dionysian expression as enthused Nietzsche, Freud only sees a doubtful and a bit ridiculous Romanticism. And, beyond this particular divergence of appreciation (that Lou does not dispute), Freud reveals himself as having limited access to true Dionysism; 'something' there 'remains mute within me'. The misunderstanding is thus very revealing.

Not that Freud is impervious to a certain tragic aspect of suffering, but for him it is defused by a form of humour. In order to appreciate the meaning of his reaction to Nietzsche's hymn, it is necessary to see that Freud reacts in a Heinean spirit. It is no accident if Freud likes Heine's poetry so much; he finds in it a 'satiric and Aristophanean lyricism'.[50] Most of Heine's poetry, in fact, defuses the effects of the deepest sorrows with sarcasm. 'There is no sorrow so great that does not imply an addition of ridicule, and it is not there to diminish it, but to give it a new grandeur.'[51]

It is thus in emulation of Heine and of Busch that Freud reacts very precisely to Dionysian lyricism. What Andler says of Heine applies well here to Freud, and gives meaning to his evocation of the head cold as a humorous antidote to existential suffering.

> Humour, at the moment when it envisions a reality, already sees the certain bearing, the imminent swoon, the sure destination .... Humour animates the thought that knows that every noble ideal is conditioned by a grossly material reality, and thought itself, by common images .... And this fragility (of the world), is considered with a laugh which transmits compassion'.[52]

We understand that this would not prevent Freud from being sensitive to other expressions of sorrow in Nietzsche, on which he has commented in other hymns.[53] But, like Heine, whom Nietzsche equally appreciated, something in Freud defuses the abandonment to the depths of sorrow, by means of raillery, as toward his own suffering.[54] In this sense he is incapable of long voyages into the irrational, so much that a reminder of material reality is sufficient to cure him of those grand desires of which Nietzsche is precisely incurable. That, without a doubt, is one of the key differences between their particular sensibilities. Where Nietzsche's soul dilates, Freud's soul 'contracts into the tiny cavity of a molar'.[55]

Thomas Mann, Herald and Mediator

If Lou Salomé has the adroit discretion not to transgress her role, one of the most active protagonists of the rapprochement between Freud's and Nietzsche's *thematics* from the years 1925–30 was Thomas Mann.

We can judge this from the essay *Freud and Modern Thought* (1929),[56] conceived as a commentary on an aphorism from *Human, All Too Human*, which announced a new relationship to culture.[57] Freud is introduced as an 'explorer of the depths (*Tiefenforscher*) and psychologist of instincts', situated 'in the lineage of writers of the nineteenth and twentieth centuries who – historians, philosophers, critics, or archaeologists – are opposed to rationalism, to intellectualism, to classicism, in a word at once opposed to the spirit of the eighteenth or even perhaps a little of the nineteenth century'.[58] This judgement of identity is founded on the idea that denotes a membership among those who 'underline the dark side of nature and of the soul' as the truly determinant and creative element of life. But right away Thomas Mann underlines two strategies in relation to this irrational element. On the one hand, this family of spirits 'cultivates' the irrational, by defending the primacy of and even advocating the 'great return to the night, to the original preconscious of life'; on the other hand, they clarify it scientifically (*wissenschaftlich hervorkehren*). It is thus a question of transcending the irrationalist attitude of exaltation by a recognition of its irrational element, not irreducible, but the object of a new scientific investigation.

All of the arguments in Thomas Mann's essay consist from this point in proposing that these two approaches proceed without contradiction from a will at once reactionary (as a return to the origin) and revolutionary (as a Will to

Progress conditioned by a return to sources). He thus distinguishes Freud's taking into account of the irrational as an 'anti-idealist and anti-intellectual will ... smashing the primacy of spirit and reason, decrying it as the most sterile of illusions, and re-establishing in triumph in their primitive vital right, the forces of shadows and the abysmal, instinctual, irrational depths'.[59]

Thus Freud appears as a sort of antidote to the suspect glorification of the irrational; specifically, he applies a rational disposition to an irrational object.

> The interest of knowing what Freud proves for the affective sphere does not degenerate into a glorification of its object at the expense of the intellectual sphere. His anti-rationalism is tantamount to an understanding of the affective and dominant superiority of instinct over mind; it is not equivalent to an admiring prostration before this superiority, to a raillery of the spirit ... his 'interest' in instincts is not a servile negation of the mind by a conservatism of nature; it converges on the revolutionary victory of reason and spirit, envisioned in the future'.[60]

In this context, Thomas Mann underlines the affinities between Freud and German Romanticism and between Freud and Nietzsche himself. Furthermore, he considers that Freud's misrecognition of literature has 'increased the force of impact of his message',[61] because he 'travelled alone the hard path of his discovery, alone and in complete independence, uniquely as a physician and a naturalist'. Thus he arrived at the irrational through his fundamentally scientific method. Freud's relations to Nietzsche are presented as simple 'unconscious affinities'. 'He did not know Nietzsche', Mann maintains, 'in whom abound on all sides, like flashes of lightning (*blitzhaft*), anticipations (*Einsichten*) of Freud'.[62]

We find in Thomas Mann a traditional representation of Nietzsche as Freud's precursor, but this text is remarkable in that Freud is cleared of 'every reactionary abuse' of modern irrationalism, by his refusal 'to sing the poetry of spirits shrouded, exalted, turned toward the past'[63] – which, paradoxically, permits him to evoke the 'Voltairean' Nietzsche[64] of the beginning of the 1880s (the period of the 'Lights') and, at the same time, to reserve for psychoanalysis an approach *by way of knowledge*.[65]

In Mann's view, Freud and Nietzsche are closely linked through the intermediary of a third term, Schopenhauer, his favourite philosopher.[66] It is no accident if, in his famous homage to the founder of psychoanalysis in 1936,[67] he characterized Freud by referring to these two associations. 'An independent spirit, "a man and a squire, somber and severe in bearing", as Nietzsche said of Schopenhauer'.[68] But in other respects it suggests a direct influence. 'Sigmund Freud, the founder of psychoanalysis ... has travelled the hard path of his discovery, alone and in complete independence, uniquely as physician and as an observer of nature. ... He did not know Nietzsche, in whom on all sides, tracking through his *work* like flashes of lightning, Freudian observations are often anticipated.'[69] Nevertheless, Mann maintains that

> what comprises the love of truth, conceived *as psychological truth*, this love whose morality is centred on the acceptation of truth without reservation, derives from the noble school of Nietzsche in whom, in fact, the identity of the concepts of *psychological* truth, of knowledge and of psychology leap before one's eyes.'[70]

It is an important idea to the literary intelligentsia attracted to psychoanalysis in the inter-war years. Nietzsche and Freud are irresistibly reconciled, notwithstanding the content of their work, by the principle of a determination of truth, a psychological *sapere aude* which comprised the veritable modern *Aufklärer*. It is no accident if Stefan Zweig places one of Nietzsche's aphorisms in an epigraph in his essay on Freud. 'How much of truth *supports*, how much of truth *dares* a spirit? That has become for me, more and more, the true measure of values'.[71]

Thomas Mann adds to this first and fundamental affinity the community of the 'meaning of illness ... as a means of attaining knowledge'.[72] It is another essential idea in the Freudian-Nietzschean literature, and one accredited by Freud himself;[73] the genius for self-therapy that founds Nietzsche's *work* paves the way for Freudian psychoanalysis.

For what is doctrinal in *content*, Mann insists significantly on the bond between Freud and Schopenhauer, presenting Freud as the 'true son of the Schopenhauerean era' and insisting on the 'close parentage of Schopenhauer to his revolution'.[74] In this way Freud and Nietzsche are twinned by a common parentage – which justifies a natural passage from Schopenhauer and Nietzsche to psychoanalysis, as existing in a 'familiar world' and a 'land of knowledge'.[75] But Schopenhauer furnishes Thomas Mann with a stable, primordial metaphysical referent, while Nietzsche and Freud furnish him with the complementary slopes of a psychological *heuristic* under perpetual construction.

Finally, Thomas Mann wonderfully represents the path that leads irresistibly from Nietzsche to Freud.[76] We should recall that his *Reflexions d'un apolitique* had won him the 'Nietzsche prize' in 1919,[77] earning him Elisabeth's congratulations on the 'aristocratic radicalism' that he expressed. Ten years later, as we have seen, Thomas Mann praises Freud's work before rendering him his vibrant final homage. So we find woven the conjunction between two thematics, wedded by a tenacious association upon which literature bestowed its titles of nobility. Freud receives from the literary intelligentsia, at the same time as an homage, the *imperative* of a rapprochement with Nietzsche.

NIETZSCHEO-FREUDIANISM: FROM GROSS TO RANK

There remain those who sought systematically *to think* this relation.

From 1924 on, Charles Baudouin maintained the thesis of a precise filiation between Nietzschean thematics and psychoanalysis,[78] one that Wittels, Nietzsche's first biographer, had raised.[79] In Freudian circles there were proposals for a *theoretical* rapprochement with Nietzsche; in 1927, Oscar Pfister remarked to Freud that his position on religion had been expressed by Nietzsche, unbeknownst to him.[80] Above all, Ludwig Binswanger, the philosopher closest to Freud, established a close parallel between the two projects. In a text dating from 1936 which summarized Freud's contributions in a solemn homage, Binswanger presented him as 'accomplishing no less radically and passionately than Nietzsche the divine mandate of his ideas, but preferring over the flash of corrosive aphorisms the rigorous and systematic elaboration of the huge empirico-scientific edifice of his *technique of unmasking*.'[81] Thus was accredited in philosophical circles near to psychoanalysis the idea of a coalescence of projects, with Nietzsche and Freud lending two voices, the one disruptive and aphoristic, the other methodical and scientific, in order to define the same *terra incognita*. Free to situate, as Binswanger was, the difference at an anthropological level, 'the rigorously naturalistic, empirico-constructive character of Freud's *homo natura* distinguishes it from Nietzsche's *homo natura* more than any opposition between Eros and Will to Power.'[82]

But it is with Otto Rank that the rapprochement is systematized. As we have seen in our preceding study, Rank is the most active mediator among the philosophers at the heart of the analytic movement.[83] Due to his solid philosophical background, he is not satisfied with vague cultural relationships, but discerns the structures of intelligibility that link Freud to philosophical systems. Interested in Schopenhauer and Freud, he will establish his own difference, beginning with his disagreement with Freud, after 1924, over an astonishing reinterpretation of the contributions of psychoanalysis in the afterglow of Nietzsche,[84] thus bringing to term a Nietzscheo-Freudian current which was manifested before the war by Otto Gross.[85]

In 1926, Rank founds his critique of Freudian therapy on the claim of a 'therapy of the Will' as we see in *Will and Psychotherapy*,[86] but not without an appeal to Nietzsche. Rank goes so far as to establish the 'therapeutic experience' on the confrontation of two wills, that of the analyst and that of the analysed, again finding in the cure Nietzsche's schema of the confrontation of wills. A 'psychology of the Will' is thus placed under Nietzsche's sponsorship, as the only one who had undertaken to situate himself from this perspective.[87]

Rank maintains that 'Freud's psychology is anything but a doctrine of will' and explicitly appeals to Nietzsche in order to recognize the necessity of a 'rehabilitation of the Will',[88] by which he means 'an organization, positive and directing, and an integration of the Ego that utilizes its instinctive tendencies, in a constructive manner – at the same time that they are inhibited and controlled'.[89] It is revealing that the appeal is to a creative and positive, constructive and integrative will (in contrast with Freudian desire, defined as an evanescent and extenuated will) as recommended by Nietzsche.

In his major philosophical work, *The Will to Happiness* (1929),[90] Rank proposes a model of articulation between psychoanalysis and Nietzschean philosophy. We might call it the first great model of Freudo-Nietzschean construction. For the first time, in fact, the contributions of Nietzsche and Freud, of whom Rank is equally cognisant, are integrated into an ambitious synthesis, conducted with the systematicity of a *Weltanshauung*. Thus it is an important document for our purposes, since Rank is determined to exhibit the force of the convergence between these thinkers, yet free to polarize them to suit the needs of his project. That this resolute amalgam could not be to Freud's liking, there is no doubt at all, but to be exact, we have (in Rank's project) an accomplished model of a synthesis that joyfully transcends the prudent representation of partial 'similitudes' in order to embrace the two thoughts in an ambitious 'worldview'. It will not be accomplished without a reciprocal readjustment between the two theories, which is valuable exactly as an indication of the cleavages that Rank claims to have overcome. Rank's attempt is important to us for this reason, for it indicates, by its very effort to complete Freud by Nietzsche, both the correspondences and the gaps between the two thinkers.

Rank presents himself as a Freudian who has evolved in the sense of a rehabilitation of the *creative* aspect of the personality. 'I have been from the beginning entirely under the influence of Freud's materialist psychology, and it is in terms of a mechanistic biology, conforming to its ideology of the natural sciences, that I have exposed my conception of the creative genius.'[91] He gives as a motive for his separation from Freud's naturalism his discovery of the 'self-creation of the individual', of 'man's creative action'[92] on the occasion of the discovery of the determinant role of the 'trauma of birth'. The complementary principle that Rank requires in light of the Freudian viewpoint is thus to specify his naturalism by a perspective of 'creation' understood as the 'independent power' of the 'intra-mental world', that is not content to be influenced by the external world, but seeks actively to modify it.

Let us take up this claim from the point of view of the creative activity of individuality as establishing the recourse, against Freud and by complement, to the point of view recommended by Nietzsche of a 'psychology of the Will'. Rank's 'creative type' is defined as 'a being endowed with an aptitude ... to utilize the elementary instinctive factors in view of a *voluntary* creation ... in order to formulate an ideal that guides and consciously dominates this creative will in the sense of a personality', that implies a considerable development of the Ego as 'creator'.[93] The Ego is defined as 'the temporal representative of the primitive cosmic force'.[94] Rank further specifies that it is 'the vigour of this primitive force represented in the individual that we call the Will'. We see that the rehabilitation of creativity that Freud would have deliberately ignored is also that of individuality against specificity and of spirituality against biology. In that way, Rank permits the introduction, against the Freudian determinism of the Unconscious, of a theory of conscious liberty that founds a *therapeutic* revision of Freudian analysis.

In fact, Rank comes to consider neurosis and artistic creation as two versions, one failed and the other successful, of the same process. Neurosis appears finally as a sort of work or art *manquée* but which proceeds from the same hypertrophied aspiration of the Ego. The therapeutic principle would thus be to convert the mode of expression of neurosis into that of creation, on the artistic model. According to Rank, Freud cannot really conceive of the creative force of art. The recourse to Nietzsche consequently takes on the convergent sense of a reference to an aesthetic point of view against the domination of the point of view of scientific knowledge in Freud.

In that, therapy encounters the problem of morality, that is to say of the character, 'good' or 'bad', of the Will, from whence proceeds the question of *guilt.* Rank, in a grand recapitulation, interprets the whole sense of the progression of the problem, from Schopenhauer to Freud, by passing through Nietzsche. To Schopenhauer belongs the merit of having objectified the bad character of the Will, to Nietzsche that of having separated the 'Will from the problem of guilt'. But with Freud we come back to a pessimistic conception, accomplished by a 'death wish', related to Schopenhauer's original point of view – which will require a final conversion that Rank will claim as his own. Thus we end up, through this test problem, at a curious quadrille that takes the form of a proportional fourth. *Rank* claims to be to *Freud* what *Nietzsche* was to *Schopenhauer*.

In effect, 'Nietzsche reacts through the affirmation of the Will to the negation in Schopenhauer's system; just as Freud's theory is, as well, against Nietzsche, as a return to a pessimism and a nihilism nearly Schopenhauerean. I do not doubt that my psychology of the Will . . . amounts, in its turn, to a response to Freud's conception of ill will.'[95] So Rank clearly defines his role: he will be the 'Nietzsche of Freud'.[96] It must not be understood as a regression to a Nietzschean point of view in an articulated progressive schema; if Rank establishes Nietzsche as having been 'up to now the only and unique psychologist',[97] he declares no less clearly that Nietzsche could not resolve the problem posed 'because the analytic experience was necessary for that',[98] and firmly reproaches him for introducing 'clandestinely . . . a scale of values in psychology'.[99]

Thus Rank denies any confusion of genres. He begins with 'psychology' and remains there; before being an ethico-axiological question, Will is for him a 'psychological fact'. But the manner in which he formulates the 'epistemological' question expresses its ethico-metaphysical stake. 'Firstly, whence comes (Will) and how does it develop in man? Yet, then, why must we either condemn it as 'bad', or justify it as 'good', instead of recognizing and affirming its necessary character?'[100] Rank's question expresses well, even by its *mixed nature*, assumed as such, the encounter between the two questions and the two modes of expression respectively of Nietzsche and Freud. That it cannot work without contradiction, to the point of an explosive encounter between two modes of expression, goes back to Rank's own appreciation of the project. The essential thing is that it defines and indicates the moment of an encounter between two fields and without a doubt materializes the stakes at base. Perhaps in effect Nietzsche and Freud did encounter each other, in order to better decide between themselves, on this test question that Rank expressed in his project as that of 'the origin and psychological importance of the Will', the one exploring it *via* the psychological approach, the other *via* the critique of morality – Rank for his part makes them converge in the therapeutic, by assigning to that the task of 'justifying the Will'.

Such is finally Rank's double importance. Historically, he is the artisan of the most important systematization of Nietzscheo-Freudianism; didactically, for our purposes, he is the catalyst for a rapprochement and one who reveals the places where a comparison may be made, in the inquiry we will conduct on the detailed articulation of the themes. Rank can, in fact, claim the role of an indicator, as well as of a rival psychoanalyst, a disciple of Nietzsche, who represents Nietzsche in comparison to Freud, and against him.

Such is the complex process that defines the attitude of Freud with respect to Nietzsche during most of a half-century. It is a sinuous and multidimensional process, but one which is organized in a contradictory coherence whose constituent elements we have reconstituted.

In the beginning, we find a *personal* bond, at once indirect and ambivalent, which is expressed by a borrowing of modes of expression and at the same time by an extension which manifests a sort of prohibition bearing on Freud's reading of Nietzsche and even on his writing about Nietzsche. Upon this matrix of personal bonds is woven the work of intercessors and mediators who constitute Nietzscheo-Freudianism, at once myth, a fact of the history of ideas, a demand and even a system, such that Freud is seen to return to this bond that he has struggled to exorcise, as an imperative of rapprochement.

It is now necessary to turn toward what Freud *says* about Nietzsche in his *work*, in order to seek from this side the materiality of this relation whose history we have reconstructed.

2

NIETZSCHE IN FREUDIAN DISCOURSE

In contrast with the ambitious syntheses those who preach a Nietzsche-Freud Ecumenism, Freud's own discourse on Nietzsche is remarkably economical and concise. Nietzsche only appears in Freud's work in the form of brief references, following the general mode of all philosophical presence there. At first glance unpredictable, brief, and stereotypical,[1] references to Nietzsche periodically breach the continuity of his psychoanalytic discourse.

As otherwise Freud claims to have read very little of Nietzsche, we are left to interpret these *traces*, which constitute the most precise form of Nietzsche's presence in Freud. We find ourselves in possession of a dozen disparate allusions,[2] but by elucidating these allusions within their context, and by going back to their sources in Nietzsche's texts (and we are free to correct or elaborate upon them where Freud approximates the reference), we can see the outline of a web of important indications concerning the points of Freud's interest in Nietzschean thematics.

We know that these references fill, in Freud's theoretical strategy,[3] the function of an anticipatory and legitimating intuition regarding the discovery of psychoanalysis. In this manner, Freud indicates the meaning to which he wishes to guide his reader, for whomever might wish to follow the path that leads from Nietzsche to psychoanalysis.

NIETZSCHE'S STATUS IN FREUD'S PHILOSOPHICAL TOPOGRAPHY

We will first examine the texts where Freud in some way invests Nietzsche with the function of a precursor.

In 1914, in the *Contribution to the History of the Psychoanalytic Movement*, Nietzsche is mentioned in a prominent position among those who anticipated the psychoanalytic theses, right after Schopenhauer.[4] It is a symbolic situation; in Freud's philosophical galaxy, Nietzsche plays the role of a satellite to the Frankfurt philosopher. We thus need to discern what, in the Nietzschean reference, reflects the influence of Schopenhauer, who had already expressed it.[5]

But we get the impression that the philosophical taboo is overdetermined in the particular case of Nietzsche, since Freud makes the strange declaration that 'the great pleasure I took from Nietzsche's work, I later denied myself (*behindert*) with the conscious motivation that I would not be entrapped, in the elaboration of impressions furnished by psychoanalysis, by any exterior representation' (*Erwartungsvorstellung*).[6] Nietzsche is thus the object of a retention of a particularly determined (and fully conscious) interest, in proportion to the enjoyment (*Genuss*) which resulted.

This declaration conforms to preceding ones,[7] insofar as it confirms the limit of Freud's knowledge of Nietzsche's work, at the same time as it confirms the privileged bond between the two bodies of thought, since according to Freud's paradoxical rationale, the imperative to abstinence from reading philosophy is more rigorous and willing than the danger of allegiance is great. Freud recognizes that his affinity with Nietzsche is particularly pregnant, thus justifying the most energetic defence measures. A strange and profound bond ties Freud to Nietzsche; placed at a distance, with determination, this supposedly barely known stranger comes back to haunt psychoanalytic truth like its shadow. Such is the peculiar mixture of affinity and alterity entertained even by Freud, and which one who analyses the relationships between Freud and Nietzsche has the delicate task of separating.

The second great text to make a reference, *Selbstdarstellung* (1925) confirms the 1914 version. This is the famous passage where Freud affirms having carefully avoided approaching philosophy, then notes his 'concordances held' with Schopenhauer. Nietzsche's position there is also symbolic; his name is somehow evoked in association with that of Schopenhauer:[8]

> Nietzsche is the other philosopher whose intuitions and apperceptions (*Ahnungen und Einsichten*) often coincide (*sich decken*) in the most astonishing ways with the painfully acquired results of psychoanalysis; for that reason (*gerard darum*) I have for a long time avoided him; I consider it certainly less of a priority than maintaining my own impartiality (*Unbefangenheit*).[9]

Thus we see confirmed:

1 That Nietzsche is associated with Schopenhauer; he is even a sort of other Schopenhauer (*der andere Philosoph*) – this does not signify that his importance is secondary, but Freud's use of Nietzsche is from the outset mediated by a filiation, such that in referring to Nietzsche, Freud always gives the feeling of referring to a *family* of familiar thought at least as far as Nietzsche's philosophy is unique or disruptive.
2 That the frequency of Nietzschean anticipations, their acuity and their gravity are strongly felt by Freud. There persists in his evocations something like admiration for Nietzsche's anticipatory 'divinations', but these are precisely of the order of a prescience or an apperception – this is why Freud takes care to oppose him once more with the 'pain' of scientific labour, which has authenticated Nietzsche's intuitions.

3 That Freud is indeed prevented from reading Nietzsche out of concern for his own ingenuity, a condition of his own impartiality – and that limits his knowledge of Nietzsche's work.

TRAUMDEUTUNG: THE THEORY OF DREAMS

Let us see, then, what these *Ahnungen und Einsichten* are that Freud himself mentions throughout his own work.

To define the scope of Nietzschean referents in the economy of Freud's work, we should begin by pointing out the precise occurrences of Nietzsche's mention by name in Freud's texts, to grasp both the context and the meaning, as well as the function for which Freud needs to interpellate Nietzsche.

Nietzsche's name appears in *The Interpretation of Dreams*, in the chapter (VII) dedicated to the 'psychology of the processes of dreams', at the moment when Freud reaches the conclusion of *regression.* It is not simply a matter of Nietzsche being one among other second-hand historical references, such as abounded in the previous chapter.[10] Here, Freud's develops some generalizations somewhat more audacious than he permitted himself throughout a lengthy analysis of technical minutiae.

Freud specifies the characteristics of regression by distinguishing between its topical, temporal and formal aspects. He affects not having wanted to conclude without confiding in a general yet insistent 'impression' that would be disengaged from the experience of dreams and neuroses. 'The act of dreaming (*Träumen*) is a sort of regression to the most precocious relations of the dreamer, a revivification (*Wiedererleben*) of his infancy; of the past motions of drives (*Triebregungen*) which have dominated him and past modes of expression (*Ausdrucksweisen*) to which he is disposed.'[11] It is an impression that confirms, among others, the famous law of the ontogenetic recapitulation of phylogenetic development. 'Behind this individual infancy, we can hope to throw a glance onto phylogenetic infancy, on the development of the human species, of which the development of the individual is only a summary repetition influenced by the fortuitous circumstances of life.'

At the same time, Freud throws a wink toward Nietzsche:

> We sense (*ahnen*) the extent to which Fr. Nietzsche's words are accurate according to which during dreams there 'endures (*fortübt*) a primitive epoch of humanity', that we can no longer attain 'in a direct manner', and we can expect to reach, through the analysis of dreams, knowledge of man's archaic heritage, to discern what is psychically innate (*das seelisch Angeborene*) in him.

Such is thus the idea that Freud recognizes as common between himself and Nietzsche, the conception that dreams provide a privileged access to the 'antiquities of the soul', a prehistoric and phylogenetic legacy whose ontogenetic sediment constitutes a trace. It is one of the most fecund intuitions by which Nietzsche perceives what the 'science of dreams' would come to confirm experimentally.

Here, Freud obviously cites Nietzsche from memory, without indicating the reference. In question is a passage from the thirteenth aphorism of *Human, All Too Human*, in which Nietzsche declares that 'in dreams there continues to be exercised within us a primordial part of humanity, because it is the foundation on which higher reason is developed and continues to develop in each person'.[12] We see that Freud has casually used quotation marks, since only the first part of the phrase is found in the original text – still, the attitude is little modified, which confirms that he is citing it from memory. As for the rest of the phrase on the indirect knowledge that dreams furnish, it is not at all in Nietzsche's text, but it functions, in Freud's memory, to summarize an idea effectively expressed just afterwards by Nietzsche. 'Dreams report to us of distant states of civilization and put in our hands the means of better understanding them'. At least the idea conforms to Nietzsche's actual thoughts on the question.

We see, then, that Freud has recognized in Nietzsche a parent idea on this point, and he pins it to his conception by excessively condensing the formulation, in order that it fulfil the function of an anticipatory reflection. If we seek to compare Freud's and Nietzsche's conceptions, we will have to add details in the places where Freud omits them, and to resituate these remarks in the ensemble of Nietzsche's theory of dreams.[13]

THE PSYCHOPATHOLOGY OF EVERYDAY LIFE: MEMORY

Nietzsche is evoked in a note in *The Psychopathology of Everyday Life*, with regard to the idea, imposed by analytic experience, 'that a resistance is opposed to the remembering of painful impressions, and to the representation of painful thoughts'. Now, the note goes on, if a series of authors has located this effect, it is unquestionably to Nietzsche that we must give the most credit:

> But no one among them has represented the phenomenon and its psychological proof as exhaustively (*erschöpfend*) and at the same time as expressively (*eindrucksvoll*) as Nietzsche has done in one of his aphorisms: I did that, says my 'memory'. I did not do it, says my pride, and it remains adamant. In the end, it is memory who cedes.[14]

This time Freud is precise; he indicates that in question is Aphorism 68, from the fourth part of *Beyond Good and Evil*.[15] Its value in Freud's eyes is to indicate, with an extreme concision due to the clarity of the aphorism, the psychological foundation (*psycholgische Begründun*) of a phenomenon, more expressively than a lengthy literature on the subject.

This aphorism enjoys a prestige and an agreement particularly striking for Freud. While taking a position on Nietzsche in 1908, during one of the

Wednesday seminars,[16] this was the aphorism Freud had in mind when he praised Nietzsche's psychological perspicacity. What is more extraordinary, though, is that clinical experience would send Freud back to this aphorism. In 1907, Ernst Lanzer, 'The Ratman', evoked the aphorism in question during the course of a session in order to express his own conflict. Calling to mind a criminal act 'that he did not himself recognize but which he remembers especially as having committed', Lanzer cites Nietzsche in order to express the conflict between memory and will,[17] an astonishing situation that insinuates Nietzsche between Freud and his patient, at the initiative of the patient himself, a distinguished *gebildet*. What is still more curious is that before entering into analysis, Lanzer had at least skimmed through *The Psychopathology of Everyday Life*. Freud had no doubt that Lanzer had occasion to read Nietzsche's aphorism in his own book, and then it had come back as an unconscious irony.[18] What had happened was that a neurotic had found his own thoughts expressed in Nietzsche's aphorism, and there was an unexpected illustration of the psychological weight that Freud had placed on it, to the point where Nietzsche's verbiage slid between Freud and his object. That symbolically ratified the commerce between the two thinkers.

But there are more precise motivations of content which are capable of founding a meeting between Freud and Nietzsche on this idea. Paradoxically, Nietzsche unconsciously copied this idea from Schopenhauer, whose psychology strongly influenced Freud. In *The World as Will and Representation*, Schopenhauer described the mechanism of madness as a conflict issuing from the Will and Intellect based on the repugnance of pride. 'We recall with what repugnance we think of things that strongly hinder our interests, our pride and our desires, with what pain we decide to submit to a precise and serious examination of our intellect, with what facility we can on the contrary brusquely turn it aside.'[19] Based on this refusal, the mind breaks 'the thread of memory', and madness results, expressing 'the repugnance of the will to allow to happen what is contrary to the light of the intellect' to the point of subjugating memory.

Thus we find in Schopenhauer an analysis extracted from the mechanism, which Nietzsche summarizes by his formula. Undeniably, it is to Schopenhauer that credit goes for the idea's paternity, and Nietzsche spontaneously plagiarized a work which had been so formative for him.[20] Nietzsche, it is true, endows the idea with an expression that concentrates in three phrases a long dialogue. Nevertheless, that tells us that we have to seek out the implications of this expressive formula in the overall conception of memory and repression where it is engaged.[21]

THE CASE OF SCHREBER: THE SOLAR SYMBOL OF THE FATHER

The following appearance of Nietzsche in Freud's work confirms its implications in the clinic, in the study of Schreber entitled *Psychoanalytic Remarks on the Autobiography of a Case of Paranoia* (1911).

Freud is in the process of examining a symbolic link between the father and the sun. In order to illustrate the relationship between 'neurotic fantasies' and 'cosmic myths', he makes an allusion to one of his cases who, having 'lost his father at an early age, sought to rediscover it in everything in nature that was great and sublime'. There Nietzsche intervenes, induced, we see, by the most vivid clinical experience. 'That,' he says, 'made him understand that Nietzsche's hymn "Before Sunrise" expresses the same nostalgia'.[22]

It is the title to the fourth text of the third part of *Thus Spoke Zarathustra*. In fact, we find there a sort of hymn to the dawn of nature, to pure Sky as the image of innocence and the great 'Yes'. By that, Zarathustra's message summarizes a benediction to 'Sky of accident', 'Sky of innocence', 'Sky of exuberance'. 'Before sunrise' symbolizes 'the great and unlimited Yes', before the coming of mediating clouds.[23]

It is curious that Freud would evoke this hymn to the sky in relation to a myth about the Sun, since, if we refer back to Nietzsche's idea, it is the sunrise that interrupts the enjoyment of innocence before daybreak. The Sky is thus the enemy of the Sun, symbolizing the paternal complex by its dazzling aspect. In fact, Freud has in mind a transparent idea that imposes the relation. As he recalls in his notes, 'Nietzsche also lost his father while still an infant',[24] a point on which Freud had insisted during the Wednesday seminar at the Vienna Society dedicated to *Ecce Homo*, and which he maintains here.[25] Zarathustra's sacred admiration before Nature's sublime is here translated into Nietzsche's paternal complex, a sublimated quest for an absent father.[26]

Once again, the rapprochement is rapid. Freud has retained from his reading of the text the exaltation of the natural sublime, and he can overstep the opposition between the Sky and the Sun, however essential to the meaning of the text, in order to seize the *document*, the analogy between the neurotic sense of the cosmic myth and its poetic expression. The philosophical poetry thus gives its mode of expression (*langage*) to the neurotic who is himself the ontogenetic expression of a phylogenetic myth.[27]

It is in this spirit that Freud uses Nietzsche's mode of expression, and assigns it a particular importance, for it expresses in all its depth the cosmic dimension of ontogenetic experience. In addition, even if the relation does not linger on the details of the content, it is no longer a banal citation. Nietzsche is not a simple cultural referent for Freud. These few fragments that he knew reside in his memory in a sufficiently vivid fashion as to be reactualized through an analogy induced from clinical experience. Independently of the diagnosis of Nietzsche's case and his own pathology, a privileged relation joins his poetic expression to the language of the depths – which naturally leads 'the psychology of the depths' to what Freud reads in it.

That is how Freud uses the text, but beyond this usage, the text contains a signification which engages the whole conception of morality and guilt. Without a doubt, Freud saw in that text one of the essential subjects with which his theory of Neurosis is compared. Thus we will have to re-read it from the perspective of this comparison.[28]

CHARACTER-TYPES: CRIME AND GUILT

At the end of a small work of 1915, *On Character-Types Met With in Psychoanalytic Work*, at the conclusion of an elaboration on 'criminals by feelings of guilt', a new analogy with Nietzsche appears.

'A friend had afterwards remarked on this point that the "criminal by feeling of guilt" was also known to Nietzsche. The pre-existence of the feeling of guilt and turning aside from the act (*Verwendung der Tat*) in order to rationalize it glitters before us in Zarathustra's discourse, 'On the pale criminal'. We will leave to future research the problem of deciding how criminals are to be counted among these 'pale ones'.[29]

Returning to the characteristics of Nietzsche's intervention in Freud's discourse, we see it placed at the end of a precise development, in order to give it a somehow typical dimension. As it occurs, the pale silhouette of the guilty criminal serves to fix it as a *type* in the psychography just previously evoked. Nietzsche appears, not fortuitously, as the portraitist of what otherwise remains an abstract type, a wonderful encounter between Freud's typology and that of Nietzsche, as a double determination. On the other hand, the same characteristics are attributed to Nietzsche's intervention; striking, sparkling, we hear that he gives his expressive touches to a type, so much so that it can guide future research, as a veritable nosographic framework. Freud is not far from proposing to designate the type of criminal-by-guilt as the 'pale criminal complex'. This text, from the first part of *Thus Spoke Zarathustra*,[30] thus serves once more as a clinical document, this time by furnishing an instrument of nosographic generalization.

Freud, again, does not ask more, but he discovers (not fortuitously) the pathways to the theory of guilt, designated by the problem that we will have to envision from the meaning of Nietzsche's general theory of the criminal.[31]

GROUP PSYCHOLOGY AND THE ANALYSIS OF THE EGO: OVERMAN

Ubermensch, one of Nietzsche's major concepts, is evoked in the tenth chapter of *Group Psychology and the Analysis of the Ego* (1921), but in an apparently confusing context.

Describing 'the crowd and the primitive horde', Freud relates 'the father of the primitive horde' to Nietzsche's Overman. 'At the beginning of human history, it was only Overman that Nietzsche expected in the future'.[32] On what does Freud base this astonishing equivalence between the originary collective father and Overman? We are tempted to think that the relationship is arbitrary and only engages the *name* of Overman, but Freud has indicated a common point to us in the context, the overdevelopment of the Ego.

In the beginning, the father of the primitive horde enjoys, in contrast to the constraint of the crowd, an exceptional liberty. 'The individuals of the crowd were as constrained as we find them today, but the father of the primitive horde was free.' Following a description of this liberty, which establishes the Overman analogy, Freud goes on to say that 'his intellectual acts, even in an isolated state (*in der Vereinzelung*), were strong and independent, his will did not need to be reinforced by that of others'. In effect, the originary father enjoys in the beginning the same supreme prerogative of self-sufficiency that Nietzsche accords to Overman in the future.

But this self-sufficiency for Freud reveals a precise reality, the sovereign development of a form of hypertrophied narcissism. 'His Ego had few libidinal attachments; he loved no one outside of himself and only loved others to the extent that they served his needs. His Ego gives up nothing excessive to his objects.' From this angle, the analogy with Overman becomes strongly revelatory. On the one hand, it contains the principle of a Freudian interpretation of Overman; on the other hand, it permits Freud to situate his paradoxical sense of the equivalence between Overman and the originary Father.

We see that the free exercise of Will to Power immediately has for Freud the sense of an an-object relation, where at the least the relation to the object is especially loose and refined. To be independent (*unabhängig*) signifies for Freud a relative disengagement from object-oriented investments. We know that the inverse development of the Ego's libido and the libido of the object characterizes Narcissism. 'The more one absorbs, the more the other is impoverished', Freud explains in his essay on Narcissism.[33] If we represent 'an originary investment of the Ego's libido, which is later on transferred to objects, but which still fundamentally persists and is borne around its object-investments, like the body of a protoplasmic animalcule around the pseudopods that it had emitted,' we find an impressive expression of this exorbitant development of the Ego's libido that characterizes super-humanity.

But at the same time, we understand the profound sense of opposition that makes Freud situate, at the origin, this sovereign privilege of primary narcissism, which Nietzsche locates in the future. The hypothesis of an 'originary father' or an 'Overman' is no longer important in itself; what matters is that the attained *type* of the most integrally conceivable narcissism is related by Freud to an interrupted and lapsed *before*, while for Nietzsche it is reactivated as the *living end* toward which becoming legitimately tends. In other words, Overman realizes a narcissism that is outlined in a supreme indifference toward the other, characterizing the master, so that the putting to death of the Father also signifies the arrest of the death of narcissism – that is why Freud neither awaits nor welcomes the coming of Overman....

This rapprochement, we can see, introduces an essential comparison of the meaning of the origin of narcissism, decisive in our comparison of Freud and Nietzsche.[34] In fact, there is more to the rapprochement between Father and Overman than a fortuitous analogy; it is one of Freud's oldest ideas. When Freud wrote his 1921 work, perhaps he had not forgotten that, nearly a quarter of a century earlier, he had already formulated the idea. In a manuscript dating from 31 May 1897 and addressed to Fliess, Freud invoked both the idea and the name of Nietzsche's Overman in order to conclude one of his first ethnological articles. There, Freud maintains that 'incest is an anti-social fact that, in order to exist, civilization has had bit by bit to renounce'.[35] In this precise place, he adds, 'Antinomy: "Overman"'.

So in this first formulation where Freud outlines his great theory of civilization and instincts, the specific reference to Nietzsche's Overman theory (to which the quotation marks attest) is imposed, not fortuitously, and remains linked for a long time to Freud's ethnological theory. Thus the 1921 allusion is a sort of reappearance; far from being improvised, it is linked to an old line of reflection.

The two allusions are mutually clarifying. In the glimmer of the development of *Group Psychology and the Analysis of the Ego*, the brief mention of 1897 takes on a precise and familiar signification. Incest defines one of the limits of collective morality, that of prohibition, while Overman symbolizes the other limit. Incest expresses, in fact, the renunciation of the pleasure principle by the masses, while Overman symbolizes the non-mediated pleasure principle, of which Freud's homology will be the chief of the horde that appeared between these two texts, in *Totem and Taboo* (1912–13).

In addition, Freud's relation to the Overman theory becomes understandable as exhibiting as an 'antinomy' the conflict between the instincts and human law, which is at the heart of Freud's theory of *Kultur*.[36] When he notices in Michelangelo's *Moses* 'something ... of Overman',[37] Freud gives Nietzsche's attribute to the very figure of the Law![38]

THE EGO AND THE ID: NIETZSCHE BETWEEN FREUD AND GRODDECK

At the moment when, in the framework of his second phase, Freud introduces the concept of *Id* (*Es*), he is advised that, even before Groddeck instituted the use of the concept, Nietzsche had already inaugurated the usage. In the text where Freud introduces the denomination, referring to Groddeck, he takes care to point out in a note that 'Groddeck himself has indeed followed Nietzsche's example, in whose work this grammatical expression is used to indicate that there is in our being something impersonal and necessarily submitted to nature in some way.'[39]

Freud does not give more precision to the term, but takes its usage as acquired. Whether a vague memory or an insistent impression, Freud thus conceives of a certain use by Nietzsche of this concept in order to designate, in Freud's words, 'das Unpersönliche und sozusagen Naturnotwendige in unserem Wesen'.

We find an analogous declaration in the third of the *New Introductory Lectures on Psychoanalysis*, in 1932, where Nietzsche is associated with the introduction of the Id. 'In establishing for ourselves the use of Nietzsche's term (*Sprachgebrauch*), and at the instigation of G. Groddeck, we will henceforth call it the Id'.[40] We can see, even in the form of this phrase, that Nietzsche's lexical intervention has had the effect of substantivizing the 'impersonal pronoun', 'particularly proper to express the essential character of this psychic province, its alterity to the Ego' (*Ichfremdheit*). As happens so often for Freud, Nietzsche intervenes by inscribing, through the force of the word, an essential determination (*Hauptcharakter*) that psychoanalytic investigation rejoinders through clinical experimentation. Thanks to Nietzsche's linguistic innovations, according to Freud, *es* has become *Es*, thus naming an apparatus in which the topic provides its meta-psychological content – that nominally seals the (Nietzschean) name to the (Freudian) thing. For this reason, Freud does not miss the opportunity to evoke him at the same time as his own discovery.

However, It was Freud himself who hypothesized borrowing the term 'Id' from Nietzsche and proposed it to Groddeck in a letter dating from Christmas 1922. 'I think that you have taken the Id (literally, not associatively) from Nietzsche'[41] and asked him for authorization to mention it in *The Ego and the Id*. 'May I also say it in my own writing?' In Freud's texts, the rapprochement is carried on to the terminological plane; by limiting the borrowing to the *word*, Freud leaves aside the more interesting question of the analogy of the content of the concepts themselves. It is, at base, the only occasion where Nietzsche intervenes in the correspondence between Freud and Groddeck. While Groddeck willingly spoke about Nietzsche to others,[42] Freud tacitly but firmly placed Nietzsche out of bounds. The most we know is that Groddeck approved of Freud's suggestion, since in a letter from 1929 to another correspondent he conceded that regarding 'something that is composed of both conscious and unconscious' elements he 'calls the Id, in reference to Nietzsche, and for reasons of commodity'.[43] In Groddeck, moreover, Freud met someone whose personal affinities were particularly linked to Nietzsche. Groddeck's father had known and even influenced Nietzsche,[44] and Groddeck himself had visited Nietzsche's tomb in 1904 in the company of Elisabeth Förster-Nietzsche.[45] But Freud seems tacitly to impose, upon those who had been close enough to touch Nietzsche, a kind of silence; that regarding Groddeck was no different from that of Lou Salomé.

For our purposes, it is necessary to break the silence. If Freud for his part wants to retain only the resonance of the word, it is necessary for us to pose the question of content. To what extent, in Nietzsche's conception of instinct and the Unconscious, is the Id 'anticipated'? That will be one of the chief principles of our comparison.[46]

THE BALANCE SHEET OF NIETZSCHEAN ECHOES IN FREUD

We see that, despite their disparate nature, the Nietzschean echoes go back, like fulguration, to basic themes: dreams, conflict, neurosis, criminality and guilt, Overman and Father, Id and the drives. Even in that, we touch the limits of what Freud can teach us about the relation between psychoanalysis and Nietzschean thought. He does not indicate to us the means of systematizing the thematic comparison, contenting himself with pointing out, at the whim of his own associations, the possible echoes. Finally, if Freud indicates certain things of great importance, he keeps silent about, or does not perceive, certain essential others.

The moment has thus arrived to embark on our comparison of the thematics according to a systematic order which is disengaged from these two monumental works. Starting out, as we have said, from the specificity of Freud's vision which has served us as an indispensable indicator, it is now necessary for us to invert the axis of our inquiry, in other words to turn back the sense of the conjunction.[47] Treating 'Freud and Nietzsche' in the preceding part, we have reported the relation to the Freudian pole that interpellates it in its own context and for its own stakes of the moment. It is necessary for us now to treat the inverse of the question, that of 'Nietzsche and Freud', that is to say to present a parallelism of two thematics, through their respective logics, which will provide us at the same time with the fundamental sense of the preceding echoes, by inserting them into an ordered comparison whose goal is an exhaustive clarification.

PART TWO
NIETZSCHE AND FREUD

INTRODUCTION

TOWARDS A THEMATIC COMPARISON: METHOD AND PROBLEMS

To compare two theories poses a series of considerable methodological problems. Two discursive objects are not naturally comparable, insofar as they constitute their own space in and for themselves and do not readily contain the means necessary for a projection on to a common field. At any rate, such would only be an artificial space which would immediately falsify the objects themselves – which constitutes the vice of every analogical approach. It is necessary for us, then, paradoxically to *construct* the space of comparison *while* leading to an explanation of the rapprochements.

In other words, it is not a matter of immediately situating one from the point of view of the other, by treating Nietzsche's contributions as those of 'Freud's precursor', which would have the problematic effect of evaluating Nietzsche from the perspective of a Law external to his own identity, by making Freud the truth of Nietzsche. But inversely, neither it is a question of placing Freud in a Nietzschean perspective, as a sort of challenge, evaluating psychoanalysis in anticipation – which goes back to judging Freud's contributions by Nietzsche's standards, and thus placing the Law in Nietzsche. It is necessary for us to go from one to the other, treating each respectively as a reciprocal limit, so that a common space-perspective can appear, which is not a given but a conflictual result. For this reason, we will resort to a dialectical shuttle that, at every given level (theme, notion), will define the Nietzschean and Freudian problematics by exhibiting them at the same time – in a chronological succession, but a logical simultaneity – the attainment and transcendence of such virtuality as is present in Freud, and the resistance to 'transcendence' as manifested in Nietzsche's idiosyncratic work.[1] Finally, as each of these problematics is defined by its own becoming, it will be necessary for us, for each level of analysis considered, to retrace the sense of genesis for both Freud and Nietzsche in order to clarify reciprocally the geneses at the level of notional homologies.[2]

However, that poses precisely the most delicate problem, that of the validity of the *homologies* and of an excavation capable of organizing an established order beyond the analogies, something like an anatomy or a comparative physiology of thematics. We have seen the judicious offhandedness with which Freud draws upon Nietzsche. He is content to designate as his right (or birthright) the points of Nietzsche's motifs that he can pin on the canvas of psychoanalysis, without lingering either to explain or to problematize the association of his officious allusions. Nietzsche is here interpellated purely and simply as the *Vortreter* of psychoanalytic truth, as a legitimating anticipation. But that leads us to underestimate the problematic *sui generis* while at the same time overestimating the contribution, since it is the contribution to psychoanalysis that permits us to give such intuitions a signifying value that does not always rightfully belong to Nietzsche.[3] In so doing, Freud indeed pins down the points of contact, as we have suggested, so that we can deploy our double thematic; he does so, however, without any order, at the will and whim of their discovery and their utility to psychoanalysis.

It is not enough simply to declare the analogies and anticipations. We must create the conditions of a dialogue, on a common terrain, where the problematics are determined in a manner that is subtly both convergent and divergent. Nietzsche and Freud are often in a position of practically *saying the same thing*, but not always *about the same thing*. What gives its full meaning to such a theoretical expression is its context in the notional body under consideration, and it only takes its significance relative to the overall approach that subtends it. Thus we must transcend our astonishment before the *echoes* in order to discover the differences in tonality. The most important thing seems to us to be to locate the somehow structural correspondences in the respective texts, in order to read the functional differences between the conceptual regimes we have engaged.

But that implies that we have located an orderly structure where an apparent dissymmetry reigns, that such-and-such an aspect of Nietzsche's thematic contains an analytic element which Freud will come to integrate into an organized thematic. It is necessary to guard against inflating Nietzsche's importance here, while also accentuating it in order to bring the correspondence to light. Inversely, what is thematic for Nietzsche may pass as an isolated element in Freud. We are thus in the presence of a puzzle of elements and themes that we must articulate both synchronically and independently, in the manner of a *palaeontology* that progressively reconstitutes two skeletons beginning with partially similar bones, of which we know that in a certain respect they belong to the same genre, but which remain under specific principles of organization. The most striking resemblances can be revealed erroneously with regard to later principles of organization, while an anodyne element may induce a profound isomorphism.

Moreover, Nietzsche's philosophy and Freud's psychoanalysis both energetically reject systematization.[4] The guiding principles are produced and articulated in and by a process of permanent constitution, which we can only establish via a lateral cadence. It is to just such a morphology that we shall now proceed, by moving from *fundamentals*[5] to the *themes*[6] and then to the *stakes* involved.[7]

BOOK ONE
THE FOUNDATIONS

1

INSTINCT AND DRIVE

A comparison between the works of Nietzsche and Freud finds a natural point of schism in the concept of instinct. Nietzsche's philosophy can be taken literally as one of instincts, while instinct (or drive)[1] forms the very foundation of Freudian psychoanalysis. That said, though, we must come to terms with this point of departure. It is not a matter of prejudging either the Nietzschean or the Freudian project by *defining* them as theories of instinct; we will take this concept only as a referent and situate it as the intersecting term in the two discourses we are analysing, whose status we derive from the extraordinary number of occurrences of the concept in Nietzsche as well as in Freud.[2] The approach is thus warranted, but we will need to specify and elucidate its contents. Our point of departure will be a pair of literal homonyms, for the terms *Trieb* and *Instinkt* fulfil a discursive *and* functional role for both Nietzsche and Freud. But, as we shall see, they do not fulfil the *same* role.

The status of the concepts in question designates more a discursive function than a semantic unity that can be immediately circumscribed. However, if the contents turn out to be indeterminate in their generality, the cleavages which the contents produce are precise and determining. We need to understand the meaning of this semantic referent by observing the conceptual effects it produces for both Nietzsche and Freud. In other words, to understand what instinct *means* is at once to grasp *what it produces* in the demonstrative strategy that invokes it.

In this way, however, we have already retreated from the attempt to define what the term *means*, especially for Nietzsche. In Freud, the term is well defined, but there it reigns as an indetermination crucial to the theoretical function of instinct in the Freudian conceptual economy. To clarify these two positions simultaneously, we need to trace the complex conceptual use of these terms. *Instinkt* is elucidated *a posteriori* by its extension, whose meaning is coherent, yet which varies according to the context that requires it.

It is possible that the *meaning* of the concept signifies less than what Nietzsche or Freud want to say when they use the term, but this claim requires an inquiry into the *genesis of use* of both the term and the concept. In fact, for both theorists *instinct* is constructed as a theoretical tool through a process of progressive development.[3] We have the best chance of understanding what the term means, then, through its progressive use, in other words through a phenomenological grasp of what Nietzsche and Freud respectively contribute to the concept. In this way we can arrive at a comparative definition, but we need to begin our inquiry first by identifying in Nietzsche, and in Freud, their original uses of the concept.

NIETZSCHEAN INSTINCT: ORIGINS OF THE CONCEPT

The first time Nietzsche uses the term *instinct* is in 1869 on the occasion of his first lecture at Basel, entitled *Homer and Classical Philology*. There, Nietzsche describes philology as a mixture, or a heterogeneous aggregate, of 'scientific and ethico-aesthetic instincts at first disparate', then 'reunited under a common denomination', which creates 'a sort of apparent monarchy'.[4]

- This first significant use of the term *Trieb* marks a regime in Nietzsche's work which will be in place for a long time, and combines in a single term several fundamental ideas which Nietzsche will henceforth always attach in some way to the idea of instinct. In this first case, instincts are presented in bundles; what dominates among them is a sort of teeming diversity, which Nietzsche will often evoke by the modality of *et cetera*.
- Here, also it is true, spaces are circumscribed and named. We can discern two major genealogical axes, one part scientific, the other part ethico-aesthetic. The categorization of the instincts thus derives from their form of activity or expression. There is a specific instinct at work in science, in ethics, in art; the Nietzschean instincts are presented as so many tiny demons which animate human activity. There is even an instinct *for* human activity, somewhat akin to the notion that, as in the animistic religions, there is a spirit in each object. We can act in such-and-such a way via innumerable instincts, according to Nietzsche, at least in the early phases of his thought. There are instincts everywhere, just as for Heraclitus there are gods everywhere, that is, everywhere that something of some importance happens.
- It is not by accident that the initial evocation of the concept *instinct* should reflect a mixed nature. Every so-called unitary activity, according to Nietzsche's philological practices, reveals a pool of instincts somehow held together (*zusammengetan*). Reality is adjudged amid this teeming diversity of instincts, and unity is dismissed to the rank of appearances. Thus, under the tranquil, unitary denomination of 'philology', Nietzsche reveals a heterogeneous diversity of instincts pulling in opposing directions. In Nietzsche's discourse, instinct functions as an impurity that rejects the homogeneity of substance. The 'Same' is revealed as an appearance that covers over a complex alloy of instincts forcibly held together.

Nietzsche explains this fact by the historical link between philology and pedagogy. Pedagogical care is obliged to operate as a sort of alloy, or 'choice of edifying elements'. What characterizes this artificial alloy is that the composing elements are at once agglomerated *and* incompatible. We get the image of a body whose composite elements are taken in a unity which is not a fusion, which obliges and constrains the elementary instincts to coexist in a state of hostility. Nietzsche speaks in this sense of 'the hostility of instincts fundamentally held together (*zusammengefassten*) under the name of philology, and yet not blended.'[5]

We should note that instincts are evoked like Democritus' atoms, unities realized in everything, and this unity is a convention which names a subjective appearance. Such is philology's finality, to forcibly obtain 'the total forgery and the reduction to unity of fundamental instincts originally hostile and only reassembled (*zusammengebrachten*) by force.'[6] The anarchic regime of instincts is illustrated by a metaphor of crooked growth (*Verwachsen*). The alternative is formulated whereby, on the one hand the harmonious growth of *Trieb*, etymologically erupts, and on the other hand an artificial becoming-one (*Einswerden*), negates of the eruption. This conception emerges in Nietzsche's discourse from the very beginnings of his use of *Trieb.*[7]

At the same time, and in the same text, the term *Instinkt* is introduced. Philology is presented as a fragment of 'natural science' in that it 'seeks to investigate (*ergründen*) the most profound human instinct, that of speech (*Sprachinstinkt*).'[8] Elsewhere, *Trieb* and *Instinkt* are concurrently produced. 'The great instincts of the masses (*Masseninstinkte*), the popular unconscious instincts (*Volkertriebe*)' appear as 'the veritable supports and activities of so-called universal history.'[9]

Instinkt designates a fundamental faculty. Instead of tiny demons animating activity, here it refers to a fundamental energy. This time, though, depth (*Tiefe*) is the adjudged characteristic. *Trieb* is itself associated with a force operating in the subterranean space of the human Unconscious. Where *Instinkt* is a calm and continuous force acting within the continuity of life, *Trieb* is the dynamic eruption; together they form the supports and activities (*Träger und Hebel*) of appearances.

Thus Nietzsche's own philological practices puts him on the path of the instincts, in three complementary ways. First, Nietzsche's philology reveals the subterranean action of heterogeneous instincts, emanating from scientific, ethical and aesthetic registers; second, it discovers in itself its own natural object, that of language-as-instinct; finally, this philology understands *language* to be the instinctive force, specific and collective, at work in history. Thus, philology is in commerce with the instincts in three ways: those instincts it activates via cognition, those it investigates via research, and those it addresses via science. In this manner instinct defines the being, the object and the activity of philology, which as a science marks a triple entry into the 'laboratories of the instinctive' (*in der Werkstätte des Instinktiven*).[10]

Philology's penetration into the laboratories of the instinctive encounters a privileged object, that of the Greek conscience. We should note that Nietzsche encountered this object prior to his writings on Greek tragedy by way of the Homeric problem, which Friedrich Wolf had firmly established in classical philology.[11] In his writing on Homer,[12] Nietzsche examines the combative instinct that 'the Greek genius valorized.'[13] Homeric civilization is held to give value (*gelten lassen*) to a fundamental instinct (*Trieb*), *Eris*. Nietzsche then works to derive from this instinct the congenial politics of a Themistocles.[14] From this angle, Nietzsche will embark on his famous dual theory of instincts articulated in *The Birth of Tragedy*, but we can already see outlined in his early work on Homer the first formulations of this theory.

Kunnsttrieb, the prototypical instinct, is grasped at once as an informing activity, as in its Apollonian manifestation. It is an important moment in the subtle genesis of the concept where instinct is understood as language, and literally assumes a body in reality. Here is the demiurgic evocation of the Apollonian instinct. 'The individual, the differentiating Apollonian instinct, creating from the forms and by the means – visibly – of individuals.'[15] Instinct is defined as an 'unconscious force formative of forms', transparent in artistic creation;[16] or better yet, the visible forms are the 'organs' which serve the instincts, created by instinct so as to make itself appear as a permanent suffering.[17] Instinct as power (*Macht*) manifests itself materially.

This is how we must understand the Apollonian and the Dionysian; they are 'artistic powers' which 'spring from the same nature.'[18] They are the instruments of immediate satisfaction of the aesthetic instinct of nature. In other words, the aesthetic instinct derives from nature. A better way of saying this is that nature is the subject of the aesthetic instinct. In this sense Nietzsche's first conception of *Instinkt* is undeniably *naturalistic*; what is expressed by instinct is none other that nature itself. The objective of *The Birth of Tragedy* is to know 'up to what point and to what extent *these aesthetic instincts of nature* are developed among the Greeks.'[19] Elsewhere, Nietzsche evokes 'these all-powerful artistic instincts in nature.'[20]

Apollo and Dionysus thus symbolize two different destinies rising out of the same source, which is no other than *Natur* itself. In this sense it is properly necessary to take the duplicity of these two fundamental instincts in analogy with the 'duality of the sexes' in reproduction.[21] Socrates, identified as the negation of instinct,[22] is presented as the destiny opposed to and the inverse of natural instinct, and finally taken in the history of this fundamentally tragic instinct, in the name of 'a form, truly speaking enfeebled by the transfiguration in the Socratism of a science oriented towards life.'[23] That expresses the essential character of instinct, which realizes itself to the point of its own negation. But where instinct realizes itself effectively, it is defined as 'the creative-affirmative force.'[24]

The contemporary text entitled *Philosophy (Art and Cognition)*[25] expresses even more clearly the status of instinct at this moment in Nietzsche's philosophy. Here the dominant axis is the opposition between science and life. Nietzsche's critique centres on an examination of the misdeeds of a special type of instinct, *Erkenntnistrieb* (instinct of cognition).[26] This is a new logical (though chronologically prior) moment in the genesis of the central instinctual thematic, where Nietzsche begins to forge the terms that will support his conception of *Trieb*. It is through a process more of revelation than of lability that he names this new instinct (which we still need to interpret). From this moment on, *Triebe* in Nietzschean discourse appear endowed with a schizogenetic mode of reproduction.[27]

If this species of instinct, *Erkenntnistrieb*, is privileged at this stage of theoretical genesis, it is because it figures as the contradictory destiny of an instinct turned back against its source, that is to say life, itself a special case of *phusis*. The hypertrophy of this instinct is thus an eminently pathological symptom of the scope of instinct. 'The instinct of cognition, excessive, insatiable ... is a sign (*Zeichen*) that life has become old.'[28] It indicates a general degeneration of the instinctive economy, in which 'the instincts in general have become feeble (*matt*) as well and no longer fasten the bridle to the individual.' But it also tells us about instinct as such; it tends to be an absence of measure, which is only another form of self-affirmation. It is the *aesthetic instinct* which must furnish the remedy for the re-equilibrium of the whole organism.

The cognitive instinct is obliged, then, to take into account this compensatory law in the instinctual totality. From this angle, Nietzsche conceives of the pathology of instinct in terms of hypo- and hyper-development of partial instincts in relation to the totality, and art takes on the role of re-establishing equilibrium by subjugating the bulimic instinct of cognition.

Alongside this, however, we find a relativization of the very notion of instinct. Nietzsche reflects on instinct as a human invention:

> Man discovers only slowly how much the world is infinitely complicated .... He leaves himself, the latest result, and conceives of the original forces just as they occurred in his imagination .... Also, he thinks he has explained something with the word 'instinct' and willingly reports the actions as an unconscious finality in the original development of things.[29]

For our purposes, this is an important fragment because here Nietzsche gives an account of the genesis of the idea *instinct*. A philosophy that postulates instincts at work at every instant in human reality simultaneously perceives its own anthropomorphic nature.

Nietzsche goes so far as to say that the concept *instinct* explains nothing. 'With instinct (*Instinkt*) one does not advance a single step towards explaining the conformity to ends (*Zweckmässigkeit*), precisely because these instincts are already themselves the result of processes pursued for an infinitely long time.'[30] The originary character of the instincts is thus in a way an illusion, an affect of a naive analogy between belated human thought and originary forces (*Urkräfte*). On the contrary, it is necessary to conceive of instinct as the product of a *process*, rather than as an immediate beginning. At the same time, it is not enough to pronounce 'instinct' like a magic word in order to explain the nature of the forces at work; rather, it is necessary to show the processes themselves at work which have carried the instinct to term.

Having attained this degree of sophistication with the concept, the *Untimely Meditations* makes polemic use of it. There we see the process of the Philistine, who incarnates the negation of 'instinct the disquieting creator of the artist',[31] in the first *Meditation*. The hypertrophic development of the historical sense is defined as a pathological symptom of civilization.

Nietzsche also postulates the existence of a 'historical instinct',[32] but the relation to the past raises it above an instinct. Left to itself, it is destructive, exhausting the sources of the present. He acknowledges a balance, again via a 'constructive instinct' which maintains history in the service of life. This has profound consequences for the conception of instincts, to which Nietzsche raises an essential critique. 'By history,' he argues, 'we implant a new habit, a new instinct, a new nature, such that the first nature dries up and collapses.'[33] Against this pathology, it is necessary to change our skin, as it were, which supposes a return to something like a first nature, now altered.

The naturalist connotation appears in the conclusion:

> The harm is terrible, and nevertheless! If youth did not have the clairvoyant gift of nature, no one would know that there was harm done and that a paradise of sanity has been lost. But this same youth divines as well, with the curative instinct of the same nature, how this paradise can be won again.'[34]

Naturally, this leads Nietzsche to formulate his pedagogical conception, which at base shares the common foundation of his preceding interventions. It emerges in the public lectures delivered in 1872 at Basel, entitled *On the Future of Our Teaching Establishments*. This savage attack on the educational system recapitulates every level of the preceding critique: the primacy of 'scientific instincts', the negation of 'true culture'[35], to the benefit of the barbaric tastes and sterile erudition.

But another essential element is specified, that of the critique of the State. It is the State that imposes the channelling of the utilitarian instincts, for its own benefit and at the price of 'annihilating those instincts whose design cannot be put to immediate use'[36]. The State thus requires barbarism, and supports it through both historical consciousness and the natural sciences.

This last element confirms the general naturalist inspiration for the concept of instinct, as demonstrated by the following passage. 'That which is lost . . . (is) the instinctive and true understanding of nature; in its place is presently instituted a cunning design (*Berechnen*) and an illusion (*Uberlisten*) of nature.[37] What functions here is the opposition of *Phusis*, as the generator of fecund and authentic instincts, to the accidental universe (*Willkür*) with its vile forms of intentionality. Politics gives its ultimate form to this *anti-phusis*, which expresses the regression of true instinct into a base calculation, from affectivity to falsehood and illusion. Thus through the historical and cultural forms that instinct develops, nature is degraded; through the promised cure, nature is repaired.

THE FREUDIAN DRIVE: ORIGINS OF THE CONCEPT

If it is true that Freud gave *Trieb* an explicitly explanatory role only after 1905,[38] that does not prevent us from finding a conceptual tool that at the least implies an instinctualist thematic (and a terminology) at work from the early years of the birth of psychoanalytic theory. Thus it is necessary at the outset, in order to grasp the origin and development of this thematic, to understand what role the idea of instinct played in those first Freudian formulations.

The *Outline of a Scientific Psychology* (1896) is a document of the first order on this point, for there Freud demonstrates his collection of conceptual tools.[39] The energetic representation inspired by the 'natural sciences' implies a consideration of 'the psychic processes as quantitative states determined by particular distinguishable materials'[40] of the nervous system, that is to say the neurons. Now, two functions take place in the 'neuronic system'. The primary function, the discharge of excitations, makes possible our adaptation to the exterior world. This function is genetically linked to 'general protoplasmic activity', while the neuronic system itself is linked to 'the irritable exterior surface of the protoplasm',[41] and makes the *principle of inertia* the fundamental principle of the nervous economy, according to which the neurons tend to rid themselves of excitations until they return to 'degree = 0'.

But one essential circumstance offsets the integral application of the principle of inertia. 'To the extent that the internal complexity of the organism increases, the neuronic system receives stimuli originating from the somatic elements themselves, those endogenous stimuli also tend to discharge themselves.' They are born in the cells of the body and provoke the primary needs of hunger, respiration and sexuality. We can say that the emergence of these fundamental instincts is narrowly coupled with the endogenous stimuli of the organism, but this emergence also effectively tempers the application of the general principle of inertia.

This second source of excitations requires a second function. 'The organism cannot escape them like it can external stimuli; it is not a matter of utilizing their quantity (Q) in order to avoid them. The excitations only cease if the already determined conditions are realized in the exterior world . . .'. *Economically*, this new demand is specifically expressed by the principle of inertia:

> In order to perform the action . . . , it requires an effort independent of quantities endogenous to and generally greater than itself, while the individual is subjected to certain conditions we might call *the urgency of life*. Consequently, the neuronic system sees itself obliged to renounce its original tendency towards inertia, that is to say its tendency to degree zero. It must learn to support a stored quantity (Q*n*) which satisfies the demands of a specific action.'

But the general demand to discharge, instead of being abolished, increases, such that 'following the way in which it works, meanwhile, the same tendency persists under the modified form of an effort to maintain the quantity at as low a degree as possible and to avoid every increase, that is to say in order to conserve a constant level.' This is a *principle of constancy*. Thus from the outset, the global representation of the neuronic economy assigns a status to the drives within the psycho-vital economy.

We began by stating that Freud's point of departure is neuronic excitation, correlative to organic or protoplasmic excitability. Excitation is thus the basic concept for Freudian theory in the period around 1895. In the second (logical) period, general excitability splits into two levels, with the appearance of endogenous excitations. Now the generative path is constituted by the fundamental instincts, or rather 'the cells of the body', a somatic substrate whose fundamental instincts are its vital expression, because of their universality, but at the price of being specified in terms of constancy.

The current expenditures of the domestic economy of the organism (the satisfaction of vital needs) requires hoarding, thus a stasis which constitutes a functional contravention of the principle of inertia. But the maintenance of excitations at as low a degree as possible is a kind of homage the organism must pay to this general principle, as a compromise between the general law and the specific conditions of the case.

We see, then, the discreet entry that instincts make into Freud's representation of the psyche. Far from being a triumphal form of vital positivity linked spontaneously to the term, they are only the somatic requisites that oblige a tempering of the general tendency towards energetic haemorrhage, without in any case calling itself into question. In the irreversible current of energetic loss, instincts are by no means principles of efficient construction, but rather salutary anti-positions of life. Properly speaking, instincts appear as instalments of investments originally unforeseen, in the pure and simple exercise of the principle of inertia; they are the 'chief of debits' in the everyday economy of the nervous system. We are a long ways from the richness of Nietzschean instinct. The Freudian psycho-organic system is chronically deficient; as for the instincts, far from enriching us, they impose themselves on us with a conjunctural and limited greed.

Instincts only appear in outline form, on the dividing line passing through the neuronic universe, and oblige us to distinguish between 'the system turned towards the outside' and 'the system which remains out of contact with the exterior world', the first having 'for its task to discharge as rapidly as possible the quantities assailing the neurons', while the second only receives quantities 'of the cellular elements of the interior of the body' (and the neurons).[42] They designate that which requires a 'specific action', or rather a lasting resolution to the tension arising from endogenous excitations which come completely from a schema of inertia.

This entropic representation of the nervous system is thoroughly *physicalist*. The irrepressible tendency to empty oneself, characteristic of the nervous elements, brings us back, we might say, to a brute state. It is the necessary consequence of the status of excitation. Excitability, recognized since Haller as the basic characteristic of living organisms, does not know how to be anything else, for Freud or for the general notion of physiology in his time, except an energetic redundancy that tends towards its own abolition, a superfluous repetition of sensible matter. It is true that at the same time, matter is the object of a sort of energetic translation, but it is precisely this dynamic that makes possible a rigorous physicalism whose dynamic is expressed by the universality of inertia.

At the base of physical loss, the organic order requires a strongly *limited retention*. The organism, properly speaking, with all its ensemble, remains itself limited; instincts do not require any dispensation. The organism thus introduces a supplementary clause obliging it to rewrite the principle of inertia as a principle of constancy.

From the outset, the physicalism of Freud's conception prevents an organicist interpretation (à la Nietzsche) of instinct. Instinct, in its positive sense, for Freud as for Nietzsche, is in itself only the proclamation of a properly vital order; it is the imperious voice of the organism-as-reality *sui generis*. For this reason, it appears self-valorizing as a vital expression, before being valorized either ethically or metaphysically. For Freud, though, instinct is not at all originally provided with this virtue; instinct is less a principle than a given or a condition. Nevertheless, it is, taking the word in its strongest connotation, a *circumstance* of the nervous system, which itself is defined on a material model. It is true that instinct is the root of the 'impulsion which holds together all psychic activity',[43] but, paradoxically, it is an impulsion which does not create. This *impetus* is like a *given*, important in itself, but which only operates with respect to the general laws of the psycho-physiological system.

Returning to the origins of Freud's conception allows us to anticipate the strange confusion between the notions of drive (*Trieb*) and excitation (*Reiz*) which dominate Freud's ultimate conceptual economy. Originally, we saw that excitation played the central explanatory role; but with the *Three Essays on the Theory of Sexuality*, the emergence of the drive displaces this function, and everything happens as though *Trieb* was invested with the *princeps* function which later returns under *Reiz*, but the relation between the two remains problematic.

A. Strictly speaking, *Reiz* is one of the determinants of *Trieb*. It is the state of tension localized as the source requiring the push of the drive whose aim is to cancel the tension by satisfying it via an *object*.
B. *Trieb*, the constitutive element of the psycho-organic system, is defined as the psychic representation of (endogenous) *Reiz*.
C. *Trieb* is invested with the function that elsewhere fell due to *Reiz*, as that which is represented in the psyche via affects and representations.[44]

Thus there are three figures in the relation between drive and excitation; *Trieb* is at the same time (1) a mode of satisfaction – a response to excitations encompassing it like a variable; (2) the psychic representation of excitation; (3) another name for excitation. Surprisingly, these formulations pass from distinction to identification by way of representation!

This ambiguity, however, will be clarified by examining the genesis of the terms. In the beginning, excitation, by nature neuronic, refers *indissociably* to a theory of the organism as well as to a conception of the psyche, in which excitability was the most general property of the organism and excitation the functional modality of the ideational nervous system. Therefore, excitation was a *given objective*, with all of the weight that an optician gives to the notion of *objectivity*. Correlatively, instinct does not have this explanatory value; as a purveyor of a specific type of excitation, it plays the role of a *condition*.

Raised to the level of an explanatory principle, however, instinct will in turn relegate excitation to the rank of a condition. This reversal of perspective is expressed by the idea of the psychic *eruption*. In emerging as the proper order of reality, psychology requires a rethinking of immediate psycho-somatic identification – thus the appearance of the thematic of representation, and consequently, of signification.[45]

However, these points of view do not necessarily follow one from the other. To the extent that an obsolescence of epistemological points of view is *not* brought about, excitation for Freud preserves the prestige of an objectivity that it possessed despite the mutation of its etiological function. This is why excitation is deployed under the diverse figures of the variable and of the fundamental represented, up to the point of perhaps usurping the function of the drive, or up to a quasi-synonymy with it.

From this curious quadrille between notions, almost to the point of utter confusion when Representation, in relation 'B' above, arises – we must nonetheless retain an essential message relative to the nature of Freud's *Trieb*. Before the 1905 turning point, it is not predominant as an organicist-vital thematic which breaks with the previous thematic to the point of differing from it *toto caelo*. *Trieb* will retain something of the nature of excitation (in its *circa* 1895 sense), and thus will inherit its function. Without at all prejudging the all-too-insistent discontinuity between these problematics, we must uncover the *content* of Freud's concept in a way that is different from the way we approached Nietzsche as regards the origins. The physicalist origin of the Freudian conception seems to immunize once and for all the concept of *Trieb*, in its received heritage, against any predominance of the vitalist conception.

At the same time, we can see through this apparently mysterious notion of eruption (*Drang*), which serves above all to characterize the drive. In the metapsychological essay discussed here, *Instincts and Their Vicissitudes*, Freud defines *Drang* as the motivating motor (*motorisches Moment*) of the drive, 'the sum of the force or the extent of the demand of work that it represents'.[46] Eruption is thus defined as a surplus of psychic activity; in economic terms, it is an *excess imposed* on the psychic apparatus.

From the perspective of the 'general property of instincts' we may grasp its effective nature, according to Freud. The most characteristic counter-sense in the interpretation of eruption would be to place it as a *primum movens* creator. Paradoxically, in place of insisting on the surplus of energy that represents and *produces* instinct, Freud defines it as a demand, imposed from the outside, to produce a surplus of work. But how can we fail to see in this idea a rejuvenated form, a full meta-psychological elaboration of the old principle of inertia? In fact, to use an anthropomorphic phrase, it is *unwillingly* that the psyche *produces*; this is the *corvée* or forced labour that informs the instinctual eruption.

True, pleasure is gratification, but it is only through effort that the psychic system crawls out of its natural lethargy.

Drang thus has none of the explosive affirmation that one might attribute to it, following the indications in a semantic history linking it with *Sturm*. Far from being the orgiastic release of a tempest, here it is presented as a heavy disturbance to psychic lethargy, a notification that *there is something to be done* that one would rather never do. It is immediately necessary, on the other hand, to guard against conferring on this representation an affective inverse tonality. Eruption is no more painful than it is enjoyable, as eruptions go. And precisely, as we saw with Nietzsche, the immanent creativity of instincts emerges, from the beginning, directly from the exaltation of tragic suffering, as *amor fati*.

To understand the idea of *demand* (*Anforderung*), it is only necessary to see it as an economic, functional and impersonal requisite. *Eruption* is that which is called 'filling a lack'. *Active*, in one way (by being a motivating motor), in another sense it is *passive* at base, allowing an event that negatively affects the economic system to designate the intervention. It is summoned as having to furnish the surplus that is lacking with regard to the global economy, a task of filling in what is absent.

The impulsive eruption appears less as a manifestation of its own productivity than as a result of a *plus* inserted into the energetic depression which created it. The eruption is only the *verso* of this *minus*, a negative economic event. Translating a lack, it is above all first a signal, then a response, whose goal is to abolish itself through satisfaction. It is only in the interval from 'a lack to be filled' to 'a lack filled' that one finds the strongest affirmation, albeit an ontologically precarious one, of *Drang* at work.

Now that we have defined the phenomenological origins of the respective regimes of Nietzschean instinct and Freudian drive, we should be able to turn to a comparison of their natures and functions. But this still supposes that we have grasped their *historical* origins.

Naturally, neither Nietzsche nor Freud invented either their terms or their concepts; they found them among the intellectual baggage of nineteenth century thought, itself the result of a long process[47]. The concept *Trieb*, whose use was established in the discourse of the eighteenth century, was eminently polysemic. As a result, several layers of meaning had been deposited with the term by the time that Nietzsche and Freud adopt it. Nevertheless, Nietzsche's and Freud's respective use of the term vary significantly from these received meanings. The examination of the historical referents that found the Nietzschean and Freudian uses will allow us to clarify one and the other, by inserting the regime of the concept into the historical problematic that constructed it.

THE HISTORICAL PARADIGM OF NIETZSCHEAN INSTINCT

Nietzsche's first conception of instinct takes shape via historically determined sources, which are important to recall in order to understand the original content of the concept and its evolution in Nietzschean thought.

The core of this notion comes from pre-Romantic Germany. By the time that Nietzsche adopts the term, it had been generalized in a literary sense since the end of the previous century, and thus its content was the result of accumulated semantic 'sediment'. The word *Trieb* flourished in the German language during the time of *Sturm und Drang*, and designates a motor which acts on human reality and demands to be invested in poetic discourse. Thus it is in a primary sense linked to *aesthetics*.

The word 'instinct' saw a generalized usage around the same time as another word, suddenly and similarly overdetermined: *genius*. This contemporaneity is not fortuitous, for their origins are in fact linked. The great pre-Romantic problematic in the aesthetic sphere was undeniably between *genius* and *instinct*. We can establish that *genius* first appeared in Germany around 1750, in the polemics surrounding Klopstock, and in the treatises of the so-called 'popularizers' of philosophy.[48] Once imported to France, the concept and the word progressively evolved during the last quarter of the eighteenth century. The semantic content of *Genius*, in this transformation, passed from rationalism and intellectualism to a form of irrationalism and sentimentalism, thus taking on the semantic air of *Trieb*.

French aesthetics of the period situated genius in *ingenium*, the penetrating faculty that is found everywhere, though in unequal degrees, and implies the vigilance of understanding. In the later German conception, *Genius* became 'a personal genius, the god that attends to you and guides you'.[49] It is thus that we came to define it specifically by the instinct, *as instinct*. As in the well-known controversy between genius and the law, we can pose the question of domesticating instinct as we see it posed in Mendelssohn and in Lessing.[50] This *instinctualist* conception, under influences coming from France (Rousseau) and above all from England (Young), triumphed in Germany with Hamann and Herder in the last quarter of the eighteenth century.

According to the great theoreticians of the time, *Genius* and *Trieb* are referred to as the alphabet of the aesthetic conception. This is the conception that the young Nietzsche inherited as a student at Pforta where, important symbolically, Klopstock, Schlegel and Novalis all had preceded him. It is thus no accident that, in Nietzsche's essay-letter of 1861 (contained in his biographical notes) we can read a vibrant dithyrambe from Hölderlin, in which Schiller's spiritual mentorship is underlined. In fact, in Schiller and Hölderlin, Nietzsche found the outline of his own theory of *Kunsttrieb*.

All Schillerian anthropology, insofar as we can extract it from his *Letters on Aesthetic Education*, returns to the opposition between two fundamental instincts, *Sachtrieb* and *Formtrieb*. *Sachtrieb* leads man toward the sensible, to reality, while *Formtrieb* leads him toward the form. This duality derives from the primary anthropological duality between the person (*das Bleibende*) and his changing states. The two *Triebe* depend respectively on two functions, which are to realize the person, the Self (*Sachtrieb*), and to give form to the reality of its states (*Formtrieb*). The two instincts are antagonistic and complementary at once; they are antagonistic because one demands the multiplication of experiences while the other demands the continuity of the person facing the sensible world; but they are also complementary in that it is by their reciprocal action (*Wechselwirkung*) that harmony between unity and diversity is realized.

Only there needs to be a third term that finally gives the reciprocal action its full fecundity, and without which the two instincts would encroach upon one another in a struggle for domination. Thus *Spieltrieb* intervenes, the ludic instinct in which man simultaneously experiences his liberty and his existence, and which resorbs the duality between sensibility and the faculty of reason which had first opened the primary duality. *Spieltrieb* unites the world with life on one side and the form and the law on the other side, in the living figure (*lebende Gestalt*) which is no other than Beauty.

Given that 'it is necessary to note the great influence of Schiller'[51] on Nietzsche, this model contains in germ form the Nietzschean theory of instinct. Apart from some profound later differences, it is here that the genetic elements of the conception of instinct, which alone interests us here, are set into place. We can say in fact:

- As far as the tendency to create the fundamental instincts by the free adjunction of *Trieb*, Schiller legitimated this practice and made *Trieb* into a linguistic sign in a new conceptual regime.
- Schiller assigned the central place of the idea of conflict in the dual, then trinary, conception of *Triebe*; antagonism and the demand for harmony make up part of the instinctualist regime.
- As for the probationary role of *Trieb* in the aesthetic sphere, it is in order to overcome the dualism of the Kantian faculties that Schiller forges his theory of instincts.[52]

This triple characteristic passes directly into Nietzsche's use of the concept, literally straight from Schiller's hand.

Hölderlin, Schiller's favourite disciple and young Nietzsche's second idol at Pforta, takes up this usage in his theory of 'genius, artistic and formative' (*Kunst- und Bildungstrieb*), which he defines, significantly, as 'a veritable service which man renders to nature'.[53] It is precisely on this paradox that Hölderlin founds his interpretation of tragedy, and therein we see the dual character of the Nietzschean conception come to life. Naturalistic, it defines art as *Trieb* derived from nature, but simultaneously it conceives *Trieb* as a response to nature which causes it to emerge exactly as *Art*. This is the double aspect of Nietzschean *Kunsttrieb*. Nietzsche's lecture *Hyperion and Empedocles* is precociously impregnated with this sense.[54]

Thus Nietzsche takes the semantic core of his notion of instinct from its pre-Romantic conception. By opposing Romanticism's enervation, which does not overcome the state of excitation,[55] Schiller and Hölderlin remain the prophets of the authentic vitality of *Kunsttrieb*. However, to this first semantic layer we must add another layer, less visible but which nonetheless demands mention if we wish to grasp the exact formula of Nietzsche's *Trieb*. Nietzsche by this time had already read the work of that American pastor's son, who broke with dogma in order to put his faith in the rich evidence of his senses: Ralph Waldo Emerson.[56]

There is in Emerson a mystique of the *eternal forces of nature*,[57] in whose name he battles every dogma and all dry rationalism. From the moment when transcendentalism is first formulated, instinct plays a determining role; it is the means of recovering the immediate sense of the world, and the law of concord between the inner human and nature. Emersonian instinct echoes the fecundity of nature in human individuality. In Nietzsche's *Trieb* as well, there is something of this mysterious 'elative sense'[58] which betrays the evidence of appearance on the side of rational mediation.

But this immediacy is not the only thing that Nietzsche inherits from Emerson. The force and the seduction come from the manner that instinct serves as a weapon in the fundamental task of the *critique of the present*. Emerson, the defrocked preacher,[59] praises the evangelic instinct that opposes the idols of the present, seen as religion, politics, the State and history. The instinctualist reference serves to de-mask appearance and illusion. Emerson has shown Nietzsche the devastating–purifying function of the theory of instinct. Thus it is no accident that, from 1862 on, in his first critique of Christianity, Nietzsche cites Emerson, and when he travels, he carries the *Essays* of the American master in his bags.

We agree with Charles Andler's judgment that 'Ralph Waldo Emerson was one of those beloved authors whose thought Nietzsche absorbed until he could no longer separate it from his own.'[60] In this close acquaintance, Nietzsche acquires a certain lability with reference to an instinctivist thematic. But with Emerson, *instinct* takes on an *ethical* and *polemical* connotation which distinguishes the aesthetic connotation. After *Untimely Meditations* this register passes to the primary level. It is true that the *Untimely Meditations* appeared in the form of an Emersonian essay or a Carlylian pamphlet;[61] they all share the same untimely function of denouncing ethico-scientific fictions and of calling for a regeneration, and of counting on one type of regeneration founded on the eternal present of a nature, incarnated by the force of great representative individualities, figures chosen from originary forces.

We can now see what Emersonian instinct adds to Schillerian *Trieb* to distinguish Nietzsche's own use of the instinctual thematic. The common base is assuredly naturalistic – how could it be otherwise for a philosophy of instincts? – but it also adds a projected critique which offers Nietzsche a potential ethic. Emerson's idealism, nourished by Plato and Swedenborg, presents definite affinities with Nietzsche's own; it colours the idea of instinct as idealist. In fact, the Nietzschean conception combines the reference to a vital originality with an ideality, and assumes an ethico-aesthetic character. The reference to a norm of naturing authenticity serves as an instrument of demystification.

Finally, Nietzsche's conception owes much to Richard Wagner, even before his acquaintance with Schopenhauer.[62] In *The Work of Art of the Future*, Wagner introduced the central concept of *Lebenstrieb*. 'In everything which exists', wrote Wagner, 'the most powerful element is the vital instinct; it is the irresistable force which binds the conditions under which beings appear, animate or inanimate'.[63] During this period Wagner essentially placed primordial instincts at the level of people, as a revolutionary motor. *Lebenstrieb* is thus instinct in its fundamental, general form; it is the *Urtrieb*.

The Wagnerian conception is clearly naturalistic; *Lebenstrieb* is *Natur* expressed as power. At the same time, *Natur* is the cosmic substance, unity and power, inexhaustible fecundity and ceaseless renewal, simplicity and innocence.[64] Its fundamental character is *necessity*. For Wagner, necessity signifies *authenticity*, the domain of *Unwillkür* (non-arbitrary or *real*) which is opposed to *Willkür* (artificial). This essential opposition is a characteristic element in Nietzsche's conception of instinct. *Trieb* is perhaps better defined as *Unwillkür*, a significant term even in its imprecision. In fact, the ensemble of Nietzsche's preceding acceptations are recapitulated in this idea, for *Trieb* is neither artificial nor arbitrary nor fictive nor unfounded. It functions by evoking a *Wirklichkeit* which marks itself off from the non-natural and unreal.

In Wagner's aesthetic, the vital instinct returns to the authentic creative power of nature and violently opposes fashion, industry, false arts, social institutions, and signs of the reign of abstract intelligence (characteristic of decadence) – by which Wagner joins with Burckhardt. Vital instinct is in fact defined as the moment when 'the bond of necessity is no longer' and where 'an unlimited arbitrariness rages'.

The appeal to the original power of nature thus plays the role of an instrument of regeneration. The work of art of the future must embody these imperious instincts which constitute man's authenticity. We can see how Wagner's instinctualism opens, as will be the case with Nietzsche, on to a theory of civilization. 'Nature, human nature, will pronounce the law to its two sisters, culture and civilization: to the extent that I am contained within yourselves, you can live and flourish; to the extent that I am not, you will wither and die.'[65]

In the beginning, Wagner relied on Feuerbach's sensualism to found his theory of *Lebenstrieb* on the primacy and fecundity of sensibility (*Sinnlichkeit*). Feuerbach's sensualist materialism will indeed serve as a weapon against Hegelian rationalism. After 1854, though, Wagner expressed his thematic in the language of Schopenhauer. This badly used term *Unwillkür*, decreed Wagner in 1871, must in fact be called 'Will, and ... *Willkür* characterizes the Will influenced and guided by reflection, what we call "the representative Will".'[66] In fact, *Unwillkür* is substantially none other than Schopenhauer's Will-to-Live, but this equivalence of registers does not abolish their distinction. In any case, it is remarkable that Nietzsche included Wagner's specification in his own conception of instinct. In Nietzsche's first conception, the determinant oppositions that Wagner established come back to life; perhaps, then, there is a place to raise the Wagnerian component in relation to the Schopenhauerian component in Nietzsche's schema of instinct. Even in the midst of his Schopenhauerian period, Nietzsche spoke more willingly and more frequently in terms of instinct than in terms of Will. It is true that the life-wish is the root of instinct, but everything happens as if the manifestation preceded the principle.

THE HISTORICAL PARADIGM OF FREUDIAN DRIVE

Turning to Freud, we can see from the very beginning a rapid evolution which leads him from an infatuation with a certain 'pantheistic *Natur*-philosophy' inspired by Goethe, to a form of materialism that turns into a scientific conception of the universe which is codified by Freud's Viennese teachers. It is at least symbolically important that Freud once declared to have chosen medicine upon reading a Goethe poem that exalted the creative power and universal curative potency of Nature.[67] However, several years of apprenticeship in anatomy–physiology sufficed to cure him of this lyrical temptation.

This conversion implies a determining choice in the conception of instinct. It is no longer a function of exalting the power of *Natur*; instead, the organism is now conceived as a system of forces whose specific mode of action is found through the physical–mathematical method. The very idea of an instinct becomes suspect if it permits the belief, through its teleological charge, that there are forces not reducible to attraction and repulsion,[68] a *physicalist* conception. Here Freud opts for an anti-teleological reductionism, such that after the drive comes to be fully recognized, it will still be affected by a physical index which prevents its hypostasis.

The pre-Romantic inspiration, which Freud did not fully escape, will be reinvested at a mythological level in order to name the fundamental drives, but at that point it is important rather to speak in terms of *principles*.[69] We can now understand why instinct, despite its determinant function, makes such a discreet entry into the Freudian explanatory model. Freud has in mind a wholly other destiny for the concept of instinct than Nietzsche had conceived.

The immediate origin of Freudian instinct is thus less plural than with Nietzsche. It is maintained entirely in the physicalist model forged from an anatomo-physiological discourse that extended from Helmholtz to Brücke.[70] Instinct is found narrowly inserted in the material system of forces which define the organism. Thus it appears as a residual and differential reality at the heart of a physical system, according to Freud's schema. It is true that the Romantic use of instinct influenced Freud as well, but significantly, Freud does not lend his first model any explanatory value at all. In particular, the word 'force' (*Kraft*) changes radically in scope when we pass from Nietzschean to Freudian acceptations. What is creative withdrawal (*ponction*) in one case translates into an expenditure in the other.

A DIFFERENCE OF DEFINITION

We can finally produce a comparative definition of the terms at stake. For Freud as for Nietzsche, instinct is indeed an eruption, whose value as a force originates in a nature endowed with sensibility and irritability and seeking to realize a goal, in and by which it realizes its own objectivity. But if Nietzschean instinct is originally creative, Freud's conception resembles a sort of energetic secretion. They feed off two models as different as Romantic life-wish and Fechnerian inertia, by nature thoroughly entropic.

This difference, in both nature and origin, has a major consequence. Right away, Nietzsche's instinct serves either to valorize a reality or to disqualify it from an ethico-aesthetic point of view. For Freud, though, instinct connotes less a value than it denotes a function. Thus its positive tenor, as an epistemological prerequisite.

This is why, for one and the other, if instinct is equally omnipresent in man, it is for Nietzsche as a means of participation in a cosmic effusion, while for Freud it is as a demand – in the sense of a necessity in a material system, a negative demand – as much universal as *minimum*. This returns us in the final analysis to a difference in the conception of objectivity, because Nietzschean instinct, like its pre-Romantic and Schopenhauerian analogues, realizes its objectivity, in the strong sense of being endowed with affectivity (*verwecklichen*), in a *Natur* that it actualizes. Freudian instinct, like its physicalist model, limits necessity to objectify a lack.

Behind the homonymy, and freed from presuppositions, we thus discern a divergence. For Nietzsche, instinct reveals a *Natur* whose 'creative-affirmative' virtue is valued by the demands of regeneration. For Freud, the drive reveals a material, incomplete nature submitted to a positive, descriptive investigation. Thus a double, differential figure emerges with this comparison: two 'naturalisms'.

2

NIETZSCHEAN PYSCHOLOGY, FREUDIAN PSYCHOANALYSIS

We have seen Nietzsche and Freud use the same term 'instinct' to designate their first object of analysis; now, we need to examine the ways that they, respectively, understand the term, in order to grasp its function and functional laws.

In the course of his analysis, Nietzsche names his hermeneutic of instincts 'psychology' and christens himself 'the first psychologist'. Likewise, Freud conceives of 'psychoanalysis' as none other than the hermeneutic science of the drives, whose parallel 'meta-psychology' describes its theoretical scope. Nietzschean psychology and Freudian psychoanalysis thus constitute forms of apprehension respectively informed and directed toward a *knowledge of instincts* – which implies an evolving status of the concept 'instinct', now promoted to the rank of an object, of knowledge as well as of diagnosis. It is at this level that we must carry our examination.[1]

THE HOMOLOGY OF 'PSYCHO-ANALYSES': THE CHEMICAL METAPHOR

Whoever seeks to compare Nietzschean psychology with Freudian psychoanalysis, with a view towards determining their respective nature and function, is aided by a common metaphor useful as a benchmark, that of *chemistry*. There is more to the metaphor, however, than a single image; its insistence indicates that we should see in it a true index of the epistemic nature of an 'analysis of the psyche', founded on a theory of drives.

The analogy is present from the very beginning of Nietzsche's psychological project. Significantly, we see an indication of it in the first aphorism of *Human, All Too Human*, aptly entitled 'Chemistry of concepts and sentiments'.[2] There, psychology is said to be a question of 'moral, religious, aesthetic sentiments, thus of all the emotions (*Regungen*) that we experience in the great and small relations of civilization and society, and even in solitude';[3] it is besieged with 'questions concerning origins and beginnings'. Psychology is thus a genealogy, but in the same manner as chemistry, which is concerned with the origins of bodies and their transformations, and which ignores metaphysics by its very nature.

In other respects, it is remarkable that, as early as 1872, Nietzsche was talking about 'chemical transformations from inorganic nature' as 'artistic processes' or 'impulses that trigger mimetic roles', either singly or several at once.[4] This nature of this artistic plasticity, that Nietzsche will henceforth elucidate in living, human nature, is ethico-aesthetic. Its atomic unities are concepts (*Begrie*) and sentiments (*Empfindungen*). A reflection in the *Nachlass*, written during the period that produced *Daybreak*, gives us an interesting indication of the links between intellectual chemistry and the chemical theory (in the proper sense) of living beings. 'In the chemical world reigns the most vivid perception of the diversity of forces. But a protoplasm, as a diversity of chemical forces, has only an imprecise and indeterminate overall perception of a foreign object'.[5] This fragmentation of the field of the real must be taken into account by a sort of 'psycho-chemistry', or, to take the term in its authentic generality, a 'psycho-analysis'!

A strange aphorism goes so far as to link moral activity to 'the modification of the chemical constitution of the body'.[6] Meanwhile, the ideational constitution seeks to transform the chemistry of representations. These forces are analogous to the corporeal forces which refract them.

Passing over *On the Genealogy of Morals*, the chemical inspiration figures more explicitly in *The Will to Power*. On the one hand, chemistry demonstrates that 'there is nothing which is not transformable'.[7] Chemistry studies the flux and transformation of the characteristics of substances, and it figures as a becoming-universal, the milieu proclaimed in *Wille zur Macht*. On the other hand, chemistry also figures as a type of order in becoming *that which exceeds all legality* – in which it can serve to explain the 'relations of force'. 'I am wary', wrote Nietzsche in this sense, 'of speaking in terms of chemical 'laws': that leaves a moral aftertaste. It is rather a question of the absolute establishment of relations of force' (*Machtverhänissen*).[8]

One may argue that, according to the very specifications of the Nietzschean project, a slippage occurs in the manner of conceiving the nature and the sense of this moral chemistry, to the extent that, increasingly, the atoms-representations become dynamized in forces, from a Boscovitchian perspective.[9] But the important aspect remains, for our purposes, the persistence of the chemical reference, which serves to identify the analytical and dynamic project.

Turning now to Freud, we find that the reference to chemistry fills a *princeps* role no less explicitly. Even the term 'Psychoanalysis', introduced in 1896 to identify the Freudian investigational project, definitively supplanting 'psychic' or 'psychological' as analytical terms,[10] is forged by an analogy with chemical analysis. Freud's precise formulation appears in a 1918 work, *Lines of Advance in Psychoanalytic Therapy*:

> The labour by which we introduce, to the consciousness of the afflicted, the suppressed psychic content, we have called Psychoanalysis. Why 'analysis', which signifies decomposition, desegregation, and makes one think of an analogy with the work of the chemist on the substances that he finds in nature and carries to his laboratory? Because from one important point of view, such an analogy is really consistent. The symptoms and the

> morbid manifestations of the afflicted are, like all psychic activities, by nature highly complex; the elements of these combinations are, in the final analysis, the activities of the drives (*Triebregungen*).[11]

The psychoanalyst thus decomposes the combinations, restores the aggregates of symptoms to their constituent elements (the actions of the drives, the atoms of a mental chemistry), 'just as the chemist separates a salt into its fundamental elements, the chemical element that became unrecognizable in combination with other elements'.

Again, we see that there is more than one image to this metaphor.[12] Freud plainly wants to make the analogy; he qualifies as 'well-founded' (*berechtigt*) 'the comparison of psychoanalytic medical practice with the labour of the chemist'.[13] Nevertheless, he takes care to specify further that 'the comparison with chemical analysis is limited by the fact that we are concerned with human psychic life in all its aspirations, which imply a compulsion towards unification and fusion', such that, hardly isolated, the elements tend to reconstitute a new synthesis.[14]

Freud then goes on to dynamize the chemical schema. The chemistry of the drives is a chemistry of forces; these elements are, in fact, endowed with a formal tendency. Analysis thus encounters the limit of the immanent tendency towards synthesis, but analysis must also push the epistemic demand precisely up to this limit, a labour that is by nature fundamentally *analytical.*

The reference to chemistry, beyond this definition of 'psychoanalysis', is omnipresent in Freud. A passage from *On Narcissism: An Introduction* makes a curious comparison.

> One must remember that all of our provisional psychological conceptions must one day be established on the ground of organic substrates. It seems likely that there are particular substances and chemical processes which produce the effects of sexuality and permit the perpetuation of the individual life of the species. It is this probability which we must hold to account, by replacing particular chemical substances with particular psychic forces'.[15]

This essential text clearly signifies that the psychic elements which make up the object of psychoanalysis are only the provisional substitutes of the basic elements of a future chemistry which will emerge. The analogy of psychology with chemistry is derived in the final analysis from what, already in the analytic investigation of the psyche, makes psychoanalysis the propaedeutic of chemistry.

In the glimmer of this insight, we need to interpret *stricto sensu* Freud's declarations relative to the scientific comparison of psychoanalysis with chemistry. Thus, in *The Psychoanalysis and Theory of the Libido*, the character of psychoanalysis as an 'empirical science' is affirmed by its relation to 'physics or chemistry'.[16] Freud will repeat this assertion up to the publication of his

Psychoanalysis (1926), which will say that 'the processes with which (psychoanalysis) is concerned are in themselves as unknowable as those of other sciences, physical or chemical'.[17]

Thus Freud and Nietzsche both consider themselves *chemists*, but chemists who handle explosive substances. It is edifying to hear Nietzsche echoed in Freud's declarations, which amount to virtual repetitions of the same idea.

We can read in Nietzsche, in *Assorted Opinions and Maxims*:

> the utility of the unconditional search for truth, without cease, is a hundred times newly demonstrated to us, such that one must perhaps without hesitation endure the noxious, slight and scarce things that the individual can suffer as a consequence. One cannot prevent the chemist from occasionally burning or poisoning himself during the course of his experiments.[18]

Likewise, Freud declares in *Observations on Transference-Love* that

> the psychoanalyst knows that he works with the most explosive forces and that he must operate with the same prudence and the same conscience as the chemist. But when has one forbidden the chemist from working in indispensable explosive substances, due to their dangerous character?[19]

Such are the profound analyses of psychoanalysis and Nietzschean psychology, manipulations of the explosive substances which are the *Triebregungen*. It remains for us to confront the nature of these substances.

INSTINCT, NIETZSCHE'S PSYCHOLOGICAL OBJECT

Human, All Too Human inaugurates a new conceptual scope for the study of instincts. The work, a 'commemoration of a crisis',[20] marks according to Nietzsche himself a caesura in relation to his preceding conceptual production. What is important to note are the terms that 'instinct' is associated with in this new context. Here we come up against an insidious difficulty, located in the status of the concept itself. An innovative use of the term is inserted into what in other respects is an astonishingly persistent thematic. We need to be careful, though, because if the content of the concept seems little changed, the new usage that bears it imposes a noticeable inflection which finally affects the content itself; it accedes to the rank of a psychological object.

This is the moment where Nietzsche declares himself to be a psychologist–historian of moral sentiments. 'Psychological observation'[21] is presented as 'a chemistry of representations and of moral, religious and aesthetic sentiments'.[22] The 'moralist' approach of *Human, All Too Human* expresses a new positional modality of the critique. From this moment on, Nietzschean discourse ostensibly presents itself as a cold, dispassionate analysis. This proclaimed change of critical attitude indicates a transformation in the relation of the concept to reality; a new category emerges, that of the *Menschliches*. The ensemble of human phonemes appear as the material of observation and diagnosis and as the object of a cold evaluation.

The diagnosis thus changes the mode of intervention. Everything happens as if the ensemble of the elements of the previous critique were related to an immanent anthropological sphere, comprising the object of a 'science' of morality. But it is at the price of a change in scope, whose importance we must acknowledge as affecting the status of the concept of instinct.

What *The Birth of Tragedy*, *Untimely Meditations*, and the collective production of the preceding epoch grasped were the manifestations in science and in art, in civilization and in history, of original forces derived in the last instance from *Natur*. Human reality was based on these instinctual forces, which manifested themselves through some sort of transference. Now, it is the layer of 'representations and sentiments' which emerge on the first plane. Instincts are found throughout a *psyche* which is the object of a *psychology*; this is the reason for the proclamation of the term. In brief, instinct is 'humanized'.

We hear that human reality is the immanent plane, not only traversed by natural instincts, but the proper place for the work of these instincts. Not that instincts cease to proceed from nature, but now, between the generative source and the expression, a structure emerges, a 'human fact'. The naturalist connotation, without being abolished, is further specified by an anthropo-psychological determinant.

We can now discern the mixture of continuity and discontinuity in Nietzsche's problematic, in the context of the period of 1876–8. On the one hand, the ensemble of the preceding analyses naturally finds its place in the new psychology, but on the other hand the theoretical posture has changed. Now the critique centres on the layer of the real and of a human moral *habitus* which has taken constancy and furnishes Nietzsche's investigation with a new homogeneity.

Thus the restriction of the general question of instincts centers around the pair selfish/unselfish (*égoïste/non égoïste*) instincts. Here, we recognize the contribution of the French moralist tradition, in particular that of La Rochefoucauld, to this new conception of instinct. In fact, for La Rochefoucauld self-love is the key which permits us to define the whole of moral life, under the masks of altruism. Nietzsche's new approach to instincts will consist in disclosing, in the play of psychic appearances (ideas, sentiments, comportments), the work of this pair of fundamental instincts.

What, precisely, constitutes this work? From the outset, we must recognize that this is an inversion of traditional philosophical method, which began with the 'man as he is' considered as *aeterna veritas*, and consequently considered the instincts of this 'man' working backwards, as the immutable facts 'of humanity'.[23] By contrast, historical psychology postulates a radical becoming. Opposing 'eternal truths', it posits 'little unpretentious truths, which have been found by a critical method'.[24] Thus Nietzsche's taste for 'the art of coining maxims', in other words, for psychological observation.

But what is the object of this observation, if not a complex material of representations under which observation discloses the work of a simple instinct, that consists in 'approaching something, or turning away from something', necessarily accompanied by a 'sentiment of wanting what is beneficial (*das Förderliche)*, of avoiding what is harmful (*das Schädliche*)', implying 'a kind of appreciation for the knowledge of the value of a goal'.[25] It comprises a simple and primary anthropological fact, which strongly resembles La Rochefoucauld's self-love. As Nietzsche would later say, 'Selfishness (*l'égoïsme*) is not a principle, but the sole and unique fact'.[26]

Everything proceeds from there. We can reconstitute the ensemble of psychological reality emanating from this selfish instinct, split from an altruistic instinct (*unegoistisches Trieb*)[27] – even though, as Nietzsche would later say, 'these words 'altruistic instinct' ring in my ears like 'iron in wood'.[28] The social instinct is itself only an extension of the instinct of Self-preservation. 'Through his relations with other men, man derives a new type of pleasure in addition to the sensations of pleasure he feels by himself; in this manner of sensible means he extends the domain of pleasure in general'.[29]

We can see the moral consequences stemming from the primacy of the instinctual principle. 'All "evil" actions are motivated by the instinct for preservation, or, more exactly, by the aspiration to pleasure and the flight from displeasure in the individual; but, insofar as they are motivated, they are not "bad".'[30] That the question of morality and sociality passes to the first plane reveals the new function of the concept of instinct.

One of the consequences of this evolution is the relative exhaustion of the inflation of instincts. Everything happens as if Nietzsche provisionally centred his investigation around the fundamental couplet selfishness/altruism, or rather on the unique principle of Self-preservation (altruistic (*un*-selfish) instinct being already derivative), which permits him to investigate instinctual multiplicity as so many expressions of this fundamental reality. The innumerable mass of instincts is divided into either selfish or unselfish instincts; as a result, moral psychology is furnished with a controlling thread in its investigation of the instinctual economy. And so there appears in the wake of this newly instituted psychology the idea–metaphor of the *Nachtrieb* (literally, an *over-drive*; but figuratively meaning a derived instinct).

We can judge this from the number of occurrences of *Nachtrieb* in *The Voyager and His Shadow*. 'The instinct that only wants to have certitudes in its domain (of first and last things) is a *religious over-drive*, nothing more – a disguised form skeptical of metaphysical needs'.[31] 'To celebrate the origin, there is a *metaphysical over-drive* which re-emerges in the concept of history'.[32] 'Vanity as an *over-drive* is a non-social state'.[33] In the repetition of the term *Nachtrieb*, Nietzsche intuits an instinct that 'belittles' or causes rejections (*Schösslinge*) to flower.[34] Psychology must therefore recognize the action of an instinct through its *over-drives* or rejections, metaphysical, religious or social. It resembles the work of the naturalist or the expert gardener who recognizes the subterranean activity of plants, but the difficulty comes precisely in that the fundamental instinct is a plant which never appears directly, but is discerned only through its rejections.[35]

Here we can compare the hedonistic postulates of Nietzschean psychology with its legitimate homology in Freudian psychoanalysis, the pleasure principle (*Lustprinzip*), where the principal end of psychic activity consists in avoiding displeasure and procuring for itself pleasure. Generally recognized as the essential principle of the 'functioning of psychic life', with the reality principle as its guiding and controlling force, it is a concept which, though only explicitly articulated in 1911, is nonetheless present from the very beginning in Freud's psychic economy. The psychic apparatus is in fact oriented by this tactic of avoiding tensions which introduce economic crises.

However, on closer inspection the analogy reveals a difference in nature between the two principles. For Nietzsche, instinctivist hedonism consists in relating every mode of human action and expression to the unique and positive end of pleasure-interest. By contrast, Freud's *pleasure principle* declares more precisely that the pleasure that determines in the last instance all psychic activity is released by the representation of action. Thus, it is better allied with the psychology and ethics of Theodor Fechner who similarly postulated a 'pleasure principle of action'.

It is true that Nietzsche, as a psychologist of instincts, provides evidence, in the wake of La Rochefoucauld, for the relation of action to the representation of an immediately perceived interest, but he relates it, via his psychological approach, to a hedonistic philosophy of human action, whereas Freud merely postulates a functional principle which he infers from clinical observation.

Otherwise, the function of Freud's pleasure principle is to specify a reality principle, by the acceptance of a detour imposed by the Real on the *princeps* demands of satisfaction. In terms of physics and economics, this implies a transformation of free energy into harnessed energy. For Nietzsche, reality here is only that which affords to selfish (*égoïste*) pleasure opportunities for self-gratification and occlusion.

THE DRIVE, FREUD'S META-PSYCHOLOGICAL UNITY

In 1905, in *Three Essays on the Theory of Sexuality*, Freud introduced instinct as an etiological concept. We have so far focused on the gap between the original theoretical writing and the adoption of the concept. Whereas *Trieb* is functional from the very beginning for Nietzsche, as if the concept was contemporaneous with the theoretical project and serving at the same time to explain it, for Freud there passes an important lapse of time[36] before the concept acquires an explicit central role. It is all the more reason to try to grasp both the scope and the function of the term and the concept from the moment when it is first introduced.

Unlike Nietzsche, Freud gives us a *definition* of the term. Under the term 'drive' we can understand nothing other than 'the psychic representative (*psychische*

Repräsentanz) of a source of intra-somatic excitation passing simultaneously (*kontinuierlisch fliessenden, innersomatischen Reizquelle*), different from an excitation (*Reiz*) produced by external and discontinuous excitants (*vereinzelte und von aussen kommende Erregungen*).'[37] But to understand this definition, we first need to see how it is introduced.

Freud begins with a *biological* opposition, or more precisely an opposition adopted from biology, between the sexual instinct (*Geschlechtstrieb*) and the nutritive instinct (*Trieb nach nahrungsaufnahme*) or *Hunger*.[38] He proposes to call the sexual instinct *Libido*, a scientific term which had just entered into common use at the time. Freud's *thesis* argues that the libido is present from infancy and that sexual union is *not* its immediate aim, but his *demonstration* centres straightaway on pathology, that is to say on the deviations (*Abirrungen*) related to the object and aim of the sexual instinct, and from there Freud moves on to perversions and neuroses. Only in this way, Freud argues, can the drive be defined. There is no single fortuitous order of exposition; the primacy of pathological manifestations indicates the status of *Trieb* for Freud. Experimenting with the pathological variations regarding objects and aims puts him on the path of the nature and function of *Trieb*.

We should stress that Freud only *starts* from the biological concept of *Geschlechtstrieb*. Through the detour of pathology the notion is transformed into the *psychoanalytic* concept of *Trieb*. The transformation is made possible through the intermediary concept of partial drives (*Partialtriebe*). At the same time, we should reflect on how it is as *partial* that the drive is inserted into the Freudian discourse, and for good reason, as the mechanism of the deviation essentially brings into play the partial state of the drive. Thus, through the pathological destiny of the drive, this partializing property asserts itself and demands an introduction.

Likewise, Nietzsche's discourse on instincts begins with and departs from a diversity of instincts,[39] but immediately this comparison suggests an important difference. For Nietzsche, this diversity is limitless, a pure plurality that merely suggests an instinct, whereas for Freud the diversity is limited by nature, which is why he asserts the drive as *a partialization of an instinctual whole*. Nietzschean instinct exhibits a characteristic tendency toward schizogenesis; each activity has its own little instinct, its own particular and demoniacal soul. Freud's *Partialtrieb* returns to a finite totality which finds its limit in somatic space.

Now, 'what distinguishes one drive from another and endows each with specific properties is their relation to their respective somatic *sources* and *aims*. The source of the drive is an existing process in an organism and its immediate aim is the appeasement of organic excitation.'[40] What limits the number of partial drives is the number of erogenous zones, themselves linked to somatic regions and organs which form a 'secondary genital apparatus' (*Nebenapparate*).[41] The partial drives are thus restored in the last instance to this specific topological space. Every drive is reattached to a topological referent with a correlative object (oral, anal), and when one drive is characterized by its aim, Freud takes pains to assign it a somatic referent.[42]

The unity of the ensemble is ensured by the primacy of the genital drive which integrates the ensemble of partial drives; here 'a new sexual aim is given, to which all the partial drives cooperate, while the erogenous zones submit to the primacy of the genital zone.'[43] In effect, the evolution of the libido resorbs the multiplicity of the drives; in other words, by being united around a privileged zone (the genitals) the partialization is resorbed. The partial acts of the drives are progressively converted into an ensemble-act (*zusammen wirken*); that is to say, the concept of partialization contains the notion of a division of labor.

Between the 'polymorphous perversity' of the infant and the integrated sexuality of adult genital normality, there is a relation between one partialized whole and another, coordinated whole, even if the partialization can survive within the coordination or can reactivate itself in *regression*.

It is true that Freud sometimes insists on the anarchic nature of the partial drives; they even seem endowed with a *conatus*. Each drive appears to operate on its own without the least concern for any other drive. Yet according to Freud there is a sort of *libidinal deception* which unconsciously works to fit the individual drives into a cohesive ensemble. But where does this cohesive tendency come from? Here is where the libidinal function intervenes; because all the drives unfold from a common source (Libido), they must be rejoined in this same source, like rivers that inexorably flow toward the sea. A text from 1908 states it clearly; we must speak of sexual instincts in the plural, because 'analysis shows that the sexual drive is composed of several components, or partial drives.'[44] The adjective 'partial' must be read, quasi-literally, as 'parts'.

In the *Introductory Lectures on Psychoanalysis*, Freud says that 'the sexual life of the infant is exhausted in a series of partial drives which seek to obtain pleasure independently of one another.'[45] Later, he insists that the partial drives 'communicate among themselves in a certain fashion, so that a drive emanating from a certain erogenous source can furnish its intensity to reinforce a partial drive emanating from another source, and that the satisfaction of one drive can replace that of another.'

This alternating tendency to place the accent at some times on the autonomy of the partial drives, and at other times on their unification, reveals a certain hesitation that, while manifested in the original theory, will continue to be further specified and clarified. In fact, what is still missing in Freud's 1905 conception is the concept of a libidinal *organization* which establishes the convergence of the partial drives toward a non-fortuitous *cooperation*. The idea of an organization has been implicit in the theory from the beginning, but everything proceeds as if Freud, in order to highlight the proper autonomy of the partial drives, has provisionally opted for what we might call the *weak theory of libidinal organization*.

The play of partial drives remains at its origin disorganized; it is the triumph of the genital drives that they impose a sort of *de facto* order. It is only in 1913[46] that Freud introduces the concept of a pre-genital organization in the anal drive. He emphasizes that each stage is presented as a type of unity of drives, characterized by the predominance of one sexual activity assigned to one erogenous zone.

Freud specifies henceforth that this predominance creates its own organization. Thus partialization is related to a general process of progressive organization, divided by the types of successive organizations. This amounts to a *strong theory of libidinal organization.*

From that moment, the definitive concept is fixed, as we can see in *The Psychoanalysis and Theory of the Libido* (1923).

> The sexual instinct, whose dynamic exteriorization in psychic life can be called *Libido*, is composed of partial drives which can be both separated and progressively united in determined organizations. The particular partial drives initially tend toward independent satisfaction, but in the course of development they always become more unified and centered.'[47]

Without ever reducing the initial plurality of partial drives, Freud tends to normalize their evolution through a generalized notion of organization. It is less a matter of a passage from a pure diversity to an organization than it is one of a genesis of organizational levels.

We see that the investigation into libidinal organization gains increasing value for Freud's conception of instinct; the partial drive calls into question the unity of the drives. We can conclude that Freud, unlike Nietzsche, does not pose the pure diversity of the drives as primary. At the heart of the Freudian conception lies the principle that we do not have to multiply the instincts in vain. It is expressed, on the one hand by Freud's refusal to postulate an instinct for each human activity (somatic space prescribes needs and pleasures assigned to limited sites); on the other hand, the idea of organization introduces a principle of unification which obliges us to identify non-resorbed diversity as *regressive.*

INSTINCT AND PSYCHE

Nietzschean psychology and Freudian psychoanalysis finally turn on the question of how to conceive of the relation between instinct and psyche. It is an essential question to bring to bear on Nietzsche and Freud, and a strong point for comparing the two conceptions. In fact, this is the same question which Nietzsche confronts at the very moment that he mobilizes instinct as an idea. We have seen, however, that he resolves the question at first in an organicist sense. For Nietzsche, instinct is a given multiple emanating from a generative source (*Natur*). Consequently, instinctual *reality* can only be a *reflection* of this *given.* Reality and human action are nothing but modalities according to which the primitive instinctual given is phenomenalized. This distinct conception derives in part, of course, from the heritage of the concept.[48]

That said, however, the Nietzschean conception will evolve to show a subtle realization of the importance of the psychic element. We can schematize this evolution in order to explain what began as only a thematic slippage. At first, instinct is conceived as the thing-in-itself, analogous to Schopenhauer's will-to-live. It extends its scope and its influence to every manifestation, natural as well as human; human reality is merely a minted form of instinct.

True, there is the authentic and the inauthentic within the family of instincts, but that is really just an axiological difference inherent to a 'natural' objectivity. It is only a reflection of the modalities of this cleavage, and notably the slippage is revealed only by the emergence of the 'critique of the present'. Instinct remains the objective motor, but the question now becomes one of a Being that is acted upon by instinct. It is displaced to the side of the question of the Real, which is that of the 'human'. The emergence of this dimension of *Menschliches* is marked by a new attention given to *motivation*. Now, in a purely naturalist conception there is no question of motivation. The subjective determinant is merely the shadow cast by instinctual reality, and motives and motifs are judged in humans simply by the *impetus* that defines them. In this sense, Nietzsche defines instincts first as 'a thought in images (*Bilderdenken*) that finally (*zuletzt*) is transformed into excitation and motif.'[49] The emergence of a 'psychological' approach comes back to insist upon a terminal, motivational aspect of the process, in other words to seize upon its symbolic logic. But we also see that this psychic autonomy is merely functional. The nucleus of reality remains localized in the organicity of instinct, which is manifested only as a motif.

When Freud comes to offer a meta-psychological definition of the concept of drive, it is in order to distinguish it from the concept of excitation. In its first approximation, 'the drive would be an excitation for the psyche' (*Reiz für das Psychische*).[50] More precisely, the drive appears as 'the psychic representative (*psychischer Repräsentat*) of excitation issuing from the interior of the body and arriving at the psyche.'[51] Thus everything proceeds as if the psychic motif, which for Nietzsche served as the terminal symptom of an organic process, must for Freud submit to a *representational* mediation.

Thus construed, Freud's definition of instinct is distinguished by the part recognized in the psychic element. The drive is *defined by* a psychic reality – in relation to another, somatic reality – a relation of representation. We can say that this conception is *mixed*, which gives rise to Freud's famous formula, produced just after the definition discussed above, whereby the 'drive is the concept of the limit between the psychic and the somatic' (*Abgrenzung des Seelischen von Körperlichen*).[52] But what stands out in this conception of the drive is the psychic element – drive *is* the psychic representative – the somatic element being present in instinct in a constituent, but *delegated*, manner.

Consequently, the nature of the Freudian drive is clarified by understanding the function of representation at work. What, precisely, does the idea of somatic *representation* signify? In fact, from the moment we encounter this notion of representation, we are faced with a polysemy; we become aware of a considerable ambiguity, which concerns the stages of the process of representation. In Freud's first formulation, the terms *seemed* clear. The representative is psychic; the represented is somatic; the drive is the sum or the relation between the two.

But then everything proceeds as if this problematic, yet intelligible, relation got further mixed up when Freud undertook a meta-psychological explanation.

In *Instincts and Their Vicissitudes*, 10 years later, we learn that 'the drive' is a limit-concept between the psychic and the somatic, in that it remains 'the measure of the demand of work which is imposed on the psyche as a consequence of its link to the body'.[53] Here the idea of the limit is taken up again, but now it is the drive that is the representative whose function, consequently, is to represent somatic excitations. Thus the earlier conception of the drive (the representative/ represented relation) is reduced to only one of the terms. This nuance is at once infinitesimal – since we continue to say that the drive consists in the representative – and considerable, because the drive from this moment on is no longer the psychic representative of represented reality, which is somatic by nature.

It seems, even, that this second version prevails in Freud's writing, in preference to the first version, but without Freud ever having judged the value of what distinguishes the two. In his monograph on Schreber, he declares that 'we conceive of the drive as the limit-concept between the somatic and the psychic; we see in it the psychic representative of organic forces.'[54] It gets better; 10 years later, when Freud modifies the first edition of *Three Essays on the Theory of Sexuality*, this latter conception carries the day. In 1938, in *An Outline of Psychoanalysis*, this is the official formulation which is once more accredited. 'They (the drives) represent the corporeal contributions to psychic life.'[55]

Yet in the margins of this interpretation, Freud accredits another. This time, it is to the second term that the drive is assimilated. It is now represented in the psyche by two elements, representation and affect. The double interpretive virtuality of the drive indicates an essential question: what type of psychic/ somatic correlation constitutes the drive?

- It is no accident that Freud always insists on taking the somatic as given, relegating the psychic to the rank of a superstructure. In other words, the drive would be something in an organic being which remains somehow indifferent to the psychic processes which delegate it in the psyche. Its psychic destiny would be as extrinsic as, philosophically speaking, the phenomenon of appearance would be to essence.
- The psychological conception of the drive, in the other direction, in effect reduces the drive to a psychic reflection, such that it is manifested in a quasi-organic effectivity. Such is in fact the status of the drive of the manifesting/ manifested type of Being.

We understand that Freud has equivocated by not choosing between these two extremes; the function of the concept creates the ambiguity, and it cannot be rescued. To 'resolve' it would only create obstacles, at the same time by the maintenance of an articulated ambivalence as by a primacy accorded to the psychological point of view, given as dominant – the organic perspective being considered recessive, marginalized but not purely and simply suppressed.

The problem of the representation of the drive, which is at the heart of Freud's analytic elaboration, stands out in our comparative study, although Nietzsche does not theorize the drive in such a manner. Nietzschean psychology, grounded on an organicist conception of instincts, considers the psychic motif as only a reflection. This is why, in correlation, psychology, while accentuating its approach through the subjective flow of motivation, does not know how to pose itself as autonomous from a theory of instincts. By contrast, Freud's meta-psychology can easily be seen as posing a 'mythology'[56] of drives, without compromising psychoanalysis as an investigation into the effects of the psychic senses.

In that, there is one difference that reflects the status of the body and the thing-in-itself. For Nietzsche, the motif appears as the imagery of the body; the psychologist inherits the infinite task of revealing, by the fugitive virtues of psychological and moral aphorisms, the activities of the instinctual body which is forever hidden. For Freud, there is an associative logic of psychic representation which makes possible an indirect, but objective, knowledge of the drive.[57]

That is why, starting with a homology of the projects indicated by a chemical reference, we must conclude with a distinction between objects and the positional form which takes them into account.[58]

3

PRINCIPLES OF THE DRIVE

A comparative study of the principles behind Freudian and Nietzschean theories would not be complete without an examination of the foundations of their respective *Trieblehre* (theory of the drives). The theory of the drives is in fact capped, for Nietzsche as for Freud, by the concept of *fundamental drives*.

This concept works in two directions:

- On the one hand, the plurality of individual drives return in the last instance to the principal drives which direct and arrange the organization and the scope of each drive. They are the 'fundamental drives', which constitute the touchstone of the entire edifice of the drives and which reveal their orientation.
- On the other hand, each individual drive, such as motion, is developed in a sort of foyer which constitutes a common source. A theory of instincts inevitably needs such a *focus originarius* to foment activity, where the drive's *matter* is formed.

There is thus a double determining criteria which will permit us to gauge the two conceptions. By a regression, we have in fact arrived at a nexus where we can approach the disjunction between Nietzschean and Freudian thought, as manifesting different responses to the question: in what does the Being of the drive consist?

THE FUNDAMENTAL DRIVES: HUNGER AND SELF-PRESERVATION

In the genesis of Freud's theory of the drives,[1] we must accord a decisive importance to the moment when the requirements of *fundamental drives* are formulated.

Strictly speaking, at the moment when Freud introduces the concept of the drives in 1905, nothing specifically requires a duality. In his exposition, Freud raises two types of drives, nutritive and sexual; he centres his investigation essentially on the second, while noting from time to time the relation between the two. But nothing yet implies that the psyche has to be structured exclusively, or at least specifically, around these two determined types of drives. It is in a second period, between 1905 and 1910, that this decisive step will take place. In fact, in 1910, in a technical essay on hysteria, a new formula appears.[2]

The context is revealing. The first time that the idea of a dualism of drives is introduced is on the basis of a psychic conflict, and this idea will forever after be linked to *Trieblehre*. Remarkably, this theory of drives makes its entry into the Freudian discourse via a very specific point of psychopathology. Having explained the psychic origins of the disturbance of vision by the contradiction between suppressed representations and the synthetic concept of the Ego, Freud asks: to what must we attribute this contrariety (*Gegensatz*) that engages in suppression? It is there that the duality of the drives intervenes. Drives will seek to valorize themselves by the animation of representations adapted to the drives' own ends, from whence arises the representational life (*Vorstellungsleben*) that constitutes the *medium* of the drives. But drives essentially exist in a mode of opposition. 'These drives do not support one another; they frequently arrive at a conflict of interests. The oppositions of representations are thus only the expressions of the struggles of individual drives.'[3] Finally, from this general conflict, a (specific) conflict disengages, which must be privileged due to its *etiological* value:

> Of particular importance for our explanatory purposes is the undeniable opposition between those drives which have a sexual orientation, which aim at sexual pleasure, and others oriented toward the self-preservation (*Selbsterhaltung*) of the individual, the drives of the Ego (*Ichtrieben*).[4]

Freud immediately expresses this opposition in terms of principles, by invoking the authority of Schiller. 'We can likewise classify, by the terms of the poet, all of the organic drives acting in our psyche as either "Hunger" or "Love" (*Hunger oder Liebe*)'. Pathogenic suppression thus originates in the intolerable contradiction between the interests of the Ego drives and the pretensions of the sexual drives.

This text marks a turning point in Freud's conception of the drive to the extent that drives begin to be hypostasized in dual principles, around which are structured the totality of psychic life. It is no accident if, at this moment, Freud cannot resist the poetic reference. But in a contrary sense, we must return to the modesty of this introduction. What led to the privileging of these two types of drives is the etiological role that they fulfil and for which they must be privileged. In this regard, it is significant that Freud does not grant to the first dualism of drives a special and autonomous explanation; he seems to discover it on his way, as an etiological hypothesis, beginning with an 'induction' on a very precise question of psycho-pathology. It is thus as an event as revolutionary as it is discreet that he introduces the dualism, which is then imposed in the Freudian *Trieblehre*.

Nevertheless, to satisfy a technical requirement, Freud resorts to a distinction which, not fortuitously, originates with Schiller.[5] It is as if the Romantic sense of the concept of *Trieb*, effectively neutralized by Freud to the status of an optional drive via scientific[6] theorization, is imposed at the global level of *Trieblehre* in order to express its mythological aspect.

Moreover, contrary to the pan-sexualist representation, we can say that love is differentially defined in relation to its antonymic principle, hunger or self-preservation. This is even the primary principle of the drive, insofar as love is originally only satisfied by the support (*Anlehnung*) of the principles of self-preservation. If it is true that 'the sexual drives find their first objects by supporting the values recognized by the Ego drives', it is by these that we must follow the examination of the dualism of drives.

It is revealing, to put Nietzsche's *Trieblehren* in a better light, to examine the status of drives in Nietzsche which, in their first dualistic formulation, fulfil for Freud the function of fundamental drives. To begin with, what is there regarding the drives of self-preservation or hunger which, we have seen, indicate the axis of a dualism?[7] They indeed exist from the beginning, among the panoply of human instincts, but beginning with *Human, All Too Human*, they acquire a central place. As far as being another name for 'selfish (*egoistisch*) instinct' or 'self-love' taken in the strong sense, they appear as the first distinction of human activity. Every human action, beyond their division into 'good' or 'bad', is submitted to the jurisdiction of a principle which consists in the 'aspiration to pleasure' and the 'flight from the discomfort of the individual'.[8] Nietzsche goes so far as to say that 'to do evil, not by the instinct for survival, but for reprisals (*Vergeltung*), is the consequence of a false judgment and to that extent equally innocent'. This is power in the state of nature, which the State itself inherits, or rather the principle of interest well understood.

But we are witness to a clear and spectacular evolution of the status of this instinct of self-preservation in Nietzsche. It is articulated in *The Gay Science*, where an aphorism declares that 'to will to preserve oneself is the expression of a situation of distress (*Notlage*), a restriction of the fundamental vital instinct, properly speaking (*Einschränkung des eigentlichen Lebensgrundtriebes*), which aims at extending one's power (*Machterweiterung*) and, in that, often broaches the question of self-preservation or sacrifice'.[9] What was once the fundamental instinct thus becomes a reduction of the fundamental instinct, hereafter localized in the extension of power.

The evolution is so pure that Nietzsche goes on to diagnose a deficiency of instinct at work in the theoreticians of self-preservation *themselves*. 'We consider it symptomatic that certain philosophers, as for example the consumptive Spinoza, had considered the so-called instinct of self-preservation the decisive principle, precisely because they were men in distress.'[10] Let us note, for our purposes, how fortuitous it is that this opinion is delivered against all theories past and to come on self-preservation, seeing that this will concern Freud himself!

But because behind this theory lurks the scientific guarantee furnished by Darwin, Nietzsche at the same time issues a challenge to the Darwinian principle. Darwin appears in fact as the modern father of the partisans of self-preservation, as the 'decisive' element of living, human nature. Nietzsche goes so far as to make Darwin echo the situation of the material distress of the English thinkers who had projected their vision of life there:

> What reigns in Nature is not poverty, but profusion (*Uberfluss*), prodigality, even foolishness. The struggle for life is only an *exception*, a

> momentary restriction of the will to live; great and small struggles take aim everywhere in preponderance, in extension, in capacity, in the manner of Will to Power, which is precisely the will to live.[11]

This conception is inscribed in Nietzsche's definition of instinct from the very beginning. Dionysian intuition is that of profusion and luxury – that is why every limitation of the instinct is an *impoverishment.* But for a long time this tropical conception of instinct accommodated the primacy of an instinct of preservation; it is a decisive moment when Nietzsche perceives the contradiction. The critique of the primacy of the preservation instinct is logically and chronologically contemporaneous with the introduction of Will to Power; it is named in the same way as it expresses necessity. This is why Nietzsche, up to the end, never misses an occasion to dismiss the instinct of self-preservation from its pretensions to supremacy, and so marks the requirement of a different principle, which will be more and more clearly affirmed to be no other than *Wille zur Macht.*

The clearest statement appears in *Beyond Good and Evil* that the clearest statement appears. 'The psychologists need to think again before affirming the instinct of self-preservation as a cardinal instinct (*kardinalen Trieb*) of organic being.'[12] This signifies that there is some force which acts *before* the individual. 'Above all, every living thing wants to give free vent (*auslassen*) to its power; self-preservation is only one of its indirect and most frequent consequences.'

Thus it is not a question of denying the importance of the preservation instinct in the economy of life, but at the same time it is necessary to guard against confusing the effect, whether it be the most frequent or the most manifest, for the cause or the first principle. It is an *interpretation* of life. Nietzsche goes on to disqualify the preservation instinct in the name of the 'principle of the economy of principles'; it is useless to encumber ourselves with a superfluous teleological principle! Here again Spinoza is accused, since it was to his inconsistency that we owe the generalization of the principle, he who was the enemy of final causes. In fact, the reduction of principles paves the way for a *coup d'Etat* by Will to Power, which will progressively concentrate every capacity. To this end Nietzsche dispossesses the dangerous rival concept of self-preservation. This is what Zarathustra means when he declares that 'I love those who do not want save themselves'.[13]

An aphorism in *Twilight of the Idols* announces an 'anti-Darwin':

> As far as the famous 'struggle to live' goes, it appears to me as a new order more asserted than demonstrated. It has a place, but as an exception; the general aspect of life is not indigence or famine, but rather richness and opulence, even an absurd prodigality – where there is a struggle, it is a struggle for *power.*[14]

A word sums up the sense of Nietzsche's intervention: 'One should not confuse Malthus with Nature.'

A brief fragment contemporary with *The Will to Power* reaffirms this precisely. 'The struggle to live' designates an exceptional situation. The rule is rather the struggle for *power*, for 'the most' and 'the best' and 'the quickest' and 'the most frequent'.[15] The relativization of the principle of self-preservation thus rests on the opposition between Darwin's *Kampf ums Dasein* and the Nietzschean *Kampf um Macht*, and that is the true answer to our question.

Nietzsche's position on the hunger drive, significantly, follows the same fluctuations. Appetite is the privileged modality under which instinct is defined. As we see in *Daybreak*, instincts follow 'laws of nutrition'. They are affirmed by their 'nutritive needs' to which experience furnishes 'nutriments'.[16] Not only is hunger a fundamental instinctive activity, but it is the mode by which instinctual willing is identified. Instinct is affirmed by reclaiming the nourishment which is its adequate mode of satisfaction. But in the evolution of Nietzschean thought the nutritive schema, while not being abolished, is relativized. *The Will to Power* provides a clarification rich in significance from our point of view. 'It is not possible', declares Nietzsche, 'to consider hunger as the primary motive, any more than self-preservation.'[17]

The primary argument is that the originary activity of protoplasm cannot be derived from a will to self-preservation 'because it madly absorbs more that its preservation requires'. Far from being originally preserved, it destroys itself; there is rather in the beginning a 'will to not be saved'.[18] The error consists in judging it by hunger, which concerns complex organisms. Hunger is thus 'the expression of a specialized, belated form of instinct, an expression of the division of labor of an instinct seen from above'; it is thus not originary, but must be 'conceived as the consequence of an under-nourishment', that is to say as the consequence of a *Will to Power which is no longer master*.'[19]

In other words,

> it is absolutely not a matter of redressing a loss; it is only later, as a consequence of the division of labour, after Will to Power has learned to succeed by every other path to its satisfaction, that the organism's need for domination (*Aneignungsbedfürfnis*) is *reduced* to hunger, to the need to replace what has been lost.

The tendency to nourish oneself by filling a lack, another facet of self-preservation, only knows how to define that life which is prior to any affirmation of power. Thus it is not at first that the organism exteriorizes its living-being in order to preserve and sustain itself. At this stage, life already has a prehistory, and what has already happened *before* is no other than the affirmation of power.[20]

LIFE AND DEATH

We know that Freud began to modify his dualism of drives around 1920. The discovery of narcissism and its consequences in 1914 had virtually undermined the principle of opposition between sexual drives and Ego drives, by presenting the formula for a sexual investment in the Ego itself. The notion of auto-eroticism thoroughly muddles the criteria for distinction.

Consequently the principle of self-preservation loses its *princeps* function. Now it is included in a new dualism of drives, the life-wish and the death-wish, which are imposed from the time of *Beyond the Pleasure Principle*. The status of this dualism does not allow for any surplus problematic being, as Freud presents it from the beginning as a detour on the way to death; to preserve oneself would only mean 'to die a natural death'.[21] Finally, Freud relates the Ego drives to the life-wish.

So Freud, in the second dualism, relativizes the idea of self-preservation just as Nietzsche did in his second phase, but the gulf between them will increase in this second stage. In fact, it now becomes a question of understanding what the one and the other mean by life and death.

These terms clearly indicate that we have regressively arrived closer to the term of our comparison of the concept of instinct, given that instinct is conceived as a vital eruption, and that the ultimate ontological question of a theory of instincts concerns the foundations that nourish it, that is: what is meant by Life and Death?

In order to understand that, it is necessary to begin with Freud's famous representation of the protoplasmic ball assailed by the afflux of external excitations, whose resistance progressively grows to the point of widening the interval between two states of death. Life is thus only that which makes possible the deferment of the return to an inorganic state. This expletive and restrictive characterization of the vital process does not surprise us, if we set it in relation to the energetic schema from which Freud began in 1896 (see above). Conforming to an entropic schema, life appears as a tendency to overcome a loss.

Formulated in positive terms, life for Freud consists in 'provoking and maintaining the cohesion between the parts of the living substance.'[22] Self-preservation is now an aspect of this general tendency, alongside the sexual drives. Hunger and love thus are found included in the family of life-wishes. Where Freud tends to confuse the life-wishes with their mythological prototype, Eros, he accentuates their active aspect. 'The aim of Eros is to establish ever greater unities, thus to conserve; it is the linkage (*Bindung*),'[23] but the error will be to conceive of the work of linkage as creative. At first, Freud opposed *free* or mobile energy, which flows toward the most immediately possible path of discharge, to *bound* energy (*gebundene Energie*) whose movement toward discharge is thwarted. That implies that the process of discharge is primary and that the 'link' is merely derived.

Correlatively, the vital linkage is only a demiurgic activity that creates order or harmony, an efficacious and provisional retardation of free energy. It is thus a point of triumphant vitalism; for Freud, to live is barely more than to control death, and every vital linkage is only an inhibited de-linking (*Entbindung*). The 'major aim of Eros' is indeed 'to unite and link', but that strongly resembles a labour of Penelope, in that it passes the time reweaving a fabric that is ceaselessly unravelled under the effect of the death-wish. It is an endless intention opposed by the aim of the 'other drive', which is 'to break off relations, thus to destroy things'.

Now that it is clear that life is defined in relation to death, we must take care not to represent Thanatos as a demoniacal principle and invest it with a positive power which we had to refuse regarding life. It is more a question of a type of a natural propensity which is opposed less to life than to death, despite the mythological formulae dramatizing the conflict, than it is a permanent denial, effected by the phenomena of repetition and aggression.

In this sense, Freud can finally affirm that every drive is, as such, a death-wish, to the point where 'the pleasure principle seems in fact in the service of the death-wish',[24] insofar as it represents the requirements of the libido. This conclusion, whose apparent paradox is clarified by its energetic origin, makes Being ultimately consist of the life-wish *in* the death-wish, and links the destiny of the libido with death.

How does Nietzsche see life? Right away, it is interesting to note that life is opposed to knowledge. A life dominated by knowledge, as Nietzsche says in the second *Untimely Meditation*, 'is much less "living" '.[25] Thus from the beginning life is defined in terms of intensity, which implies that certain of its forms are valorized, as manifesting 'the true life', such that it is 'more alive', which further implies that life is a 'plus' that we should preserve from any diminution. Moreover, life is linked to illusion. Life is no other than that which 'wills illusion' (*Täuschung*).[26] These two characteristics are combined in the representation of a zigzag vital process. 'Life consists in particular moments of the highest importance and of numerous intervals'.[27] In other words, 'the epochs of life are these short latency periods (*Stillstandes*) between a rise and a fall (*Aufsteigen und Absteigen*).'[28]

In addition, Nietzsche's intuition of life is one of an indomitable profusion. On the one hand, life is posed as something impenetrable (*Unergründliche*);[29] on the other, the 'global aspect (*Gesammt-aspekt*) of life is not the state of necessity (*Notlage*), but of riches.'[30] Where *Lebensgefühl* is referenced, 'The poor in life enfeeble it, the rich in life enrich it.'[31] Here is a true axio-ontology, given that 'our degree of vital feeling gives us the measure of our "being" ',[32] or even 'Being' as a generalization of the concept of 'life'.[33] At the limits, the notion of Being is only the metaphorization of life; life is only Being without quotation marks.

If we seek to define life, we see that what we call 'life' is really 'a plurality of forces, linked by a common process of development',[34] or even that 'life is defined as a durable form of the process of the establishment of forces'. In fact, it is Will to Power which will result in a 'new fixation of the concept of "life" '.[35] From this moment on, Nietzsche's concept of life loses its autonomy, in the double sense that everything that life contains is taken in charge by Will to Power and that Will to Power serves to define a true 'outside of life'.

'Wherever I have found life' asserts Nietzsche, 'I have found Will to Power'.[36] It is no mere coincidence. 'Life itself is Will to Power',[37] or even that life is only 'life insofar as it is Will to Power'.[38] This can be expressed in several ways, such as, 'life is specifically a will to accumulate power';[39] or even that 'life is only a particular case of Will to Power';[40] or that 'life is the expression of the forms of belief of power'.[41] Moreover, by an ultimate reversal, Will to Power defines a transcendence which makes necessary an outside to life as such. But even in transcendence, *Wille zur Macht* is no other than life in its movement necessary to overcome itself, a radical immanence.

In this way the heterogeneity of the conceptions of life which operate in both Nietzsche and Freud becomes visible. One is profusion and infinity, the other a capacity of limiting links; one is power, the other necessity; one is valorizing, the other functional; and so on to the point where Nietzsche can diagnose in the Freudian conception of life the symptoms of reactivity and debility!

We can confirm this attainment by examining Nietzsche's conception of death. What is universally striking about the way in which Nietzsche arrives at death is his refusal to pose it as a *problem*; death appears as a natural given, transformable into action by suicide, defined from the outset as a legitimate recourse. Voluntary death is understood, in a Schopenhaurean inspiration, as a truly vital act.[42] In addition, death appears from the outset in an ethical, even a casuistic, register. From this point of view, death is valorized as the Dionysian *back side* of life, the limits of existence abutting death, without intervening as a specific principle.

In fact, Nietzsche only conceives of death as a 'decrease of power' in the physiological sense. With *Zarathustra* there will appear the polemic thematic against the 'preachers of death',[43] who preach the 'renunciation of life', 'consumptives of the soul' who 'scarcely born they already learn how to die'.[44] Against this death that poisons life, Zarathustra opposes the 'free death', 'accomplishment', 'motivation' and 'promise' for the living,[45] the 'speedy death'.

Finally death, related to the register of Will to Power, becomes the indicator of an organic economy, knowing that the wasting away and partial disuse of organs can be seen as the 'index of an increment of power and of a movement towards perfection'. Death is thus related to 'conditions of a true progression; that which appears always under the form of Will and of direction towards *the most considerable power*.'[46]

Such is thus the triple figure of death in Nietzschean thought: a natural event, a stake in ascetic evaluation and a condition of progress of *Wille zur Macht*. Under this heading, the idea of a death-wish is alienated in its conception even from life, for two precise reasons. On the one hand, to transform death into a positive principle is the symptom of an ascetic conception of life; on the other, death is indeed intimately present in life, but it only serves to measure the quality of life. To the chronic recessive virtuality that Freud's death-wish represents is opposed the Nietzschean idea of *progressus zur grösserer Macht*.

LIBIDO AND WILL TO POWER

If we now carry the comparison of the content of *Trieblehre* on to its *form*, we will note a new and significant divergence. Freud has always maintained a *dualist* representation, indispensable to a theory of *conflict*, and explicable by a separation between the two types of drives. Apart from a brief temptation during the transition phase between the two dualisms,[47] Freud is suspicious of any monism. By contrast, the Nietzschean synthesis proceeds *towards* a monism. For Nietzsche, conflict is not the fundamental motor, and it is Will to Power which will furnish the global and discriminating principle to the drives. That is why there is no contradiction among the principles of the drives, as there is for Freud, but rather an opposition between the *affirmation* of Will to Power and its *negation*, as a Will to Nothingness.

If we nevertheless ask ourselves to what principle does the unifying role of the drive dynamic return, for Freud and Nietzsche, we notice a remarkable functional homology between Will to Power and Libido. Thanks to the intervention of this principle, the inflation of instincts is reattached in the Nietzschean dynamic to a unifying principle; every instinct becomes in the last instance a specific articulation of Will to Power. Likewise, for Freud every drive activity comes back to consummate the libido; thus it appears that *Libido* and *Will to Power* play a homologous role, respectively, in Freud and in Nietzsche. In order to understand the determining sense of this homology, we should begin by taking a look at the essential enunciations that introduce the concepts.

In the first place, Libido is present as an economic concept; affirming its quantitative character, Freud makes it the very centre of the psychic economy. We can see this in a passage from *Three Essays on the Theory of Sexuality* where he justifies the introduction of the notion. 'We have established the concept of Libido as a variable quantitative force (*quantitativveränderlichen Kraft*) which could measure (*messen*) the process and the transformations (*Vorgänge und Umsetzungen*) in the domain of sexual excitation.'[48] The quantitative aspect is confirmed as central in the final definition. 'Libido is an expression derived from the theory of affectivity. We call it the energy considered as a quantitative mass (*quantitative Grösse*) of such drives – which is not actually measurable – that is at work in everything that we can understand as love'.[49]

Freud has nonetheless taken care to distinguish a qualitative aspect. 'But this libido, we distinguish it from the energy which is implied at the base of the psychic processes in general, in relation to its own origin and we accord it equally a qualitative character.'[50] It is no other than the sexual specification which obliges him to distinguish 'libidinal energy from all other psychic energy'.

This double character accords the libido its etiological function; it is its 'production, augmentation and diminution, its repartition and displacement which must offer us the possibilities of explicating observed psycho-sexual phenomena.'[51] The transformations provide the means for taking into account every psychic phenomenon. 'The task of a theory of the libido of neurotic and psychotic disturbances must consist in expressing every phenomenon considered and their inferred processes in terms of a libidinal economy (*in den Terminis der Libidoökonomie*).'[52]

The libidinal register thus gives psychoanalytic explanation its mode of expression. Every articulation relative to psychic phenomena must be able to relate back to it and to be expressed in libidinal terms. This etiological power founds the synthetic value of an explanation in terms of Libido, as that to which in the final analysis every phenomenon must be related, as what gives it its principial appearance and its paradoxical indetermination, as a definition by which everything else is defined and understood as *drive*, and finally as the primary energetic material, the matter out of which even the drives, the primary elements, are cut. It is also that which founds the necessity to pass by 'way of speculation' in order to pursue a theory of the libido.

If we now turn to the text of *Beyond Good and Evil*, where Nietzsche invokes Will to Power, we find this enveloping character solemnly affirmed in a principle founded on a similar quantitative character. *Wille zur Macht* is in fact designated as the term which permits one 'to determine without equivocation (univocally, *eindeutig*) every active force' (*alle wirkende Kraft*).[53] In other words, it is another name for *energy*, but specified and qualified, that out of which every human phenomenon is formed. Those transformations, repartitions and displacements (to paraphrase the Freudian formulae relative to the libido) can give way to a global explanation, at once synthetic and varied; this is what is developed in Nietzsche's diagnostic psychology.

But we also understand why speculation is imposed here as well. The principle of Will to Power is like Freud's Libido, simultaneously a postulate and a regulatory ideal. It is significant that, in this programmatic text, Nietzsche poses a conditional requirement, a necessity to promote:

> To suppose that one could relate every organic function to this Will to Power, our whole instinctive life (*gesamtes Treibleben*) as a development and a ramification (*Ausgestaltung und Verzweigung*) of *one* fundamental form (*Grundform*) of willing – that is to say of Will to Power, conforming to my proposition; to suppose that one can relate every organic function to this Will to Power and to find in it as well the solution to the problems of procreation and of nutrition – it is a problem – one would have thus proved even the right to determine every force acting univocally: *Will to Power*.

This is precisely the task to which Nietzsche's grand unfinished synthesis is applied; it is ordered around this formulaic requirement in paragraph 36 of *Beyond Good and Evil*.

The comparison of these foundational texts indeed permits us to speak of a functional homology of the two concepts which function, in each respective conceptual economy, *at the same level*. Freud's Libido and Nietzsche's Will to Power are both invested with the *princeps* function of exhibiting an energetic and qualified explanatory principle which immediately permits the subsumption of the entire ensemble of anthropological phenomena.

But in that way, the ultimate divergence of the principle of these two drive doctrines is situated, given that they are in fact two heterogeneous principles: a principle of domination on the one hand, and one of pleasure on the other.

We will see, however, in the inquiry which follows, that this divergence is thematically specified. Nevertheless, we have located the *major* ethical effect of this divergence.

Like Libido, Will to Power is valuable as an interpretive principle; henceforth everything is related to the *libido dominandi*. 'The movements are the symptoms, just as thoughts are symptoms; behind one and the other we can find desires, and the fundamental desire, which is the will to dominate.'[54] In other words, it is a quasi-physiological hypothesis; 'That which is the most developed in man, is Will to Power.'[55] This is conceived as what gives desires their unity. Nietzsche even defines it as the 'strongest of all instincts', as 'that which even now directs all organic evolution'. It is what drains all meaning; 'All signification is Will to Power'. But if Will to Power is the supreme interpretation, it is so to the extent that 'the organic process presupposes a *continuous interpretive activity*.'[56]

We can now see what becomes of our point of departure, instinct, from the moment when Will to Power becomes the primary fact-principle. Nietzsche gives us one final definition. 'The instincts are the *superior organs*, in the sense that I give to these words: actions, sentiments and states of sensation entangled one with the other which organize and nourish each other',[57] as so many significant metamorphoses of Will to Power, 'expressions and metaphors of the same will inherent in every phenomenon, Will to Power.' Instincts are thus the 'judgements founded on previous experiences', 'sensations of strength or weakness'.[58]

Consequently, the teleology of the notion, still virtual in the utilitarianism of the preceding conception, is definitely rejected. Nietzsche ends by affirming that 'the instincts cannot be placed from the point of view of utility'. Far from being economical and prudent, 'in acting, it sacrifices its strength and that of other instincts'. Thus the *mechanism* of the Nietzschean conception is completed, which takes the form of an antidote to the initial Romantic accusation.

It is remarkable that the advent of Will to Power affects the hedonistic conception and the status of happiness. Where the first formulations placed happiness in the perception of the atemporal,[59] in reason[60] or in the 'quickness of the senses and of thought', it is hereafter related to power. To the question 'What is happiness?', the *Antichrist* responds, 'the sentiment of the fact that power increases, that a resistance is overcome.'[61] In other words, 'Happiness is an auxiliary appearance (*Begleiterscheinung*) in the exercise of power.'[62] Thus 'happiness' is henceforth the shadow cast by power, as an increase in power or a discharge of force, which Nietzsche designates as 'a fortunate organization'.

For this reason, Nietzsche's last formulations relativize happiness and its panegyrics. Nietzsche diagnoses in the discourse of 'supreme happiness' the aspiration towards *sleep* of beings who are weary and suffering.[63] He denies the universality of the eudemonic tendency (*Streben nach Glück*), by inverting the eudemonic formula whereby 'man does not desire 'happiness' – as his true desire',[64] which means that 'happiness is not the aim, but the sentiment of power' (*Machtgefühl*).[65] Consequently, 'liberty signifies that the virile instincts, the joyous instincts of war and of victory predominate over the other instincts, for example over those of "happiness" ',[66] a word which will hereafter appear only in quotation marks.

Overman, in overcoming life, transcends his own will to happiness, which is to say that Nietzsche's Will to Power is truly *beyond the happiness principle*, much as the Freudian death-wish is *beyond the pleasure principle*. In the inverted echo of these two formulae we can measure the ultimate meaning of the divergence of the two theories of instinct.

BOOK TWO: THE THEMES

Now that we have located the drive edifice which structures and defines both the Freudian and Nietzschean discourses, we can carry our examination on to the thematics which they derive from the principles of the drive.

These thematics are deployed along a triple axis which has long interested readers of Nietzsche and Freud. Freudian psychoanalysis has effectively been defined in terms of theories of sexuality and the Unconscious, while at the same time it is seen as the science of the interpretation of dreams. On these three key themes, Nietzsche seems to us to be a singular and unique 'precursor'.[1] Put into perspective by relating the principles of the drives which subtend them, these themes can now be re-examined, to see how the difference between Freud and Nietzsche plays out on the level where the principles are actualized and specified.

1

LOVE AND SEXUALITY

The comparison between Nietzschean and Freudian *Trieblehren* revealed, as much on the question of the fundamental drives as on that of the libido, the importance of *sexuality* as a differential indicator.[1] It is now a question of seeing how this differential choice, at the level of principles, influences the status of sexuality itself.

EROS AND DIONYSUS

What is the status of sexuality in Nietzsche's vision of the instinctual economy?

Not fortuitously, *The Birth of Tragedy* opens with an image of the duality of the sexes in procreation, symbolizing the aesthetic duality of Apollo and Dionysus.[2] Sexuality exemplifies the cosmology of the will-to-live; thus we must locate it at the level of the principle of life, and not simply as blind desire, which a contemporary text tells us is a 'sign of baseness' (*Gemeinheit*).[3]

With the advent of the hedonism of *Human, All Too Human*, sexuality is understood, conforming to a general reduction to the immanent plane of naturalism, as a variety of interpersonal pleasure (*Lust*). The sexual relation is evoked as an example of the acquisition of a 'new type of pleasure' which the individual acquires when he establishes contacts with others, and 'as such is an extension of the sensation of pleasure in general.'[4] In a universe regulated by the principle of selfishness (*le principe égoïste*), sexual attraction plays the part of an extensive form of self-interest (*l'égoïsme*).

Starting with *Daybreak*, a new interest in sexuality appears, as a moral stake. Setting himself up against the 'demonization of Eros' by Christianity, Nietzsche reaffirms his hedonism:

> Within oneself, sexual feelings have in common with pity and adoration the notion that one human being can benefit another human being through one's own pleasure – one does not often find such a benevolent arrangement in nature! And that is precisely what is calumniated and corrupted by a bad conscience![5]

But behind this pleasure a special instinct is at work, which is a mischance (*une fatalité*). A contemporary fragment declares that 'the illusion of sexual instinct is a thread that, when it is broken, always repairs itself.'[6] But Nietzsche takes care to distinguish Eros from procreation. He goes so far as to say that 'sexual instinct has no necessary relation to procreation', neither in 'intention' nor as a 'necessary consequence'. At most, it is the occasional consequence of the sexual instinct's modality of satisfaction. Nietzsche conceives of the sexual instinct as 'antisocial' and the negation of 'general equality and of the equality of value between human beings'. Paradoxically, the sexual instinct puts two individualities into relation, as 'the individual type of passion'. 'The sexual instinct goes to the meaning of individuation.'[7] Consequently, he can say that 'the separation of the sexes is not a fundamental one'; rather, 'individual pleasure' constitutes sexuality, while 'procreation is not essentially sexual'.

Such is the paradox that the species reproduces thanks to the absence of a *telos*. 'Humanity would be wiped out if the sexual instinct did not have such a character: blind, lacking in foresight, impatient, destitute of thought. In itself, its satisfaction is not absolutely linked to the propagation of the species.'[8] It is only through a moral *lie* that such a linkage is made necessary.[9]

Disengaged from its immediate organic substrate, sexuality comes to be inserted into the overall human economy. It is thus that Nietzsche finds himself on the path of a perspective whereby sexuality extends its hold well beyond its jurisdiction, as a special instinct. We recall the famous aphorism from *Beyond Good and Evil* (in which Freud might find a seductive echo), which states that 'the degree and nature of human sexuality is raised to the highest summit of the spirit.'[10] From the same perspective, Nietzsche speaks of 'sublimated sexual love', as a characteristic cultural phenomenon.

The theory of *sublimation* is formulated with an astonishing precision in a fragment contemporary with *Daybreak*; this text, which figures in the *Nachlass*, demands to be examined closely for its affinity to Freud. 'When an instinct becomes *intellectual*', writes Nietzsche,

> it acquires a new name, a new trait and a new evaluation. It is often *opposed* to the older instinct as its contrary .... A number of instincts, for example the sexual instinct, are susceptible to a great *refinement* (*Verfeinerung*) by the intellect (love of humanity .... Plato thinks that the love of knowledge and philosophy is a sublimated sexual instinct). Alongside it remains its old and immediate action.'[11]

Sublimation is a way of perfecting the instinct and rendering it useful. We should understand the sublimation of the sexual instinct as a process of intellectual refinement which makes possible its redeployment in 'higher' tasks. Notably, it is 'under the influence of Christianity' that 'the sexual instinct is sublimated as love.'[12]

Twilight of the Idols reaffirms this insight. 'Only Christianity, with its fundamental resentment towards life, turns sexuality into something impure', while 'for the Greeks the *sexual* symbol was a venerable symbol in itself, the truly profound interior meaning of all ancient piety.'[13] The 'mysteries of sexuality' held for the Greeks the function of a pagan revelation of 'the eternal return of life'. *Ecce Homo* speaks in this sense of 'the perpetual *war* of the sexes',[14] and denounces the poisoning of nature in sexual love by all 'idealism'[15] and contempt for sexual activity, everywhere tainted by the idea of 'impurity', as 'the true sin against life, the true sin against the Holy Spirit of life'.

It now remains to assign a place to the sexual instinct in the ultimate philosophy of Will to Power. A prior text had already put the sexual instinct in relation with a 'thirst for power'. 'Sexual excitation, when it appears, maintains a tension (*Spannung*) which is discharged in a feeling of power (*Durst nach Macht*); preservation and nutrition and often the pleasure of eating are presented as substitutes (*Ersatz*).'[16] We understand the sense whereby in Antiquity 'sexuality was religiously venerated',[17] and valued as a sign of health by ancient civilizations. Thus it is no accident if one of Nietzsche's first writings was dedicated to the principle of the Homeric struggle (*Wettkampf*); the sexual instinct is posed as *Wettkampf* whose stakes are no other than those of becoming and of life itself.[18] Everywhere that it is neglected or underestimated, there occurs a crisis of power which is to be feared.

Thus the sexual instinct did not suffer as radical a relativization in the evolution of Nietzsche's thought as did the instinct of self-preservation. For all that, though, it does not usurp the force of Will to Power, but rather occupies a privileged status *within* Will to Power. It is an important indicator (*Zeichen*) of the thirst for power; if it remains on the side of the higher forms, where *Wille zur Macht* is raised above even Life itself, sexuality manifests the forms incorporated in some way in the becoming-vital of the dynamic of the will.

The Will to Power thus recapitulates the various levels of intervention of the sexual instinct in human reality. It is a function of sublimation, 'pity and love of humanity as a development (*Entwickelung*) of an sexual instinct'[19] (*ethical*). '*The desire for art and beauty* is an indirect desire for the enchantments of the sexual instinct communicated to the brain'[20] (*aesthetic*). The correlation between art and sexuality is strongly marked. 'Artists, if they value something, are (equally physically) strongly constituted, prolix, powerful, sensual beasts; without a certain overheating of the sexual system, no Raphaël could be conceivable.'[21] Elsewhere, Nietzsche is even more explicit. 'It is one and the same force which one expends in the conception of works of art, as in the sexual act: there is only *one* kind of force.'[22]

We can see that the unity originates in the last instance from a common source of power. In this spirit, Nietzsche reinterprets his first theory of Dionysian *intoxication*; literally speaking, it 'is sexuality and sensual pleasure'.[23] But the primitive analogy is further specified. The one and the other are the shadows cast by *Wille zur Macht*, which consequently founds their organic relation. It is a matter of the 'high points of life' that 'the religious sentiment of intoxication and sexual excitation' are 'admirably coordinated'.[24]

The sexual drive is, along with intoxication and cruelty, one of the privileged states through which man arrives at the state of lucidity (*Verklärung*) and plenitude.[25] It is 'notably in sexual love' that the sentiment of perfection or accomplishment is produced, which carries with it 'the extra-ordinary extension of a feeling of power'. But we need to recognize that this feeling of perfection is expressed less by a satisfaction sequential to filling a lack than as an impression of 'richness' and of overflowing. It derives from a state where the 'cerebral system' is overloaded (*überladen*) by sexual impulses.[26] The orgiastic sensation is thus an endogenous sensation of an excess rather than of an equality; or rather, the equality is in itself only realized by a transfer of cerebral energy.

Such is Nietzsche's last word on sexuality; defined as a superfluity, sexuality somehow schematizes the fundamental economy of Will to Power. There we recover its characteristics, refracted, it is true, by the limits of life which sexuality, in the last instance, transgresses.[27]

EROS AND LIBIDO

The Freudian discourse on sexuality begins from the moment when Freud examines a definition of sexuality restricted to genitality. The theory of infantile sexuality revealed in *Three Essays on the Theory of Sexuality* requires us to dissociate the physiological function, made possible by puberty, from the pregenital activity of the libido. Now, three characteristics stand out with respect to infantile sexuality: a relation of support (on the self-preservation drive), the existence of erogenous zones and the primacy of auto-eroticism.[28] These characteristics are bound together, since drives are partial by nature,[29] and because they are supported by the self-preservation drive, the original drive (oral) loses its object and becomes auto-erotic. Sexuality remains forever marked, in Freud's conception, by this original auto-eroticism, even when it makes itself the object of choice by the mediation of narcissism,[30] the moment when the Ego becomes the erotic object.

In that way, the idea of sexuality comes to be considerably enlarged in relation to the 'popular' conception,[31] which is bound to an exercise of the procreative function. The term *Libido* is used specifically to avoid this restriction, and otherwise to abandon the term 'sexuality' to connote a genital exercise. It is important to note that, amazingly, 'we are not yet in possession of a universally recognized sign that permits us to affirm with certitude the sexual nature of a process.'[32] Let us not hesitate to say that for Freud sexuality is an unknown – even if it is itself determined – given that no sure psychological criteria permits us to assign it to a given process. The sexual is thus what is accomplished through the genitals, but which is already there in 'the localized pleasure of the organs'. It is the application of a biogenetic principle, according to which the product of a process of development derives, in its mode of existence, from the existence of the process itself. At the limits, the sexual is neither the result of a (genital) process, nor its (pregenital) beginning, but rather the 'reason' for the process.

The determining role of sexuality for Freud thus proceeds paradoxically from its indetermination and its non-exclusivity; that is because the libido continually encounters an antagonistic principle that attests to its power in psychic life. There would be no such conflict for pure Libido; in other words, it is as an *alterity* that it expresses its power, as a contradiction to opposed drives, or to the reality principle.

With the emergence of the second dualism, sexuality is redefined on the basis of the mythological principle *Eros*, which appears as the prototype of the life-wish without eliminating it, and which is opposed to the principle of death. This hypostasis colours the Freudian Eros with a demiurgic aspect that could pass for a mythical cousin of Dionysus.

But Eros is none other than the libido; simply put, 'the libido of our sexual drives will coincide with the Eros of the poets and philosophers.'[33] Freud even presents it as a terminological change; henceforth, it will be necessary *to say* Eros when we speak of libido,[34] while justifying the adoption of a Greek term by a prudence with respect to its suggestive power. There is, in fact, as indicated by the Platonic connotation, an idealistic semantic charge which goes so far as to sublimate the term *Libido*, whose connotation is by contrast, 'materialistic'.[35] However, Libido remains the major concept from an explanatory point of view, from an *economic* standpoint; Eros symbolizes the effects of sexuality from a *dynamic* standpoint, in the framework of Freud's last theory of conflict. Moreover, Eros serves to produce a generic class of drives which encircle it, as an eminent modality of the life-wish.

For Nietzsche, sexuality serves to attest to the eminence of the Dionysian explosion of instincts. For Freud, it serves to *explain* phenomena experienced for the most part as conflictual. That is why, by correlation, Eros as the emissary of Dionysus is for Nietzsche a weapon against Christian asceticism, among others; his hedonism in this sense takes on a polemic import. For Freud, paradoxically, we do not find an equivalent valorization. Eros is a salutary and sympathetic god, but never sublimated nor valorized as such. It is an efficient adversary to Thanatos, but not invincible. Likewise, the libido through its horrors of development produces neurosis, such that it is evoked as an explanatory concept from a pathogenetic perspective, while Nietzsche evokes it as the salvific antidote in the framework of the rehabilitation of the Body.

Finally, sexuality is itself derived from Will to Power, which constantly absorbs it, and which thoroughly limits its autonomy; it is in the last instance merely the shadow cast by *Wille zur Macht*. For Freud, if Eros serves to produce life, it resides in the alpha and omega of human experience.

We can see how to specify further this divergence on an otherwise remarkably analogous thematic, via the activity of *cognition*, a terrain on which we feel the power of the drive in its sublimated form – given that this 'love of knowledge' reveals the affinity between love and cognition.

COGNITIVE INSTINCT AND THE DRIVE TO KNOW: BETWEEN LIBIDO AND POWER

Very soon there appears in the instinctive problematic a privileged question, that of the cognitive instinct (*Erkenntnistreib*).[36] We can grasp, from Nietzsche's enunciation of his theory of instincts, the meaning of this choice. The cognitive instinct is, first, the return of instinct to its source, life; but at the same time it expresses the power of the instinct, since knowledge is verified to be dependent on the instinctive eruption. That is why the *Erkenntnistreib*, or its doubles (*Wissentrieb* especially), is concurrently evoked by Nietzsche in two registers, as the mortal negation of life (knowledge as sickness) and as the manifestation of the generic power of instincts.

In *The Birth of Tragedy*, Socrates appears as the incarnation of the cognitive instinct, as the type of man for whom this instinct, monstrously developed, has eclipsed all others. But at the same time there shows through an admiration for this voracious logical instinct, this 'natural force, as we only meet in our surprise, full of fright at the greatest of the instinctive forces', this 'prodigious motor' which animates the quest for knowledge.[37]

In the collection of fragments entitled *Philosophy* (*Art and Cognition*), the cognitive instinct is systematically dismantled. There, we find the most pre-cise formulae of its function and sense. 'The cognitive instinct, enormous, insatiable . . . is a sign (*Zeichen*) that life has become old; the danger is also great that individuals will become ill (*schlecht*), and that is why their interest becomes greatly attached to the objects of cognition, whatever they might be.'[38] This hyper-development is expressed as a general qualitative decline. 'The instincts in general have become weak (*matt*) as well and no longer serve to rein in the individual.' Nietzsche here is thinking in particular of the German for whom 'the unlimited cognitive instinct is the consequence of an indigent life.'[39]

Another fragment hazards an analogy which carries for us a particular value in our comparison with Freud. 'The cognitive instinct without discernment' writes Nietzsche, 'resembles the blind sexual instinct, a sign of baseness.'[40]

The remedy is proposed there, again, by reference to Greek civilization; Greek philosophers are distinguished from the moderns in that 'they subjugate the cognitive instinct',[41] while the moderns are submerged in an 'unchained'[42] cognitive instinct, in both a proper and a figurative sense. The word of the day would thus be 'Mastery (*Bändigung*) over the cognitive instinct'.[43] Such is the superiority of the 'philosophy of tragic knowledge' which puts 'knowledge in the service of life' thanks to aesthetic expression.[44] It is also the secret behind the Italian Renaissance, as Burckhardt had revealed to Nietzsche.

Philosophy in the Tragic Age of the Greeks elaborates this conception. 'The uncontrolled instinct for knowledge is in itself as barbaric as the hatred for knowledge (*Wissenshass*) . . . . The Greeks, out of their respect for life . . . had mastered their own insatiable instinct for knowledge – because everything they learned, they also wanted to live.'[45] Inversely, the blind instinct for knowledge along with its rejection (erudition and barbarism of taste) led to the modern gymnasia which Nietzsche had criticized in the conferences of the same period. It is quite true that, as a note in the same vein says, 'the pleasure of thinking does not demonstrate a desire for truth'.

The misdeeds of the cognitive instinct are denounced in the first two *Untimely Meditations*, by way of the philistine science incarnated in D.F. Strauss. But it is the historian, as the 'physician of civilization',[46] who appears for Nietzsche to materialize the greatest of the misdeeds of a liberated instinct. The hypertrophy of the historical perspective manifests the negative effects of the cognitive instinct.

The desire for knowledge and cognition is naturally accompanied by a hypertrophy of memory and a decline in the function of *forgetting*. The historical instinct derives from the cognitive instinct and produces the same destructive effects. 'One rejoices that "science has begun to rule our lives" ... A life thus dominated is not worth much, because it is much less "living" and carries the seed less of life to come than of the former life, ruled not by knowledge but by instinct and powerful illusions.'[47]

The psychologist of *Human, All Too Human* naturally encounters the cognitive instinct in human instinctual psychography. It appears exactly that 'knowledge can only allow motives of pleasure and pain, utility and damage'[48] – we understand by this authentic anthropological knowledge, that of 'psychology'. From this moment the cognitive instinct, previously a symptom of decadence, becomes the object of close psychological analysis.

Then it appears that the sage, who wished to establish himself through his unique instinct for truth, is in fact 'made from impure metal', composed of 'a complicated interlacing of diverse motives and stimulations.'[49] It is thus a question of showing at work, under the apparent uniformity of mono-instinctualism, a dynamic developed amid a throng of petty instincts (*Triebchen*). The cognitive instinct is deceived into squandering itself, under the action of psychological analysis and the chemistry of representations.

Daybreak treats the cognitive instinct as an obstacle to the enjoyment of 'a strong, solid illusion' which consists of barbaric happiness.[50] This perspective opens with the diagnosis of *The Gay Science*; knowledge, far from being in reality something essentially opposed to the instincts, is only *a certain relation of instincts among themselves*.[51] More precisely, it is 'a result of different and contradictory instincts of laughter, pity, malediction'. It is pronounced and thought of as an event, insofar as the intellect, while seeming to decide, only registers a pondered solution which is disconnected from the debate among the instincts.

In the same work, Nietzsche remarks that it is paradoxically a fundamental error in the nature of knowledge which causes it to progress. This thought comes from Spinoza, for whom knowledge was 'something disinterested ... in which man's bad instincts would absolutely not participate.'[52] It is not by chance that, at this level of theory, the name of Spinoza is frequently invoked; it is he who, in giving knowledge the seal of joy, while donning it with disinterest, marks the instinctual implication of the cognitive instinct while denying it an impassioned character. At the same time, the cognitive instinct is characterized as an instinct of appropriation (*Eigentumstreib*) in the manner of the instincts of the hunt or of nourishment.[53]

This analysis shows that the cognitive instinct depends on a more fundamental activity. In *Beyond Good and Evil*, while examining the motivation of the philosopher, Nietzsche declares that 'I do not believe that an "instinct for knowledge" (*Trieb zur Erkenntnis*) is the father of philosophy, but that another instinct, here as elsewhere, only serves cognition (and mis-cognition!) as an instrument.'[54] For the sage, the instinct for philosophical knowledge proclaims a myriad of instincts, 'inspirational geniuses' which 'have already practiced philosophy'. It is to the extent that each instinct tends to dominate that it 'aspires to philosophize'. What is identified as the cognitive instinct is thus literally only Will to Power of the dominant instinct.

Nevertheless, this is not a simple fiction; Nietzsche immediately concedes that according to the sages 'one can truly have something like a cognitive instinct, something like a tiny independent clockwork that, well wound, works courageously without the essential participation of the reunited instincts of the sage'. In other words, the cognitive instinct has an alternative destiny of either being decomposed by the dynamic of the instincts which carry it, or to function apart, as a tiny autonomous mechanism which does not implicate the true 'interests'.

The *Erkenntnistrieb* is thus finally split for Nietzsche into a parallel routine, something like a 'complex' or an inoffensive *habitus*, on the one hand, and an expression derived from the spiritual Will to Power (*geistige Wille zur Macht*) on the other, while thought is once again reduced to a 'relation between the instincts'.

An aphorism from *The Will to Power* furnishes the final formulation to the question of *Erkenntnistrieb*. 'The so-called cognitive instinct is restored to an *instinct of appropriation and domination*.'[55] That is the purest enunciation of the evolution that Nietzsche ends by placing it between quotation marks, in order to signify that it only serves to refract the intellectual form of Will to Power. But at the same time, it appears as the origin from which emanates, through its development, every form of cognition (meaning, memory, etc.). The last word on the subject of cognition tends to link *knowledge* to *power*, by the phenomenon of the will refracted in the instinctive drive.

The instinct for knowledge, which Nietzsche denounces in detail throughout his work, Freud seems to encounter in his investigation of infantile sexuality. But this homonymy is an occasion for seeing two conceptions converging on the same object.

In the second of the *Three Essays on the Theory of Sexuality*, dedicated to infantile sexuality, Freud remarks that 'in the same period that the sexual life of the infant attains its first stage, from the third to the fifth year, we can locate the beginning of an activity which we attribute to the drive to seek or to know (*Wiss- oder Forschertrieb*).'[56] Freud is careful to add that 'it is not a theoretical interest, but a practical one' which carries this theoretical drive; it is the riddle of the sexual Sphinx which sustains this living interest.

However, having introduced the idea, Freud immediately specifies that 'the drive to know cannot be counted among the elementary compositional drives'. We recognize in that the Freudian principle of the limitation of drives. Where for Nietzsche *Wissentrieb* and *Erkenntnistrieb* constitute instincts in themselves,

Freud is careful to hierarchize the drive levels. *Wisstrieb* is thus not an autonomous instinct; it is not a drive in the same sense as sexuality or self-preservation. But we do not know, for that, how to derive it purely and simply. It cannot be 'submitted exclusively to sexuality', even though 'the relations to sexual life are very important'.

Wisstrieb thus poses a problem of identification. From whence does this non-sexual drive, intimately linked to sexuality, proceed? 'Its activity (*Tun*) expresses, on the one hand, a sublimated mode of mastery (*Bemächtigung*), while on the other hand it works with the energy of the pleasure of vision (*Schaulust*). It thus combines a requirement for mastery with an intellectual voyeurism. The drive to know thus arises from a drive for mastery and is fed by a pleasure linked to vision.

Freud is in accord with Nietzsche in linking this drive, elsewhere associated with the birth of intelligence, to a pathological phenomenon. In the theoretical considerations which accompany the study of 'the Ratman', Freud remarks that one regularly discovers in the histories of obsessional neurotics 'the apparition and precocious repression of the sexual drive of vision and knowledge.'[57] Thus the principal symptom of mental rumination (*Grübeln*) is that 'the process of thought itself is sexualized, whereas sexual pleasure which ordinarily is related to the content of thought is directed towards the very act of thinking and the satisfaction exhibited in attaining a cognitive result is like sexual satisfaction'.

The dysfunctional hyper-development of the cognitive drive is thus founded for Freud on a substitutive function of sexual satisfaction – just as for Nietzsche it expresses a disturbance in life and a refusal of the vital drive. But we have already seen that Nietzsche speaks of *Wissentrieb*, where Freud uses the term *Wisstrieb*; Nietzsche denounces the predominance of the tendency *to knowledge*, while Freud studies the overdevelopment of the tendency *to know*. It is true that in the two cases the imperious desire for knowledge is implicated for there we encounter the Freudian concept of *Wissbegierde*, which is adequately translated by the expression *libido sciendi*, literally, knowledge as the object of concupiscence. In a more restricted sense, it is synonymous with *Wisstrieb*.

In the fourth of the *Five Lectures on Psychoanalysis*, Freud signals that the desire to know is detached from the active form of the pleasure of vision, while the passive form of the pleasure of vision (*Schaulust*) gives birth to artistic and dramatic displays.[58] The pleasure of cognition is thus distinguished for Freud from the sensible aesthetic pleasure by the active character of the drive at work.

In his study of Leonardo da Vinci, Freud articulates a law for defining this type of instinct. In the case of an emotionally disturbed subject, a single instinct is found to be developed with an overdeveloped force and intensity, such as the desire for knowledge in Leonardo, and it is necessary to postulate that this 'overpowering' (*überstark*) instinct is apparent in the earliest infancy of the subject and that it owes its sovereignty (*Oberherrschaft*) over the other instincts to the representative function of the sexual drive. Moreover, Freud specifies further that this overdevelopment has the same effects in the case where the overdeveloped instinct is completely other than the drive for knowledge or seeking (*Förschertrieb*).[59] There is no denying that it is, not fortuitously, this type of drive which gives way to the articulation of the law of compensatory overdevelopment and that it is on this terrain that Freud's enunciations most closely resemble those of Nietzsche.

The particular imperialism of the cognitive instinct is linked to what is, according to the expression of a later text, 'a rejection of the drive for control (*Bemächtigungstrieb*) sublimated and elevated to the intellectual plane.'[60]

We see particularly well on this point how Nietzsche's and Freud's analyses manifest a remarkably convergent thematic in defining a common field, by means of two distinct interpretive principles.

2

THE UNCONSCIOUS AND CONSCIOUSNESS

If it is true that sexuality finds its mode of expression (*langage*) in the *Unconscious*, then we need to move our 'dialogue' between Freud and Nietzsche on to this new theme. This will also provide a means of coming to terms with the question of the relation between the drives and the psyche, posed in relation to a new principle[1] centred on the notion of the Unconscious, as the psychic translation of the drive.

THE UNCONSCIOUS IN NIETZSCHEAN PHILOSOPHY

The idea of an Unconscious appears in Nietzsche even as early as the inaugural lecture *Homer and Classical Philology*. Evoking the Homeric question, Nietzsche remarks that 'the intellectual (*Einsicht*) penetration into the fully heterogeneous laboratories of instincts and consciousness displaces the manner of posing the Homeric problematic.'[2] We should note that here the idea of *Instinktives* is opposed to that of consciousness; it is said that an equivalence is spontaneously postulated between instinct and the Unconscious. Instinct is that which is by nature definable in the *un*-conscious element; on the other hand, instinctive/unconscious and consciousness are two registers or orders which are symmetrically and radically opposed. These contraries constitute two incompatible processual modalities – whence the significant term *Werkstätte* – qualified by a respectively opposed taxonomy. Between these two *genres*, no *metabasis eis allo genos* is allowed. That is why their distinction, with all the attendant consequences, is the methodological point of departure for philology as Nietzsche conceives of it, beginning with the classical Homeric problem which for Nietzsche was so revelatory. The lack of clear discernment in philology consisted in confounding these two registers by reducing one to the other.

Nietzsche's point of departure follows directly upon this confusion. He posits a *princeps* requirement which gives substance to the formal differentiation of the instinctive register. Taken together with the account of the formal positional modality of the *un*-conscious, the Unconscious is thus installed from the outset at the heart of Nietzsche's thematic, with the instinctive register at its very epicentre. The Unconscious is in this first sense the most characteristic property of instinct, its universal predicament and, at the limit, its equivalent, its other name.

However, we will note, in Nietzsche's use of the term the Unconscious is not immediately hypostasized in principle, even if it functions as a principle. That the Unconscious *would* act as a principle is, in the extension of Schopenhauer's perspective (and as an element in the pre-Freudian conception of the Unconscious),[3] a constituent characteristic. But the inventory and analysis of the occurrences of the term in Nietzsche's work does not reveal any tendency, as it does for, say, Hartmann,[4] to substantialize the Unconscious by raising it to the level of a first, supremely explanatory, principle. In other words, unconscious determination is omnipresent, that is to say it is implicated everywhere that the instinctive register intervenes, but everything proceeds as if it is not detached from what could be posited as *upokeimenon*. We could summarize this general impression, which is disengaged from the economy of the term in Nietzsche's work, by saying that the unconscious is everywhere in natural, human reality, but we never actually encounter it directly, in whole or in part.

So it appears, in *The Birth of Tragedy*, that Dionysus gives free rein to instinctive and unconscious forces, while Apollo is weighed down by the demands for form imposed by consciousness. 'The dialectic' says Nietzsche in this sense, 'carries an optimistic element, which celebrates its triumph in every argument and which can breathe only in the cold clarity of consciousness.'[5] We see that the 'cold clarity of consciousness' is associated with Apollonian (and Socratic) values, against the hot opacity of Dionysian tragedy. Form clarifies, to the extent that it organizes; in that, it is associated with consciousness. In the other direction, the outburst of instinctive forces is deployed in a privileged manner in the Unconscious. But the Unconscious is not, properly speaking, a central concept in *The Birth of Tragedy* (in the same way as instinct or intelligence figures there); we hear it designating less a formal category than the shadow cast by Dionysian phenomena. More than the Unconscious itself, it is *to be unconscious* with respect to instinct that Nietzsche valorizes.

In another respect, for Nietzsche the Unconscious affirms the identity and the dynamic of people (*Völker*). He refers to a collective identity which holds hidden cultural riches. Nietzsche discovers this popular unconscious at work in the Homeric epic, in Greek tragedy, and when he engages in his 'critique of the present' the popular unconscious is the touchstone that gauges the health of a civilization. The hypertrophy of memory linked to a modern historical sense goes together with the primacy of conscious values. Inversely, the great Greek people, who know how to forget when they need to, conceal a vigorous Unconscious. Historical memory is associated with consciousness, just as the function of forgetting expresses the Unconscious. It is no accident that the second *Untimely Meditation* opens with the evocation of the herd, an image which links unconsciousness with innocence,[6] nor is it accidental that Nietzsche, a critic of the German schools and an opponent of scientific philistinism, adored the false values of trans-lucidity, 'this salutary unconsciousness, this collective sleep which preserves a people's health.'[7] He opposes this to the slogan of popular culture – 'Wake up!' – as the authentic 'measure of the health of a civilization.'

In such a way Nietzsche links sickness and consciousness, health and unconsciousness. Consciousness, in place of being synonymous with liberation, will be linked to trickery, while the Unconscious will be invested with curative virtues (*heilsame Unbewusstsein*).

With the advent of the psychological project, the function of the Unconscious is modified at the same time as its level of intervention changes. If, as Nietzsche says in *Human, All Too Human, the individuum is a dividuum*,[8] that is to say a coupling of a selfish (*égoïste*) instinct with the motivation that conceals it, the Unconscious is placed at the *nexus* of this dividuum. Humans love themselves with a distracted love, but he acts through motivations that mask this primary motor from themselves. In the wake of La Rochefoucauld, the moralist intervenes in this precise spot where self-love is signified by its mask. The moralist pitilessly leads the mobile Unconscious to consciousness, and rejects the conscious motif. In this way, the moralist demystifies by discovering the 'vile, despicable matter' hidden under 'the most magnificent colours'.[9]

We can see how the intervention of the Unconscious is modified. In the preceding perspective, it designated the mode of inherence of instinct, as revealed in tragedy; it served to valorize the authentic mode of existence, that of obscurity. That is why it was grasped anonymously, in the collective Unconscious of a people, even as an apparatus of human nature – thus its salvific virtues. The Unconscious designated the intra-individual breach relative to an ideal nature, less an effusion than a dissimulation.[10] This is the sense of the manifestations of the Unconscious throughout *Human, All Too Human*, *The Voyager and His Shadow* and *Assorted Opinions and Maxims*. Each aphorism, sentence or maxim points to an aspect of these manifestations.

Again, the Unconscious is less a principle than the chronic regime of human action, the scission endlessly reactivated between the will and the deed, the true and the false, the said and the unsaid. It always designates *illusion*, but grasped nevertheless in the immanence of moral comportment. That humans would forever do something other than what they think they are doing, constitutes the *misrecognition* at the heart of human reality and universalizes the Unconscious as the mode of expression (*langage*) of this chronic misrecognition.

But Nietzsche returns, as before, to dismiss consciousness from its pretensions to the status of a principle. This implies a reversal of the conscious–unconscious relation that constitutes misrecognition; what is originally given as primary is only the most superficial, which conceals the true principle. From this perspective Nietzsche will engage in a battle against *conscientious-ness*.[11] In every significant text, Nietzsche effects this reversal. We can see, in the glimmer of what preceded it, the meaning of Nietzsche's focus; the primacy accorded to the Conscious is the principal signal of the structure of misrecognition. Thus Nietzsche engages a complete anthropology which he must overtake and reject because of this bias toward consciousness.

From the two preceding positions, it is necessary to keep in mind two overlapping requirements; first, to reject the illusion of misrecognition, and second, to conceive of illusion as Being itself. This explains how 'the

Unconscious, the mode of expression (*langage*) of illusion' is used, alternatively or simultaneously, by Nietzsche in order either *to denounce illusion or to valorize it*, in the two cases that produce the phrase. By correlation, the Unconscious will be thought of as a *mask* and *means to health*, opposed to consciousness as mask and malady. It is during the period of *Daybreak* and *The Gay Science* that this conception is established.

'"Know thyself",' says an aphorism, 'is all of science',[12] but this science is, to be precise, predicated on the formal capacity of *non-conscious* experience. Self-awareness implies a becoming-conscious of the subordination of the Conscious to the Unconscious. An aphorism in *The Gay Science* precisely states a long-developed conception. 'Consciousness is only the last and the latest stage in organic development and as such is less developed and less strong.'[13]

Consciousness and the Unconscious are thus judged with respect to a developing organic system to which they are related as constituting two moments. Within this developmental regime (*Entwickelung*), consciousness appears as a belated acquisition. The development of the organic system is taken to mean a continuing adaptation which goes along with a relaxation of the morphological structure. What comes later in the history of the organism comes in decreasing degrees of perfection.[14]

We have touched the very heart of Nietzschean physiology. It should be represented as a hierarchical organization whose *centre* is 'the preserving bonds of instincts'.[15] It is there that we must locate the Unconscious, but we must not thereby locate consciousness only at the periphery, subordinated to the centre. Every disturbance of the relation of forces generates a *pathology* whereby 'the Conscious gives birth to innumerable mistakes which make an animal, a human, perish sooner than is necessary.'[16] In other words, if the 'regulatory' Unconscious were not 'also excessively more powerful' than consciousness, humanity would succumb to the least peccadillo; the least idea would be lethal. Consciousness is thus a function acquired very late which is neither mature nor developed; for this reason it is a threat to the organism. It is thus salutary that it should be 'thoroughly tyrannized'.[17] Such is the Unconscious, the organism's providential tyrant.

That is the proper representation of the organism. General misrecognition consists in taking consciousness for a great constant, to which we attribute the unity of the organism, where we would need to speak of intermittences. Against this illusory conscientiousness, we need to return consciousness to its subordinate role of a *variable*, reserving the status of *constant* for the unconscious instinct. That is the salutary return of organic mathematics, the true Copernican revolution which will discover that the Conscious revolves around the Unconscious.[18] Nietzsche expresses this with a remarkable clarity.

Returning to the 'problem of consciousness' in a later aphorism, Nietzsche expresses well the modality by saying that it appears from the moment when 'we begin to understand how we might escape it.'[19] He evokes the physiology and history of animals as support. As a result, consciousness is only a non-necessary and non-universal predicate of life and action.

> In fact, we would like to think, feel, will, remember, we would like as well to 'act' in every sense of the term; nevertheless, none of that requires that we 'enter into consciousness' .... All of life would be possible without regarding ourselves in such a mirror. And so the greater part of life is in fact played out for us without any such mirror – and most assuredly this is the case for our thinking, feeling, willing life, however vexing, for us as for philosophers of old.

In sum, 'consciousness is *superfluous* with respect to essential things' (*Hauptsache*).

Nietzsche goes so far as to imply that consciousness is only developed under the pressure of the 'need to communicate' as a consequence of social life. Thus 'the thought which becomes conscious is only the most infinitesimal part, we can say the most superficial, the worst, because there is only this conscious thought which has *a place in speech*, that is to say *in signs of exchange*.'[20] 'Consciousness does not truly belong to individual human existence, but to a common nature and to the existence of the herd.'[21] Beyond what is expressed as consciousness, thought loses its individual and personal reality; it is reduced to a specific approximation which irreversibly distorts it. That is why 'the growth of consciousness is a threat.'[22] This is a fundamental text, where we see that access to individuality passes for Nietzsche through the Unconscious, the non-falsifying mode of expression (*langage*) of the instinctual centre; it is what gives individuality its formal *value*. But we must point out that, in this text, the Unconscious is present *in absentia*; the Conscious is alone rejected. The Unconscious is implicitly omnipresent as a function of instinctive regulation, but Nietzsche does not claim too deterministic a role for it, at the price of impoverishing this other sphere not exhausted by that of the Conscious. It is sufficient to suggest that the Unconscious designates this region in which the 'essential things' of human reality happen. Where the Conscious begins to speak, the essential has already happened – and is lost or concealed behind a mask.

In the same movement, Nietzsche expels the most profound instinctive activity at work in consciousness. In *Beyond Good and Evil*, it is not fortuitous that he proceeds to a demonstration by the example of the philosopher. Already in the preceding text, *The Gay Science*, Nietzsche had evoked the image of the traditional philosopher suffering when the pretensions of the Conscious are humbled. Conscientiousness, for Nietzsche as for Freud, is the transgression of philosophy. The philosopher is the 'artisan' of the Conscious, and philosophizing activity is the supreme pretension of conscious activity. That is why Nietzsche diagnoses that

> we can include the greatest part of conscious thought among instinctive activities, even in the case of philosophical thought ... 'conscious being' is not *opposed* in some decisive sense to the instinctive – the greater part of the conscious thought of the philosopher is secretly driven by his instincts and constrained to follow determined paths.[23]

This is not to call back into question the conscious/instinctive registers, but to indicate, on the contrary, their natural consequence. The primacy of instinct (conforming to the preceding physiological theory) implies the derivation, in the last instance, of the Conscious from the Unconscious. It comes back to affirm that *there is no pure Conscious*; it is inhabited by the instinctive as a sort of un-Conscious.

As *On the Genealogy of Morals* further specifies, human consciousness resembles a narrow window,[24] a precarious breach in 'the machinic activity' whose motor is no other than the *Instinktives*. Notably, this implies the outcry of consciousness, reduced to a 'bundle of affects';[25] thus we hear that the great principal activity of the organism (*Haupttätigkeit*) is unconscious.[26] 'Consciousness only habitually appears when the whole wishes to be subordinated to a higher totality.' This *princeps* activity is thus ramified in every activity, even the most conscious thought.

Nietzsche constantly returns to the metaphor of surface (*Oberfläche*) in order to characterize the Conscious.[27] The Unconscious thus appears correlatively as the foundation or the interior. It *figures* in this sense as the thing-in-itself, posed beyond the question of its status in the philosophy of *The Will to Power*. At the moment when the ultimate synthesis is constructed, where is the Unconscious?

We first find there the diagnosis we already knew: 'Consciousness expresses an imperfect and frequently ailing personal state,' while 'every perfect act is precisely unconscious and involuntary.'[28] It is thus necessary to denounce as erroneous the idea according to which 'the value of an action must depend on what rises in consciousness,'[29] or rather '*becoming-conscious* is a sign (*Zeichen*) of the fact that true morality, that is to say the instinctive certitude of the action, has gone all to Hell.'[30] Morality is here an example of a fundamental physiological law. 'In every becoming-conscious is expressed an ailment of the organism.' It is in fact the proof of something new that implies the pangs of consciousness, which in turn implies *tension*.[31] Thus it is necessary to conclude that perfection only arises from the Unconscious, and reject as false the 'presupposition' that 'consciousness is the higher, superior state.'[32] On the contrary, 'the intensity of consciousness is found in an inverse relation to the lability (*Leichterei*) and celerity of cerebral transmissions.'[33]

Nietzsche comes back to reject the pretension to objectivity of the 'pretended' facts of consciousness,[34] on which is founded Self-observation or introspec-tion; that is why the real question is one of becoming-conscious (*Bewusstwerden*). If consciousness can only *pretend* to the primacy that it claims for itself, it is necessary to put 'becoming conscientious' in relation to the dynamic of the organism that requires and *proportions* it, as only the becoming-conscious of what is felt to be, in principle, *useful*.[35] Pathology begins when the threshold of consciousness is overstepped.

The process of becoming-conscientious implies one of simplification, of schematization, of adaption, which expresses the 'phenomenality of the interior world'. In other words, 'everything that becomes conscious is an ultimate phenomenon, a conclusion, and thus the cause of nothing.'[36] Here we glimpse the meaning of Nietzsche's final theory of consciousness; by dismissing these pretensions, we take away the efficiency that is reported in *Wille zur Macht*. Consequently we see that the insistence on unconscious givens is further specified, as an invaluable indication that the Conscious is the *cause* of nothing, and thus that *Will to Power* is in the last instance the final *cause*.

Consciousness is conceived as a 'process' which, lured by the coordination of external sensations, is progressively centred on the biological individual through a process of deepening and internalization;[37] in this way, it must be understood as being related to the 'overall organic process'. 'All of conscious life "labours" above all in the service of a vital nobility' (*Lebensteigerung*).[38] That is to say that, 'in the enormous multiplicity of internal events of the organism, the part that becomes conscious for us is only one path among others.' Nietzsche goes so far as to envision that consciousness, whose role is only secondary, 'nearly indifferent and superfluous', is 'destined to disappear and to be replaced by a perfect automatism', by nature unconscious.[39] This clearly signifies that consciousness is only a precarious intermediary formation; *our relation with the 'external world' developed it.*[40] Far from being 'the superior case', it is only 'a means of communicability'.[41] We understand that it is developed as a result of the requirements of communication (*Verkehr*), and thus not the rudder but merely a sounding device (*une organe de la direction*) for the organism.

The theory of *Will to Power* denounces the 'capital error' of psychologists and philosophers who endow consciousness with a measure of clarity and who consider 'non-evident representations as an inferior modality of representation'.[42] It is necessary to affirm it against what is only the unilateral point of view of consciousness itself, that 'what moves out of our consciousness and so becomes obscure to us can still be perfectly clear'. This reversal, demanded from the point of view of the will, leads us to reject 'the insensible overestimation of consciousness.' This is sometimes posed as a superfluity – insofar as 'the greatest mass of movements have nothing to do with consciousness;'[43] and sometimes as a sickness – 'the degradation of life is essentially conditioned by the extraordinary capacity for error by consciousness.'[44] Finally, sometimes consciousness is posed as a fiction, given that 'all of our conscious motives are surface phenomena; behind them lurk the struggles of our instincts ... the struggle for power' (*Kampf um die Gewalt*).[45] In other words, 'that which we call "Conscious" and "Mind" are only the means by which *a conflict tries to survive.*'[46] In this sense, it is 'an organ in the same sense as the stomach.'[47] At the limit 'there is in man as many "consciousnesses" as there are essences which constitute the body.'[48]

We can conclude that the devalorization of the Conscious, present since the beginning in Nietzsche, takes in its final meaning a valorization of Power. The Unconscious is implicated in the intersection between a Conscious, relativized and subordinated, and a Will to Power established in *ultima ratio*. The rejection of the 'conscious world' is founded, in the final analysis, on the fact, sufficient to constitute an axiology, that it cannot be valued as a point of resolution *for value*

(*Wertausgangpunkt*), that is to say that it cannot satisfy a *princeps* requirement, the 'necessity of an objective axiological position'.[49]

However, by the same token we see that the Unconscious is for Nietzsche more of a stake than a central concept. It is found somehow along the path to the capital problem; it conditions it, but to a secondary degree. That is why the substantive *Unbewusstsein* is relatively rare in Nietzsche; the Unconscious intervenes much more often as an adjective than as a principle. The basic opposition is one between consciousness, or the Conscious (*Bewussheit*), and instinct (or the instinctive); later, it comes to be between consciousness and Will (to Power). So it is that Nietzsche can write that 'one must have *a mixture of consciousness and will* in any complex organic being.'[50] In the first opposition, consciousness is subordinated to the instinctive; in the second, we are told that 'the end is not an amelioration of consciousness' but 'an elevation of Power'.[51] In the two cases, the Unconscious is an important condition, but it is only a stake.

In the first case, the Unconscious indicates an instinctive determination; in the second, it manifests the fundamental Will. It thus expresses the work of fundamental forces, but as a shadow cast by those forces (instinct, Will, Power). It is the nodal point whereby consciousness is continually resorbed, and whereby the instinctual Will originates and derives its impulse. It is, under this double heading, a greatly revealing intermediary, as an indication that something essential is at stake in human reality. In this sense, the importance of the unconscious processes in man manifests their real nature, which is instinct and Will. But it is also the limit-point. 'Will to Power: to become conscious of the Will to Live . . .',[52] indicates Nietzsche, writing in 1888. While *Will to Power* is simultaneously given as the principle of the Unconscious, we read it in both its necessity and its transcendence, because insomuch as it is Will, it is the Unconscious of the Will to Live, as well as its becoming-conscious.

TOPICS OF THE UNCONSCIOUS IN FREUD

With Freud, the Unconscious ceases to be a *principle* and becomes the object of a meta-psychological codification, a double point of view, at once *topical* and *dynamic*.

From the first point of view, Freud's primary concern is to make known the existence of a 'system' or an instance of the psychic apparatus that is endowed with formal characteristics and functionally distinguishable from others.[53] In addition, what might have passed, in the pre-Freudian lens, as a degree of consciousness of the Other by metaphor, for Freud the Unconscious as a system is set apart from psychic co-systems (Conscious, Preconscious). That is why what for Nietzsche is a spatial metaphor becomes for Freud a structured topics, a fiction of knowledge charged to represent the function of the psyche as 'psychic space'.

From the second point of view, the word Unconscious functions to designate a type of specific psychic process and conflictual relation, which situate in the unconscious psychic system those 'psychic contents' which could not be acceded to the Preconscious–Conscious system, such that the very notion of the Unconscious is literally derived from a repression. This constitutes the fundamental psychic action which functionally requires an unconscious system. Indeed, even though the repressed does not fully comprise the Unconscious, repression serves to define it.

In that way, Freud is clearly opposed to the Nietzschean conception of the Unconscious as an actualization of the positivity of instincts. The reactionary regime of instincts is indeed characterized by a process analogous to repression, but it is precisely a matter of Nietzsche's pathology of instincts, of which morality gives such rich illustrations.[54] For Freud, repression serves to designate the unconscious process in its dynamic reality. What is produced by repression is essentially unconscious; this is the principal contribution of Freudian clinical practice.

In this sense, Freud is able to affirm that 'the theory of repression is the cornerstone on which rests the whole edifice of psychoanalysis.'[55] It is the main process that governs the relation between the Conscious and the Unconscious. In that way is necessarily posed the question of *representation*, which we saw above is sidestepped by Nietzsche,[56] but we understand at this level of comparison the meaning of this difference in conception.

For Freud, the contents called Unconscious are the *representatives* of the drives. Here repression specifically refers to representatives–representations; the materials of repression are none other than the contents of the Unconscious system. But repression 'properly speaking', as an action, is preceded somehow passively in time by an 'originary repression' by which is constituted a refused content which goes on to exercise a mechanical attraction and requires the reactivation of repression. This unconscious labour is manifested by the 'return of the repressed' in which the psychic content seeks a means of return. The schema implies a fundamental reactivity of the Unconscious which contrasts with its Nietzschean homology.

This difference is confirmed from an *economic* point of view in which the meta-psychological representation is achieved. The Freudian Unconscious is economically characterized as a 'primary process', which implies that representations allow psychic energy to pass, in opposition to the 'secondary process' characteristic of the Preconscious–Conscious system, to which psychic energy is linked before passing from one representation to another.

We see that the economic reality of the Unconscious only expresses the originary principle of Freudian economics. It is in sum the most privative characteristic – an absence of obstacle and clearing – which serves to characterize the Unconscious. We are finally at the antipodes of Nietzsche's valorization of the Unconscious, as the direct mode of expression (*langage*) of instinct.

This allows us as well to understand that for Nietzsche the Unconscious is not properly speaking a *psychological* concept, while *representation* properly characterizes consciousness and even indicates its limits. Nietzsche's organic Unconscious is much richer in that it transcends all responsibility. It is only the shadow cast by the thing-in-itself, instinct and then Will to Power. In contrast, for Freud the Unconscious designates a certain regime of representation (primary process). Additionally, the drive can name the thing-in-itself; the Unconscious, which is its mode of expression (*langage*), designates a representational sphere accessible to a psychological, clinical investigation. In this way, the concept ceases to be simply descriptive or overly connotative, in order to become explanatory. At most, Freud owes a debt to a tradition going back to Schopenhauer and culminating with Nietzsche, which had denounced the reductive 'conscientiousness' of psychism, but that only comes into play as an incitement to raise the Unconscious to the rank of an explanatory concept.

THE ID AND THE SELF

If sexuality and the Unconscious are for Freud something other than principles, this raises the problem of the nature of what Freud designates as the Id in the second topic, where the Id seems precisely to possess *a nature*, rather than characterizing a structure or designating a process as before. We need to reconcile this with what Nietzsche presents as a principle, for in many respects Nietzsche's *Selbst* bears a remarkable resemblance to Freud's *Es*. Freud himself saw this as a major analogy, as we have already seen.[57]

The Self forms with the Ego a homology to the Freudian couple Id–Ego. The relation is described through the use of an anthropomorphic vocabulary. We can see this most clearly in a passage from *Thus Spoke Zarathustra*, where we find this dialogue: 'Your "Self" mocks your Ego and its arrogant restrictions .... The Self says to the Ego: "Suffer now!", so the Ego suffers .... The Self says to the Ego: "Rejoice now!", so the Ego rejoices.'[58] So the Self in this instance is present behind consciousness, whose 'sense and spirit' are only 'playthings' for the Self. 'It governs and is also the master of the Ego.' The Self is characterized as 'the groomer of the Ego and the prompter of its ideas'.

This characterization corresponds literally to Freud's Id, and so the analogy could only have been imposed by Freud himself. We remember that in *The Ego and the Id* we hear the Superego 'whisper' commands to the Ego in order to signify the dependence of the latter on the former. 'Be thus', 'don't be thus'.[59] Indeed, the Ego appeals to the Id for love in the Ego-Ideal. 'Look, you can love me, I resemble so much an object.'[60] The Ego lives under a double dependence, a first, silent one which comes from the Id, and a second, verbalized dependence which provides the moral reference. The Id is thus the motor of the Ego, in the direction of the drives, but it is taken in relation to the Law. If the Id breaches the Ego's privilege, as 'in the non-personal things virtually necessary by nature in our being,'[61] it is just as much a 'chaos' that limits the Superego.

There is a naturalistic connotation in the idea of the Id as a reservoir of drives, but everything proceeds as if Freud forestalls this latent idea of nature by a description of the processes and effects, which only impose a functional dependence. For Nietzsche the Self is immediately valorized by serving to argue for the authenticity of the *Body* as the *ultima ratio* of consciousness reduced to the rank of an artifice:

> 'Ego', you say, and you are proud of this word. But there is a greater one – which you do not wish to believe – it is your body and its great reason. It does not say 'Ego', but it makes the Ego . . . . Behind your thoughts and feelings . . . , there is a powerful governor and an unknown sage, whose name is 'Self'. It lives in your body, it is your body.[62]

The Self is thus the corporeal identity of the individual, which is also domination (*Herrschaft*) and materializes Will to Power, the body being the creation of Will (*Herrschaftsgebilde*). Thus it is the *truth* of the Ego, defined at the same time as power and wisdom.

We now understand in what way Nietzsche's conception is fundamentally *physiological* and somatic in the strong sense. The Id, if it fills a comparable function vis-à-vis the Ego, is nevertheless *not* the Body, an entity which does not have a status for Freud. It is the root of the drive, which itself is the limit of the somatic and the psychic. In addition, its effects do not express a providential teleology – such that the Body is defined by Nietzsche as material Providence; at most, one can say that the Id is 'open at its extremity from the somatic side.'[63] And even though everything depends on it, it wants nothing – 'it does not promote any general will';[64] even though all order proceeds from it, 'it has no organization' in itself; even though it gives being to every psychic motion, the Id is revealed as a remarkable vacuity.

So, if the Id seems to be analogous to the Self, it comes back to an entirely other reality, shown by the fact that for Nietzsche the Self forms an exclusive couple with the Ego, draining all authentic need-to-be, whereas for Freud the Superego imposes its own specific mode of domination. From the beginning of Nietzsche's writing corpus, the call to the Self is a command: 'Wish for a Self!'[65] It leads the campaign against those who deny the body, who deprive themselves of the health furnished by the great wisdom of the Body. All of morality, seen as a sickness, is in this sense a negation of the voice of the Body. The Superego would thus only be a sickness, an infection in the wisdom of the Body; that is why it would be a pathological symptom rather than an apparatus!

Consequently, we understand that the Ego can only reflect the order of the Self in a minimal interpretation; it expresses the vital norm of instinct. For Freud, there is a *sui generis labor* of reaction formations. On the other hand, the Ego's health is only an aspect of its linkage to the Self. For Freud this remains a problem which is at the same times a requirement. 'Wo Es war (where Id was) soll Ich Werden (Ego shall be).'[66] Indeed, it is a demand that is also *cultural*.[67]

In other words, for Nietzsche the Ego's wisdom lies in the recognition of its true master. As an emanation from the Body–Self, the Ego's only authentic vocation is to be absorbed by the principle which precedes it by nature; it must immerse itself in the flow that produced it. What a contrast, finally, with the Freudian image of drainage; the Id drains, like the Zeider Zee, but in bits and pieces[68] it would be absorbed, a movement that is the inverse of Nietzschean refusion.

SUBJECT AND ILLUSION

Nietzsche supports his critique of the 'overestimation of the Conscious' on a critique of the substantialist illusion of 'the subject' which attains its fullest development in his last writings.

Naturally, the central object of the critique is the Cartesian *Cogito*:

> 'There is thought; therefore there is a thinking subject', that is what Descartes argues. But this only in turn poses as 'an *a priori* truth' our belief in the concept of *substance*. To say that there is thought, there must also be something 'that thinks', which is only a means of formulating, proper to our grammatical habits that suppose an acting subject for every act.[69]

Now 'the error in observation is to believe it is *I* who "does" this, who "suffers" that, who "has" this, who "possesses" such-and-such a quality.' On the contrary, 'if we renounce the soul, the "subject", the preliminary condition of substance completely disappears.' This even calls into play a 'critique of the concept of cause'[70] in terms of a substance-cause.

It is important to understand that 'the "subject" is not a thing which *acts* but a simple fiction,' a declaration which, for Freud, inscribed Nietzsche as the fundamental opposition to the tradition of philosophical conscientiousness that resisted the psychoanalytic theory of the Unconscious.[71] Nietzsche's whole critique of substantialism thus clears the way for Freud.

However it is helpful to remember the stake of the critique within Nietzsche's project itself. It is no accident that the critique is systematized from the point of view of *Wille zur Macht*. By destroying the claim in the belief in the subject as artificial, the critique seeks to attain the notion of 'reality' or 'being' from which the subject is derived. The positive counterpart is the affirmation that 'the degree of our feelings of life and power ... give us our measure of "being", of "reality".' Thus it is the reality of all reality.

The critique of the fiction of the 'subject' is thus destined to diagnose 'the terminology for our belief in those moments of our highest feelings of reality.' The hypothesis of identity gives birth to a high feeling of mastery and of identification with reality. If Nietzsche affirms that 'the "subject" is the fiction that many *similar* states within us are really the effect of the same substrate', it is in order to accentuate the fact that 'it is we who have created the "identity" of these states.' The phenomenality serves here to support the creativism of *Wille zur Macht*, whereas for Freud the impossibility of the 'subject' only denotes a lack. In other words, if Nietzsche and Freud seem remarkably close in the critique of the idea of the 'subject' as a conscious substrate, the ends of each critique are quite different. For one, the ruins of the subject gives way to feelings of willed power; for the other there is only a lack, which Freud will name the *death-wish*.[72]

3

DREAMS AND SYMBOLISM

The Unconscious, in its symbolic value, finds its 'crowning' expression in *dreams*. Not fortuitously, this theme is the site of some essential developments, for both Nietzsche and Freud. Our thematic comparison thus will pass through dreams, to find a kind of recapitulation there.

THE APOLLONIAN CONCEPTION OF DREAMS

Beginning with Nietzsche's first great work, *The Birth of Tragedy*, dreams play an essential role, serving to characterize the 'aesthetic world' relevant to the Apollonian principle, as opposed to the aesthetic world of Dionysian *intoxication* (*Rausch*).[1] Dreams are thus one of the four terms around which the whole work develops.

'Dream worlds' rest on the compelling idea of the plastic arts and poetry, of the 'beautiful illusion', which goes back to an enjoyment taken in 'direct comprehension of form'. The Apollonian artist, as a practitioner of beautiful illusion and form, exploits an aptitude that Nietzsche presents as pertaining to an anthropological basis. 'Our most intimate being, the common foundation we share with all, experiences dreams in itself as a profound pleasure and a fortunate necessity.'[2]

Apollo figures as the deification of 'this fortunate necessity of oneiric experience.' In other words, that which is experienced (in a quasi-physiological sense) as the dreamer's pleasure is elevated to the rank of *an aesthetic value* under the name of Apollo. In this way, the 'inner world of imagination', of which dreams are the privileged instances, is consecrated. We can see how, from the very beginning, Nietzsche makes a tight link between dreams and art. It is more than an analogy, for dreams are experiential necessities which find their organ and 'language' (*langage*) in aesthetic (essentially plastic) expression.

Thus dreams are naturally valorized as the vestibule of aesthetic creation, and even as an expression of the good life. 'The profound consciousness of a helpful and beneficial nature in sleep and dreams is at the same time the symbolic homology of the gift of prophecy and of the arts in general, by which life is rendered possible and worth living.'[3]

It is really not important what type of aesthetic creation is involved; the ones linked to dreams are those in which the *formal* and *figurative* elements dominate. We can find a 'principle of individuation' at work in dreams which organizes their diversity by imposing limits of measure, whose form is precisely unity. The 'affectivity of the dream' is thus the accession, via the scintillation of the senses, to the level of appearances.[4]

In Greek tragedy, the Apollonian oneiric element effectively expresses the 'state' of the artist, that is to say 'his unity with the intimate substrate of the universe' in terms of *symbolic oneiric images*.[5] The organizing representative element ponders Dionysian excess by elaborating it in form. In the first use of the concept, the register of dreams is opposed to that of intoxication; it is reattached to a formal expression of variety. That is why Nietzsche paradoxically makes Apollo, the god of light, into that of dreams. In the deep gloom of night, where is instituted 'the Apollonian state of dreams, the world of the day is veiled, and a new world, clearer, more comprehensible, more tangible and yet more shadowy is offered to our eyes in a continual state of change.'[6]

This conception is based on an inversion of the waking/dream axis, to the benefit of the second term.

> Though it is certain that of the two halves of life, the waking part and the dreaming part, the first seems to us incomparably preferable, more important, more estimable, more worthy of being lived and even alone to be lived, I would like, though it appears paradoxical, to advance precisely the opposite opinion of dreams in favour of this base, full of the mystery of our being, of which we are the mere appearance.[7]

It is not so much that the dream constitutes, insofar as it is appearance, a lesser degree of being with respect to reality, but for Nietzsche dreams express the essence, the core of truth around which human reality gravitates, whose manifestations are only appearances. In the last analysis, dreams hold this privilege by constituting *the appearance of appearance*.[8] Reality being appearance, dreams are such only to a second degree; for this reason, they are valued as 'yet higher satisfactions of the universal aspiration to appearance' (*Suchen nach dem Schein*).

In the first use of the idea of dreams, they designate a mixture of an aesthetic principle and concrete experience; at the same time, there is a question between dreams as a metaphysical mode of being and dreams as a daily activity. This intimate union of psychology and metaphysics characterizes a usage which would later be transcended. In the works which follow the Beyreuth rupture, everything proceeds as if Nietzsche will again turn his attention to the positive characteristics of oneiric activity, whence, as we will see, his attention to the physiology of the dreamer. That does not mean that the metaphysical *aura* of the concept will immediately disappear, but the stakes will be displaced, while an immanent analysis of oneiric experience will be developed. Nietzsche's *psychology* also includes a *Traumlehre*. In one of the first aphorisms in *Human, All Too Human*, Nietzsche links metaphysical illusion to oneiric experience, speaking in this sense of 'misunderstanding dreams'.[9]

Oneiric experience is related to a truly *ethnological hypothesis*. 'During dreams, man believes in common, elementary ages of civilization in order to get to know a *second real world*; here we find the origins of all metaphysics.' Without dreams, we would not have found the occasion for a scission from the world (*Scheidung der Welt*). The decomposition of body and soul (*Zerlegung in Seele und Leib*) is equally reattached to the oldest conception of the dream, as it is to the hypothesis of a corporeal envelope for the soul; it is thus the origin of all belief in the spirits and probably also of belief in gods.

The dream is evoked here as the primordial experience, in the primitive Unconscious, that founds the metaphysical belief in another world. But we must take this hypothesis in a realistic sense; primitive revery is the process which acts upon the real world and reveals there a breach. Through this shift, from oneiric experience to conscious (*vigile*) experience, the metaphysical fiction of another world is introduced, thanks to the process of *Scheidung/Zerlegung* (scission/decomposition).

Through the mediation of the dream, Nietzsche's critique of metaphysics finds its *anthropological* foundation. The conclusion of the aphorism clearly indicates that '"the dead continue to live *because* they appear alive in dreams": thus people formerly reasoned for centuries.' Nietzsche openly borrows this hypothesis from one of the most celebrated contemporary theories of the origin of religious belief.[10]

A little later on, two aphorisms develop the ontogenetic hypothesis formulated in the first aphorism; we see there the further specification of the articulation between the metaphysical critique that permits Nietzsche's *psychology* to be posed, on the one hand, and the theory of dreams on the other. This development in turn works in two directions; one, to determine the relation between 'dreams and civilization,'[11] and two, to analyse the 'logic of dreams.'[12]

Haeckel's hypothesis, according to which 'ontogeny recapitulates phylogeny', is given free rein.[13] Remarking that 'the function of the brain which is the most affected by sleep is memory,' Nietzsche immediately adds that 'memory does not rest during sleep, but is reduced to a state of imperfection analogous to the way it could have been in the very earliest periods of human history.'[14] In other words, the modern human brain will regress to an archaic mode of activity assimilable to primitive humanity, rediscovering in oneiric nocturnal activity a former state of waking primitive activity. It is difficult to draw out more clearly the consequences of an ontogenetic principle. The dream is a voyage of daily return to the original *mentalité* of the species by means of memory, the faculty at work in this regressive process. The terms *imperfection* and return–regression (*Zurückbringen*) attest to the evolutionist connotation of this conception. An individual's oneiric cerebral activity in any given moment of evolution recapitulates that of the species at a corresponding moment, within the space of a dream.

Consequently, Nietzsche outlines an analysis which compares the individual's evolved oneiric logic with the species' archaic waking logic:

> Arbitrary and confused as it is, it constantly confounds things on the foundation of the most fleeting similitudes; but it is with the same

> arbitrariness and the same confusion that people forge their mythologies, and even now voyagers are accustomed to observe the extent to which the savage is inclined to forget, how his mind, after a brief tension of memory, begins to reel to and fro and how, by simply relaxing, he produces falsehoods and absurdities. But we completely resemble this savage in our dreams; the defective recognition and erroneous assimilation (*schlechte Widererkennen und irrtümliche Gleichsetzen*) are the cause of the defective reasoning of which we are capable in our dreams, and we ourselves are as frightened of what we find in dreams as we are of madness.[15]

The analogy of the 'civilized' dreamer with the wakeful 'savage' pushes the evolutionist hypothesis to its term. The defectiveness of oneiric logic is reconciled to the deficient psychic economy of the savage, who is drained in the short term and is dissipated of strength after the least tension. The psychic energy at work in dreams is thus assimilated to a very poor activity, in the manner of a spring endowed with very weak possibilities of action, which is unwound and produces only partial movements which fail to organize themselves into coherent sequences. This clearly signifies that for Nietzsche, oneiric logic is degraded and recessive; a short voyage into delusion leaves a disquieting impression in the reawakened dreamer.

The brief oneiric delusion reproduces the state of primitive hallucination, the archaic mode of perception during times when desire is indistinguishable from reality.

> The perfect clarity of every representation in dreams, which presupposes an unconditional belief in their reality, again recalls for us the situations in humanity's past when hallucinations were extraordinarily frequent and from time to time possessed entire communities, entire peoples. So, in sleep and in dreams we once again relive the thought (*Pensum*) of past humanity.[16]

Without any contradiction, Nietzsche can attribute clarity to the same dream whose confusion he comes to describe. Oneiric representation is precisely a non-sense which is perceived as coming from the Self; this is the definition of a *hallucination*. Indeed, oneiric perception is in this sense, to paraphrase Taine's famous formula, a true hallucination.

From this base, Nietzsche proceeds toward a veritable *physiology* of the oneiric mechanism, indicating that it is important to take literally the idea of a cerebral function which he puts as the point of departure in his theory of dreams. The point of departure is a theory of co-anaesthetic impressions. 'During sleep,' he remarks, 'our nervous system is continually in excitation from multiple internal phenomena.'[17] There follows an evocation of multiple intra-organic events which populate the sleeping body. From this endogenous murmuring, created by organic activity, the movement of the blood and the position of limbs, there are born 'a hundred motivations for the mind to be surprised and to look for the *reasons* for these excitations.'[18] This is what permits Nietzsche to define dreams as '*the search for and the representation of the causes* of sensations thus unveiled, that is to say from presumed causes.'

According to Nietzsche, that is the psycho-physiological genesis of dreams. Cerebral activity tends to identify the causes of consecutive proprioceptive excitations with their effects on the organs. We should note, however, that it is thus a question of a form of intellectual activity, but one that is in some way inferior and reflexive; the mind aspires (*suchen*) to know what is happening, that is to say from whence emanate the excitations that it perceives from within the body. To this end it emits a 'hypothesis' (*Hypothese*) which becomes 'a belief accompanied by an imagined representation (*bildlichen Vorstellung*) and a poetic invention' (*Ausdichtung*). The spontaneous quest for causes only imitates scientific inquiry; hypothesis becomes a figured belief, thus the affinity between the oneiric form and the poetic work. 'Excited imagination' stylizes the sensations, and gives appearance its symbolizing function. Nietzsche supports this conception with known examples, where rags become serpents, or sounds turn into tolling bells or cannon shots.

It is in this sense that Nietzsche speaks of a 'logic of dreams'.[19] It has the form of a scientific inference, but the inductive mind of the dreamer 'always leads to falsehood'. It testifies to a temerity which contrasts with the mind in an awakened state, 'reserved, prudent and sceptical with regard to hypotheses.' Yet concerning this astonishing resolve towards an aberration, Nietzsche asks: how does it come about that 'the first hypothesis suffices for an explanation of a feeling'? How does it come about that the same mind would demand the awake to take the first reason to come along for the best, and to believe it immediately in its proposed truthfulness, to take it as 'money in the bank', from the moment when it is dreamed?

Here is where ontogenetic theory intervenes again. 'I think that as, even now, man reasons in his dreams, so humanity reasoned *in an awake state* in centuries past; the first cause which is presented to the mind in order to explain something which needs an explanation will suffice it and take on the value of truth.' The contemporary testimony of travellers is again evoked to support this theory. We understand this from the vivid articulation of the ontogenetic theory of dreams with the Nietzschean idea of a dream logic. It actualizes an infantile intellectual regime in humanity.

Nietzsche applies this theory to the letter, to the point where it makes the dreams of contemporary 'civilized' people into an ethnological instrument:

> In dreams there continue to be exercised within us an ancient part of humanity because it is the foundation on which all higher reason is developed and still develops within each human; dreams tell us of the distant states of human civilization and put to hand the means for better understanding them.[20]

The individual dream is thus the vestige of an archaic collective patrimony. We see here the same valuation; it permits us to see the foundation on which the development of superior reason is established. We saw above that this is one of Nietzsche's texts which most struck Freud.[21]

Oneiric activity testifies to a sort of apprenticeship of the species. 'To think in dreams (*Traumdenken*) is for us so easy, because we have been well trained to do just that, during the immense periods of human evolution, to think in this fantastical and shoddy mode of explanation that takes off from the first idea, whatever it is.'[22] This return to the immediate forms of thought even has a *recreational* function. 'To this extent, a dream is a recreation (*Erholung*) for the brain which during the day has to satisfy the strict requirements of thought, such as are established by a superior civilization.' Dreams, in this new definition, function as a cure, outside of the constraints of society, in a protected zone of permissiveness.

Now the presence of dreams in man has the significance of a monument to an irrational form of thought that lies even at the heart of logical (diurnal) thought.

> We can conclude from these phenomena *how belatedly* the more rigorously logical forms of thought, the strict search for cause and effect, has been developed, if our rational and intellectual functions *even now* take up again these primitive forms of reason and if we live approximately half our lives in this state.[23]

Here, dreams clearly serve to dismiss rationalism from its pretensions to reduce psychic activity to its rational manifestations.

To the theme of the regressive activity at work in dreams, there is added a valorization which gives dreams to thought, independently of purely rational thought – which reconcile them, from one point of view, to aesthetic activity. 'The poet and the artist *impute* to these sentiments and states causes which are not at all true; they recall in this measure our ancient humanity and can aid us in understanding it.' Dreams and works of art appear jointly as archaeological documents of originary thoughts, as the double mode of expression (*langage*) through which they are actualized in contemporary humanity.

A brief aphorism in *Assorted Opinions and Maxims* shows the immediate revelatory sense that the hermeneutic of dreams reveals. '*To interpret through dreams*. What we sometimes neither know nor feel during our waking hours ... in dreams we understand absolutely, unequivocally.'[24] But what is the nature of that revelation? Nietzsche is specific; it is a matter of whether 'one has a good or a bad conscience towards someone.' Thus the message of the dream is placed on the terrain of culpability, or guilt.

In other words, we should note that what is laid bare, immediately and evidently, is one's true moral disposition toward others. For Nietzsche, dreams are thus moral and psychological instruments of truth. This is why they occupy space in 'assorted opinions and maxims'; dreams are moments for exploitation and interpretation, when, in the eyes of the subject himself, the mask falls from one's intimate dispositions, in the context of interpersonal commerce.

In the aphorism dedicated to dreams in *The Voyager and His Shadow*,[25] Nietzsche formulates an analogy between the oneiric chain of representations and literary narrative. 'Our dreams ... are the chains of symbolic scenes and images (*symbolische Szenen- und Bilder-ketten*), in the place of a discourse in the form of a literary narrative.' We find in this definition of dreams the triple character that Freud will assign to dreams: associativity, symbolism and figuration. What is more, the analogy with the narrative suggests the idea of a logic of oneiric association, developing in a common source with aesthetic creation.

But this analogy has a particular meaning for Nietzsche. Everything proceeds as if the energy in the dream was turned back from its aesthetic use. Here he insists on the demiurgic audacity of dreams, which 'modify (*umschreiben*) the things we have experienced (*Erlebnisse*), our hopes or even our affairs, with an audacity and a poetic precision such that in the morning we are always astonished on our account when we remember our dreams.' However, aesthetic performance only imitates true creation, and for this reason Nietzsche concludes the analogy with an ironic remark. 'We consume too much aesthetic meaning in dreams – and that is why during the day we are often so poor.'

Such a witticism indicates that, fascinated at times by the symbolic logic of dreams, Nietzsche nevertheless conceives them as a waste. Dreams appear to him in this context as works of art that are spoiled because they are *mutilated*. In the same text, he notes that 'habitually, dreams are botched works' or 'a botch job' (*Pfuscher-Arbeit*). While frequently the analogy between dreams and works of art serves to valorize the aesthetic value of oneiric activity, for Nietzsche it turns, as we see here, in disfavour of the dream. So the analogy, which puts the accent on the symbolic connections that dreams suggestively make to raise the stake of creative meaning, is turned back by Nietzsche. Indeed, he makes note of the symbolic connections, but it is in order to reserve them for the case where 'as an exception, they are successful and perfect'. Most of the time, they are as abortions which are not carried to term.

We must pay attention to this relativization in Nietzsche's judgement on oneiric creativity; its chronic tendency toward abortion and its substitutive function puts it back into a subordinate place. Full aesthetic creation is not a creation of dreams. The beautiful symbolic tapestries of dreams thus sustain for Nietzsche a mixture of admiration and condescendence, as if the ingenuity dispensed there were suspected of only producing false appearances.

In fact, this conception, taken in all its meaning, refers to the evolutionist conception which subtends it, and whose formulations we find just prior to it, in the text of *Human, All Too Human* that we have analysed. The poetic fiction returns, through its affinity with dreams, to its archaic usage in mythology. We recall in this respect its *arbitrary and confused* character. The term *unvollkommen* (*imperfect*) must be reattached more radically to the notion of *Unvollkommenheit* (*imperfection*), which is attributed as the characteristic of the originary state of humanity. This is from whence the lacunary and defective aspect of oneiric connections proceed.

A long aphorism in *Daybreak* takes up again the question of dreams. The preceding physiological theory is repeated; dreams are presented as 'interpretations of our nervous excitations (*Nervenreize*) during sleep, but they are very liberal and arbitrary interpretations' of our endogenous affects.[26] Meanwhile, Nietzsche's reflections have progressed. A new question has arisen: how does it come about that 'this text which remains in general very much the same from one night to the next is commented upon in such different ways?' How does it come about that 'inventive reason (*dichtende Vernunft*) is represented yesterday and today by such different causes for the same nervous excitations'?

In that, there is an important moment in the genesis of Nietzsche's conception of dreams where he considers problematic a too-complete conception. Nietzsche considers showing evidence of a logic of dreams, as a mode of explanation, as an abstraction, as if there were not a principle assigned to play in this register. This new question, however, requires us to pass from the theory of the mechanism of dreams to a theory of their meaning, in brief from the *how* to the *why* of oneiric activity, and this is precisely the point where the theory of dreams rejoins that of instincts.

In fact, instincts which seek forever to be satisfied in human life find in dreams a means of realization. Nietzsche represents the ensemble of instincts as famished and in a permanent quest for 'nourishment'; when they cannot find their pasture during the day, they are satisfied in the field of dreams. These are in the first place 'instincts called "moral"' which, contrary to their physical homologies like Hunger, can be satisfied via a substitutive path. Thus a new definition, this time taking the form of a diagnosis. 'Our dreams have precisely for their value and sense to compensate, up to a certain degree, for the lack of nourishment experienced during the day.' Putting dreams into poetic forms responds to this function; 'imaginings' (*Erdichtungen*) permit the moral instincts to procure for themselves a space of play (*Spielraum*) and of discharge (*Entladung*). This is what creates the difference in tonality between the dreams of one day and another (prank, affection, adventure) and the correlative variety of objects in dreams.

Behind inventive reason, which seems to be, in the preceding texts, the exclusive subject of dreams, there appears according to Nietzsche's happy expression, a different 'prompter' (*souffleur*) each night, an instinct which today 'wishes to be satisfied, to be occupied, exercised, restored, or discharged', one which in the continuous flow of instincts is found to be 'the most strongly in flux'.[27] Each dream lends its mode of expression (*langage*) to the instinct in service tonight in the general economy of instinctive flux, and inventive reason lends its virtues to this chosen instinct at last to furnish it with its own mode of expression (*langage*), in order to be represented in an intimate sense.

This text marks the evolution of Nietzsche's conception of dreams under another point of view, that of its relation to wakefulness. Previously, Nietzsche had insisted on the distinction between the oneiric and the awake; now, he tends to mark their continuity. If he confirms that 'life in waking hours does not have the *liberty* of interpretation that dreaming life has', that it is 'less poetic and unbridled', it is in order to add immediately that 'our instincts in an awake state do nothing other than interpret nervous excitations and to establish "causes" conforming to their needs.' The quotation marks indicate that the causes called 'real' are only less suspected of unreality than those presumed and reputedly fictive causes in dreams. Consequently 'there is no *essential* difference between being awake and dreaming'; there is only a difference of degrees of liberty in the interpretive process. Waking logic is distinguished by a coefficient of slightly superior restraints, a cog that resists the liberty of interpretation, which is given free rein during dreams.

From this moment, dreams are seen less as archaic islets in a real world than the pure expression of a universal illusion which is a quality of being. The sphere of experience (*Erleben*) bleeds into the sphere of imagination (*Erdichten*), and dreams attest to their confusion.

We have arrived at the moment in Nietzsche's thought where the relativization of moral values begins to make felt the radical effects of ontological derealization. The status of dreams is a major indication, so that previously where Nietzsche permitted a core of illusion and irrationality to provide consistency to a sphere of rationality and reality, hereafter the frontier vacillates. Suddenly the domain of the legislation of dreams is extended to the essential. 'Our judgements and moral considerations are only images and phantasms (*Bilder und Phantasien*) concerning an unknown physiological process within us, a sort of language useful for designating certain nervous excitations'; 'so-called consciousness is only a more or less fantastical commentary on an unknown, perhaps unknowable (although sensed) text.' From this moment, dreams take on a more decisive and less specific significance; they serve to exhibit no longer just a vestige at the heart of 'civilized' beings, but the general mode of inherence in the world and the relation between values. What takes place during dreams could well be the key to what happens in every human event, that is, the arbitrary grafting of meaning on to physiological excitation. The logic of dreams could well be isomorphic with that of morality, that is to say of the mode of being-in-the-world.

Beginning here, the importance of dreams doubles; as a laboratory of aesthetic sense, they appear more the laboratory of ethics themselves. The implication of dreams in the question of morality is confirmed by the aphorism dedicated, in the same work, to dreams and responsibility.

Nietzsche rejects with an exclamation mark the thesis that dreams are innocent. 'You want to be responsible in everything! But when it comes to your dreams you do not want to be!'[28] Against this denial, he is led to restore to dreamers the ownership of their dreams, which implies the taking into evidence of their expressive function. 'What miserable weakness, consequently what a lack of courage! Nothing is *more* your own (*Eigen*) than your dreams! Nothing is more *your* work! Content, form, duration, actors, spectators, in these comedies you are all of these things yourself!'

Furthermore, Nietzsche suspects in this denial a resistance founded on a feeling that an unavowed part of the Self is expressed in dreams. 'And it is precisely here' he adds, 'that you are afraid and ashamed of yourselves,' and thus the tendency to remove the culpability from this paternity and to create a destiny independent of the Self. Not fortuitously, the reference to Oedipus is imposed here, in that 'already Oedipus, wise Oedipus, knew how to draw consolation from the thought that we can never be sure about what we dream! I conclude from this fact that the majority of men must be conscious of having abominable dreams. If it were otherwise, how would we be able to exploit to the benefit of man's arrogance his nocturnal poetry?' So dreams remain analogous to poetic fantasies (*Dichterai*), but something otherwise important in the ethical order is mixed into this form; the equivocal eruption of the instincts serving appearances dresses up their desires.[29]

After having solidly imputed to dreamers responsibility for their dreams, Nietzsche delivers the aphorism which nonetheless comes around to a deterministic thesis. 'I must add that wise Oedipus was right that we are not really responsible for our dreams – but as little responsible while awake – and on the fact that the doctrine of free will has for its father and mother arrogance and a feeling of power (*Stolz und Machtgefühl*).'[30]

There is no contradiction in denouncing the belief in the irresponsibility while affirming the determinism; only after having affirmed the idea that something in the Self is expressed in dreams is it possible to grasp the mechanism by which it works. From this point of view, Nietzsche joins the course Freud takes, imputing dreams to humans, reinserting them into a psychic continuum in order to discover, at a later point, their laws. Paradoxically, the ones who are too willing to acquit themselves of responsibility for their dreams are the ones who misrecognize their determinism. Nietzsche assigns the same resistance to arrogance and to the feeling of power to recognize the sense of dreams, on the one hand, and the determinist truth on the other, a double injury which affects the same faculties.

From this point, Nietzsche holds to the idea that there is a sense to dreams, that something is at stake there, that it is not necessary to misrecognize it. He expresses it in a very brief aphorism in *The Gay Science*. '*Dreams*: One does not dream or, if one dreams, it is interesting.'[31] That is to say that there is an inherent interest in oneiric activity as such-and-such because it is not in vain that the mind is put to dreaming; its expressions are motivated. It is not a waste of energy, but an investment, always lucrative on the symbolic level.

If Nietzsche recalls this principle, it is in order to give oneiric activity to waking activity as an example. In this sense we must think about how we dream, with the same requirement. 'One must learn to be so while awake: Nothing, or interesting.' The 'free spirit', spoken of in *Human, All Too Human*, wants itself to be positively awake. Paradoxically, it is the dreamer it must take as a model. The worst state is that of somnolence without images, that thinks it should be able to be permitted to one who is awake. This brief maxim on the dreamer in the use of wakefulness indicates, discreetly, the function acquired by dreams in the ethics of *The Gay Science*.

In Nietzsche's philosophy, dreams thus take on an active significance, not only as an object of psychology, but as a mode of the transmission of truth. Zarathustra uses a dream to announce 'the great Noontide'.[32] In the arsenal of the forms of prophecy and the economy of degrees of truth, dreams have a precise function; they permit us to anticipate the truth that continually suffers from not being able to be told. Continually delayed enunciations can be *realized* in dreams, appearances in which *the real* is fused to *the possible*. Dreams will thus be one of the forms of prophecy.

We can divine this function of dreams in the narrative from the third book of *Thus Spoke Zarathustra*, entitled 'Of the Three Evils'.[33] It is a dream dreamt at the threshold of daybreak; Nietzsche evokes it as a 'dream of the morning', at the temporal frontier of the present, which the jealous daybreak has come to interrupt. 'My dream, an audacious navigator, half-vessel, half-storm, as silent as a butterfly, as impatient as a noble falcon, such patience and such leisure as it had with which to measure the world.'[34] Such is the privilege of the dream, which is the organ of intimate revelation; it possesses, outside of temporality, the virtues of patience and leisure which permit it to weigh the world by placing itself 'beyond the world'.

Zarathustra speaks of his dream as an ingenious and beneficent principle which he has lived. He testifies to recognize it and proposes to 'imitate it in broad daylight' in order to 'learn the best of its lessons'. Such is the *lesson* of the dream, to reveal the world 'measurable for those who have the time for measuring, weighable for good scales, carried by powerful wings, transparent for heavenly seekers.' What the dreamer does, the wakeful must learn how to do. That is why dreams will be one of the modes of expression (*langues*) of the new gospel.

An aphorism in *Beyond Good and Evil*[35] takes up again the theme of the continuity dreaming-awake in order to argue for the active function of dreams in waking life.

> What we experience in dreams, suppose that we would experience it often; in the end, that relates to the general economy of our soul, in the same way that something important is 'really' experienced, by which we are richer or poorer, we need more or less, and we finally become on a grand day, and even in the most serene moments of our soul, somewhat held in check by the *habitus* drawn from our dreams.

There is the idea of the elaboration of the *habitus* drawn from dreams into lived experience and conscious behaviour. Indeed, the domestic economy of the human mind permits these oneiric manifestations; they are fixed in real dispositions in the soul.

Nothing is astonishing about the point in Nietzsche's last works where, editing the notes to *Will to Power*, Nietzsche gives a prominent place to dreams. They appear as the daily revelation of the 'phenomenalism of the inner world'. In the aphorism which carries this title, Nietzsche substantially takes up the genesis of dreams. 'All our dreams are interpretations (*Auslegung*) of complex feelings (*Gesamt-gefühl*) seeking possible causes, and in such a manner that we are not initially conscious of them before the discovered causal chain has entered into consciousness'[36]

But it appears that the whole psycho-physiological theory of dreams rests in turn on a theory of 'inner experience'. This, adds Nietzsche,

> consists in the proposition that a cause of the excitation of nervous centres is sought and represented – and that the first cause discovered enters into the Conscious; this cause is in no way adequate as the true cause, but is only a groping along the foundation of formerly 'internal experiences', that is to say, of memory. But memory conserves as well the *habitus* of waking interpretations, that is to say of erroneous causality, such that 'internal experience' carries with it the consequences of all of the ancient fictions of false causes.

At the final moment in Nietzsche's philosophy, when phenomenalism must be radicalized in order to leave the *tabula rasa* to the dictatorship of Will to Power, dreams again take up these characteristics, but at a superior level; their role is to manifest the legality of this inner world (*Innenwelt*) which exhibits the internal condition of every perception of the world.

In this context, in one of the last fragments which crystalize Nietzsche's thought, the Apollonian–Dionysian opposition returns.[37] Distinguishing two drives derived respectively from two principles, themselves expressions in human art of the power of nature (one has vision, the other orgies), Nietzsche specifies further that they are represented in a weakened form in normal life, the one in dreams and the other in intoxication. While intoxication relates to passion, dreams are associated with the values of vision, union and poetry. Such is the final condition of dreams, the form representative on an everyday scale of the compulsion to vision (*Zwang sur Vision*), derived from the Apollonian form of expression in human art of the power of Nature (*Naturgewalt*).

With these final texts, the buckle is fastened. Dreams fill for Nietzsche, with the vicissitudes that we have followed, the double function of an aesthetic principle (the echo of the Apollonian principle) and a psychological principle (manifestation of an inner world). Under these two roles, they lie at the heart of human experience.

DREAMS AND THEIR INTERPRETATION: FREUD'S ONEIRIC OBJECT

The preceding inquiry has shown the importance and the richness of the Nietzschean thematic on dreams, which paved the way for an interest in oneiric activity that will engage Freud throughout his career. But it also showed that Nietzsche's approach is taken, as with the thematics of the Unconscious and of sexuality, in the double limit of physiological explanations and instinctivist valorization, whose axis is *aesthetic*, under a Romantic inspiration.

Freud's *Traumdeutung* identifies oneiric activity as does Nietzsche, as the ontogenetic reproduction of a phylogenetic heritage. There it is, as we saw in the first part, one of the officially recognized anticipations of Freud by Nietzschean thought.[38] But for Freud, the work of 'elaboration of dreams'[39] is studied for itself, as an ensemble of modalities by which the *princeps* function of dreams are found realized as the 'realization of a desire',[40] beginning with 'elements of infantile origin'.[41]

While a dream is not simply a document which links the individual to the instinctual life of the species, it is resolutely conceived on the ontogenetic plane, as a mode of expression (*langage*) of individual desire. That is why, we should point out, Nietzsche nowhere elaborates a systematic interpretation of dreams as expressions of desire; at most, he divines, in the Romantic tradition that we have located, what links the dream back to desire, but for Nietzsche it is rather a new proof of our participation in a generic Unconscious. For Freud, the idea emerges of a logic of individual desire expressing itself in an oneiric mode (*langage*).

For this reason, the analysis of the mechanisms of the 'work' of dreams is inseparable from the meta-psychological elaboration of the Unconscious. It is precisely the idea of a *primary process* which operates the passage from the register of the Unconscious to that of the dream, and makes possible a twin theory of unconscious oneiric activity, where Nietzsche could only have an aesthetic theory of the analogy between dreams and the Unconscious.

Dreams appear from here on as a regulated energetic regime centred on the free circulation of (primary) energy along associative chains linking *representations* to *affects*. Consequently, a positive study of the work of distortion to which materials (notably remaining diurnal) are treated becomes possible. It is important to note that this role operates through *displacement* and *condensation*, whose technique can only be defined insofar as it is related to the primary process.[42]

Here it is necessary to attach the greatest importance to Freud's affirmation, according to which the essential aspect of dreams consists in the work that they accomplish, more than the dream content itself which relates to some 'mysterious Unconscious'.[43] That is to say that for Freud dreams are something other than the immediate reflection of the Unconscious (which it was for Nietzsche); it is nothing other than this treatment, above all not creative but mechanical, which elaborates a *latent content* in a *manifest content*. This essentially founds that which was untimely before Freud, an '(interpretive) science of dreams' (*Traumdeutung*), requiring from now on that dreams be seen as autonomous activities regulated by a technique. We could argue that at the limit, Freud's profound originality was to have emancipated dreams from the Unconscious, by which we mean that Freud treated dreams as a *sui generis* labour, approached as the producer of given and impenetrable effects, and not as a reflection of an Unconscious. It is nothing more than the sequence of procedures which extend up to a *secondary elaboration*, by which dreams are finally reshaped into scenarios, coherent and intelligible.

In other words, what for Nietzsche remains a thematic of the dream, becomes for Freud a theory of oneiric activity as a specimen of unconscious psychic activity. For Nietzsche, a 'dream-world' is immediately valorized aesthetically, while for Freud it is a question of a material which founds an explanation and a diagnosis.[44]

A determinant stake in the question of dreams permits us to accomplish a comparison, namely the status of the dream, correlative to the requirement of visualization and figurability (*Rücksicht auf Darstellbarkeit*). It is remarkable that Freud relates this requirement to the general phenomenon of *regression* (at once topical, formal and temporal). It is conditioned by the inversion, during sleep, of the succession of excitations from the pole of motility to the pole of perception. To clarify, the image for Freud has a fundamentally regressive status; the image is an *impoverished* form of psychic expression, and in this sense it is characteristic of the general regression of dreams, related to hallucinatory types of experiences.

In correlation, the image returns to a sort of sensory and representative *receptivity*. This status links repression to the image; the one and the other act as originary nuclei which exercise an attraction that polarizes psychic life – what links the dream to the originary scene and permits it to be defined as 'the transfer to the present' of an infantile scene, as a reactive substitute.

We saw that for Nietzsche, if the physiological theory returns to the idea of receptivity,[45] it is elaborated by a valorization of *Phantasie* in an aesthetic sense. In that, the image and its Dionysian colours serve, in a typical Nietzschean metaphor, to exhibit the luxuriance of instinct; by contrast, for Freud, understood literally, dreams only express a regressive, and as such a more significant, mode of expression.

Indeed, for Freud the image expresses the regressive status of desire, defined most precisely as 'psychic motion' which seeks to 'reinvest the mnemonic image' of an expression linked to an 'experience of satisfaction'.[46] This mechanistic definition bars the way for every exaltation of the desire principle, and severs the ties once and for all between Freud and the figures of this exaltation, which Nietzsche elaborates in his approach.

BOOK THREE: THE STAKES

Having seen the deployment of the *principles* which set the scene for our comparison, and the *themes*, the basic canvases or decor that stand out within that scenery, we must now consider the dramatic action and dénouement itself. In fact, the principles and thematics lead to an essential stake, the *diagnosis* of human reality, as developed by Freud's psychoanalysis and its Nietzschean homology of 'moral pathology'. The diagnosis is the real test of the theory of instincts and its corresponding anthropology, but we also find a diagnosis of *Kultur*, a theory of civilization that appears to be a stake forming the horizon of the diagnosis, but in all truth was present from the very beginning. The inquiry leads back to this second diagnostic; beginning from the principles, *Kultur* itself is revealed as the end. Finally, given that the diagnosis indicates a *therapy*, it is on that terrain that we must seek out the natural term of our inquiry, as a response to the question of pathology.

1

NEUROSIS AND MORALITY

NOTIONS OF WELLNESS AND ILLNESS

Given that we can speak of a Nietzschean psycho-pathology, it is useful to define in some positive terms Nietzsche's acceptation of the notions of health and illness.

Human, All Too Human, affirming the 'value of illness' as generative of 'wisdom',[1] underlines a contempt for 'counsellors' who tend to the ill.[2] The 'utility' of illness is affirmed in the same way; it procures 'an extremely acute sense of health and morbidity in works and actions, one's own as well as those of others.' Paradoxically, it is the 'tone of health' that is extracted from writings on illness, even more appropriately than the robust species 'of the philosophy of spiritual health and convalescence.'[3]

With regard to this science of health through illness, *The Voyager and His Shadow* mentions 'the faith in sickness' that Christianity has inculcated in the human species.[4] When Nietzsche recommends 'reflecting on the kindnesses and considerations that one can bestow upon his friends and enemies alike'[5] as a sedative against the distresses of the soul, he alludes to something other than charity, to a form of 'diversion' which avoids aggravating the illness by the remedy, by creating resentment. Moreover, too long an illness dulls one's compassion, leading Nietzsche to infer that the patient *deserves* his illness.[6] Thus at base, 'a little health here and there, that is the best remedy for illness.'[7] This witticism expresses well the relativity of the two notions.

At the same time, the relativity is expressed by the coincidence of illness-as-reality and the idea of illness, such that to treat the patient is not just to treat the illness, but also to appease the patient's imagination, 'so that at least he ceases to suffer from thinking about his illness,'[8] as Nietzsche says in *Daybreak*. The basis of illness thus appears to be an 'affliction and misery of the soul' (*Trübsal und Seelen Elend*) which even art is not sufficient to cure.[9] In these types of afflictions, *nihilism*, the supreme illness, makes its entry into the Nietzschean universe, long before its being taken into account as such.

But let us beware of translating these formulae into saying that for Nietzsche, all illness is psychological. It is necessary to understand simply that illness is an indissociably organic and psychic *reality* – to the point where illness serves to metaphorize the solidarity between body and soul. *Daybreak* gives us a definition in this sense. 'Under the term "illness" we should understand an untimely approach of old age, of spite and pessimistic judgements – things which are implied (*zueinander gehören*) by "illness".'[10] That is why, for Nietzsche, the term 'illness' implicitly recalls an ensemble of significations, at once somatic and moral. The term is thus taken jointly and severally, in the strictly medical sense of an organic affection, as well as in a moral acceptation, where it points toward the idea of mental illness.

The more the critique of morality is sharpened, in the 1880s, the more the pathological metaphor will be developed, until the critique raises the notion of illness to the rank of a true *category* of the critique of morality. Zarathustra's declaration of war against the 'infirm' as enemies of the human species[11] completes this evolution, in terms of which illness is invested with an axiological function as a counter-value revealing values.

We can see from this presentation the difference in the originary points of view between Nietzsche and Freud regarding illness. For Nietzsche, illness involves an axiological discourse, for Freud, an explanatory one. However, this banal opposition in no way hinders an astonishing convergence on a psycho-pathological approach, as if every discourse on the normal and the pathological encounters the question of values and norms, and the correlative question of interpretation.[12]

In fact, we could say that paradoxically the idea of *illness* does not, any more than its correlative *health*, constitute operative categories for Freud. What exists before everything is an ensemble of psychic *processes* answerable to a certain *regime* of function and dysfunction. *Pathology* appears privileged in that it reveals, by way of dysfunction, the functionality of the system. It is a question, conforming to the initial formulation of 'ambitions', of 'discovering what form a theory of mental functioning assumes when one introduces there the notion of quantity, a sort of economy of nervous forces, and secondly, to draw from psycho-pathology some benefit for normal psychology.'[13] In fact, it is the first ambition which founds the second. At its limit, the *qualitative* concept of illness disappears in that it designates a kind of anthropomorphic entity; *quantity* functions for Freud as a concept of illness in terms of a process by degrees.

The theory of neurosis is founded, from its origin, on this pretentious quantification, which is supposed to immunize the idea of psycho-pathology from any valorizing connotation. Neurosis is at first a disturbance in the mental economy, which relativizes the antinomy health/illness, but via a different path from Nietzsche.

For Nietzsche, concepts never cease having a valorizing function, even if they are themselves variable; for Freud they only name descriptive figures, leaving to processual phenomena the exclusive explanatory function. If nevertheless a convergence is possible, it is because for Nietzsche evaluation becomes an exploration of the process, while for Freud the evaluation is no less so for not having to be objectified (see below).

MORAL PATHOLOGY AND THE VICISSITUDES OF INSTINCTS

We now turn to Nietzsche's analysis of moral pathology, which is distributed throughout *On the Genealogy of Morals* under the types of ill will (*ressentiment*), bad conscience and the ascetic ideal. For our own, circumscribed interests, it is a question of understanding the *psycho-pathological* conception which subtends these diagnoses.

There is in fact a truly clinical scene which Nietzsche paints throughout the three essays that comprise the *Genealogy*. What interests us is to explain the presentation of the psychic apparatus which makes possible a symptomatology in search of 'something unhealthy' (*etwas Ungesundes*)[14] that Nietzsche locates at the foundation of morality.

Ill will (*das Ressentiment*) is born under conditions where 'true reaction, that is to say action, is impossible', and thus constitutes 'an imaginary vengeance'.[15] Ill will is born paradoxically when that which is deprived – the inhibition of action (*Tat*) – becomes 'creative' (*Schöpferisch*), implying an inversion of the relation subject–action–world; for the person of ill will, it is necessary 'in physiological terms, to have external excitations in order to act.' In other words, 'one's actions are at base *reactions*,' thus the 'passive'[16] character of the conception of happiness, that is to say the fulfilment of the Self; thus its representation as 'narcosis–drowsiness (*Betäubung*), peace, "Sabbath", relaxing one's mind and stretching one's limbs.' Inversely, health consists in spontaneous thought and action, and thus the *activity* that this implies, itself founded on a 'complete assurance in the function of unconscious regulatory instincts.'

The characterology of ill will expresses this primary reactivity as character traits. 'One's soul squints, one's mind loves the recesses, the subterfuge, and the hidden doors.' The favoured psychic modalities are 'silence, not forgetting, expectation, the act of provisionally belittling oneself, of being humiliated', so many expressions of the dominant status of one's psyche, which is postponement. In effect everything proceeds such that the affect is not immediately discharged through activity, which then triggers a *toxic* mechanism. It is in terms of poisoning that Nietzsche evokes this effect by which what cannot be discharged through a motor reaction, creates a real site of infection which takes over the ensemble of the psyche. Such is the illness of ill will, which works in the manner of 'vermin' who 'infest a house'.[17]

In correlation, ill will is expressed as a disturbance in the mental economy. It is, in effect, an overabundance of plastic forces, 'regenerative and curative', which characterize health, and make possible a kind of chronic renewal of energy. Contrary to what we might expect, in the pathology of ill will there is a localized over investment, and thus an overdevelopment of *memory*. It is necessary to understand this mnemonic overdevelopment as the inverse and proportional effect of the functional underdevelopment of motor functions. It is no accident if Nietzsche comes to compare ill will to the accumulation of a 'dangerous explosive'. The *symptom* is none other than the modality according to which the explosion is discharged, at the same time as it makes up the economy, while the 'cache' (*Verstecktes*) is the dominant mode of expression (*langage*) for this *defensive* strategy. We understand, in effect, that in the case where activity does not gradually exhaust the expenditure, as in the pathological case of ill will, a memorization–symbolization function is developed which has no place in health. Illness is precisely the state where 'one comes to be rid of nothing' and where 'every event leaves its traces', where memories degenerate into 'suppurating wounds'.

We cannot escape the impression that what Nietzsche theorizes as ill will is no other that what Freud, from the beginning, theorizes as *neurosis,* such as it is. That said, we are not interested in external analogies here, but rather in the overall schema of definition.

The basic concept which permits Freud (and Breuer) to define the symptomatology of hysteria and to propose an etiology is *abreaction* (*Abreagieren*). Preliminary communications show that the goal of *Studies on Hysteria* was to 'justify an extension of the concept of traumatic hysteria.'[18] The authors sought to establish that 'the hysteric suffers in large part from his reminiscences' (*Reminiszenzen*).[19] Now, what makes a lived event become or not become a pathogenic reminiscence depends strictly on the process of abreaction by which the subject discharges the *affect* to which the event is attached. That is why, in order to pass judgement on a remembrance, it is important in the first place to know whether 'the triggering event did or did not provoke an energetic reaction.'[20] Reaction is defined as 'the series of reflexes, voluntary or involuntary, thanks to which . . . there is a discharge of affects, ranging from tears to acts of vengeance.'

It is only when the reaction is hampered that the possibility of a pathological destiny comes into play. 'When this reaction is found to be hindered, the affect remains attached to memory.' Where the normal subject is able, via action, speech or an associated context, to cause 'the concomitant affect' (*begleitenden Affekt*) to disappear, for the neurotic 'the pathogenic representations are maintained . . . in all their freshness and always charged with emotion,' because 'the normal wear and tear, due to an abreaction and to a reproduction in the states where associations are not disturbed, is rendered impossible.'[21] That constitutes a memory which is never finished with anything. The *Nicht-Vergessen* of Nietzsche's ill will is nourished from the same source as the *Reminiscenze* of Freud's hysteria, a radical functional disturbance marking the impossibility of any process of abreaction.

Bad conscience (*schlechte Gewissen*), as we know, constitutes the elaboration and the transcendence of ill will in Nietzsche's pathology. This passage takes place by a process that Nietzsche clearly characterizes. 'All the instincts which cannot be discharged on the outside are turned (*wenden*) *toward the inside* – which is called the internalization (*Verinnerlichung*) of man.'[22] Such is the radical transformation (*Veränderung*) which will create an illness that is at the same time acute and chronic, 'man sick of man, sick of himself'.[23]

Such a radical illness proceeds from a blockage of the 'instinct of liberty', which is submitted to a treatment in the course of which it is 'rendered latent by force, reinforced, repressed, returned to the interior (*zurückgedrängte, zurückgetretene, ins Innere eingekerkerte*) and finally is discharged and released only upon oneself.'[24] Cruelty, expressed in ill will by vengeance, is converted into a 'will to torture oneself'. Thus the appearance of a new register – disinterest, abnegation, self-sacrifice – where the Self (*Selbst*) is both executioner and victim. Finally, culpability expresses this paradoxical suffering administered upon oneself.

This is the moment when the Self is represented as needing to expiate a symbolic debt. What the ascetic priest designates at this level is precisely the victim. 'You are yourself guilty'. That implies, in Nietzsche's specification, that 'the direction (*Richtung*) of ill will is transformed.'[25] The projected 'responsible cause' becomes literally *intro*-jected.

It is remarkable that Freud analyses under the name of 'vicissitudes of instincts' (*Triebschicksale*), besides repression and sublimation,[26] two processes which, not fortuitously, seem engaged in the intimate mechanism of ill will and of bad conscience in Nietzsche's analyses.

Freud speaks of 'turning back on the person proper' (*Wendung gegen die eigene Person*)[27] in order to designate the process by which the drive abandons the exterior object in order to be borne by the person himself, and so setting itself up as *object*. He speaks of the 'reversal of contraries' (*Verkehrung ins Gegenteil*)[28] in order to designate the process by which the *aim* of a drive is transformed into its opposite, thus passing from activity to passivity. At the same time, he insists that these two procedures are so closely linked that it is difficult to distinguish one from the other. It is no accident, then, if the privileged example to exhibit this process is sado-masochism, while the passage from love to hate serves to materialize the reversal of contraries.

In the process which gives activity to ill will, and bad conscience, everything proceeds as if we had seen this process spiral inward. In 'internalization' we saw the directional change consummated, end-for-object. From this point on, the sado-masochistic tonality of bad conscience takes on all the signification of a drive.

Freud shows that the passage from sadism to masochism consists in an 'activity of violence, a manifestation of power originally borne toward another person taken as an object, which is abandoned and replaced by oneself; but at the same time a transformation is accomplished by which an active aim of a drive is changed into a passive aim'[29] – which requires an object to administer the punishment. In bad conscience, the subject himself produces the suffering, borne against himself in the manner of a repressive other.

THE THEORY AND PATHOLOGY OF MEMORY: MNEMONIC TRACES

Outside this remarkable economic–dynamic homology, we can discern an important *topical* reconciliation, founded on the representation of the psychic apparatus that explains the pathology of memory. In order to understand Nietzsche's theory of memory, we must consider the aphorism where he declares that 'there is no formal organ of "memory".'[30] This is indeed why we do not know how to speak of 'memory' outside of quotation marks. Memory is in fact less a specific faculty than a diffuse function whose substrate is physiological. 'All the nerves, they specify ... they remember previous experiences.' It is thus necessary to speak of an organic memory immanent to the body, which is preserved by *nervous traces* that allow excitations to pass. 'Each word, each number is the result of a physical process,' to which we do not know how to assign their proper places, to the extent that it truly does not matter where they are in the nervous circuit. In effect, 'everything that the nerves have experienced in confusion (*anorganisiert*) continues to survive in them.' Here we find precisely the articulation between memory and the Unconscious. Memory, properly speaking, is only the moment where the latent life of experiences, surviving in the Unconscious, erupts into the Conscious.

There is more. Memory is the echo of the life of the drives; that is to say, it only 'notes the facts of instincts'.[31] It fills the function of revealing the transformations of drives in the presence of objects. We literally remember only why our instinct finds itself engaged or has found an 'interest'. There is only an affective memory, that is to say one related to drives.

That is why Nietzsche insists on the necessity of changing our conception of memory. We err in 'postulating a "soul" which reproduces atemporally, recognizes, etc.'[32] In fact, 'what was experienced continues to live "in memory";'[33] that is to say, there is a conservation of the mnemonic traces of events. Memory does not know how to be called to the rescue in order to witness the persistence of a soul; it is only 'the sum of everything experienced (*Erlebnisse*) throughout an organic life: living, organizing, mutually fashioning, battling, simplifying, pushing together and transforming into a multiplicity of unities.'[34]

As to whether that experience returns, Nietzsche specifies, 'I can say nothing, the Will does not intervene ... something arrives that I take for consciousness. Now an analogous thing appears – who calls it? who awakens it?' Assuredly not an "I", but something like an "It".'

It is no accident if we cannot find a theory of memory *per se* in Freud, for in the passage from psychology to psychoanalysis, memory lost its unity as a faculty; it is no longer an affair of traces or mnemonic residues (*Erinnerungsspuren* or *Erinnerungstreste*). There are homologies to Nietzsche's 'multiple unities', whose rumbling mass forms what we conventionally designate by the name 'memory'.

Nevertheless, Freud very soon needs to find an order to these unities. Not fortuitously, the first image of the mind that comes to him, in the *Studies on Hysteria*, is one of stratification (*Schichtung*). The memories of hysterics are revealed to be 'archives kept in good order'[35] that only remain to be uncovered. These archives are deployed according to a triple order, chronological, thematic and logical. In fact, what so stratifies the mass of mnemonic traces is the existence of a pathogenic, unconscious 'central nucleus'. 'The most exterior of the strata concern recollections (or bundles of recollections) which can the most easily return to memory and are always clearly conscious',[36] while the pathogenic core of the psyche corresponds to memories properly unconscious, which can only be reached by what Freud compares to an 'infiltration'.

We could speak of a duality of memories (conscious–unconscious) only if the concept of a mnemonic trace were not destined to transcend this representation.

Rather, it would be necessary to say that these traces are organized into 'systems' – Conscious, Preconscious and Unconscious in the first topic; Id, Ego and Superego in the second – that will define these types of memories, extending the functional scope of mnemonic traces, which will allow further qualification.

The 'systems' or 'instances' thus constitute the dimensions or principles of order for the archives of memory. Thus it is remarkable that where Nietzsche gives memory to thought as a plurality of unities spontaneously self-organized, Freud subsumes the multiplicity of mnemonic traces under principles of ordination.

The model for Freud's theory is found in the famous letter of 6 December 1896, where Freud discloses to Fliess that

> in my work, I start from the hypothesis that our psychic mechanism is established by a process of stratification; the materials present under the form of mnemonic traces are found from time to time revised according to new circumstances. What is essentially new in my theory is the idea that memory is present not once but several times and that it is composed of various types of 'signs'.[37]

What is new is that the reconciliation with Nietzsche's conception permits us at least to temper it, given that memory declares itself equally in a series of *registers* (*enregistrements*).

Freud's true originality is found rather in the elaboration of a *topical* codification of this conception, but this conception is maintained up to the end by being specified. In *Traumdeutung*, by representing the psychic apparatus as an apparatus reflexive at both extremities, perceptive and motor, Freud defines memory as the function of retaining traces and relates them to a system specifically charged to register the modifications. A chain of systems is organized whose spatial order represents the temporal order of the circulation of excitations. Thus there is a division of labor between two 'organs of the psychic apparatus'.[38]

Later, Freud maintains that 'consciousness is born directly in the place of the trace of the recollection', in other words 'the inexplicable phenomenon of consciousness is produced, in the system of perception, at *the site* of permanent traces.'[39] Freud takes pains, up to the end, to think through the character of the psychic apparatus that on the one hand 'possesses the limitless gift of receiving new impressions', and on the other 'creates the continuity of mnemonic traces, durable if not unalterable.' It is on this type of prodigy that Freud's reflection is exercised again in 1929: how is it possible to conserve impressions in the psyche, in the manner of an archaeological site?[40]

GUILT AND DEBT

Freud's pathology is further specified via a sentiment with a double connotation, both *ethical* and *clinical*; for Freud, as for Nietzsche, there is a theory of guilt, equally central to their respective thought. But it is a question of discerning the most positive acceptation of this notion for one and the other, in order to determine the points of convergence and divergence. At the least, the first point in common is related to a perspective that emerges from psychopathology, taken in the highest sense. Thus we need to examine the clinical acceptation as it appears in the registers, respectively, of Nietzsche and Freud.

Naturally, guilt takes its meaning for Nietzsche in the context of the critique of morality. For our own purposes, we need to isolate the specific diagnosis which bears guilt as such, understood in some clinical regard.

In an aphorism in *Daybreak*, guilt appears linked for Nietzsche to the notions of praise and blame (*Loben und Tadeln*); the judgment of guilt is related to the 'excessive need to praise and blame'.[41] It is thus a means of proving that one has a sense of power, whether in holding another as guilty, or in provoking guilt. We find the same thing in *The Gay Science*, where the fictive character of all guilt is affirmed, related to a judgment of arbitrary value. In the same sense, 'before sunrise', Zarathustra hails this moment of the serenity and innocence of the sky, in its point of overhang, while 'below . . . constraint, purpose, and error condense, like rain'.[42] It is a question, as a contemporary aphorism says, of being convinced of the 'innocence of becoming', at last to 'gain a feeling of a complete "irresponsibility" and of gaining independence from praise and blame, from every man and everything in the past'.[43] So we find in Nietzsche, even before an analysis of guilt, a radical relativization of the notion in relation to the social–psychological notions of 'praise' and 'blame'.

It is only in the second period that guilt, fictively diagnosed, is made the object of a genealogical analysis. There, evidence of a juridical connotation appears. 'It is in this sphere of rights and obligation that the world of moral concepts like "fault", "conscience", "debt", "sanctity of obligation", finds its point of origin.'[44] Guilt points toward the cruelty of the Law; in other words, 'the feeling of debt, of personal obligation, took its origin . . . from the most ancient and most primitive relations between individuals, the relations between creditor and debtor.'[45]

Guilt is thus related to an archaic juridical relation where measure and evaluation reigned. There is no guilt without harm (*Schaden*), an event in the relation between creditor and debtor (*Glaübiger und Schuldner*). The guilty party is thus 'a debtor who not only does not reimburse the advances made to him, but even attacks his creditor'.[46] He is a 'cause of rupture, a treaty violator, lacking in intercourse with the community', which places him 'outside the law' and brands (*Strafe*) him as a criminal (*Verbrecher*), a breaker (*Brecher*) of the debt engagement.

From this perspective, Nietzsche comes to reject the idea according to which 'punishment should have the property of awakening within the guilty party the feeling of being at fault',[47] maintaining on the contrary that 'it is exactly punishment which has the most powerfully *retarded* the development of the sentiment of guilt'.[48]

That conveys a tentative summary of the phylo-genesis of the idea of guilt. Nietzsche places at its origin

> the conviction that the species subsists exclusively thanks to the sacrifices and the productions of its ancestors, who must be *paid off* (*zurückzahlen*)[49] by sacrifices and productions; we recognize a *debt* that only grows because our ancestors (who survive as powerful *spirits*) never cease to interest themselves in the tribe and accord it, through their force, new advantages and new advances.[50]

Such is the 'sort of logic' of the debt, which makes each increase in life to be expressed as an inflation of the debit – a radically inverse image of the idea of progress, since whatever one earns is as much as what is *owed*, up to the point that the supreme debt becomes localized in *God*, supreme creditor, who assumes the universal debt.

What do we make of this? Nietzsche's response is vivid:

> It would be necessary that, finally, the impossibility of ever being free from debt engenders 'the impossibility of expiation', which engenders the Christian idea that God offers himself in sacrifice in order to pay the debts of man; God will pay it himself, God achieving by himself the liberation of man from what for man himself has become irremissible, the creditor offering himself for his debtor out of love (who would believe it?), out of love for his debtor.[51]

There is nothing left from the moment when the ascetic priest gives an artistic form to this brute sentiment, in the idea of *sin* (*Sünde*), which consists in assigning a cause to an internal suffering. From that point, a person 'must seek within himself, for a fault committed in the past, and it is necessary that he himself interpret his suffering as a punishment.'[52] It will suffice to *name* this internal feeling 'sin'.

In opposition, Nietzsche will dream in *Ecce Homo* of a 'god who would come to earth' in order 'to do nothing other than injustice'. 'To take for himself not punishment, but *guilt*, that would be truly divine.'[53] *The Will to Power* will pose, as a primary and salutary negation, the 'struggle against the feeling of guilt' (or of debt);[54] Nietzsche's physics, metaphysics and psychology all get their meaning from this struggle. The thesis of 'the absence of objective value (*Wertlosigkeit*) of the whole concept of guilt'[55] is the alpha and omega of Nietzsche's conception of guilt.

For Freud, the feeling of guilt is naturally related from the outset to sexuality. In hysteria and obsessional neurosis, Freud discovers (in his writings of the 1890s) the mechanism of self-reproach that 'the subject addresses to himself because of an anticipated sexual discharge (*jouissance*)' in the aid of the 'unconscious psychic work of transformation and substitution'.[56] All ulterior guilt gets its efficacy from reinvesting the prehistoric mnemonic trace of this more or less active experience of pleasure. It is no accident if obsessional neurosis, where the experience is partly active, becomes the site of a detailed analysis of *Schuldgefühl*, where the work of internalization is the most literally *active*.

The exaggeration of the 'original attitude of sexual passivity' establishes *masochism*. It is no accident if the relationship is imposed, via the feeling of guilt, between obsessional behaviour (*Zwangshandlung*) and religious ritual (*Religionsübung*).[57] Religion gives its sublimated form to obsessional debt. 'Social anguish' and guilty conscience are interpreted in the ensemble of analyses of narcissism, as a transfer of homosexual libido. Even the anguish of death is derived from the feeling of guilt.

In the meta-psychological essay on the *Unconscious*, Freud asks himself about the meaning of the strange union of terms, 'consciousness of unconscious guilt'.[58] The expression only makes sense in relation to the relation of affects and representations in the mechanism of *repression*. What is more, Freud asserts that 'there is no doubt that one can see in the Oedipus complex one of the most important sources of the feeling of guilt.'[59]

Under the form of the 'need for punishment' (*Strafbedürfnis*),[60] the therapeutic encounters the feeling of guilt, sustaining negative reactions. What is remarkable here is that Freud proves this need via a new theory of guilt. In a study dating from 1919, he asks 'from where does the consciousness of guilt itself emerge? The analyses yet again say nothing about it.'[61] He comes to compare it to a 'scarification' (*Narbenbildung*). In fact, it is the new topic which will clarify the relation; 'we will attribute it,' he says prudently in 1919, 'to an apparatus which, as critical moral conscience, is opposed to the rest of the Ego.'

In reality, *The Ego and the Id* is the canonical text for the feeling of guilt, in its study of 'Ego dependencies' (*Abhängigkeiten des Ichs*),[62] where guilt is related to the tension between the Superego and the Ego by way of the Id's drive-related stakes. Guilt is defined as 'the perception which, in the Ego, corresponds to the critique' of the Superego (*die dieser Kritik entsprechende Wahrnehmung in Ich*).[63] Beginning with this common matrix, normal, obsessional, and melancholic versions of guilt are put into place. There, guilt finds its axis in the correspondence of instances. In its obsessional version, The Ego is set against guilt, while the Superego submits to influences which remain unknown to the Ego; in the melancholic version, the Ego no longer raises any resistance and becomes the expiatory victim dedicated to the holocaust.

Moreover, with the new function of masochism, in the ensemble of the theory of the death drive, guilt acquires a new role, because part of the death drive is 'psychically linked to the Superego'. The feeling of guilt, insofar as it is anguish in the face of the Superego, is only a 'topical variation' of anguish.[64] Finally, the feeling of guilt is taken up by Freud at a phylogenetic level. It is no accident if an exceptionally long development is dedicated to guilt in *Civilization and Its Discontents*, as 'a perception, imparted to the Ego, of its surveillance'[65] by the Superego. *Kultur* is founded on this 'collective Superego' (*Kultur-Uber-Ich*) which is assured of its control by the production of these social sentiments.

What overhangs this onto-phylogenetic conception of guilt is the famous parable of *The Death of the Father* which concludes *Totem and Taboo*. The feeling of guilt is thus the reproduction on the individual plane of guilt derived from the originary collective scene and transmitted phylogenetically.

> Society rests from that point on a common fault (*Mitschuld*) relative to the death committed in common; religion, on guilt and repentance; morality, on the necessities of this society on the one hand, on the needs for expiation (*Buben*) engendered by the consciousness of guilt on the other.[66]

In clearer terms, the cement of the 'social contract' is guilt, derived from the 'father complex'. This is the source of the family of sentiments that Nietzsche designates as reactive; they are remorse and repentance (*Reue*), 'constituting the reaction of the Ego in a given case of guilt'.[67]

Nietzsche and Freud both arrive, not fortuitously, at asserting the importance of *debt* (*Schuld*). However, if this thematic becomes central for one and the other, it is because the critique of morality and the diagnosis of neurosis meet on the way to their encounter with the category of debt.

Without a doubt, Freud has best captured the blocked dialectic of neurotic debt in the case of the 'Ratman',[68] where he encounters in effect the clinical reality *in concreto* of the symbolic stake of neurotic debt. The complex scenario described by Freud consists, for the neurotic, in deferring (through a network of ruses) the reimbursement of the debt, while simultaneously affirming the necessity of debt as so much reassurance. In this monstrous ambivalence, the neurotic deploys precisely this double valence of debt, an expression of the requirement of repayment and its impossibility, exposed to a double sanction; what is distinctive about debt is the threat of sanctions for the subject who does not repay it, as well as the valuation of debt as a sanction *per se* – such that the subject is exposed and suffers as much in repaying the debt as in shirking it. Symbolic debt only exists with regard to the debtor, so that while the real debt is erased by its repayment, symbolic debt persists in the being of the debtor, who maintains its existence, to be at fault and with a bad conscience.

In other words, debt links the subject to himself, which constitutes the best definition of *guilt*. The reconciliation, conforming to the double sense of the word *Schuld*, is made explicit by Nietzsche as one of the etymological signs of a genealogy of morals. 'The essential moral concept of "guilt" draws its origin from the wholly material idea of "debt".'[69] Everything proceeds as if the mode of expression (*langage*) of neurosis clinically develops this analogy, implicated in an economic postulate. If it is true that nothing is more difficult for man than to renounce an 'enjoyment already experienced', it is necessary to conclude that 'truly speaking, we only know how to exchange one thing for another.'

CRIME AND PUNISHMENT

We are now in a position to better understand the significance of Nietzsche's theory of criminality, which had caught Freud's attention. Zarathustra's famous declaration, with its tone of provocation and scandal, is the best document on the matter.[70]

In question is a text from the first part of *Also Sprach Zarathustra* entitled 'On the pale criminal'. It is presented as a profession of faith for the criminal, which could be interpreted as an apology for crime. In fact, it expresses the criminal point of view, instead of considering crime from the point of view of the judges. In this way it presents the grandeur of crime as an identity of thought and act in the commission of a crime. It expresses the depth of human contempt, of the radical misanthropy of the criminal who, far from subordinating crime to some conditional motif (such as theft), relates it to its own end, the 'the knife's thirst for fortune' and for blood.[71] But it is also the tragedy of guilt, the impossibility for the criminal to support the image of the crime.

This text is like a document of Nietzschean criminology, a contribution to a science just in the process of being constituted.[72] There we discover the relativization of Good and Evil, and an analogy between crime, madness and illness. 'Whoever falls ill today is the victim of the evil which is evil today; he wants to do evil with what makes him evil. But in other times there was another Evil and another Good.' It is a Dostoevskian text which challenges narrow-minded, fixist conceptions of morality, and which is destined to illustrate the Nietzschean immoralist in what we naively attribute to him as a bloody existence.

It is, in fact, the symbolic projection of axiological iconoclasm, which evokes the Shadow that accompanies Zarathustra in the last part. 'I have smashed what my heart has always respected, I have turned back all the boundaries and reversed all the images, I have pursued the most dangerous desires – in truth I have transcended at a single stroke every crime.'[73] The criminal comes to long for the security of prison.[74]

However, in order to grasp the sense of this text which caught Freud's interest, it is necessary to remember that in this text, there culminates a thematic which appears throughout Nietzsche's work, haunted by the parable of the criminal. 'Our crime toward criminals,' Nietzsche had already written in *Human, All Too Human*, 'consists in that we treat them like scoundrels.'[75] We should recall that between bad and good actions there is only a difference of degree from the moment that we consider them in conformity to necessity. Certainly, 'the complete irresponsibility of man with regard to his actions and to his being is the most bitter pill the scientist must swallow.'[76] We can perceive the meaning of the 'rehabilitation' of the criminal; it is meant to reverse the common canon, which consists in 'seeing in responsibility and duty the titles of human nobility'. In addition, irresponsibility figures in oneiric activity,[77] and it is only extended to wakeful acts.

This reflection goes back to examine the 'virtues of prejudice' demanded by 'social groups' in their defence. *The Voyager and His Shadow* remarks that 'every criminal forces society to return to degrees of a previous civilization, to the moment where the crime was committed; they act backwards.'[78] Such is the virtue of crime, that it reveals this regressive potentiality, the sacrifice of the individual in order to attain social goals.

Daybreak recalls that 'the criminal very often gives proof of a mastery over himself, of a spirit of sacrifice and of an exceptional intelligence, and that he maintains these qualities for those who fear them,'[79] in order to oppose it to 'those intoxicated by dreams', otherwise noxious to humanity. The criminal also evokes a possible future in which the criminal 'publicly dictates himself his own punishment' with respect to the law which he has promulgated himself.[80]

Above all, we find a remarkable aphorism in which Nietzsche attacks the 'abominable criminal code, with its grocer's balance sheets and its will to compensate guilt by penalty',[81] and opposes it to a diagnosis. 'Scarcely have we begun to reflect on the physiology of the criminal, than we find ourselves already faced with evidence that there exists no essential difference between criminals and the mentally ill'.[82] Then he asks us to draw the therapeutic consequences, envisioning a strategy of cure in relation to the interests of the ill and discountable prejudices. At the same time, our attention is called to the cynicism of the criminal. 'All those who have much frequented the prisons and jails are astonished to observe how rare it is to encounter an inmate who is unequivocally 'remorseful', but much more frequently one encounters a nostalgia for the dear old crime, badly or well loved'.[83] Such is the strange 'affliction' of the criminal that defies the categories of morality and strains notions of universality.

That leads to the opposition between the crime and the conscience of the criminal. 'The criminal,' writes Nietzsche in *Beyond Good and Evil*, 'often is not equal to his act; he diminishes and calumnies it.'[84] As for the lawyers, they are 'rarely artists enough to turn the glorious horror of crime to the profit of their clients'.[85] But seen from the perspective of society, Nietzsche raises as 'a point of deliquescence and of an unhealthy sensibility' the moment when 'society itself takes part in that which harms it, for the criminal' where 'to punish him seems unjust, to everyone the least idea of chastisement, the obligation to punish makes society suffer, makes it afraid' – a symptom of 'gregarious morality'.[86]

Likewise, in *Twilight of the Idols*, the portrait of Socrates will be compared with the anthropomorphic file of the criminal in order to illustrate decadence.[87] There we find the outline of a criminal typology in which 'the criminal type is a type of man strongly placed in unfavourable conditions, a type of man made ill'.[88] If he is banished from society, it is thus that he is uprooted from this form of existence where the instinct of a strong man is required. Such is 'the formula of physiological degeneration'. Those who become criminal 'are obliged to do secretly what he knows best, what he prefers, for a long time and with great tension, with precaution, with pretence', constrained, in order to avoid 'anaemia', to turn his sensibilities back against his instincts – feeling thus like 'the victim of fate'.[89] Dostoevski is explicitly evoked here as the great artisan (*orfèvre*) of criminals, who knows from what wood they are cut.

In an aphorism in *The Will to Power*, Nietzsche reveals the importance, and permanence, of the theory of the criminal. 'The criminals with whom Dostoevski lived in jail were generally and particularly of unbreakable natures; do they not thus have a hundred times more value than a "broken" Christ?',[90] which brings crime back to the heart of humanity. 'Who among us, given the favour of circumstances, would not have passed by way of the whole scale of crimes?'[91] Such is the glory of the criminal, 'the man of courage' and 'violator of contracts',[92] who 'prospered during the epoch of the Renaissance'.[93]

We find in *The Ego and the Id*, in the chapter dedicated to the feeling of guilt, a passage that summarizes the psychoanalytic position on crime:

> It was a surprise to discover that an elevation of the feeling of guilt could make a man into a criminal. But it is undoubtedly so. A potent feeling of guilt can be observed in many young criminals, which existed before the crime, thus guilt is not a consequence, but a motive for crime, as if it was a relief (*Erleichterung*) to be able to link this unconscious feeling of guilt to something real and present.'[94]

This idea-force of Freud's conception of crime had been developed in the article on *Criminals and Their Feelings of Guilt*. Crime serves, paradoxically, to relieve the sentiment of guilt 'of an unknown origin' by reattaching it to 'something definite'.[95] It is on the same occasion that Freud mentions that such a genesis was not unknown to Nietzsche.[96]

CRUELTY AND PITY

It is necessary to search for the importance of cruelty (*Grausamkeit*) for Nietzsche in his conceptions of people and of life. It appears linked to the Dionysian conception of life. 'The same cruelty that we find in the essence of each civilization is also found in the essence of each powerful religion and, in general, *in the nature of power* (*in der Natur der Macht*) which is always bad.'[97] Right away, we see that cruelty is the sign of power.

Human, All Too Human consigns cruelty to the phylogenetic heritage of the human species, as a trace of an archaic idiosyncrasy to which it bears witness.[98] For this reason, it is very quickly opposed, in the ethical register, to its antonymic virtue, pity (*Mitleid*). The evocation serves to recall that what now appears to us as a vice was originally a human *virtue*. We see this in an aphorism in *Daybreak* that evokes 'the enjoyment (*jouissance*) of cruelty' (*Genuss der Grausamkeit*).[99] 'Cruelty,' Nietzsche diagnoses, 'belongs to the most ancient festivities (*Festfreude*) of humankind,' as a recreation that the human community takes for its anguish. In the ancient spectacle of the voluntary martyr giving himself to the gods, Nietzsche makes us consider an essential fact. 'The cruel enjoy the highest form of secret (*Kitzel*) joy, of feelings of power (*Machtgefühl*).' It is thus a refraction of the most positive sentiment for Nietzsche, as, prior to the formal introduction of the concept, the shadow cast by *Wille zur Macht*.

For that reason, Nietzsche locates cruelty at the heart of morality. Behind its apparent virtues, he reveals at length in another aphorism in *Daybreak* that it acts secretly; 'virtue is just a refined form of cruelty', which comes from an 'instinct for distinction' (*Auszeichnung*) that draws pleasure from 'doing ill' toward others by arousing envy, 'the feeling of one's impotence and degradation.'[100]

Consequently, *The Gay Science* will evoke cruelty in terms of sanctity[101] and of necessity.[102] Cruelty is also associated with greatness. 'Whoever possesses greatness is cruel with respect to his virtues and secondary considerations alike.' Zarathustra defines 'man' as 'the cruelest of animals',[103] who created for himself heaven on earth by inventing Hell.

There is thus an essential stake to 'change ones opinion toward cruelty and open one's eyes', as we are invited to do in *Beyond Good and Evil.* 'Nearly everything we call "higher civilization" rests on the spiritualization and the deepening of *cruelty* – that is my argument, that this "savage beast" has not been defeated, but it lives, it prospers, it alone is deified.'[104] The reference to tragedy takes this theme in all its meanings, from one end to the other in Nietzsche's *work*; cruelty is the mainspring of tragedy's 'voluptuous sorrow'. But there, Nietzsche gives us the lineaments of what we can identify as his theory of sado-masochism.

We should note at the outset that the examples to which Nietzsche always returns pertain to collective psychology. On the other hand, he ends the aphorism just described by furnishing us with an outline of an ontogenetic theory of this pleasure in cruelty. 'It is necessary here for us to finally dispel the vulgar psychology which not so long ago knew only how to teach about cruelty as being born from the spectacle of the suffering of *others*; there is also an abundant enjoyment, more abundant than suffering itself, in the suffering that one inflicts on oneself' (*Sichleiden-machen*).[105] There, Nietzsche locates sado-masochism, through the 'vivisection of conscience' at work in all asceticism, including the act of cognition – if such is the case that 'in every desire to know there is at least a drop of cruelty'. Further on, Nietzsche analyses the manifestations of 'this type of cruelty that makes up intellectual taste and consciousness.'[106]

Nietzsche examines the trajectory of cruelty in detail in *On The Genealogy of Morals*, where the motor is the process of internalization by which 'the instinct for cruelty is turned back (*sich rückwärts wendet*), and afterwards is no longer able to be discharged (*entladen*) to the outside'.[107] We understand from here on that cruelty is ranged, in Nietzsche's final synthesis, to the side of sexual instinct and vengeance, among the 'states in which we pose a clarification and a plenitude in things'. By the rejoicing that it procures, cruelty expresses an extension of the feeling of power.

In fact, we need to understand that cruelty, properly speaking (turned toward the outside), expresses a profusion of energy that demands to be discharged. 'Cruelty is the relief (*Erleichterung*) of tense and arrogant souls, those who forever treat themselves severely. It is a rejoice for those who do ill.'[108] We can grasp the complex relation between cruelty and pity; 'cruelty toward the insensible is the opposite of pity; cruelty toward the sensible is the highest expression of the power of the one who pities'.[109] In other words, 'cruelty is a sensibility displaced and become spiritual'.[110] It is true that 'there are many cruel people who are too weak for cruelty',[111] and that 'one must also be as compassionate as cruel in order to be able to be sometimes both'.[112]

In summary, cruelty is taken by Nietzsche in two registers, in the originary given of nature and in its ethical valorization. From the first point of view, he never ceases to repeat that 'an enormous cruelty exists from the moment of origin of every organism'.[113] Consequently, 'we must be as cruel as compassionate; we must guard against becoming poorer than Nature is'.[114] But at the same time, cruelty appears as a symptom of defence, as a 'remedy (*Heilmittel*) for wounded pride'.[115] Only it is a positive sign, and from here on it is useful to distinguish two cruelties, for it is true that an axiological difference crosses the concept. 'There is a cruelty of sick souls (*böser*) and also a cruelty of vile and petty souls (*schlechter und geringer*)'.[116]

Nietzsche's axiological opposition between cruelty and pity functions very clearly, and is assimilated to a 'hypochondriac illness',[117] to the 'most profound abyss'[118] which expresses an ethico-religious reactivity, reduced in the last instance to 'the praxis of nihilism'.[119] The devalorization of cruelty is simultaneously expressed by an *overvalorization* of pity.

For Freud, cruelty expresses a typically sado-masochistic experience, and pity appears most often, behind its moral appearances, as the reaction-formation of a sadistic tendency, developed in reaction to an aggressive desire that is repressed *and* in a contrary sense. Pity as *Reaktionsbildung* thus appears as the conscious counter-investment of a force equal to, even if in the opposite direction from, an unconscious aggressive investment.[120] From this point of view, the procedure appears typically obsessional and will be related to the Superego as a moral case.

It is precisely on this point that we can see the convergence of these two diagnoses, but up to that point they are expressed differently. Nietzsche shows cruelty asleep in pity in a form that is sublimated but never transcended, thus locating a reactionary doubling and rejecting the trickery of *Mitleiden*. But he responds by reverting it to a reaction-formation and by naming cruelty as a counter-value. This emerges on an ethical condemnation of pity and an apology for 'good' cruelty. For Freud, it is sufficient first to locate the reaction-formations, then to relate the affect to its effective process, so that the obsessional who experiences his repressed aggression as a sympathetic effusion will be found assigning a real origin to his affect. That has in the last instance the goal of pacifying the affect and the drive which is expressed by it. An apology for cruelty would be, in Freud's eyes, a sort of second-degree reactionary return.

On the other hand, we can locate in the economy of drives what Freud conceives as a particular drive whose status is specified in many respects; he calls it *Bemächtigungstrieb*. *Bemächtigen* designates the action of *taking over* by mobilizing one's Power (*Macht*); we might call it a *drive to expropriate*. A question looms for whomever reflects on Nietzsche: is it not the case that Freud's drive to expropriate is really something like the principle of cruelty, the Freudian homology to *Will to Power*? The question only acts here to stimulate an examination of the concept of *drive to expropriate*, for it is true that, as part of an analogy, the comparison of Freudian and Nietzschean theories can be realized only by transcending the analogy, by discovering a *nexus* at a totally distinct level, of which the analogy is only an index. It is thus a question of grasping the conceptual function of the *drive to expropriate* in the economy of Freudian thought in order to give satisfaction, consequently, to the analogy that is served, even if to deconstruct it.

The *drive to expropriate* is marked from the outset by its special status in Freud's taxonomy of drives. We saw, in fact, that Freud's passage of drives, which lacks the tropical luxuriance of its Nietzschean homology, is structured along two crestlines, the fundamental drives (Hunger/Love, Life/Death) on the one hand, and the partial drives out of which the sexual drive is minted on the other. The *drive to expropriate* seems to be distinguished by an exceptional atopy at first. The psychic apparatus on which the drive's jurisdiction depends appears to allow it a certain vagueness that imparts a particular autonomy to the drive – relatively independent of the vicissitudes of the great dualist structure itself. Must we thus see in it a local heteronomy in the general economy of drives? This question indicates in any case the interest in clarifying the status of the drive, otherwise important for our comparison with the Nietzschean concept which provides it with a sort of 'vis-à-vis'.

Freud introduces the *drive to expropriate* from his reflections on the partial drives of voyeurism and exhibitionism (*Schau- und Zeiglust Triebe*) on the one hand, and of cruelty (*Graumsamkeit Triebe*) on the other. Moreover, it is rather a question of tendencies, whose 'relations internal to genital life would only appear later'.[121] The one and the other manifest the exercise of a *drive to expropriate* which is still unlimited. It functions in a primitive manner, anterior to genital development, and, above all – a considerable derogation to the topological principle – of 'sexual activity linked to the erogenous zones'. It is interesting that in 1905 Freud could only point out the existence of this *drive to expropriate*, conceding that 'no thorough psychological analysis of this drive has yet been known to succeed.' It is only in August of 1915 that he is able to formulate a hypothesis. 'We can admit that the tendency to cruelty derives from the drive to expropriate and makes its appearance during a stage of sexual life in which the genital organs have not yet taken their definitive role.'[122] So the *drive to expropriate* is at once originary *and* linked in a way both intimate and negative to sexual life; it is an important element of our initial sexual life without referring to sexuality, properly speaking.

The intelligibility of the concept of *drive to expropriate* progresses through the mode of the activity/passivity of drives. The privileged theme here is obsessional neurosis, characterized by a strong regression to the *anal–sadistic* stage. Thus we read in *The Predisposition to Obsessional Neurosis* (1913) that pregenital organization is characterized by 'the opposition between tendencies toward active and passive goals'; the first are related to anal eroticism, while the second return to our *drive to expropriate*. 'Activity rises from the drive to expropriate in general, what we specifically call *sadism*, when we find it in the service of the sexual function.'[123]

We can see how the sense of intervention stands out with regard to the *drive to expropriate*; its function is to take charge of and to signify the activity of the drives, or better stated, *drive as activity*. Consequently, we can explain it by saying that Freud was constrained in his manipulation of this type of drive, both by the latent duality of the particular nature of the drive and by its general function. From the first point of view, we must say that partial drives exist which one can characterize by their own drive to expropriate; from the second point of view, an expropriating function exists that represents 'partial drives *in general*'.

Freud is correct in holding these two levels at once, because, if the *drive to expropriate* does indeed return to the function of a *princeps* activity, it is a question of not hypostasizing it *in principle*. It is not a matter of unifying the whole psyche around itself; that is why Freud's *drive to expropriate*, by its conceptual nature, is incomparably more modest in its extension than Nietzsche's Will to Power. It is also why Freud wants to apply the general scope of partial drives to the *drive to expropriate*, which supposes, conforming to the topological rule, to assign it a somatic substrate, homologous to the erogenous zones. Thus it is that, in a 1915 addendum to the *Three Essays on the Theory of Sexuality*, Freud assigns an *organ* to the *drive to expropriate*, that of the musculature (intestinal mucus serves the organ in a passive capacity).

Freud again brings up the idea that sadism marks a later development than the original *drive to expropriate*, via a union between this drive and a sexual end. In *Instincts and Their Vicissitudes*, from the same period, violent domination (*Uberwältigung*), which along with abasement and the administration of pain characterizing the aim of sadism, implies a *drive to expropriate*; with sadism, *Bewältigung* becomes *Uberwältigung*.

It is remarkable that the advent of the second drive-related dualism will have the effect of rendering useless the idea of a specific *drive to expropriate*. In fact, sadism is no longer explained principally by the development of an original *drive to expropriate*, but instead by a derivation of the death-wish toward the object, by which it 'enters the service of the sexual function'.[124] We thus discover an *expropriating function*, active everywhere that the death-wish exerts its *power*, from the time of its expropriation of love in the oral stage up to the mastery of the sexual object in the genital phase. At the same time, we can postulate the manifestation of a *drive to expropriate* in those phenomena where it is a question of mastering traumatic excitation. The essential thing, however, is that the *drive to expropriate* has in some way split; its various rejections are no longer only the manifestations of a general expropriating function.

Freud thus finally determines, from *Beyond the Pleasure Principle* (1920), the thorny alternative that the *drive to expropriate* poses; in the end he refuses to make it into a special drive, even less an originary one. That is to say that *there is no autogenetic Freudian principle of power* (*Macht*). The expropriating function indeed exists, but it constitutes a determinant of the drives' stake; it is found actively working, even linked to a drive activity, without itself explaining anything *per se*. The second dualism of the drives effectively applies even more rigorously the principle of the limitation of drives; the jurisdiction of the death-wish again reduces the pretension to the secession of little, independent drive principles. It is thus that with the new government of the drives, the *drive to expropriate* can no longer discover its own identity, but will be surrounded and dissolved in a new general function, or rather required as a 'supplement' (*Zusatz*), when the vital drive generally needs a 'helping hand' in order to master its object. Moreover, Freud would not know how to praise expropriation, in the same way that Nietzsche praises cruelty.

THE PERPLEX OF MORALITY: A GIVEN OR A PROBLEM?

What is most striking about Freud's general (and personal) attitude toward morality is, paradoxically, his refusal to pose it as a *problem*. Morality, for Freud, is what comes from the Self, or, in the words of Theodor Vischer (whom Freud strongly appreciated), 'whoever is moral always conceives of himself'.[125] In this sense, morality is a given whose existence, Freud declares, affects his ability to explain it.[126] When morality is placed in the global perspective of history, Freud acknowledges an analogy. 'The moral tendencies of humanity, whose strength and importance it would be futile to dispute, constitute an acquisition of human history and form, to an unfortunately very variable degree, the hereditary patrimony of humanity today.'[127]

Consequently, when Freud is prevailed upon to take a position on the problem of ethics, under pressure from such of his interlocutors as Oscar Pfister and James Putnam,[128] who were preoccupied with this question, he always presents a double principle. On the one hand, Freud refuses to mix questions of ethics with those of fact, investigable by a positive and scientific approach; on the other, he refuses to objectify what precisely came from the Self by some speculative postulate, such as the notion of a 'universal order'.[129] At most, the ethical is 'a species of marching order in use in relations between humans'.[130] Finally, when the moralist insists, Freud suggests that behind the claim of noble natures, one would have no difficulty finding some reaction-formation against unconfessed drives; so morality joins religion in the panoply of means of defence and of sublimation that allow humanity to transform its demanding drives and to impose reason upon them.

It is difficult to be further from Nietzsche's approach, against which, as we saw above, Freud did not hesitate to apply the diagnosis or the suspicion that he reserved for pastors and sons of pastors. For Nietzsche, in fact, morality is the contrary of a peaceable and autonomous given. Moreover, Nietzsche had taken care to relate, in order to distinguish them, two approaches to morality, as we can see in an aphorism from 1885. 'A moralist is the contrary of a preacher of morals; he is a thinker who sees morality as suspect, doubtful, in short as a problem', quickly adding that 'the moralist, for the same reason, is himself a suspect being'.[131]

This permits us to gauge the radical difference between Freud's and Nietzsche's points of view. For Freud, morality is not problematic, and whoever speaks of morality resembles a preacher, and comprises a 'moralist'; at the limits, all discourse, either *of* morality or *on* morality, is 'suspect'. For Nietzsche, the true negation of morality consists in a critique of morality of which the moralist, for whom morality is *the* problem, is the authentic instrument.

'*To see*, and *to demonstrate* the problem of morality: that seems to me to be the new task, the essential thing.'[132] For Freud, it is neither essential, nor new, nor a task, but rather the most ancient *fact*, ahistorical or prehistorical, at once the most fundamental and the most anodyne, the most visible and the most implicit. To demonstrate morality is thus to transgress it. In addition, there is an idiosyncratic difference. 'I will not rest', declared Nietzsche, 'until I have clarified the immorality of a thing. When I grasp this immorality, I feel my equilibrium come back to me.'[133] Nietzschean conscience is expressed by a hypersensibility toward immorality; morality is thus, inverse to the Freudian sense of the Law, what comes *least* from the Self.

That is thus the strange statement to which a literal comparison of these two approaches leads. On the one hand, what is at the heart of Nietzsche's psychopathology (morality) is for Freud the least problematic aspect; yet we find that Nietzsche's diagnostic work explores the illnesses of morality in terms of mechanisms remarkably homologous to those which Freud locates in his elucidation of the logic of drives, which led precisely to the study of neurosis.

This strange perplex demands to be thought as such. It challenges the immediate analogy between neurosis and morality by recalling that they are related to heterogeneous presuppositions. At the same time, however, it can serve to found, in a certain sense, an encounter between Freudian and Nietzschean diagnoses. It cannot be a simple coincidence if Nietzsche and Freud encounter and theorize, each from their own perspective, homologous mechanisms, as if Nietzsche had theorized neurosis (in the Freudian sense) as morality, and as if, like an echo, Freud diagnosed a conflict of morality (inspired by Nietzsche) as neurosis.

Neurosis, a 'sickness of desire', expresses in effect the fundamental conflict with prohibition, such that neurosis is fundamentally explained by morality, emanating from an originary conflict, Oedipal in nature. In order to explicate this conflict, and this pathology, we must now take our examination to a cultural level.

2

CULTURE AND CIVILIZATION

There is for Nietzsche, as for Freud, a theory of civilization (*Kultur*) which is at the same time a theory of the illness or *malaise* of civilization. From the moment that we see this theory as a necessary and natural extension of the theory of individual illness, it is impossible to reduce it to a mere appendix; rather, it is for both theorists an essential, and even in some ways an originary, moment.

INSTINCT AND CULTURE

For Nietzsche, it is enough to recall that he starts out with a theory of civilization, by way of his theory of Greek art and his critique of modernity. As for Freud, if *Civilization and Its Discontents* was written only late in his career, Freud encountered the problem of *Kultur* from the beginning, from the moment that the problem of neurosis appears to him as a conflict with the values instituted by civilization.

For both theorists, the problem of *Kultur* reflects *the* central problem, that of instinct and its satisfaction. *Kultur* is thus an apparently natural implication of *Trieblehre* as both its extension and its stake; that is why Nietzsche and Freud both approach civilization in terms of illness. Civilization is not only unwell, it *is* the illness, as soon as it emerges as a chronic obstacle to the satisfaction of instincts.

But there is a further specification that allows the problem of instinct to be paired with that of civilization, that of the neo-Darwinian principle (as stated by Haeckel) according to which ontogeny (individual development) recapitulates phylogeny (species development). This law is taken seriously in two senses since, first, collective development serves as a document which renders individual development intelligible, and second, it helps clarify development accordingly. By virtue of this biogenetic principle, a sort of natural *nexus* is established for both Freud and Nietzsche between the two problems of drives and *Kultur*, coupled by an irresistible necessity.

That explains why, throughout our examination of the preceding thematics, we have encountered applications of the Darwinian principle, and why, if we wish to complete our inquiry into an overall thematic, the theory of *Kultur* constitutes the natural term, of which instinct, a term that we have left behind, constitutes the other extremity, significantly configured as a serpent chasing its own tail. This is also the moment of the *diagnostic* which extends the examination of neurosis and morality.

Starting from a reflection on Greek civilization, Nietzsche's first aim is to extract the deepest reasons for the strength of Hellenism, which serves simultaneously as a model that permits him to judge modernity, by contrast. Immediately, Nietzsche encounters (the problem of) the authenticity of *Kultur* relative to the strength of instinct which is expressed there, in contrast to the degeneration of modernity which seemingly expresses a decline of instinctual strength. Thus Nietzsche defines civilization in the antinomian terms of strength and weakness, functionally correlative to the instinctual register. The notions of strength and weakness are dimly defined by Nietzsche, who is content to present them merely as a symptomology.

Kultur, for these reasons, is defined from the beginning by the quality of instincts which, being expressed there, adjudicate the proper mode of being. The conflictual duality between the Apollonian and Dionysian instincts constitute the *being* of Greek *Kultur*; this representation finds its distant origin in the tradition (following Herder) of fundamental instincts that express the authenticity of the *Volk*, specified by the vision of Burckhardt's *Welgeschichte*, which Nietzsche knew from his days at Basel.[1]

The whole of Nietzsche's analysis is centred on an examination of the symptoms and causes of the illness by which the characteristic health of Greek civilization became corrupted. Here, Socrates serves to define and name the syndrome; the intrusion of reflection into the noble, spontaneous totality of the *polis* seems to be at once the cause and the principal symptom of this *decadence* (*Verfall*), to put the process in Burckhardtian terms. It is expressed by a progressive debilitation of the fundamental instincts, an idea which is also found in Wagner. Nietzsche's analysis comes back to examine the fate of civilization as a mnemonic expression of instinct, of the fate of human instincts (an even better expression), or rather as an immediate reflection of instincts.

We now understand in what way *Untimely Meditations* extends *The Birth of Tragedy*. The latter describes the state of health and the causes of its alteration; the former details the signs of modern illness, undermining the myth of progress and classifying its syndromes (philistinism, historicism). The second *Untimely Meditation* is exemplary in its analysis, beginning with the hypertrophy of historical meaning, the manifestations of decadence. The veneration of the past is decoded as the hypertrophy of the vital strengths of the present. Not accidentally, at the same time Nietzsche takes his critique to the level of pedagogy, the mode of domesticating the instincts toward a 'cultural' end. Nietzsche concludes his critique by saying that 'culture is something other than an embellishment of life', that it is necessary to conceive of it as 'a new nature', a 'harmony between life and thought, appearance, and will'.[2]

This thematic runs throughout Nietzsche's work. The entire critique of morality is presented as a reflection on the mechanisms of civilization considered as the management of instincts. In this sense, Nietzsche's genealogy of morals is fundamentally an *ethnology*, tending to treat the conditions of collective morality as an instinct-proof institution.

The final problematic of *The Will to Power* locates the opposition between *Kultur* and *Zivilisation*,[3] and postulates an 'antagonism' between the first, a time of profusion and corruption, and the second, epochs of 'forced and voluntary socialization', a period of intolerance toward artistic natures. In that, 'culture' is opposed by its finalities to 'civilization' as an enterprise of domestication. The great epochs of *Kultur* for Nietzsche are those (such as Greek antiquity or the Italian Renaissance) of artistic sublimation of the most vigorous instincts.

We can glimpse, through an allusion in the correspondence with Fliess in 1897,[4] that Freud had grasped, at the same time as the importance of instincts in neurosis, their conflict with civilization. From then on, Freud's reflections on *Kultur* would be centred on the pathogenetic question of the conflictual relation between the sexual drive and social taboos, through its neurotic manifestation.

The most significant text from this point of view is the article on *'Civilized' Sexual Morality and Modern Nervous Illness* (1908). There, Freud examines the prejudice (*Schaden*) that cultural requirements impose on the individual's sexual drive. He then proceeds to an examination of the damage inflicted by civilization, which 'is constructed on the repression of the drives'[5] and 'cultural gain' (*kulturelle Gewinn*), susceptible to taking the place of an acceptable 'compensation' (*Entschädigung*),[6] in a state of civilized morality where society is achieved, and characterized by the institution of monogamy. These terms are significant in Freud's discourse on culture, in order to evaluate, in a sort of debit–credit system, what *Kultur* substitutes for drives and what it cuts out. Without denying the necessity for a mediation of drives, he underlines the damage and concludes by asking himself 'whether our "civilized" sexual morality is worth the sacrifices that it imposes on us',[7] thus warning against a premature ethical condemnation on those, perverts and neurotics, who are deficient and thus, as those judged to be damaged, are punished for their symptoms.

We see that Freud approaches the problem of the relationship instinct–civilization, dear to Nietzsche, from a different angle which modifies the terms of the problem. Nietzsche begins with civilization in order to demonstrate the fate of instincts to which the individual is subject; Freud situates himself from the perspective of what civilization costs the individual.

In other words, the reflection on the possibility of neurosis as an intolerance of social taboos founds a theory of civilization that *Totem and Taboo* will develop some years later, on the basis of a principle of onto-phylogenetic correlation which permits Freud to explain primitive life via his analytic experience with neurosis. The essential thing remains, in Freud's ethnology, the process by which the individual is situated in relation to cultural taboos, whose prototype (and principal explanatory tool) is incest.

For Freud, the *malaise* of civilization is first of all a malaise of the individual, a being based on drives, faced with civilization. That implies postulating a cultural requirement, as an uncontested statement, and then situating the individual against this given – which allows Freud to diagnose it without proposing to reform it.

The trajectory of *Civilization and Its Discontents* (1929) is thus clarified. Freud begins with the contrast between the principle of individual pleasure and the external obstacles to happiness. There, the neuroses intervene, which 'threaten to undermine what little happiness has been acquired by the civilized human'. The neurotic is thus a revelation in that 'people become neurotic because they cannot maintain the level of renunciation (*Versagung*) demanded by society in the name of its cultural ideal'.[8] Otherwise, civilization is a simple fact that Freud defines as 'the totality of works and organizations whose institution distances us from the animal state and which serves two purposes, to protect man from nature, and to regulate the relations among men'.[9] *Kulturversagung* is another fact.

> It is impossible not to take into account to what a large extent the structure of civilization rests on the principle of renunciation of drives, and to what point it postulates the non-satisfaction (through repression, suppression, or some other mechanism) of powerful instincts'.[10]

Such is the origin of the chronic and constitutional malaise of civilization, which Freud explains as the struggle between Eros and Thanatos and the development of aggressiveness as an obstacle to cultural organization.

This thematic is taken up again in *Future of an Illusion*, where Freud writes that 'it seems that every civilization must be constructed on the constraint and renunciation of instincts'.[11] The 'decisive question' on which the 1929 essay closes is that which closed the preceding essay. 'Will we succeed, and to what point, to lessen the burden that the sacrifice of their instincts imposes on people, and to reconcile people to sacrifices which will remain necessary and to compensate for those sacrifices?'

In more precise terms, the burdens are frustration (*Versagung*), 'the fact that an instinct may not be satisfied'; reduction (*Einrichtung*) 'which establishes frustration'; finally privation (*Entbehrung*), 'the state which interdiction (*Verbot*) produces'. Freud's problem is to balance the relational formula *Versagung/Einrichtung* = *Entbehrung*, which is the key to the culture–drive arithmetic.

However, it gets more complicated. Beginning in 1912, Freud declares that 'as strange as it seems, I believe that one should consider the possibility that something in the very nature of the sexual drive is not propitious to the achievement (*Zustandekommen*) of full satisfaction (*Befriedigung*)'.[12] Something is lost *ab ovo*; primary satisfaction is rendered impossible by 'the incest barrier', and every satisfaction is a substitute; on the other hand, the plurality of composing elements introduces a diversity that can never be resorbed into a perfect unity.

As a consequence, 'it would be necessary, perhaps, to get used to the idea that to reconcile the demands of the sexual drive with those of civilization is simply impossible'.[13] In other words, 'the dissatisfaction that civilization brings with it is the consequence of certain particularities that the sexual drive has made its own under the pressure of civilization'. But Freud will reaffirm up to the end the 'dissatisfying nature in itself' of drives, independent of 'external influences'; 'there is always something lacking for complete discharge, and satisfaction *in waiting for something that will never come.*'

Freud diagnoses, throughout *Civilization and Its Discontents*, an irreducible antagonism between the two processes of individual development and the development of civilization.[14] It is thus impossible to subscribe to the prejudice according to which 'our civilization is indeed the most precious thing that we can acquire and possess'.[15] For all that, the conclusion of the essay is not pessimistic.

That is because at the same time Freud postulates an isomorphism of developments. 'Both are similar in nature, even if they are not identical processes, being applied to different objects.'[16] This establishes an astonishing 'finalism'. 'As one planet rotates on its axis while revolving around a central star, the isolated individual participates in the development of all humanity even while following the path of his own views'.[17] The functional harmony of individual and collective libidos founds a final hope in equilibrium, however precarious, on the model of the individual! Not fortuitously, the postulate of a 'collective Superego' permits such a hope, insofar as it is true that for Freud we can do nothing, in the final analysis, without the Law.

SUBLIMATION AND LABOUR

The success of a civilization rests, in the last instance, on the efficacy of a major process, the *sublimation* of drives. Between frustration and immediate satisfaction, Freud envisions a 'capacity to exchange the original sexual aim for another aim, which is no longer sexual but which is psychically related'.[18] Such is the means available to the individual for reconciling the demands of the drives with those of rationality.

The term *Sublimierung* is equally present in Nietzsche, and expresses the same metaphor of an evaporation[19] of instinct. It is in other respects a particular case of Nietzsche's inspiration through chemistry. From the beginning, Nietzsche's moral psychology encounters the process of sublimation at work in lived experience; 'unselfish (*non égoïste*) conduct' and 'disinterested contemplation' are said to be '*Sublimierungen* in which the fundamental element appears nearly volatilized (*verflüchtigt*) and no longer reveals its presence except under the closest scrutiny'.[20] The *Grundelement* being instinct as self-love, sublimation appears as the essential ethical process, consisting of occultation and 'spiriting away'.

Beginning with this principle, the whole critique of morality rests on an analysis of the tactics of sublimation, whose aim is the retrieval of the instinctive *Grundelement*. It comes back to invert the process of sublimation, by retrieving a solid, beginning with a vapour. From this point of view, from *Daybreak* to *On the Genealogy of Morals*, Nietzsche never does anything else but try to outwit the process of sublimation.

At the same time, however, the discriminating faculty of the Nietzschean moralist implies the sublimation of his own instincts, as expressed in a contemporary aphorism. 'My task: to sublimate all the instincts of the type that perceives the stranger from afar and still remains linked to pleasure'.[21] It is thus a question of a fundamental sublimation that contorts the pleasure principle in order to grasp the motivation of the *Other*.

Thus we see that, without some inflection, we would not be able to confuse Freud's version of sublimation with its Nietzschean homology. For Freud, sublimation is the conversion of the aim of a drive (for the individual) which permits energy to be channelled towards the ideal (collective) cultural given. For Nietzsche, sublimation converts a motive which misrecognizes its own (individual) nature as a mask (of altruism). The ideas are indeed closely related, but the function is different.

Freud needs to postulate a mechanism in order to account for the renunciation of the drive in its own interest, which explains its socialization and efficacious conditioning. Nietzsche has no need for such a mechanism in order to pass from one plane to another (from the individual to society), for the good reason that the cultural ideal is not *given* as such. It is *valued* as a travesty, fictive by nature, behind which individual instinct is at work.

That is why Freud's sublimation is a useful and efficacious mechanism that manages the drive–civilization antagonism (by opposition to the neurotic outcome), realizing a coalescence (instead of a harmony) between the two motivations. Nietzsche's sublimation is rather a process in the service of selfish (*égoïste*) instinct in order to make it believe that it does not exist.

In both cases, it is a question of a useful illusion, but one that for Freud is a resolution integrating individual libido into the orbit of civilized humanity – the least contradictory form of an intractable contradiction – while for Nietzsche it is a *lie* about which it is no longer useful to be ignorant, and necessary to unveil it, even if this is accomplished by a selective (further) use of illusions.

In addition, civilization appears as a construction that is nothing less than moral. 'Nearly everything that we call high culture rests on the spiritualization and deepening of cruelty'.[22] Aggression is not only an obstacle to civilization, as it is for Freud, but rather it is its idealized substance.

If it is true that *labour* is the sublimating motor of *Kultur* in modernity, the thought of both Nietzsche and Freud concerning labour are important revelations.

The central text for Nietzsche's conception of labour is the aphorism in *Daybreak* where he sounds out 'the apologists of labour':

> In the glorification of 'work' (*Verherrlighung der 'Arbeit'*), in the untiring discourse on the 'blessing of labour', I see the same ulterior motive that is at work in the praises addressed to those impersonal acts of benefit to all: to know the fear of everything that is individual ... such labour constitutes the best police force, maintains everyone in their own bridle, and is understood

to be a powerful hindrance to the development of reason, of desires, of the taste for independence. Because it consumes an extraordinary quantity of energy which is diverted from reflection, meditation, revery, worries, love and hate.[23]

Such is the ulterior motive of all valorization of labour, the devaluation of the *individuum.*

Moreover, this is an old idea for Nietzsche, who takes it in its Greek conception, which he maintains treats labour as a defamatory activity.[24] The activity of labour is a defamation to individuality; at most, the individual is inestimable as such, to the extent that 'one can never deduce a single merit' of the individual by starting with the products of his labour. In consequence, the overvaluation of labour is important as a symptom of decadence, which explains the emergence of a sort of herd civilization whose ideal of *Kultur* resides in the erasure of individuality. We understand, in contrast, that a sane *Kultur* is wary of work, to the extent that labour is organized entirely within a regime of individuality. Enemy of *Kultur*, labour is rather the policing tool of *Zivilisation*, an instrument of training and integration, which aims at 'rendering alike'.

Freud poses at the base of *Kultur* a 'constraint in labour' (*Arbeitszwang*), emanating from the 'renunciation of instincts' (*Triebverzicht*). One is proportional to the other; the degree of labour constraint which the industrial form of society has achieved can serve to measure the degree of instinctual frustration. Labour thus serves to socialize the drives, and therefore to deny their individuality, for Freud as for Nietzsche.

Nevertheless, this first idea, undeniably present for both theorists, is counterbalanced by Freud with a strong insistence on the positivity of the stratagem, as revealed in an important note in *Civilization and Its Discontents.* Freud emphasizes 'the importance of labour for the libidinal economy', to the extent that 'no other technique of vital conduct attaches the individual more solidly to reality than the accentuation of labour that is incorporated at least as a part of reality, in the human community'.[25] Freud briefly outlines a theory of labour as a *princeps* form of cultural sublimation, as the 'possibility of transferring the constituent forms of Narcissism, aggression, or even the erotism of the libido'.

There is in Freud's words a resonance which could be made to rank, at a first reading, among those praisers (*Lobredner*) of labour whom Nietzsche so despised. In fact, however, Freud produces in this text a diagnosis taking up the efficacy of the sublimating function such as labour attains, rather than justifying labour itself. Moreover, he sets this efficacy in opposition to the unpopularity of labour, 'little esteemed by men as a path toward happiness'.

It is not a problem if this difference in tone signifies a divergence of appreciation regarding labor. For Freud, renunciation is a necessity of *Kultur*, as painful as it is *functional.* From this last point of view, it is a *fact* that is necessary to accommodate, and labour is yet one of the least evil means of reconciling the requirements of gratification of the particular (*Einzelne*) with the general (cultural). If Freud does not glorify labour, he indeed recognizes it as the means of pacifying the inexpiable contrariety between desire and culture. For Nietzsche, in contrast, labour is identified as the alarming symptom that the contradiction is aggravated for the individual. An estimable remedy for the illness of civilization, as an antidote for aggression for Freud, labour for Nietzsche is a symptom of the illness and an aggravation by which social terror is carried on to individuality. For Freud, the individual saves what can be saved from the drives through their management, by the same means by which the individual is lost in Nietzsche's eyes.

RELIGION AND KULTUR

The theory of Kultur naturally leads to an examination of the great forms of manifestation incarnated in the trilogy *religion, art, science.*[26] The Being of *Kultur* consists precisely in 'the price attached to higher psychic activities, intellectual, scientific, and artistic productions'.[27] Nietzsche and Freud both intend to explain the essence of civilization by way of these 'higher activities'. But in order not to force the comparison at the outset, we need to recall the conception of civilization on which this theory depends.

For Freud, *Kultur* is founded on a material need for protection and the regulation of human relations. Because of this need, the most precious fruits of *Kultur* are developed, such as art, religion, philosophy and science. For Nietzsche, *Kultur* is somehow implicated from the outset in the theory of the higher forms of the mind, akin to the way that, for Burckhardt, culture appears as one of the three determinants of universal history, alongside religion and the State, while at the same time being the universal essence of 'civilization'.

We can thus confirm that Nietzsche has no need for an explicit theory of sublimation in order to explain the passage from one plane to another, as if from the outset, and by its very nature, *Kultur* is *already* sublimated. This nuance is important to the extent that the theory of the great forms of culture intervenes at a different level than does the theory of *Kultur*. We can grasp this best by looking at the conception of *religion*.

Religion is naturally the touchstone of Nietzsche's critical conception. The strength of religion comes from what are 'measures of value (*Wertmesser*), of scales (*Massstäbe*)'.[28] Therein resides its importance, such that a theory of *Kultur* as value finds its centre of gravity in the critique of this valorizing function.

Religion seems like a narcotic; as such, it comes close to art, but it reproduces debilitating illusions. We can say in this sense that Nietzsche's *Religionslehre* is only a deployment of his pathology of instincts.[29] The religious *habitus* is present as the cultural and phylogenetic homology of instinctual illness on an ontogenetic plane. Religion, from this point of view, serves Nietzsche in a continuous polemic usage, to name the illness, as art names the salvation.

But this meditation on religion is complicated in that religion exhibits a *strength*, even as a Will to Weakness; it is well defined in this sense when *Ecce Homo* characterizes the founder of a religion as 'one of those horrible, hybrid beings composed of illness and Will to Power'.[30] Such is the mysterious base of religion for Nietzsche, Will to Power placed in the service of illness.

The malaise of Civilization, in a Nietzschean sense, is the same as the neurosis of culture. It is the same thing that was developed in the whole critique of morality analyzed above[31] and which is given literally a clinical formulation. 'Religious neurosis *appears* as one form of "ill-being", of that there is no doubt'.[32] In other words, the question of decadence, central to Nietzsche's theory of *Kultur*,[33] is present as an inquiry into the religious type – the priest – as one who 'wishes for decadence'.[34]

Freud's conception of religion is related to the 'psycho-mythological' conception articulated in his well-known letter to Fliess[35] and taken up again in *The Psychopathology of Everyday Life*. Nevertheless, it is no accident if the examples in support of this explanation are borrowed from religion. 'One could be given the task of decomposing, from this point of view, the myths relative to paradise and to an original sin, to God, to evil and good, to immortality, etc., and so to translate metaphysics into meta-psychology.'[36] The 'construction of a supra-sensible reality' by the projection of an 'endo-psychic perception', analogous to paranoia, thus finds in religion a prime point of application.

Yet when Freud seeks to characterize religious deportment in terms of drives, and no longer merely to elucidate the projective mechanism, he imposes the analogy of neurosis, as seen in *Obsessive Actions and Religious Practices*. 'In virtue of these concordances and analogies, one could hazard the conception of obsessional neurosis as a pathological appendage (*pathologisches Gegenstück*) of religious formations, and to qualify the neurosis of individual religiosity as the religion of universal obsessive neurosis.'[37] The two compulsive ceremonials, religious and neurotic, converge on a common aim, 'the fundamental renunciation of the exercise of instincts'. At most, Freud specifies further that these repressed instincts could be considered, in the broadest sense, as 'selfish' (*égoïstes*) in the case of religious behaviour, which revert to their strictly sexual forms in the case of neurosis.

Totem and Taboo specifies the analogy between magico-religious behaviour and neurosis: 'one, the absence of motivation regarding prohibitions; two, their fixation in virtue of an internal necessity; three, their facility of displacement and their contagiousness regarding prohibited objects; four, the existence of ceremonial actions and commandments proceeding from these prohibitions'.[38]

This semiological affinity refers to a common etiological foundation. In his analysis on Leonardo Da Vinci, Freud experiments with the bond between religion and the 'paternal complex':

> Psychoanalysis has taught us to recognize an intimate bond uniting the paternal complex with the belief in God; it has shown us that the personal god is nothing other, psychologically, than the transfigured Father (*erhöhrer Vater*) .... In the paternal complex we recognize also the root of religious need. God, just and all-powerful, and benevolent Nature appear to us as the grandiose sublimations of the father and mother.[39]

As a result, religion seems to us as a 'protection ... against neurosis'. 'It discharges from the parental complex to which it is attached the feeling of culpability of the individual as well as of all humanity, and it resolves them for us'.

That expresses the fundamentally ambivalent nature of the relation. 'In this endless conflict existing, on the one hand, between nostalgia for the father, and filial fear and defiance on the other, we have seen the important characters and decisive evolutions among religions.' In addition, the study of the mechanism of 'demoniacal neurosis' reveals an aptitude of the infantile psyche for grasping the Father as Devil.[40]

Such is Freud's diagnosis of Christianity; Christ, by his death, has the mission of making amends for original sin. Now, 'sacrifice in itself signifies expiation for an act of murder', which is no other, symbolically, than the murder of the Father. It is thus a question of reconciling with the dead Father, but by 'the psychological fatality of ambivalence', the son 'becomes himself god alongside the father' or, more precisely, in the place of the father. 'The religion of the son is substituted for the religion of the father',[41] to the point that Holy Communion repeats the primitive murder that it was supposed to expiate. Thus, 'the Christian Communion is only, at base, a new expression of the father, a repetition of an act in need of expiation'. Christianity merely gives its dramatic form to the Oedipus conflict, by producing 'formations of compromise' by which, on the one hand, the murder of the father must be expiated, and on the other, benefits of the murder must be confirmed'.[42]

The Future of an Illusion inaugurates another genre of discussion on religion. There, Freud poses a new question; it is a matter of situating religion in *Kultur* at last to understand why it is held in such high esteem, as well as to judge 'what is (its) real value'.[43] Religion is specified as an *illusion*. 'We call an illusion a belief when, in its motivation, the realization of a desire is prevalent and when we cannot hold to account this action, from the relations between this belief and reality.'[44] Religious doctrines only express an intense need for consolation. 'It is a formidable relief for the individual soul to see the conflicts of infancy emanating from the paternal complex – conflicts never entirely resolved – removed, and to receive a solution acceptable to all,'[45] or in other words, 'the recognition of the fact that this (infantile) distress lasts one's whole life, that one is fastened to a father, a father one hundred times more powerful' (than the real father).

By refusing to concede to Roman Rolland that the origin and the basis of religion is an 'oceanic' feeling, a 'sensation of eternity, a feeling of something limitless',[46] Freud resolutely mobilizes a paternal model. Nothing is more instructive than the discussion by which Freud is able to submit the efficacy of Christianity as therapeutic, while Nietzsche discredits it from the outset as an aggravation of an illness.

The doctrine of 'universal love', in Freud's eyes, contradicts the primitive anthropological fact of the search for personal happiness, such that it would be 'indispensable to submit the amorous function to a vast modification in the psychic order'.[47] That implies a 'displacement of value' which relates the love for a particular object to the fact of love in general. The commandment 'love your neighbour as yourself' is at once a measure of the strongest defence against aggression *and* the best example of the anti-psychological processes of the collective Superego, as an inapplicable and derisory commandment. 'What a potent obstacle to civilization aggression must be, if to defend against it renders everything as unfortunate as it does to reclaim it'. Thus Freud condemns Christianity as a strategy for defeating the drives, all things considered.

The diagnosis of the illusion of 'after-worlds' in the Nietzschean sense allows us to measure the difference between these diagnostic points of view. In his writings on the two principles of psychic functioning, Freud cites 'the doctrine of recompense in the life Beyond in order to renounce the pleasures of the world here' as 'the mythical projection of this revolution of the mind' that is 'the substitution of the reality principle for the pleasure principle'.[48] According to this curious idea, Christianity struggles to facilitate the renunciation of the pleasure principle in the name of reality by referring to 'the promise of a future life'. Now, that is a poor calculation.[49]

ART AND KULTUR

What do we make of *art*, then, whose avowed element is exactly illusion?

For Nietzsche, art takes the whole of its meaning from the place of illusion and truth in existence and in people. Aesthetic pleasure, at the heart of the opposition between Apollo and Dionysus, is born of the joyous hope that the prison-house of individuation will be overthrown, and of the presentiment of a restored unity.[50] It is therefore at the heart of instinct, and thus of life, to the point that Nietzsche's aesthetic reflects *Trieblehre*.[51] The play of appearance is what teaches us to take pleasure in existence,[52] by endlessly plunging us back into infancy.

From this perspective, art appears as the sign of health in a *Kultur*, so that the hyper-development of rational activities comes to express the symptoms of decadence. In consequence, Nietzsche imposes art as an antidote to the illness of morality and as an alternative to science. Against its scientific fate, he calls for a regeneration through art. In this sense, art is the true enemy of the ascetic ideal, in 'sanctifying ... the *lie*' (there where science exalts the truth) and in 'putting the Will to Deception alongside the clear conscience'.[53] That is why the treason of the artist who becomes a vassal to the ascetic ideal, like Wagner, constitutes for Nietzsche the homology of religious sin and of scientific non-sense. The corruption of the artist appears as an anti-value.

So, as a stylization of the noble appearance or a remedy for decadence, art seems to be the alpha and omega of Nietzsche's *Weltanschuang*. It is the scheme, on the sensible plane, of Will to Power at work in authentic *Kultur*.

Here again, the article *The Claims of Psychoanalysis to Scientific Interest* characterizes in some essential formulae the meaning of artistic activity. Psychoanalysis 'recognizes in the practice of art an activity which is said to appease

(*Beschwichtigung*) unsated desires'.[54] This brief characterization turns out to be remarkably mechanistic; in other respects, it is why Freud sidesteps the problem of 'the aptitude for creation' which is at the base of the activity by declaring purely and simply that 'it is not a psychological question'. At most, it is a question of a transformation (*Unformung*) that attenuates the affectations of an individual's desires, which makes the work of art a sort of blueprint which does not even retain all its colours. The enjoyment of the spectator is itself a 'suppressed desire' which is recognized in the Other by means of the work of art. The content of the work is itself only the product of an artist's 'infantile impressions' and the works are only 'reactions to these excitations'. It is difficult to be more opposed to a creativist conception of art.

Throughout, artistic activity is none other than neurotic activity. 'The strength of the drives (*Triebkräfte*) of art are the same conflicts which push other individuals into neurosis'. Let us take this formula literally; a common matrix, energetic and dynamic, accounts for both art and neurosis. In addition, we could say that neurosis is in its way a work of art of the drives, as if neurosis and art must be defined as the two destinies of the same process.

Even the *Introductory Lectures on Psychoanalysis* present the artist as 'an introvert who is not far from being neurotic'.[55] Freud links art to a frustration of 'overdeveloped drive-related needs' which, unsatisfied, are turned away from reality (*Wirklichkeit*) and concentrated on 'desiring formations of an imaginative art'. The artist resembles the (barely) avoided neurotic, who permits himself 'to give his waking dreams a form such that they lose all personal characteristics capable of rebuffing a stranger and become a source of enjoyment for others'. This is accomplished by means of an essential process which confers upon its 'representation and unconscious fantasy' a quantity of pleasure sufficient to mask or to suppress, at least provisionally, the repressions.

Aesthetic pleasure is thus born of a fantasy which makes possible the provisional lifting of a repression; it is rushed to censure. Art is deliberately inscribed within the logic of repression, as a punctual and illusory liberation. The artist appears as one whose fantasies are served through the admiration of others, by procuring for others the means of again drawing some relief and consolation in the sources of enjoyment, become inaccessible in their own Unconscious.

In fact, this is a point of view acquired from Freud's technical writing which introduces 'the two principles of psychic becoming'. After having made explicit the opposition between the pleasure and reality principles, Freud introduces art as exhibiting 'a reconciliation between these two principles'.[56] The work of art in effect permits the pleasure principle to be gratified by contorting it, at the same time as gratifying reality, the inhibitory requirement of the reality principle, and to be compensated via an 'imaginary world' for the dissatisfaction imposed by reality.

Beginning with the development of a more solidly supported theory of civilization, the problem of art is renewed for Freud. In *Totem and Taboo*, the analogy between art and hysteria is introduced, the work of art being characterized as a sublimated hysteria, and hysteria as a 'deformed work of art'.[57]

Above all, art is presented as 'the sole domain where the omnipotence of ideas has been maintained up to our day'.[58] Likewise, in *The Future of an Illusion*, art is presented as giving 'substitutive satisfactions in compensation for the most ancient cultural renunciations, those which are the most deeply felt, and for that reason are not reconciled for man by the sacrifices made in the name of civilization'.[59] Art is at once the narcissistic mirror and civilization's supreme *ersatz.*

Finally, in *Civilization and Its Discontents*, art is ranked in the first level of *Ersatzbefriedigungen*[60] – a term also used by Freud to designate the substitutive formations of neurosis! In the *New Introductory Lectures on Psychoanalysis*, art is presented as 'nearly always inoffensive and beneficial, not pretending to be anything other than an illusion and never attempting an assault upon reality'.[61] In all this, art never seriously challenges the rights of the supreme power, *science*, which reigns without contest, but art is always in its shadows.

We find in Nietzsche an astonishing anticipation of the hysterical etiology of the artistic disposition, an idea dear to Freud. 'The *modern* artist, physiologically close to the hysteric, carries this morbid sign in his character as well.' Following a sort of clinical description comparing their deportments, Nietzsche adds that 'the hysteric is false – he lies for the pleasure of lying, he possesses an admirable art of dissimulation', joined to a 'vanity', a 'permanent fever that requires sedatives and does not draw back from any voluntary illusion'.[62] Nietzsche characterizes the artist by 'the absurd irritability of his system, which transforms the least experience into a crisis and which introduces "drama" to the slightest accidents of life, imparts every conceivable character to these reactions'.[63] Nietzsche does not omit a plastic aptitude for identification ('He is no longer one person, he is at most a meeting of several persons'); nor theatricality ('for this reason he is a great actor'); nor suggestibility ('virtuosity of their mimicry', 'art of their transfiguration', 'facility with which they enter into whatever character is *suggested* to them').

But we also note that Nietzsche argues in parallel against the *modern* figure of the artist; hysteria is thus valuable as a symptom of modernity-as-illness. The authentic artistic creation would therefore be conceived as the transcendence of hysteria, an expression of a corruption in the artistic vocation. Moreover, the Nietzschean clinical praxis is centred on *physiology*, conforming to the conception of *Wille zur Macht.* This double restriction hinders the production of a psychography of the artist, who Nietzsche understands as both a physiological and cultural type.

SCIENCE AND KULTUR

Is there something in *Kultur* beyond illusion? Here we encounter *science.*

The problem of science is contemporary with Nietzsche's reflective production. In the preface to *The Birth of Tragedy* written near the end of his life, Nietzsche presents his first work as having posed 'the problem even of science', such that science was 'conceived for the first time as problematic, as questionable'.[64] In clearer terms, this is to say that Nietzsche's philosophical course was inaugurated by a suspicion of science as a type of knowledge; he asks how Socrates, the 'mystagogue of science',[65] was possible? The desire for the search for the truth more than the desire for truth itself, which constitutes the 'fundamental secret of science',[66] has invested science with a decisive authority. This is the movement that is critical to reverse.

It must be accomplished by recalling from the outset that the 'man' of science and the 'man' of culture participate in two different spheres,[67] and then to submit scientific *habitus* to the lights of psychological analysis (in the Nietzschean sense). We discover in this way that the sage is not made of a pure metal, but an alloy 'of various motives and diverse attractions'.[68] That does not discredit science, since scientific activity represents 'an increase in energy'; it is very important, Nietzsche says in this sense, to have been a student of science.[69] Again, it is not necessary to be ignorant of the fact that scientific interest feeds from an instinctual source, so that it tends to take itself for its own ends. That is the beginning of the scientific *illusion*.

The Gay Science gives three illusory reasons which have justified the advancement of science: first, science as a means of 'better understanding the bounty and wisdom of God'; second, as a means of promoting 'the intimate union of morality, science, and happiness'; third, as 'an inoffensive, disinterested thing, sufficient unto itself'.[70] Zarathustra encounters on his path the figures of science become instinct, conscientious of spirit, who never want to know anything halfway, to the point where they make their kingdom in the brains of leeches,[71] and end by defining science as the name given to fear, the primordial human emotion. Science is only this 'ancient fear, charged by intelligence'.[72]

Within the framework of the philosophy of Will to Power, an insistent register will intervene concerning the ethical overdetermination of science. From the beginning, as we have seen,[73] Nietzsche insists on the development of the instinct for knowledge, which reaches a level of chronic pathology in science. Here the diagnosis becomes more radical; modern science is only 'the newest and most noble form'[74] of the ascetic ideal. Its fundamental agnosticism becomes a reflection of nihilism, the supreme illness of values. Nietzsche even makes science into a chosen ally of the ascetic ideal. Not creating any value by itself, it 'needs an ideal value, a value-creating power it can serve and which gives it faith in itself';[75] by its 'exaggeration of the value of truth', it comforts the ascetic ideal. That is why 'the epochs where the sage passes to the first rank' are 'the epochs of exhaustion' where 'the certainty of life' is eroded.[76] In fact, 'this 'modern science' . . . is for the moment the *best* ally of the ascetic ideal, because it is the most unconscious'.[77]

That is Nietzsche's real conclusion toward science; it takes its place alongside the Will to Nothingness by its very axiological neutrality. This does not preclude the possible use of science to aid in founding a transformation; did Nietzsche not plan a serious project of 'devoting ten years of study of the natural sciences in Vienna or Paris' in order to seek in 'the study of physics and the constitution of the atom'[78] the confirmation of the eternal return, the touchstone of Nietzsche's cosmology and axiology? So science is capable of being put into the service of a conception of the world liberated from the ascetic ideal, on condition that it change its axiological scope.

For Freud, *science* is opposed to world-visions (*Weltanschauungen*); in addition, it is presented as the solution (and dénouement) to the contradictions of religion, of philosophy and even of art. Science is what holds their promises, by *realizing* them through their adaptation to reality. We are a considerable ways from Nietzsche, who is quick to denounce scientific illusions.

The most significant text is Freud's work on the pleasure principle, where he opposes the religious strategy (which refers to the heavens) with that of science 'which comes closest to succeeding in the conquest' of the pleasure principle. 'Science also offers an intellectual pleasure during its labour and promises a practical gain in its end.'[79]

That is why science regularly appears in Freud as an alternative to religion – a role that for Nietzsche was delegated to art. The fictive dialogue that concludes *The Future of an Illusion* demonstrates this well. It is an apology for science, in which 'we have, through numerous and important successes, furnished the proof that it is not an illusion'.[80] There is no glorification in this fragment, but simply the idea that humanity has the most to expect from science. Science is not a 'revelation', but 'such as it is, it is all that we can have'.[81]

There is for Freud two cultural strategies for the drives. The 'principle function of the psychic mechanism' being 'to deliver the creature from tensions engendered in it by its needs', there are two possible tactics, whether to extract satisfaction from the external world through its 'domination' or to seek it in illusions. Those are the two poles incarnated in science and religion. If Freud's preference is for science, it is due to its functionality, as it 'constitutes the most perfect renunciation of the pleasure principle (*Lossagung zum Lustprinzip*) of which our psychic labour is capable'[82] in the present, while religion refers to the things of the hereafter.

THE DESTINY OF KULTUR

We can now understand the differential physiognomy of *Kultur*, following its function through each of its great productions. If religion is for both Nietzsche and Freud the site of illusion, the future of civilization consists in 'transcending' it by two very different means. For Nietzsche, it consists in following the channel of noble and sweet illusion proffered by art; for Freud, it means trusting in science, which is decidedly the least illusory means available to human society (where Nietzsche saw only a modern illusion). On the other hand, where Nietzsche diagnoses 'decadence' and calls on the salutary reaction of instinct, Freud diagnoses the effects of the death-wish that the life-wish can overcome, and science is one of its bulwarks. That brings us to the final question: what do we do?

3

THERAPEUTICS

Having described the symptoms of the illness of both individuals and of civilization, Nietzsche and Freud naturally turn to confront the final question which will close the process. *What does one do* in order to remedy the illness? How does one treat the illness and formulate a therapeutics?

There are, in fact, several levels to the therapeutic. The first corresponds to what we might call a dietetics of instinct. Since instinct, the first principle, is also the root of the illness, it is necessary to change its *regimen.*[1]

NIETZSCHE'S INSTINCTUAL DIETETICS AND THE PSYCHOANALYTIC CURE

In an aphorism in *Daybreak*[2] we find the most complete exposition of what could be called a Nietzschean therapy. There, Nietzsche poses the question of mastery over the Self; what does one do in order to combat 'the violence of an instinct'? This is the key question the Nietzschean psychologist must envision once he has described the laws of an instinct. With a concern that is interestingly exhaustive, Nietzsche seems to want to furnish us with a formula, a short technical breviary of self-therapy, by listing six methods of controlling an instinct.

The first solution consists in extinguishing the instinct by a sort of functional asceticism. 'To avoid occasions for satisfying the instinct, and weakening it by extended and always longer lapses of time' between satisfactions, it is a way of allowing the instinct 'to wither away'.[3] It is a radical solution that kills instinct through extreme neglect, or by progressively frustrating it into obsolescence.

Failing that, it is conceivable to regulate satisfaction by a disciplinary regimen that strongly resembles a dietetic of drives. 'One can make for oneself a law of strictly regulated order regarding satisfaction.' Moreover, it is both a substitute and a propaedeutic for the first method; in fact,

> by introducing regulation in oneself in this way and by restraining the flux and reflux of drives within the limits of fixed times, one gains some intermediary periods of time where the drive is no longer a disturbance, and beginning with that, one can perhaps pass on to the first method'.[4]

Whereas previously it was necessary to deprive the instinct of its pasture, in this method it is a question of balancing its grazing time.

The third solution, by contrast, attempts to gorge the instinct by an unrestrained satisfaction, as a way of inducing a salutary nausea. 'One could deliberately give oneself over to a savage and unbridled gluttony of an instinct, in order finally to reap a distaste for it and thus attain some control over the instinct.' This procedure strongly resembles a purge of drives through excess satisfaction. Nevertheless, Nietzsche takes care to indicate the risks attendant on this procedure, by underlining that 'the rider who beats his horse to death ... (often) breaks his own neck'.

The next procedure consists in an 'intellectual artifice'; it is a matter of 'linking the gluttony (of a dangerous instinct) to some generally troublesome thought, so firmly that, after a certain period, the thought of satisfaction provokes nearly always an instantaneous unpleasant sensation'. The detoxification here comes back, in Freudian terms (of whom the analogy is not fortuitously invoked here), to discredit the representation of satisfaction by linking the representation to a disagreeable affect. That implies a disruptive intervention in the cycle of the desire for self-reproduction in the instinct, founded on an association between a representation and an agreeable affect. Once affected by a bitter aftertaste, the satisfaction enters into a contradiction with itself and comes to be disinvested.

The fifth method resorts to a diversion, a matter of dislocating an instinct's potential strength by imposing some particularly difficult and demanding labour on the instinct, or by deliberately submitting it to new excitations and new pleasures. In topical terms, it is a question of considering new possibilities, 'of turning the thoughts and the play of physical strengths toward other paths,'[5] a curiously homœopathic method of treating drives. The method consists in treating one instinct by another through the production of a conflict; 'when one temporarily favours one instinct, one procures frequent occasions for its satisfaction, and thus one pushes it to dissipate its strength, without which the first instinct becomes dangerous in its violence.' We are aware that this implies a globalist conception of an instinctual economy, where the consummation of one part is proportional to that of the whole. It comes back, finally, to serve up to other instincts what the one overly voracious instinct claims that it 'would like to play the master', thus calling 'the tyrant' back to rationality. Here, democracy appears as a functional requirement for the health of the drives!

If every one of these procedures fails, there remains one final solution, resolutely ascetic, which consists at base in completely discrediting the entire instinctual machinery, thus putting every instinct outside the state of harm from being satisfied. It is a resort to 'weaken and oppress the *ensemble* of one's physical and moral organization', in order to 'weaken at the same time a particularly violent instinct', a radical, and in some ways a desperate solution, whose efficacy is obtained at the highest price a cure that amounts to psychic death.

Such is the panoply of graduated treatment in Nietzschean therapy. We see that it is 'an avoidance of occasions'; an 'implantation of regulation'; a provocation of 'satiety and distaste'; an establishment of links to 'a torturous idea';

a 'dislocation of strength'; finally, a 'weakening and general exhaustion'. We can only treat our instincts by gradually extinguishing them to various degrees.

That said, however, in what does the technique actually consist? We know that it is presented as a sort of self-therapy, to be administered according to one's own perception of the relations of force and instinctual needs. The Nietzschean instinctual subject is his own physician. We can gauge the difference from Freud's point of view by trying to imagine Freud counselling his neurotics to practise these methods. These are precisely what neurotics are *the least capable* of doing; a third term is required between the subject and his drives, that of the analyst.

On the other hand, and in correlation, it seems to imply an aptitude for manipulation and a relative control over one's instincts. However, in order to restrain the voluntarist aspect of this minor 'discourse on methods' of drives, Nietzsche adds at the end of his exposition the question that whether 'one *would want* to combat the violence of an instinct, that is not in our power' to judge. It is not at all a question of some deliberate strategy, but one of a pragmatic usage; the 'risk' and the 'success' decide the validity of the method, which strongly resembles a kind of pharmacopoeia of expedients, without any 'scientific' ambition for a systematic cure.

What demands treatment is not the opposite of instinct, but rather a 'rival', contrary instinct. The Will to Cure emanates from one instinct (rest, shame, love) that 'complains about another'. The intellect is no guide, but rather only a vacillating arbiter in a combat of instincts, one which gives the 'cure' its dramatic aspect. By this qualification, Nietzsche forestalls any interpretation of a treatment that would consist in *curing ourselves of our instincts* under the pretext of tempering a particular instinct; any asceticism here is purely functional.

But how do we *not* identify here, under this general requirement, Nietzsche's own personal problem, when Nietzsche's whole life can be explained in terms of his illness (and the proliferation of remedies),[6] right up to the point where he surrendered himself to his own final remedy, given that by an extraordinary effect of language he had *defined* in this text, with clinical precision, the very illness that soon would carry him away? 'General paralysis' had not been otherwise defined by psychiatric discourse than as this 'weakening and general exhaustion' (*die allgemeine Schwächung und Erschöpfung*) which Nietzsche formulates as the ultimate remedy. This is a magnificent illustration of Freud's praise–diagnosis of Nietzsche's gift for self-diagnosis, if it is true that the remedy only projects an existential experience of paralysis.[7]

Opposite Nietzsche's self-diagnosis,[8] we can situate the psychoanalytic *cure*, which is indeed, by contrast, an 'allotherapy'. For Nietzsche, the intervention of a *third party* expresses the socialization of desire (which knows well enough its own alienation), whereas Freud founds an analytic institution as this third party which is introduced between desire and the subject in order to re-establish the link.

The cure, significantly, is defined as 'a sort of re-education (*Nacherziehung*) that teaches the patient to overcome internal resistances'.[9] We can take this term in its formal sense, given that analysis intervenes in the conflictual process between civilization and the drive. If it is centred on sexuality, it is because 'nothing else, neither civilization nor education, has caused so much damage'. It is thus a matter of repairing in some way this damage, in a sense of recivilizing the subject. At the same time, the definition articulates the basic conditions for recruiting candidates for therapy. 'We must refuse those among the ill who possess neither sufficient education nor a sufficiently self-assured character'.[10] The primary condition is thus educability (*Erziehbarkeit*). To be outside the civilizing process – what Freud calls degeneration (*degenerativer Konstitution*)[11] – is to be excluded from psychoanalytic re-education.

Thus if Freud claims to recognize neurosis and civilization's responsibility in its genesis, he also seeks to effect, through the psychoanalytic technique, the return of dissident desires to a culturally accepted expression (*jouissance*), given that there can be no expression outside *Kultur*, even if *Kultur* itself prevents any perfect expression. For want of loving this civilization that demands so many sacrifices, it is necessary to re-establish a dosage (of expression) consisting in the least evil. This schema combines Freud's confidence in education (*Aufklärer*) with an awareness of the strength of the drive that rejects any social mysticism.

The analyst is at the crossroads between desire and *Kultur*, a progressive representative of the civilizing process, and even 'representing a conception of a free and enlightened world',[12] imposing the requirement of a cure which goes so far as to prescribe a salutary abstinence. 'Psychoanalytic treatment must as much as possible take place in a state of frustration, of abstinence.'[13] The 'priest of secular souls'[14] chases the secondary gains of the illness, in order to remove from the patient the primary gain that is the illness itself, but at the price of recognizing the order of desire and of justifying neurosis as the contravention of *Kultur*. That implies, however, a relation of forces, materialized by the necessary manifestations of *resistance* and *transference* which express the dialectic of the confrontation that self-therapy ignores.[15]

CURE AND OVERMAN

Following that, what exactly is a *cure*? Remarkably, Freud and Nietzsche do not formulate the problem in the same way. We can express this by saying that the further we go, the more we suspect 'man' even of *being* the illness in Nietzsche's representation, especially the illness called morality and its historical form of *nihilism*.[16] From that point, the remedy can only be *super* human; so Nietzsche, by naming *Overman*, only does so to articulate the gap between the illness and the 'cure'. We could as well characterize Overman as the figure of the cure or as the Beyond of the illness, and thus of morality.

Overman thus permits Nietzsche to unveil a regime of new instincts. In this manner he passes from the dietetic discussed above to a typology of a Beyond to the illness and the cure, where Overman designates both a *desire* and a *word*. It is the wish that just once all of the dead gods would 'live as Overman'.[17] 'Let me give birth to Overman!'[18] 'Overman' is what *we must say* 'while gazing out over distant seas',[19] even if there has 'never yet been an Overman'.[20] Overman is what *could* be created.[21] Zarathustra thus crosses a space that runs from Being-ill to a Being who would no longer have to be cured, who would have transcended the figure of the priest who inoculated the illness and who created the remedy–poison called *religion*. The priest never ceases making illnesses and administering panaceas. Overman's *health* must not be conceived as that of a cured being, at least he would not be the *same* one who was ill; he escapes all dialectics of illness in order to be positioned opposite the immediacy of Being and of Becoming.

Such is in effect the major *proof* in which Overman is revealed as the incarnation of Will to Power. To support the barest and hardest truth, that of the *eternal return*, a demoniacal truth according to which 'everything will return, and return in the same order, following the same merciless succession',[22] such that 'the eternal hourglass of life will be turned over and over without respite'. It is pure cosmic repetition which engages the pure repetitiveness of *Wille zur Macht* as both challenge and revelation. 'Do you want that? Do you want it again? Once? Always? To infinity?' Such would be Overman, who would love life to the point of 'no longer desiring any other thing than this supreme and eternal confirmation'. In that, 'the heaviest weight' (*das grösste Schwergewicht*) is also the lightest for the lightest heart, that of the infant-Overman, accessible to the pure presentation of becoming, 'the thought of thoughts'.

But in addition, this thought, insofar as it is experienced and lived, defines the supreme state of health. We should note that it excludes all re-presentation except its own return which is an eternally present presentation. In that, as far as we can conceive it, every figure of mediation disappears – remorse, regret, resentment, and their derivatives, guilt, bad conscience, and finally every type of ethico-religious psychopathology, up to *pity*.

Supreme health, as 'hyperborean' as it is, expresses the narcissistic schema of omnipotence, that is to say of infinite satisfaction. Overman names an infinite satisfaction whose sole rationality and morality is reduced to *noch einmal, encore!* We understand why its revelation is for Nietzsche a monstrous mixture of harsh enjoyment and sacred terror, given that pleasure in its infinite repetition sounds like damnation. Such is the content of the revelation at Sils-Maria where Nietzsche discovered the most implacable verdict, that of an integral narcissism, of which it only remained to draw out its consequences, whose principal figure is Overman himself.

We could make better sense of it if we take up again the difference encountered above, between the paternal model of Freudian guilt and its absence in Nietzsche. That is expressed, briefly speaking, by the absence of a theory of the *Superego* in Nietzsche, apart from a truly topical elaboration of what Freud would call the 'psychic apparatus'. In correlation, there is thus no theory of *identification* as an elaboration of the paternal model. That is why originary guilt, for Freud, flows from its primitive extraction to the Law, which is supported simultaneously by an aspect of the Law, that of the Father.

For Nietzsche, the model, we could say by way of contrast, is fundamentally *maternal*. It is the schema of a primitive innocence of becoming, a primary enjoyment of the desire for inclusion, that a progressive infection has spoiled whereby the *Other*, the figure of the *intruder*, is introduced between desire and its enjoyment, in the figure of the ascetic priest, before finally being internalized and festering (*consommant la gangrère*). That is why there was never developed an endogenous instance charged with the mastery of the paternal model, such that guilt is inoculated from the outside, by the *priest*, who plays the role of a Father introjected by force.

For the same reason, there is for Nietzsche no originary Oedipal scenario, no specific, dramatic moment where, under the figure of the Father, desire is confronted by the Law. In the end, Nietzsche conceives of only two states, that of a desire of a pure life (health), indifferent to the Law and its significations (guilt), and that of an infected desire. Thus the Law only appears as the figure of illness–morality in Nietzsche, while Freud institutes it as a sort of dialectic of desire, where the Law appears as a necessary term of identificatory constitution. Such is finally the difference in diagnostics between Nietzsche and Freud. For Freud, neurosis is a bad relation between the Law and the paternal complex, which the cure functions to readjust; for Nietzsche, moral illness is the illness of life consecutive to the accession of a point of view of the Law that is lethal to life, of which it is a question of *transcending*, by a radical transvaluation, on the side of becoming-being symbolized by the camel and the lion, a return to *infancy*. Conforming to Zarathustra's famous parable, the cure leads from the heaviest weight to liberty and so to 'innocence and forgetting, which is a recommencement, a wheel that turns by itself, a first movement, a sacred "yes".'[23]

This transvaluation implies a return to a form of apprehension that implies at the same time the transcendence of guilt and a strategy of identification. Nietzsche's Overman possesses in effect a major virtue in an aptitude for veneration (*Verehrung*) and for respect (*Ehrfucht*). It is a question of everything but a banal sentiment, a characterological sign all the more determinant – in that nihilism and decadence are expressed *a contrario* by an impotence to admire, to honour, to *venerate* in the strong sense of the term (an *affirmative* sentiment in which Will to Power is affirmed) – so that the man of *ressentiment* no longer knows what it means to venerate. Zarathustra, in a world where 'no one knows any longer how to venerate', presents 'the great despisers as the great veneraters'.[24] *Beyond Good and Evil* defines the same 'aristocratic soul' via 'self-respect' (*Selbstehrfucht*).[25]

To venerate thus appears as a complex and subtle mixture of respect and scorn in which is crystallized the *lived experience* of Overman, beyond any conformist morality or Will to Nothingness. In this we grasp a type of resolution experienced as a moral antinomy; to be in good health is to know how to venerate. This sentiment clearly has its roots in a form of *narcissism* that extends the salutary innocence of the infant. Freud points out its origin in the principle or 'instance'[26] that he calls the *Ego-Ideal*.

In fact, within the framework of his general theory of narcissism, Freud analyses the sentiment of 'self-esteem' (*Seblstachtung*) – which Nietzsche lavishly praises. That implies, according to Freud, that the subject had 'established in himself an *ideal* against which he measures his Ego *such as it is*'.[27] Here Freud perceives the transference onto this 'ideal Ego' of the self-love that the *real* Ego enjoyed in its infancy, implying that the subject 'does not want to do without the narcissistic perfection of his infancy'. 'What is projected before him as his ideal is a substitute for the lost narcissism of his infancy', from the time when he 'was himself his own ideal'.

There is a double interest in this rapprochement. On the one hand, Freud shows the narcissistic matrix of Nietzsche's Overman; to confide in the innocence of becoming comes back to a discovery of the sense of veneration, derived from self-esteem – which constitutes the basic *élitism* of Nietzschean morality. On the other hand, it permits us to understand that, inasmuch as morality in the Freudian sense means to seek in the direction of the Superego, so Nietzsche's superior 'morality' means to seek in the direction of the Ego-Ideal or the ideal Ego.

Insofar as the Superego implies a recognition of the (Oedipal) Law, the introjection of the Father, and the imposition of guilt as a necessary moment, and even as the motor of the whole scenario, so the Ego-Ideal is an extension of originary narcissism. For this reason, it erases every mediation, and leaps above guilt (which is none other than the lived experience of this mediation) in order to repeat a *before* that is wished for without fracture, but can only be experienced *shamefully*[28] as a fracture, since this *before* is defined as *no longer* being.

Here we touch upon an essential cleavage between the two conceptions. In other respects, it is remarkable that Freud ended, after having distinguished them, by identifying the Ego-Ideal to a critical instance or a 'moral conscience' that he christens the Superego.[29] Nietzsche's wager is *in toto*, by contrast, to conceive of an Ego-Ideal that is no longer a Superego. He aspires to those privileged moments that consecrate 'the re-entry of the Ideal in the Ego, its reconciliation with the Ego', a moment when 'the individual discovers contentment in himself', from this 'magnificent festival'[30] where all tensions between the Ego and its ideal figure are annulled.[31] This is the festival that Nietzsche dreams about, while for Freud it can only be the paranoid projection of an impossible reconciliation. That is why Nietzsche's festivity is opposed to the sober enjoyment of Freud's Law.

COMPULSIVE REPETITION AND ETERNAL RETURN

That introduces the figure of repetition.

Remarkably, the theme of repetition is introduced in Nietzsche's conception of history from the outset, even before the discovery of the eternal return. Pythagorean theory is evoked as a reservation to the idea that 'whatever was formerly possible could not be reproduced a second time'. It is, at the least, symbolic that the first evocation of repetition in Nietzsche is cosmological in nature, yet also concerns the 'linkages between motifs'. Immediately, the restitution of the connection between motifs is apprehended as a modality of the 'connection between causes and effects.'

Nietzsche's thematic of repetition resorts to the fundamental category of the *return of the same* (*Wiederkunft des Gleichen*). When this truth is revealed a second time, it is proved, conforming to Nietzsche's experience at Sils-Maria, and reported in *The Gay Science* as 'the heaviest weight' to bear.[32] This time, it is a Self who has to live the repetition that is addressed as a stake and a challenge. The return of the same is also that of suffering, of pleasure, of thought, of breath even, and is balanced by an ultimatum to wish. 'Do you want that? Do you want it again? Once? Always? To infinity?' The tragedy and the grandeur of this challenge come from what it engages, jointly and severally the love of life and *amor fati*, because if this is the hardest truth to bear, and one that we can at first only murmur, it is also our strongest hope. 'Ah! How it should be that you love it yourself and that you love life in order *to no longer desire any other thing* than this supreme and eternal affirmation and confirmation' (*Bestätigung und Besiegelung*).[33]

It is thus the eruption of Will to Power, which effectively *dramatizes* what was previously only a theme, present in order to be articulated among others in Nietzsche's Hellenic heritage. From this point on, the function of the (cosmological) return of the same will be to represent or 'schematize' the repetitiveness at work in *Wille zur Macht*.

It is remarkable that Freud also experiments with repetition (*Wiederholung*) from the beginning, under two apparently contradictory types, the repetitiveness of the neurotic symptom, and the pleasure of repetition in puns and humour. We can see the outline of a conception of a pleasure-of-repetition (*Wiederholungslust*).

Beginning in 1914,[34] the activity of repetition is taken into account and theorized in itself; at this time, the phenomenon of repetition endlessly encountered in the psychoanalytic material is organized around the central concept of a 'compulsion for repetition' (*Weiderholungszwang*). The activation of repressed memory outside the process of recollection during the cure is made under the form of repetition. The patient 'does not reproduce it as a memory, but as an act, naturally without knowing that he is repeating it'.[35] Compulsive repetition is thus investigated in an elective relation with transference and resistance. Freud notes that by foregrounding this new notion, he has not introduced any 'new fact', but has only endowed his conception with unity. It is essentially a question of drawing out the consequences of the analyst's tactics, which must transform the automatism of repetition into a 'motif of memory'. The analytic check consists in rendering the repetition inoffensive by procedures of transference, which create a truly transferable repetition.

This inaugurates a third moment in Freud's theory of repetition, when Freud tries to derive compulsive repetition experimentally, from the outset of his investigation into an inherent property of the drives. This stage is capped by an essay entitled *The Uncanny*, and by *Beyond the Pleasure Principle*, written during 1919–20.

At the base of the sentiment of *Unheimlich*, Freud locates 'the factor of repetition of the similar' (*Wiederholung des Gleischartigen*),[36] derived from infantile psychic life. It is the occasion of an important generalization. 'In the psychic unconscious we recognize the domination (*Herrschaft*) of a compulsion for repetition emanating from instinctive drives, and which probably depends on the most intimate nature of the drives' and 'strong enough to be affirmed above the pleasure principle'.[37] This is the source of its 'demoniacal character' that colours lived experience – the sentiment of *unheimlich* draws its character by manifesting this latent compulsion for repetition.

The text is so much more remarkable for our purposes because it raises the temptation to analyse Nietzsche's personal experiences as a formidable revelation of a latent compulsion for repetition in Nietzsche himself and his lived experiences, on the scale both of the world and of a person.[38] But it is, naturally, elsewhere that we must carry this comparison, on the scale of a fundamental conception that the theory of repetition carries for Nietzsche and Freud, respectively.

We know that for Freud, the compulsion for repetition points toward the death-wish. We have seen that the concept was acquired six years earlier, when Freud proceeded to a reorganization that allowed him to include the totality of known facts; now this quantitative inflation is simultaneously expressed by what strongly resembles a change of *meaning*, so that the idea of repetition seems to have been enriched with signification – even though its content, *stricto sensu*, has not been modified. Everything proceeds as if this notion, originally omnipresent throughout psychic phenomena, has been progressively autonomized in order to be posed as a central revelatory concept.[39]

To understand the fundamental sense of Freudian repetition forces us to re-evaluate our understanding of this phenomenon which pushes us to repeat, no longer only, as previously, via technical effects, but via what it reveals as 'most intimate' regarding the nature of the drive, as Freud invites us to witness. That implies that henceforth we must investigate in a regressive manner what there is about the drives that is at play in repetition.

Right away, Freud insists on the fact that the tendency toward repetition imputes it to an 'unconscious' repression, that is to say to the content itself, and has for a motor the conflict between the Ego and the repressed elements. From then on, closer and closer, from transference to eventual neuroses, to traumatic neuroses and infantile play, it is the 'eternal return of the same' (*ewige Wiederkehr des Gleichen*) which manifests its power.

But we will discover on the plane of repetition the same divergence as at the plane of the Law and of Overman. Whereas Nietzsche's repetition has a value of immediacy – that is why it resonates as authenticity and innocence – Freud's repetition presents a *reflexive* mechanical aspect, as an irrepressible character that one rejects and that returns with a tenacity that is troublesome more than painful, and which takes its whole meaning in the return of the repressed. The apparatus of the cure, taken as a whole, is centred on this compulsive process to the point where it is only a management of a triple procedure of recollection, activation (*Agieren*) and working-through (*Durcharbeiten*) – it is a repetition as representation, repetition as action, and repetition as a riposte of resistances.

Far from being the figure of a naked enjoyment, repetition must be conceived as the work of a process, such that the 'cure', far from being a return to the innocence of the infant, implies the re-elaboration of the infantile and of its chemical processes within us. In addition, the subject does not walk away from the cure with a feeling of virginity that returns him to a pure becoming – Freud has always defied the psychotherapies of rebirth – but with the feeling of a digestion reproduced in reverse.

TRANSVALUATION AND THE LAW

In the last resort, the relation to the Law distinguishes the two projects even in their dénouement. The common image of tablets (*Tafeln*) can serve as a scheme in order to illustrate in some way the *ultima verba* on the subject of illness and its cure. It is enough for us to read this difference by setting side by side the iconoclastic gospel that marks the climax of *Zarathustra* with the image of Moses fashioned by Michelangelo, on which Freud meditated.

Zarathustra's cry is that of the prophet who waits seated 'surrounded by ancient broken tablets and tablets half covered in writing'.[40] The enunciator of Overman articulates the two conditions by which he might disappear and come to shatter the tablets in order to create Overman. 'Oh my brothers, break them, break for me these ancient tablets!'[41] shouts Zarathustra. So the authentic creation becomes possible and thus it is possible to fill new tablets. The transvaluation passes by the image of the fracture and the rewriting elsewhere.

On the face of things, the symbol that refracts Freudian identity is that which he delivers in his interpretation of Michelangelo's statue of Moses. The image of the prophet is that of Moses 'seated, trunk facing me, the head, with its powerful beard and regard, turned to the left ... , The right arm holds the Tablets of the Law'.[42] But Freud perceives in this immobility a return. 'The tablets are here, the head lower, a singular treatment of sacred objects. They are felt to be, above, below, and in an unstable equilibrium on a single point.'[43] That permits him to imagine an astonishing cinematic, in the course of which the primitive immobility (Moses holding the Tablets) has been interrupted by a disorder (the toppling over of the Tablets under the effect of the violence of the reaction succeeding the reports of disorder),[44] yet the movement of retention that prevents the Tablets from falling on the ground and shattering readjusts them in reverse. Here, therefore, is not a fracture, but a return that carries the symbolic trace of the *risk* of fracture. Not new tablets, but the rotation of the old ones, a readjustment that nevertheless carries a trace at once indelible and overcome from an impassioned vacillation of a desire made to rock.

To Nietzsche's transvaluation, which breaks the tablets in order to overcome them, is opposed Freud's decentring that overcomes the fracture. To the death of the Law immolated by Overman is opposed the salvation by the Law that subjugates desire and saves it from itself. To the creative arbitration of Will to

Power that is eternally repeated, life, is opposed the repetition articulated in the Law, the supreme proof of death. For Nietzsche, to cure man is to overcome both the 'Man' and the Law, while for Freud, to cure is to overcome the *gap* between desire and the Law; a gap where, truly speaking, we all are.

CONCLUSION

What constrains us, is that Nietzsche has transformed being ('ist') into duty ('soll') ....
Freud

THE LOGIC OF OUR APPROACH

We have followed step by step the genesis of the homologies and differences between Nietzsche and Freud. Throughout and beyond the thematic content, we can characterize the type of approach that subtends this process. There appeared from the outset a common posture, an initial matrix differentiating these two projects.

Who is Nietzsche, in the end, if not a *philologist*, whose competence enables him to construct a new and *original* thing, on condition of leaving the space instituted by that knowledge? We can see the same gap in Freud, between his formative period and the event of the discovery of his 'thing'. We find one and the other in the same situation of constituting a field which had not yet found its place within institutional space, and of inventing *their own* discipline. This assumed atopy marks both thinkers as specimens of a new type, the *Selbstdenker*. Here is a professor of philology who became Nietzsche, because of whom a new project becomes possible, which we call 'psychology', 'critique' or axiology;[1] there is a physician, a product of the schools of the natural sciences who became the founder of a field named by a neologism, 'psychoanalysis'.[2]

Their common untimeliness is the measure of their originality, in the radical sense of an aptitude for giving names to things that have never been named.[3] From that derives the jealous care with which they defended their property. 'I guard my own house' says Nietzsche;[4] 'the psychoanalyst *farà de se*,'[5] proclaims Freud. Likewise, both exhibit an equal defiance regarding influences, and a concern to refer every consideration to their own great work. From this point of view, we can declare a common ambivalence toward the philosophical 'thing'. For Nietzsche as for Freud, the philosopher is the Other, that *which one is not* that serves to measure *a contrario* what one truly *is*. Moreover, Nietzsche and Freud come from elsewhere to encounter their own creation, which already appears to them to be their destiny. But they also encounter in their common and problematic object a quest for the *origin*. To what extent can we reconcile this double quest? Is it a question of *the same origin*? In examining this question, in the glimmer of what we have acquired from the preceding inquiry, we can address it by way of conclusion.

GENEALOGY AND ARCHAEOLOGY

In the end, Nietzsche names his project a 'genealogy', a merciless inquiry into 'the origins of moral prejudices', which must lead to the source, the 'valuation of values'. This is also the source that Freud seeks when he looks for the unique principle of his 'general theory of neurosis'; when he believes he has located it in the event of primitive seduction, *Ur-szene*, he claims victory, saying that he now holds 'a capital revelation, something akin to the discovery of the sources of the Nile of psychopathology'.[6]

For Nietzsche, as for Freud, it is a question of finding the prehistoric *before*, and their respective discourses are organized around this quest, to reveal anew that by which everything begins for the human species. But, significantly, Freud resorts to the privileged metaphor of 'archaeology' in order to illustrate this quest. What leads us to compare these two theorists' origins is the invocation of the *genealogist* and the *archaeologist*.

The one and the other seek a *before* that can account for the present, which is valued as an *after*, and following the ramifications which lead them to the source by going upstream. But the genealogist conceives of the past as flowing *in the veins of the present*, whereas the archaeologist envisions it as a past which sleeps *under the present*. The genealogist seeks the origin in order to demonstrate the sense of filiation, in order to qualify or disqualify it, that is, to *evaluate* it. The archaeologist tends to exhume the past in order to *explain* the present.

Assuredly, what defines the past is to be passed, bygone; however, the genealogist demonstrates, in a sense, that it has not passed, since he can attest to its *presence* in the present. The exhibition of the past serves to show that the present is by nature the origin. In contrast, the archaeologist resorts to a dead past, separated from the present by the distance that one seeks to fill. Certainly, Freud takes care to specify how the psychoanalyst is concerned with a living past,[7] since it endures in the present and even explains it. But there can be no archaeological metaphor without reference to a space divided into two distinct strata – that there is a below (in some way *dead*) as well as an above (*alive* in a proper sense).

For this reason, Freud refers to psychoanalysis as an 'abyssal psychology' or a 'psychology of the depths', institutionalizing in a way a reference to archaeology, because it is necessary to *excavate* under the surface in order to discover the 'truth' which lies below, covered over by the present, and finally to extract it. The past as such must be bygone, so that the present can appear as its debris and ruins. The genealogist believes more in a diachrony of filiation than in a spatial dependence; if one digs, one does not dig deep, for the art here is to grasp the continuity by exploring the surfaces.

By articulating this difference, we must admit that the psychoanalyst is also a genealogist, and the Nietzschean psychologist is in some small way an archaeologist. But it is also necessary to establish that these two, respectively, refer to significantly distinct registers in their dominion. Genealogy consists in *making visible* the past in the present, in order to reveal the present as duped. Archaeology tends to *reattach* the lost past to the present by re-engendering the present beginning from the 'true' past. Thus if the voyage runs from one to the other, it is neither in the same sense nor with the same intention.

The genealogist uses the past in order either to dismiss the present from its pretensions or to establish them; in this sense, both the distance and the distinction are annulled. The archaeologist aims at a past *as such*, by regenerating it as the *truth* of the present; far from annulling the distance, it is confirmed as the space of the path, and/or the time of the symptom, all the while filling that space via a readjustment. In other words, if we look closely, for a genealogist the present *causes the problem*, since it is its own dupe. We understand why Nietzsche must begin with a critique of *modernity*, since the recourse to the *Unzeitmässig* appears as a remedy against the illusion of the present, modernity being the present as an illusion. For the archaeologist, it is *the past* that causes the problem, since it is a question of retrieving and reconstructing it; in the ideal of the cure, the restitution of the past (in recollection) dissipates the anomalies of the present. Is this not to say, following the archaeological metaphor in its material aspect, that the present is only the past, incomplete and mutilated?

So if there is a dupery of the present for Nietzsche *and* for Freud – that of the illness – it is for two very different reasons. The present for Nietzsche is only ill from believing itself distinct from its origin, while for Freud the present is ill from confusing itself with the past. In correlation, the therapeutic recourse to the authenticity of the origin for one and the other is borne by two distinct philosophies of health. For Nietzsche, the recollection of the origin delivers the present from its own lie, while for Freud the same recollection makes it impossible to maintain illusions about the past, by restoring it as such. From the Id-origin, the subject must (re)appear.

This raises the problem of the very *reality* of the origin. What type of reality does the origin have, and to what extent does it *exist*? Paradoxically, this question, we are told, will necessitate a quest for the origin, to the extent that the origin is conceived as a *fiction*, that is to say a *sense*, or as a real event, that is to say a *cause*.

The genealogist poses, at the same time as the quest for the origin, its mythical character; to prove legitimacy is to refer to something that is unverifiable yet constraining, such as an interpretation of a primitive meaning. The arbitrariness of this choice suspends the validity of the genealogical quest. Thus Nietzsche proceeds to a philological definition of the terms 'good' and 'bad', and he works out the consequences of this arbitrary choice by *naming* it 'Will to Power'.

The archaeologist postulates, by contrast, that *there was* something that is capable of being recovered in the end. Freud thus behaves like an archaeologist when he seeks the reality of an originary scene, and maintains until the end a 'thread of reality' when he comes to suspect its historicity.[8] We understand now how close he comes to achieving that end in speaking of a transmutation relative to this crisis of reality[9] in the discovery of the reality of the meaning behind reality. At the other end of this trajectory, Freud integrates more and more fiction into his conception of the cure. But that must not cause us to lose sight of the fact that for Freud, meaning remains both *cause* and interpretation, balanced by an explanatory ambition; he never gives up the hope of exhuming Rome!

Such are the divergent destinies of these two hermeneutics, of which one (Nietzsche) genealogically makes explicit the arbitrariness of interpretation, up to the point where it is incarnated in the violence of the great genealogist of *Wille zur Macht*; the other (Freud) remains borne by the significant project of reconstructing the archaeological monument. In that, we can grasp the sense of the epistemological opposition between two types of object-position, which correspond to two types of conception of the *knowledge of meaning*.

In the text analysed above,[10] where Freud speaks the longest about Nietzsche, we can point to a remark made in passing that carries the full weight of the present discussion. We see in the text a critique of Nietzsche's approach that allows Freud to situate his own psychoanalytic approach in relation to it. In actual fact, this critique takes place in three phases, but it furnishes us a significant site by which to judge Freud's position in relation to Nietzsche, such as he expresses it himself, which moreover obliges him to abandon momentarily his diagnostic neutrality. 'What constrains us is the fact that Nietzsche has transformed "being" (*ist*) into "duty" (*soll*), but such a "duty" is a stranger to science. In that, Nietzsche remained a moralist and thus was unable to free himself from the theologian.'[11] That, for Freud, constitutes the radical *limit* of Nietzsche's *psychology*, and where he locates his own *psychoanalysis*. The reservation intervenes at the moment when Freud comes to recognize in Nietzsche an exceptional, even unique, perspicacity, all the more reason to situate the divergence between these approaches elsewhere than in the pertinence of their particular supports, but rather in their approach and method of approaching human reality.

To suggest that Nietzsche, the son of a priest, remains an incurable theologian and moralist is to denounce his psychology as an illicit confusion of *Sollen* with *Sein* that makes possible a *metabasis* of the second to the first – the effect of which would be to put their attainments, even if 'legitimate' in themselves, *outside science*. Opposing this confusion-translation, Freud presses once more the psychoanalyst's ambition to the status of a scientist. That is my ultimate difference from Nietzsche, Freud signifies, 'for my part, I reject as illegitimate any hypostasis between *Sein* and *Sollen*.' There is no endo-psychic projection here, but *Sein* alone as Fact and as Law.

What is Freud really aiming at in Nietzsche's approach by detaching *Sein* from *Sollen*? How can the 'scientific' approach of psychoanalysis avoid this detachment and claim the products as 'similitudes and anticipations' in order to take them up again in the pure sphere of a *Sein* that never commits the sin of promoting *Sollen*?

To be sure, it was a matter of clear judgment, an important key (as indicated by Freud himself), with which we grasped the points of convergence and divergence between Nietzsche's and Freud's constructions of objectivity, and recapitulating the whole preceding inquiry. In formulating this claim not to overdetermine *Sein* by *Sollen*, Freud articulates the requirement of the objectivity of 'natural science'.[12] For whomever claims the rights and obligations of *Naturwissenschaft*, as psychoanalysis does, it is no small thing not to confuse value judgements with judgements of reality. Nietzsche's error was thus to inscribe, *in* his declarations on 'reality', an evaluation.

FROM ONE COPERNICAN REVOLUTION TO ANOTHER

It is remarkable that at the moment when Nietzsche and Freud come to define their respective projects, they both refer to themselves in terms of a neo-Copernican revolution. Both cling to Copernicus as the one who consummated the decentring of 'man'.

'Since Copernicus' writes Nietzsche, 'it seems that man has found himself on a descending slope – he always rolls further and further away from his point of departure toward ... – Where is that? –Towards nothingness?'[13] Or in more concise terms, 'since Copernicus, man has been rolling away from the centre towards X'.[14] Likewise, Copernicus is the parabolic figure of the loss of the origin in Freud. Freud associates the name of Copernicus with 'the ruin of the narcissistic illusion', that deprives 'man' at once of 'the central position of the earth' and of 'the guarantee of his predominant role in the universe', his role as 'master of the world'.[15]

Both theorists relate this first wound to a second that Freud implies but Nietzsche makes explicit. 'Man's tendency to belittle himself, his will to shrink, is this not, since Copernicus, man's continual progress? Alas! That is what happened to his faith and his dignity, in his unique value – he has become an animal.' Freud echoes this declaration. 'The work of Charles Darwin has put an end to man's pretension ... man has become nothing but an animal; he is himself descended from a series of animals' which oblige him to humiliate himself in the contemporary world. It is the same idea as *Verkleinerung*.[16]

This is the state in which Nietzsche's transvaluation and Freud's psychoanalysis approach humanity; the illness is no other than the loss of the origin and the misrecognition of this loss. Nietzsche names it 'nihilism', Freud, 'neurosis'. Their intervention is consequently paradoxical, in that they aggravate the ill in order to alleviate the illness.

Thus it is no accident if transvaluation begins by crossing and radicalizing nihilism, nor if Freud is presented as aggravating disillusionment by announcing to a stricken humanity (already twice disappointed) that it is not even the master 'of its own soul' such that 'the Ego reaches the limits of its power in its own house, the soul',[17] that which is named the Unconscious. But at this level, the differential relation to the origin is registered, which permits us to distinguish the modality of the loss.

If there is in Nietzsche and Freud a declaration of human decentring, for the former the eccentricity is evoked as a fall into infinity–nothingness in the manner of a planet that is ejected from its orbit and abandoned to an endless drift. For the latter, the loss of the centre, if it is latent, only results in a modest translation, despite its considerable effects – a displacement which only means a change of situation. Consequently, for Nietzsche the loss of the centre eectuates the caducity of all centres – this is why the necessary consequence of nihilism can only be a transvaluation of values, whose radicality is recognized as containing a critique of all centre-based rationality. What is Will to Power and its Overman support, if not that which creates, on the foundation of an integral relativity demonstrated by nihilism, the only point of view that can do without a centre?

For Freud, by contrast, we note a pedagogy that, having weathered the grief incurred by its odyssey of a return to the centre, takes leave of this loss in order to consummate it (by the Unconscious) before inflicting it on humanity as a lesson, whose morality must be accommodated. Along with a nostalgia for the centre is assumed the deception of desire, which *neurosis* conserves. But it is a matter of returning to the point; we are tempted to represent a cured humanity turning in proximity to the lost centre and founding its new wisdom on the renunciation of the centre. Everything proceeds as if humanity was decentred, and never again to be recentred, but nevertheless remains planted *nearby* its lost position.

'SEIN' *AND* 'SOLLEN': FROM DRIVES TO THE SUBJECT[18]

In this sense two images are opposed in striking fashion. In Nietzsche, we see a new, tenacious mobilization to create in order to pass from the centre; for Freud, a pacification born of serenity emanates from the revelation of not having to look for a centre where there is none. Thus there are two distinct versions of the Copernican revolution. One is axiological, metonymizing *Sein* into *Sollen*; the other upholds *Sein*, even if to erect it in *Sollen*, and erecting in consequence the requirement for a cognizance of ethics.

We understand now the divergence between Nietzsche's and Freud's strategies which furnish the ensemble of the preceding comparison its differential key, at the same time as the extraordinary convergence by which they both explore the frontiers of the same *terra incognita*. But these two theorists of the origin have prospected, in part, in the same earth, and they have each returned there with incisive tools without wanting either to seek or to see the same thing. That is why, to follow them step by step along the landmarks of their prospecting, we have witnessed the strange scenario of two prospectors who work unceasingly, one on the heels of the other, locating the same traces, raising analogous indications, establishing records of discoveries sometimes identical to the letter, but at the same time reciprocally neglecting the minerals judged precious by the other and inversely digging veins that the other had left fallow.

But despite the resemblance of the paths, is it not the *same* route, since explored with a compass and from heterogeneous categories? Even if the double exploration has swept across a synchronous field, therein lies one of the ruses of thought which has established the notion of our time, associating the names of Nietzsche and Freud in the management of the same theoretical capital.

Our inquiry, borne by the project of evaluating the alliance thus tied between them, can attest to the vanity of such an accredited eclecticism, given that we have shown, point by point, in the lining of an echo, the suture lines that inscribe the difference of both context and categories. But also, we have *established* the analogy by systematizing the convergence, and thus assigning the *nexus* of two revolutions which have affected, each in their own way, the position of objectivity that determines the stakes for modern thought. Nietzsche and Freud are like two discourses set up face to face that, despite their different codes and distinct keys, nevertheless cross the same zones of language and there determine the forms, each radical in their fashion, of subversion.

In the groundwork we have undertaken of the referents that structure our theoretical present, by following the thread of an inquiry at once timely and continuous,[19] we have constantly kept close to the problem, perhaps an impossible one, with which the theory of the subject[20] must be explained; it is the question of materiality itself and of the status of the drives and desire as a posture in materiality. But it is an 'impossible' whose very theory is an instrument of instruction. Piercing the cleavage between Nietzschean and Freudian theories of the drives, we can see an antagonism between them over the status of knowledge and interpretation that actualizes the question of the very being of the drive and of its mode of inherence to the given, to the point where *Sein* and *Sollen* cross. Thus they sketch the contradictory modality by which a theory of drives can make a contribution as a *non-dialectical* theory, and which merits being fully considered, and understood *from the dialectical point of view.*[21]

Nietzsche and Freud have in fact invested and marked the field of drives with distinct instruments and heterogeneous principles. We thus understand the paradox that comprises the dialogue between them, since their respective fecundity is invested by two distinct readings of the same text given to thought, that of the effects of the materiality of the drives, whose traces Marx has pointed to in his own way, in the historical dialectic, as we have previously demonstrated.[22]

We do not hope to reconcile the heterogeneous principles of our three referents, and our trilogy in no way stresses a reconciliatory theoretical teleology. But to exacerbate the divergence of the principles in order to prevent the ideological effects of eclecticism, we have disengaged a field of contradictions which makes possible a rediscovery of what, in reality, demands to be thought through, outside of ideological confusions, by a methodological approach with which we have sought to test. Such is the most important task incumbent on theory, to mobilize the allogenic referents and to test them out *elsewhere* in order to progress in our efforts to render intelligible the material aspects and implications of our most perplexing effects and ruses of logic,[23] those which radically (re)interrogate the status of the *subject.*[24]

NOTES

Translator's Preface

1 *Daybreak*, tr. R.J. Hollingdale (Cambridge University Press, 1982), p 5.

Preface to the 1998 Edition

1 Paul-Laurent Assoun, *Freud et Nietzsche* [PUF, 'Philosophie d'aujourd'hui', 1980, 1982].
2 Paul-Laurent Assoun, *Freud, la philosophie et les philosophes* [PUF, 'Philosophie d'aujourd'hui'; 1976; 2nd, revised edn, 'Quadrige' no. 180, 1995].
3 We have expanded this inquiry with our works *L'entendement freudien* [Gallimard, 1984], and *Freud et Wittgenstein* [PUF, 'Philosophie d'aujourd'hui', 1988; 2nd revised edn 'Quadrige' 1996].
4 On the link between Freud and Schopenhauer, see our *Freud, la philosophie et les philosophes* ['Quadrige', op cit.], pp 225f.
5 *Freud, la philosophie et les philosophes* ['Quadrige'], 3rd part, pp 357–8.
6 See our *Freud et Wittgenstein*, op cit.
7 On this effect in general, see *Freud, la philosophie et les philosophes*, op cit., pp 282f.
8 See our *Introduction à la métapsychologie freudienne* [PUF, 1993].
9 On this gift of Nietzsche, see below, Conclusion, pp 282f.
10 See below, in Part One, Ch. 2, 'Nietzsche in Freudian Discourse'.
11 *An Autobiographical Study* (1925); *GW*, XIV, 86.
12 This interview with Freud was published on 14 August, 1933 ('Neurosis, the Illness of Our Time'); it was translated into French in the *Revue internationale d'histoire de la psychanalyse* [no. 5, 1992, PUF, pp 613–17], from a text discovered in 1989 by Früh Ekhart.
13 Karl Hildebrandt presented an elegaic account of the Second Meditation on 7–8 July 1877, at the moment when Nietzsche set out on his 'desert crossing.'
14 It is necessary to note here that the *Leseverein* was dissolved for 'threatening public order.' Its liberalism was sufficient to make it appear subversive.
15 Nietzsche's Viennese admirers took advantage of his 33rd birthday to address to him, on 15 October 1877, their enthusiastic declaration of 'allegiance'.
16 This circle had been founded in 1867 by Engelbert Pernerstorfer, who was also among those who signed the October, 1877, letter to Nietzsche.
17 *Ecce Homo*, *SW*, VIII, 339 ('Why I Write Such Good Books,' Section 2). The same assertion is made in *Nietzsche Contra Wagner*, *SW*, VIII, 51: 'I have my readers everywhere, in Vienna . . .'. The same list of places follows, and then the conclusion: 'I have none in Germany, that dull land in Europe.'
18 Letter from Nietzsche to Paul Rée, dated 19 November, 1877, in Nietzsche, Rée, Salomé, *Correspondance* [PUF, 1979], p 38.
19 Sigmund Freud, *Lettres de jeunesse* [Gallimard, 1990], letter to Eduard Silberstein dated 13 March, 1875, p 143.
20 On the importance of this letter (in Lettres de jeunesse, op cit., pp 143–7), refer to our *Freud, la philosophie et les philosophes*, op cit., p 8 and pp 279f.

21 It is true that Brentano's exposé was interrupted (by the unexpected arrival of his colleague Simony; op cit., p 146); Nietzsche was nonetheless certainly not foreseen in Brentano's programme of philosophical education.
22 Letter of 7 March, 1875, in *Lettres de jeunesse*, p 138, where Freud speaks of the 'struggle in favour of our verities.' On the link with Feuerbach, see *Freud, la philosophie et les philosophes*, pp 350–1.
23 On the link between Freud and Voltaire, see *Freud, la philosophie et les philosophes*, pp 330–4, and our contribution 'Freud, lecteur de Voltaire. Candide inconscient' in *Furor* no. 26, [Geneva, 1994], pp 7–21.
24 This review manuscript, of which all traces have disappeared, seems to have had an ephemeral existence. Freud evokes it in a letter, dated 6 December 1874, to Eduard Silberstein (*Lettres de jeunesse*, pp 110–11) and announces its 'death' in late January, 1875 (see note 26 below). This issue contained a critique by Freud himself of Lipiner's 'teleological argument', an article by Paneth on 'the foundations of a materialist ethic' and an article by Emmanuel Löwy on Spinoza's proof of the existence of God and 'some words on the definitions.'
25 Siegfried Lipiner, a Galician Jew, a student in Vienna where he had lived since 1871, was the same age as Freud and obtained his baccalaureate two years after him (1875). Notably, he was the author of a poetic work entitled *Prometheus Freed From His Chains* (*Der entfesselte Prometheus*), which Nietzsche received with enthusiasm. Their contact, beginning in 1877, did not last long; the rupture took place in 1878 and Lipiner, thus rejected by Nietzsche, turned toward Wagner.
26 Letter from Freud to Silberstein, 30 January 1875, in *Lettres de jeunesse*, p 126.
27 We need to remember that it is in this pastor's sermon, on the fall of a student who was a victim of repression, that the assimilation of 'philistines' (in the biblical sense) with the bourgeois enemies of students is imposed.
28 *Der alte und der neue Glaube. Ein Bekenntnis.*
29 It is the title of a work by Otto Rank, *La volonté du bonheur. Au-delà du freudisme*, French translation, Stock, 1975. The original title was *Wahrheit und Wirklichkeit (Vérité et réalité)*, 1934.
30 In April, 1926, Rank offers Freud a parting gift in a way, a copy of the works of Nietzsche (23 volumes bound in white leather). We are sure, at least, that by this date Freud possessed, in his library, Nietzsche's Opus! The irony is that this 'gift' is made at the precise moment when this conceptual divorce (for reasons of legitimating references) is produced where Nietzsche is implicated by the adverse party . . . .
31 Sigmund Freud and Arnold Zweig, *Correspondance, 1927–1939* [Gallimard], p 115.
32 Beyond Good and Evil, Ch. IX; *SW*, VII, 197f.
33 *The Will to Power: An Essay on the Transvaluation of all Values*, *SW*, IX, pp 630–3 [Book IV, § 943]. We find enumerated there no less than 23 'traits' characterizing the 'noble'.
34 *Human, All Too Human*, *SW*, III, 161 [Second part, *Assorted Opinions and Maxims*, § 397].
35 *The Gay Science*, *SW*, V, 195 [Book IV, § 294].
36 *Thus Spoke Zarathustra*, *SW*, III, 50 ['Of War and Warriors'].
37 *Beyond Good and Evil*, *SW*, VII, 212 [Ch. IX, § 265].
38 *Nietzsche Contra Wagner*, *SW*, VIII, 70 [The Psychologist Speaks'].
39 *Human, All Too Human*, *SW*, III, 161 [II, § 397].
40 *Ecce Homo.*
41 Letter to Ludwig Binswanger.
42 See our preface to Paul Rée, *De l'origine des sentiments moraux* [PUF, 1982, Collection 'Philosophie d'aujourd'hui'].
43 *The Will to Power*, *SW*, IX, 633 [Book IV, § 944].
44 *Daybreak*, *SW*, IV, 147–8 [Book III, § 173].
45 *Civilization and Its Discontents*, *GW*, XIV, 432 [Section II]. See also on this point our contribution 'Freud, lecteur de Voltaire: Candide inconscient' in Furor no. 26, [Geneva, 1994], pp 119–31.

46 Letter from Freud to Oskar Pfister, dated 9 October 1918, in *Correspondance de Sigmund Freud avec le pasteur Pfister* [Gallimard], p 103. On Freud's notion of the ideal, see our *L'entendement freudien. Logos et Ananké* [Gallimard, 1984].
47 *On the Genealogy of Morals*, I, § 9.
48 The letter from Freud to Fliess is cited in the original in Max Schur, *La mort dans la vie de Freud* [Gallimard].
49 Minutes of the Vienna Psychoanalytic Society, vol II, pp 30f, meeting of 28 October, 1908. See below, Introduction, the section 'Nietzsche in the Wednesday Seminars (2)'.
50 See our work *Freud, la philosophie et les philosophes.*
51 On this point, see our work *Le Freudisme* [PUF, collection 'Que sais-je?', 1990], p 27.
52 Lou Andreas-Salomé, *Carnets Intimes.*
53 See our work, *L'entendement freudien.*
54 See our *Introduction à la métapsychologie freudienne* [PUF, 'Quadrige', 1993].
55 On this question and its enormity, we refer back to our discussion in our work *Psychanalyse* (PUF, collection 'Premier cycle', 1997), Book III, § 4, pp 254–81, where we examine the question of the 'drive for power' in Freud, in his discussions with Adler.
56 In *A Difficulty in the Path of Psychoanalysis* (1917), Freud evokes the 'will for power' (*Machtwillen*) (*GW*, XII, 4). In the account of the analysis of the Wolf Man (*From the History of an Infantile Neurosis*, Section III) in 1918, Freud speaks of *Willen zur Macht* ('wishing for power') or the 'drive for affirmation' (*Behauptungstrieb*) as 'motives of power and privilege' (*Macht- und Vorrechtmotive*) (*GW*, XII, 46). In *An Autobiographical Study* (1925), Section VII, always in reference to Adler, he speaks of a 'striving for power' (*Machtstreben*) (*GW*, XIV, 779). We remain in the Adlerian register of 'drives to valorize' (*Geltungstriebe*) as varieties of 'self-preservation drives'. The turn to *Wille zur Macht* is taken in the writings after *Beyond the Pleasure Principle* (although chronologically we can note a certain 'overlap', maintaining the anthropological reference to Adler). See especially the decisive passage in *The Economic Problem of Masochism* (1924), whose main points are confirmed in *Civilization and Its Discontents* (1930).
57 *The Economic Problem of Masochism*, *GW*, XIII, 376. See also *Civilization and Its Discontents*, Ch. VI, *GW*, XIV, 478.
58 On the question of criminology in Freud and his confrontation with the Nietzschean conception, see our *Psychanalyse* [PUF, collection 'Premier Cycle', 1997], pp 595f.
59 See our synthesis in *Psychanalyse*, op cit., Book III, § 3, 'Desire and prohibition: the unconscious function of the father', pp 225–49.
60 Freud, *Leonardo da Vinci and a Memory of His Childhood*, Section V, *GW*, VIII, 195.
61 'My Life', II (1861), in Friedrich Nietzsche, *Premiers écrits* [Le Cherche Midi éditeur, 1994], p 50.
62 Ibid., III, p 52.
63 Ibid., p 56, 18 September 1863.
64 Ibid., p 59, 1864.
65 Ibid., p 24, written between 18 August and 1 September 1858.
66 Ibid., p 59, 1864.
67 Ibid., p 45.
68 *Ecce Homo*, *SW*, VIII, 299 ['Why I Am So Wise,' § 1].
59 Ibid., p 307 [§ 5].
60 *Vue d'ensemble des névroses de transfert* [Gallimard, 1986].
71 See below, Introduction, the section 'Nietzsche in the Wednesday Seminars (2),' and Part One, Ch. 2, the section 'The Case of Schreber.'
72 An aphorism from the period of *Human, All Too Human*, *Daybreak*, *The Gay Science*, and *Zarathustra*, reproduced in *Music/Art/Literature*, *SW*, X, 189 [§ 499].
73 Ibid. [§ 498].
74 See our contribution 'La reconciliation avec le père' in *Esquisses psychanalytiques.*
75 *The Economic Problem of Masochism*, *GW*, XIII, pp 381–3.
76 *The Gay Science*, *SW*, V, 199 [Book I, § 300].

77 *The Acquisition and Control of Fire*, 1932.
78 See the Freud-Putnam correspondence in *L'introduction de la psychanalyse aux Etats-Unis* [Gallimard].
79 *The Economic Problem of Masochism*, *GW*, XIII, 383.
80 *The Ego and the Id*, *GW*, XIII, 282 [Ch. V].

Introduction

1 See below, '"Nietzsche" in the Wednesday Seminars (1)', and in Part One, Ch. 1, 'Thomas Mann, Herald and Mediator.'
2 In the section of *Twilight of the Idols*, entitled 'Skirmishes of an Untimely Man', see Aphorism 16, which denounces German Philistinism:

> What I cannot understand is an 'and' in a bad alloy (*berüchtigtes 'und'*): The Germans say 'Goethe *and* Schiller', and I fear they will say 'Schiller *and* Goethe' . . . There are even more injurious 'ands'; I have heard with my own ears, but only among University professors: 'Schopenhauer *and* Hartmann' (*SW*, VIII, 141).

3 *Freud, la philosophie et les philosophes*, PUF, 1976. We consider the present work a direct continuation of that work. We will indicate at every important point the correlation between the two works, so as to mark the extensions.
4 See below, the mediators '"Nietzsche" in the Wednesday Seminars (1)', and in Part One, Ch. 1, 'Lou Salomé, A Natural Link.'
5 Op cit., pp 136–7.
6 Op cit., Part Two, Ch. 5, pp 205f.
7 Whence the status that we have reserved for Nietzsche in the general framework of our inquiry into (the relation between) Freud and the philosophers (op cit.), by simply pointing out its presence in our previous work, insofar as the general regimen of Freud's relation to philosophers is applied. From this point of view, Freud's relation to Nietzsche confirms the overall schema. On the other hand, the particular case of Nietzsche deserves to be disengaged and treated separately, as it involves an overall comparison of problematics. In this sense, the first part of the present work extends the approach taken up in the preceding work, by applying it to Nietzsche, while the second part investigates the two problematics independently of an immediate reading of Freud. See below, pp 49.
8 Nietzsche was born in 1844; Freud in 1856.
9 See notably the debut of Nietzsche's celebrity in France and his contacts with Georg Brandes in the spring of 1888. As Halévy says, 'it is during the same months, by a single encounter, that the fire started in his brain and in the masses, until then inert, of the public' (*Nietzsche*, p 528).
10 See Geneviève Bianquis, *Nietzsche en France*, an inquiry awarded a prize by the *Nietzsche Gesellschaft* in 1928 (published in 1929).
11 See below, p 19, the letter dated 21 September 1897. In a manuscript dated 31 May, 1897, Freud uses the term 'Overman'; see below, p 43.
12 *Friedrich Nietzsche in Seinen Wercken*, Wien.
13 *Das Leben Friedrich Nietzsche*, Leipzig, vol 1: 1896, vol 2, I: 1897, vol 2, II: 1904. The work reappeared in abridged form in 1912 and 1914 (in 2 vols).
14 Published in Leipzig, by the editor Naumann.
15 Prior to the First World War, Elisabeth's grip on the management of her brother's work was undertaken according to an unrelenting process. In 1893, she had stripped Peter Gast (pseudonym of Heinrich Köselitz) of his claims to her brother's work – free to use him later, after Koegel's repudiation. She brought permanent action against Overbeck, accusing him in the end of having lost the manuscript to *The Will to Power*, never finished, which lasted until his death in 1908. At that time she obtained the

exclusive literary rights to her brother's works, including the correspondence, thanks to a decision by the Jena tribunal that forbade the publication of any extract from Nietzsche's private correspondence without the authorization of the author, which prevented Bernoulli from publishing in the second volume of his work (see below, [p 12], note 17) the important letters from Gast to Overbeck (in 1895, Elisabeth had wrested from her mother the rights to Nietzsche's literary property). A Nietzsche Foundation was officially recognized on 23 May, 1908, as a not-for-profit scientific and cultural institution, which had benefitted from the generous donation of the Swedish patron Ernst Thiel.

- Whatever the distribution of Nietzsche's works, we should recall that, during the philosopher's life, the circulation of his work did not exceed a few thousand copies. Witness the quarrels between Elisabeth and her brother's publishers in 1891. Schmeitzner declared that he had sold off his unsold inventories. Naumann enumerated 2,800 copies sold out of 6,200 printed of the four works, *On the Genealogy of Morals, Beyond Good and Evil, The Case of Wagner* and *Twilight of the Idols*, and Nietzsche remained in debt. The balance sheet of Fritsche, Nietzsche's third editor, was no more cause for rejoicing. In 1893 everything changed. Naumann announced to Elisabeth an influx of demand for Nietzsche's writings which necessitated a new edition of the works and a biography. The income to the author from the first volumes published was considerable. French, English and American editions were anticipated, a tendency that reached its zenith during the war: 11,000 copies of Zarathustra were sold in less than six weeks, and 40,000 were sold for the year 1917!

16 *Das Nietzsche-Archiv, seine Freunde und Feinde*. We find in a brochure dating from 1910, *Nietzsches Werke und das Nietzsche-Archiv*, appearing in Leipzig, an account of the work of the foundation, a document of the 'Weimar tradition' (Andler, *Nietzsche, sa vie et sa pensée*, vol 2, p 8, note 1).
17 *Franz Overbeck und Friedrich Nietzsche*, Jena, 2 vols, 1908.
18 *Friedrich Nietzsche, sein Leben und sein Werk*, 1903.
19 *Friedrich Nietzsche, sein Leben und seine Werke*, 1913.
20 *Nietzsche, Versuch einer Mythologie*, 1919.
21 See below, Part One, Chapters 1 and 2, p 37 and pp 61f.
22 Meeting of the Vienna Psychoanalytic Society, 1 April, 1908; in *Les premiers psychanalystes*, Gallimard, vol 1, p 372. [Translator note: minutes of these meetings were published in English as *Minutes of the Vienna Psychoanalytic Society* (New York: International Universities Press; vol I, 1906–8 (1962); vol II, 1908–10 (1967); vol III, 1910–11 (1974); vol IV, 1912–18 (1975). Citations hereafter abbreviated as *Minutes*, with volume and page numbers. For the meeting indicated here, see *Minutes* I:359.]
23 Meeting of the Psychoanalytic Society of Vienna, 28 October, 1908; op cit., vol 2, p 36. [*Minutes* II:32.]. [Translator's note: this may have been a defensive posture more than an objective fact. According to Peter Gay, Freud had read Nietzsche as a university student. See his *Freud: A Life for Our Time*; French edition translated by Tina Jolas (Hachette, 1991), vol 1, p 105. See also the 1998 Preface to the present work, above.]
24 *GW*, X, 53, in *On the History of the Psychoanalytic Movement* [See *SE* 14:15].
25 *GW*, XIV, 86, in Selbstdarstellung [See *SE* 20:60].
26 See the second part of this work.
27 Published in France under the title *Les Premiers Psychanalystes, Minutes de la Société psychanalytique de Vienne*, Gallimard, vol 1: 1906–8; vol 2: 1098–10; vol 3: 1910–11 (French translation 1976, 1978 and 1979). [For the English edition of these minutes, see note 22 above.]
28 Otto Rank, secretary of the Society, was charged with recording the meetings. On Rank's important role between Nietzsche and Freud, see below, in Part One, Chapter 1, 'Nietzscheo-Freudianism: From Gross to Rank.'

29 Minute no. 45, op cit., vol 1, p 368 [Minutes I:356].
30 Op cit., p 369 [*Minutes* I:356]. [Translator's note: in all fairness, it is useful to point out that this contrast did not go unrecognized by Nietzsche himself. 'At the bottom I have already undergone the test of my own view of life: many more will have to do it after me. Up to the present my spirit has not been depressed by the unremitting suffering that my ailments have caused me,' wrote Nietzsche to Peter Gast (Köselitz) in September, 1879. He continues: 'Just read this last manuscript through, my dear friend, and ask yourself whether there are any traces of suffering or depression to be found in it. I don't believe there are, and this very belief is a sign that there must be powers concealed in these views, and not the proofs of importence and lassitude after which my enemies will seek . . .' (Peter Klossowski, *Nietzsche and the Vicious Circle*, tr. Daniel W. Smith, The Athlone Press, 1977, p 17). In the psychoanalytic movement, Nietzsche's erstwhile champions and advocates would come to seek similar proofs.]
31 Hitschmann takes the term literally, since he specifies further that 'we do not know of any (sexual) relation he had with a woman, apart from the occasional prostitute' (ibid.) [*Minutes* I:357].
32 Op cit., pp 369–70. [*Minutes* I:357].
33 *Beyond Good and Evil, SW*, VIII, 12 (Part One, aphorism 6).
34 Op cit., p 370. Sadger goes so far as to say that *Herrenmoral* (morals of the master) is related to the fact that Nietzsche 'was the only male member of his family' (ibid.) [*Minutes* I:357].
35 Op cit., ibid. On the meaning of Nietzsche to Adler, see below, in Part One, Chapter 1, 'Nietzsche and the Attack on the Libido.'
36 Op cit., pp 370–1. [*Minutes* I:358].
37 'These works constitute a self-treatment' (op cit., p 371) [*Minutes* I:358].
38 Op cit., p 372 [*Minutes* I:359].
39 After Freud, Rank spoke as well, insisting on the importance for him of 'the sadistic (masochistic) drive and its repression', which would account for the double aspect of his character attested by the biographies: on the one hand, 'his finesse, courtesy and sweetness'; on the other hand, 'his glorification of cruelty and the thirst for revenge' (*sic*). The gift of self-therapy is explained by an interiorizing transference (op cit., pp 373–4) [*Minutes* I:361].
40 Op cit., p 372 [*Minutes* I:359].
41 On these attempts, see below, p 20.
42 See *Freud, la philosophie et les philosophes, passim.*
43 [*Minutes* I:359–60]. To reconcile this declaration with later ones, see below, Part One, Ch. 2, 'Nietzsche's Status in Freud's Philosophical Topography.'
44 See the role of the philosophical referent as an anticipating and legitimating intuition, analysed in our preceding work, *Freud, la philosophie et les philosophes*, second part, pp 125f.
45 Op cit., p 373 [*Minutes* I:360].
46 Minute No. 56, reproduced in *Les premiers psychanalystes*, vol 2, pp 30f. [Cf. *Minutes* II:25–33]. Present were Adler, Deutsch, Federn, Hollerung, Joachim, Rank, Rie, Sadger and Steckel. *Ecce Homo*, the canonical text of the Weimar hagiography, had just been re-edited in 1908, in a de luxe limited edition.
47 Op cit., p 34 [*Minutes* II:29].
48 At the same moment at the beginning of the century, there appeared the work of Augustin Cabanès in France, of G.M. Gould in the USA, and above all that of Paul Möbius in Germany. On this trend, see Grmek's exposition, *Histoire des recherches sur les relations entre génie et folie*, reproduced in the *Revue d'Histoire des Sciences* XV, no 1, 1962.
49 *Psychiatrie und Literaturgeschichte*, Leipzig, 1901.
50 It was, in fact, Möbius who had made public the diagnosis of progressive general paralysis in his monograph published in 1901 in Wiesbaden, *Über das Pathologische Nietzsche*. At this time, the health bulletins of the sanitaria at Jena and at Basel had not

yet been published: they would only appear in 1930 in Heidelberg by Erich Podach, in *Nietzsches Zusammenbruch*. We point out that Elisabeth Förster-Nietzsche was opposed to this thesis, in *Der einsame Nietzsche* (1914) and up to 1932 (P. Cohen and E. Förster-Nietzsche, *Um Nietzsches Untergang*). See also Karl Hildebrandt, *Gesundheit und Krankheit in Nietzsches Leben und Werk* (1926).

51 Op cit., vol 1, p 368 [*Minutes* I:355].

52 Op cit., vol 2, p 35 [*Minutes* II:30].

53 Note the diversity of diagnoses during the two meetings, which run from obsessional neurosis to paranoia.

54 An allusion to the state of euphoria that, according to the psychiatric diagnosis, precedes the crisis of cerebral paralysis. In fact, during the weeks which preceded his collapse, Nietzsche expressed a particular experience of well being, which peaked around October 1888, three months before the crisis of 3 January 1889 (see the anthology assembled by Karl Jaspers in his *Nietzsche*, Book I, Gallimard, Collection 'Tel', p 104). See also the euphoria that followed the crisis: Overbeck found Nietzsche 'in his furnished room (in Turin), singing, proclaiming his glory, banging the piano with his elbow to accompany his clamours and roars' (in Daniel Halévy, *Nietzsche*, p 526). For a psychoanalytic approach to general paralysis, see Ferenczi and Hollos, *Zur Psychoanalyse der paralytischen Geistesstörung. Beihefte zur internationalen Zeitsschrift für Psychoanalyse*, no. 5.

55 Freud was opposed to the dominant thesis that leans toward the interpretation of a precocious pathology in Nietzsche (cf. Möbius, Hildebrandt, Podach). See Paul-Louis Landsberg, 'Essai d'interpretation de la maladie mentale de Nietzsche' (1934), in *Problèmes du personnalisme* (1952), pp 194–7.

56 See below, in Part One, Ch. 1, 'Arnold Zweig and the Impossible Discourse,' Freud's final objections to a similar enterprise.

57 In *The Claims of Psycho-Analysis to Scientific Interest*, *GW*, VIII, 407. On the principle of philosophical psychography, see *Freud, la philosophie et les philosophes*, pp 84f.

58 A basic objection reaffirmed up to 1934; see below, p 22f.

59 'In his infancy, one thing dominates: he lost his father at a very young age and grew up in a family of women ... in his autobiography, Nietzsche kills his father one more time' (ibid.) [*Minutes* II:31].

60 'Completely cut off from life by his illness, he turns toward the only object of search remaining to him and to which, as a homosexual, he is in every way closer: the Ego. And so he begins, with a great perspicacity – with a perception we could call endo-psychic – to explore the recesses of his self' (pp 35–6) [*Minutes* II:31].

61 See the letter to Fliess dated 12 December 1897, and *The Psychopathology of Everyday Life* (see our *Freud, la philosophie et les philosophes*, Part One, Book II). Nietzsche's value lies in that he expressed prototypically the mechanism of philosophy, which consists of projecting 'toward the exterior, as an exigency of life (*Lebensanforderung*) what he has discovered in his own self' (p 36) [*Minutes* II:31]. Compare this with the genesis of the 'endopsychic myths': 'The obscure perception internalized by the subject of his own psychic apparatus sustains the illusions that, naturally, are found projected onto the outside' (*La naissance de la psychanalyse*, p 210).

62 On the meaning of the formula from *Human, All Too Human*, see below, Part Two, Chapter 2, 'Instince, Nietzsche's Psychological Object.'

63 *La vie et l'œuvre de Sigmund Freud*, vol 2, p 365.

64 Text from *The Will to Power* dating to 1887 (XIV, Part Two, § 227, Kröner ed. French translation by G. Bianquis, vol 2, p 61, § 159).

65 Op cit., p 37 [*Minutes* II:32].

66 Op cit., p 36 [*Minutes* II:32]. On these attempts, see below, p 20.

67 See below, in Part One, Ch. 2, 'Nietzsche's Status in Freud's Philosophical Topography.'

68 See some of these aphorisms, below, Part One, Ch. 2. [Translator's note: in an astonishing anticipation of Freud's own attitude as a reader of Nietzsche, the latter had

written in *Daybreak* that 'a book such as this is not for reading straight through or reading aloud but for dipping into, especially when out walking or on a journey; you must be able to stick your head into it and out of it again and again and discover nothing familar around you,' (tr. R.J. Hollingdale, Cambridge 1982, Aphorism 454).]

69 After Nietzsche's stays in the sanitaria, he lived in Naumburg, after the death of his mother in 1897, in the villa that his sister had bought in his name near Weimar with help from Meta von Salis (for details of the affair, see H.F. Peters, *Nietzsche et sa sœur Elisabeth*, Chapter 18, 'La villa Silberblick' pp 234f.).

70 Goethe lived in Weimar (1776–1832), where he held a prestigious salon (which, according to Nietzsche, his grandmother attended), thanks to the Duke Karl-August of Weimar. Elisabeth dreamt of winning over the Duke Wilhelm-Ernst to the cult of Nietzsche, the Goethe of modern times (see in this regard, the autobiography that Nietzsche composed near the end of his life for Georg Brandes).

71 Op cit, vol 2, p 90.

72 Bernard Förster, a disciple of Wagner, knew Elisabeth in Beyreuth, married her in 1883, and took her to Paraguay where he directed a German colony that expected to regenerate Germany, the *Nueva Germania*. He ended his life by suicide in 1889 after the financial collapse of the enterprise. See Peters, op cit., notably the second part, pp 147f. Nietzsche never cared much for his brother-in-law.

73 She was presented to him by Bjerre. See below, in Part One, Ch. 1, 'Lou Salomé, a natural Link,' on Lou's role as one of Nietzsche's mediators.

74 It was in the course of this stay in the summer of 1882, in Nietzsche's sanctuary, that their adventure culminated, of which we know the avatars (cf. Lou's *Lebensrückblick*, H.F. Peters' *Ma sur, mon épouse*, second part, pp 79f.).

75 H.F. Peters, *Ma Sur, mon épouse* Gallimard, p 275.

76 Peters, ibid.

77 H.F. Peters, *Nietzsche et sa sœur Elisabeth*, p 248.

78 Peters, op cit., p 282.

79 See Peters, op cit., Chapter 22, pp 280f. Nietzsche's funeral services were very solemn affairs, and in 1924 there was even talk of a monument and an Olympic stadium!

80 Op cit., pp 274–5.

81 Op cit., vol 2, p 90. See the analysis of the Putnam episode in our preceding work, pp 46–9.

82 In the form of a diagnosis, in the meeting of the Vienna Psychoanalytic Society on 1 April 1908: 'Nietzsche's sister reminds him of those patients who prepared themselves (for each analytic session) to prevent the possibility of anything becoming known spontaneously (uncensored)' (op cit., p 373) [*Minutes* I:360]. That characterizes the defensive and dogmatic attitude of interpretation of the Weimar school, with which he forged diplomatic relations a little later.

83 First part: 'Freud and Nietzsche'.

84 Second Part: 'Nietzsche and Freud'.

PART ONE: FREUD AND NIETZSCHE

Chapter 1 The Genesis of an Encounter

1 This is the formula from the Prologue to *Twilight of the Idols*. See also Aphorism 62 of *The Antichrist*: 'Today's date? Transvaluation of all values! . . .' (*SW*, VIII, 283). In Nietzsche's design, this book would have constituted the first volume of a project entitled *Transvaluation of All Values*, which, starting in summer 1888, replaces the title *Will to Power*. On this concept, see below, Part Two, Book III, Ch. 3, 'Transvaluation and the Law.'].

2 In a curious omission, the French translation does not mention values, content only to speak of a 'general collapse' (*La naissance de la psychanalyse*, p 193). By contrast, Jones gives a complete translation, without omitting the axiological acceptation (op cit., vol 1, p 391) and revealing a 'paraphrase of Nietzsche' (note 1). Emphasis added to Freud's text.

3 *GW*, II–III, 315, in *Traumdeutung* ('Dream-work').

4 Op cit., p 335.

5 *GW*, II–III, 667, in *Uber den Traum* ('On Dreams').

6 On Koegel, see Peters' study of Elisabeth Nietzsche, pp 178f and pp 196–233.

7 This letter is not included in the collection *La naissance de la psychanalyse*, but Max Schur cites it in *La mort dans la vie de Freud*, p 248. See p 646 of Schur's work for the complete German text. [Translator's note: interestingly, this statement is made in the context of an announcement to Fliess that Freud had purchased an edition of Nietzsche's Complete Works. See Gay, op. cit., p 105.]

8 See below, in Part One, Ch. 2, 'Nietzsche's Status in Freud's Philosophical Topography,' and above, pp 4f.

9 See above, p 10f.

10 See above, p 7f.

11 On Zweig, see note 18 below.

12 Cited by Jones, op cit., vol 3, in *Extraits de la correspondence de Freud*, p 517.

13 Op cit., ibid., note 1. On the details of Nietzsche's travels, see Guy de Pourtalès, *Nietzsche en Italie* (1929).

14 Freud makes allusion to Paneth in *The Interpretation of Dreams* ('my friend Joseph', *GW*, II–III, 486). It was he who had advanced Freud the money with which to get married and who succeeded Freud at the Institute of Physiology in Vienna as an assistant-teacher (demonstrator) in 1882. He died of tuberculosis.

15 The passion for Italy is a common trait between Freud's and Nietzsche's sensibilities. But, truly speaking, it is not the same Italy that attracts one and the other: we know of Freud's love for Rome, which Nietzsche hardly shared. See Pourtalès, op cit., p 143: 'a detestable, rather than an Eternal city, for Nietzsche', who briefly visited it in 1883. Contrast that with Freud's sense of marvel – exclusively before pagan Rome, it is true – on discovering Rome in 1901 after a long hesitation. During this period when he refused to travel to Italy, Freud strongly appreciated those who would speak of it. Paneth was among those.

16 *SW*, VI, 224 (Book III, § 11, 'Of Old and New Tablets').

17 Letter from Paneth to his wife, reproduced in Carl Albrecht Bernoulli, *Franz Overbeck und Friedrich Nietzsche*, 1908, vol I, pp 358–60, and in French in *Nietzsche devant ses contemporains*, texts collected and published by Geneviève Bianquis, ed. du Rocher, 1959, pp 112–15.

18 Arnold Zweig (1887–1968), a writer who corresponded with Freud from 1927, who took refuge in Palestine in 1933, and ended his days in East Berlin. His reflection on Nietzsche takes place in the context of his ideological resistance to the usage which had begun to be undertaken with the Nazis, with the support of Elisabeth Nietzsche.

19 Op cit., vol III, p 217.

20 Cited by Jones, op cit., vol III, p 516.

21 Op cit., p 517. Freud cites in reference to this Podach's work, which contains the latest information on the case of Nietzsche (see above, 'Introduction,' note 50). We note an analogy between Nietzsche... and Moses, that is established on this occasion in Freud's mind. In fact, in a letter dated 30 September 1934, Freud evokes the beginning of his *Moses and Monotheism*, and declares that 'my book's title, *The Man Moses, a Historical Novel* (a more exact title than your novel on Nietzsche)' (in *Correspondance*, 1873–1939, Gallimard, pp 458–9). In other words, Freud conceives of Moses as *his* Nietzsche . . . .

22 Freud is thus faithful to his position, formulated a quarter of a century earlier on the same question (see above p 22). Elsewhere, Freud adds: 'At any rate, if one is not a specialist, the details of an illness present very little of interest.' It is also a means of

willingly flattening the problem on technical grounds: decidedly, 'The case of Nietzsche' is an affair of 'specialists', a *de facto* question (interpretation of his paralysis) preliminary to any speculation, even psychoanalytic.

23 Cited by Jones, vol III, p 217.

24 In support, Freud evokes the hypothesis: 'One knows that he was a passive homosexual and that he had contracted syphilis is a men's bordello in Italy,' a rumour on which Freud does not speculate. 'Is it true: *quien sabe*?' Already in 1908, Freud and the other Viennese analysts had considered this fact, in the seminar of 28 October: 'A certain sexual anomaly is certain. Jung claimed to have learned that Nietzsche had contracted syphilis in a homosexual bordello; that is of no importance' (*Minutes*, op cit., II, 35) [In the English edition, see *Minutes* II:30]. By 1934, Jung had become 'one', but Jung seems to be one of those who accredited this hypothesis to the core group of the analytic movement.

25 For Freud it is a matter of a brute pathology. 'Writers are authorized to change the brute pathological facts.' 'I ignore them,' he adds. 'They are not in general very docile people.' One cannot be more prudent than that in psychography.

26 Letter dated 11 May 1934, ibid.

27 In a letter dated 15 July, Freud declares not to believe in 'the half of what Zweig writes on his subject in his *Account*'; that is, his *Account of German Judaism: An Essay*, which contains a ringing praise of Freud.

Compare the identificatory formulae which are addressed to Freud's masters (Brücke and his associates): 'Helmholtz my idol'. But for Freud the scientific ideal is regulatory; one can hope to approach it, but the philosopher (here: Nietzsche) reveals an inaccessible nobility, being in another place, perhaps fictive. Around 1885, in any event, these two ideals were able to coexist for Freud.

28 Freud has in fact always overestimated the continuity of his relationship to philosophers, and reduced his interest to an anodyne attraction of youth (see *Freud, la philosophie et les philosophes*, p 15).

29 Nevertheless, it is at the same moment (1911) that Weimar pays official homage to Nietzsche, that Adler quits the psychoanalytic movement.

30 Letter to Oscar Pfister dated 26 February 1911, *Correspondance*, p 86.

31 It is only, it is true, an expression. Manès Sperber, who refers to Adler, has well noted the differences in categories: Adler's 'will to power' is anodynized in relation to that of Nietzsche (*Alfred Adler et la psychologie individuelle*, Gallimard, pp 122–6). The substitution of aggression for sexuality is nonetheless in itself a revelation: see below, Part Two, [p 90f].

32 Sigmund Freud, C.-G. Jung, Correspondance, French Translation Gallimard, vol 1, letter 46J dated 25 September, 1907: 'Dr. Gross tells me that he would immediately get rid of transference in medicine, by turning men into sexual immoralists . . . The state that is truly sound for the neurotic is sexual immorality. In that, he associates you with Nietzsche' (pp 143–4). Gross (1877–1919), Kraeplin's assistant in Munich, thus represents a form of mixed therapy (Freudo-Nietzschean), a variety that compares to such Freudo-Schopenhauerean hybrids as that of Juliusberger (cf. *Freud, la philosophie et les philosophes*, pp 182–3). See also Rank's point of view, below, in 'Nietzscheo Freudianism: From Gross to Rank.'

33 Letter 170J dated 25 December 1909: 'I would willingly tell you many things on the subject of Dionysus . . . Nietzsche seems to me to have suspected a good part of all that' (op cit., vol 1, p 364). On this point, see below, Part Two, Book II, Ch. 2.

34 Letter 291J dated 2 January 1912: 'Mme Lou . . . through her relations with Nietzsche, has a literary reputation which is not to be disdained' (op cit., vol 2, p 242). See below, in "Lou Salomé, A Natural Link."

35 Letter 303J, dated 3 March 1912: 'I let Zarathustra speak for me' says Jung (op cit., vol 2, p 259), citing the last chapter of Book I, 'Of the Gift-Giving Virtue', 3 (*SW*, VI, 83–4), which contains the famous statement: 'Now, I order you to lose me and to find yourselves, and only when you have rejected me, will I return to you.'

36 Letter 304F, dated 5 March 1912, op cit., vol 2, p 260.
37 Op cit., vol 2, p 188.
38 Cited by Jones, vol 3, p 243.
39 Lou knew Nietzsche in 1882–3, and met Freud in 1911.
40 Lou-Andreas Salomé, *Correspondance avec Sigmund Freud*, Gallimard, p 245, the letter dated 8 May 1932. In a letter dated 4 May, Lou evoked the necessity of publishing his *Memoires* 'because of some points regarding Nietzsche' (ibid., p 244). In question is the attack that Elisabeth Nietzsche had launched once more against Lou, contesting all the facts alleged by the old acquaintances of her brother, a campaign that ended in her writing *Nietzsche et les femmes de son temps*, where she presented Lou as a vulgar adventuress. In the same letter, Freud clearly takes Lou's side and urged her to respond: 'You have always let it pass because you have been too great a lady; will you not finally defend yourself in a more dignified manner?' Doubtless since the meeting of 1911 (see above, in the 'Introduction,' 'The Weimar Encounter: Nietzscheo-Freudian Chronicles'), Freud's opinion on Nietzsche's sister was still degraded.
41 It is moreover without pleasure, and at Zweig's insistence, that Freud made this approach in favour of a project that, as we have seen, Freud himself disavowed. On 16 May 1934, he wrote her: 'A dear friend, Arnold Zweig, author of *Grisha*, wants to work out and present a Nietzsche (note the sceptical tone!). He knows that you would be an incomparable advisor, but would you want to? Out of principle, I have advised him against taking up this subject' (op cit., p 250). The least that one can say is that he does not encourage her to accept it. Lou's response, dated 20 May, flatly states that

> this participation is *absolutely unthinkable* as far as I am concerned, and even the smallest role would be impossible. For me, it is not to be touched; I reject this idea with dread. I ask you to tell him straightway with the greatest energy and finality. As you have moreover reason insistently to advise him against this Nietzsche project (pp 250–1).

Thus Freud and Lou were accomplices in a refusal to take up Nietzsche!
42 See the *Journal d'une année (1912–1913)*, p 338. On the importance of this text, see *Freud, la philosophie et les philosophes*, pp 18–19.
43 *Lebensrückblick*, Ma vie, PUF, p 170.
44 In question is one of Lou's poems entitled *Prayer to Life* that enthused Nietzsche, who saw in it the echo of his own sensibility and put it to music. 'They will sing it later, one day, in memory of me', he said of it in 1888 (*SW*, VIII, 372).
45 'The text, I am fond of saying it expressly because there was a misunderstanding on this subject: the text is not mine. It is due to the astonishing inspiration of a young Russian with whom I have become friends, Mlle. Lou Salomé. For whoever is capable of grasping the meaning that is attached to the last verse of this poem, it would be easy to guess why I would accord him my preference and my admiration. It has grandeur (*Grösse*). The sorrow is not presented as an objection to life: "If you have no more happiness to give me, alas your torments remain" (*SW*, VIII, 372). Freud is not among those who are 'capable of grasping the meaning that is attached to the last verse of this poem', whose 'grandeur' escapes him.
46 See Wilhelm Busch (1832–1908), *Balduin Bählamm*. Busch was a humourist much appreciated by Freud.
47 *GW*, XIV, 434, *Civilization and Its Discontents*. On the Schopenhauerean sense of this passage, see *Freud, la philosophie et les philosophes*, p 201.
48 Cf. the 'turning point' of 1920.
49 This is the term used by Jones (op cit., vol 1, p 20). 'The latter's well-known aversion to music constitutes one of his idiosyncrasies.' This aversion takes acute forms. Entering a place where an orchestra was playing, Freud 'wasted no time stopping up his ears so as not to hear' (ibid.). A letter from Rome, dated 22 September 1907 states that Freud is

bothered by the loudness of the orchestras (cited by Jones, op cit., vol 2, pp 39–40). In a letter to Jones, dated 22 September 1912, he notes, as a fact foreign to his nature, that 'music touches the ears of certain people' (ibid., p 101). At the beginning of his study on *Michelangelo's Moses*, Freud gives a reason for this musical phobia: The first condition for artistic enjoyment is to be able to 'contemplate at length' the works of art in order to 'understand them after their nature', that is to say in order to 'grasp that by which they produce an effect', which is the case for 'literary works or the plastic arts'. 'When I may not do so, for example with music, I am nearly incapable of enjoying it. A rationalist, or perhaps an analytic disposition struggles in me against the emotions when I do not know why I am moved, nor what has seized me' (*GW*, X, 172). In any case, there is a trait clearly different from Nietzschean idiosyncrasies.

50 See Charles Andler's study *La poésie de Heine* (1948), p 89. Andler is the author of the first general survey of Nietzsche to appear in French, *Nietzsche, sa vie et sa pensée*. Nietzsche appreciated Heine as well, but with another sensibility that accentuated the Dionysian aspects, while Freud is more sensitive to what Andler calls the 'Aristophanean' Heine. Regarding Marx's influence on this aspect of Heine, see our *Marx et la répetition historique*, pp 71f.

51 Andler, op cit., p 72.

52 Op cit., p 191.

53 See below p 68. It is true that it is a question of a sort of diagnosis.

54 See Freud's attitude towards his own illness.

55 According to Busch's expression, in Balduin Bählamm, cited by Freud in An Introduction, *On Narcissism*, *GW*, X, 148–9 (II).

56 Cf. the volume of essays published by Aubier-Flammarion, pp 106f.

57 Human, All Too Human, I, 26, *SW*, III, 39–40: 'Reaction as Progress'. *Daybreak*, III, 197, *SW*, IV, 165–7: ('The Hostility of Germans Toward the Enlightenment').

58 Mann, op cit., p 115.

59 Op cit., p 127.

60 Op cit., pp 141–2.

61 Op cit., p 143.

62 These are literally Freud's own words. See below, Part One, Ch. 2, 'Nietzsche's Status in Freud's Philosophical Topography.'

63 Op cit., p 149.

64 We know that *Human, All Too Human* was dedicated to Voltaire.

65 It is nevertheless necessary to mention Freud's moderate reaction, who reproached T. Mann for having linked him to Romanticism.

66 See, notably, Mann's introduction to his anthology of the 'immortal pages of Schopenhauer'.

67 In question is the speech read before the Akädamische Verein für Medizinische Psychologie on 8 May, 1936, then read to Freud on 24 June. It is entitled *Freud and the Future* (reproduced in French in *Freud. Jugements et témoignages, présenté par Roland Jacard*, PUF, pp 15f).

68 Op cit., p 18. Here is an allusion to Dürer's tableau *Le Chevalier et la Mort*, whose importance in Nietzschean iconology Ernst Bertram has demonstrated (*Nietzsche. Essai de mythologie*). Mann assures the transmission of this Nietzschean symbol to Freud.

69 Op cit., p 17.

70 Op cit., p 18–19.

71 In *La guérison par l'esprit*, French translation (1940), p 223.

72 Op cit., p 19–20.

73 See above, p 23.

74 Op cit., p 22.

75 Op cit., p 26.

76 Thomas Mann is interested early on in Nietzsche, around 1895, and he encountered psychoanalysis around 1925. See Louis Leibrich, 'Thomas Mann et Nietzsche' in *Etudes*

et témoignages de cinquantenaire, Société française d'Etudes nietzschéennes, 1950. pp 221f. See also Jean Finck's *Thomas Mann und die Psychoanalyse* (1973). We should also point out that in his last novel, *Doctor Faustus*, Mann represents Nietzsche's last days through the character Adrien Leverkühn.

77 It was a prize of 5,000 marks offered by the counsel Lassen to the best book written in the spirit of Nietzsche, in the context of a great pro-Nietzsche movement just after the First World War. We note that the title recalls the formula in *Ecce Homo* where Nietzsche defines himself as 'the first anti-political German' [*Ecce Homo* 'Why I am so clever' § 3]. We can also read the name of Thomas Mann in the Guest Register of the Silberblick villa; he had personally made the pilgrimage to Weimar.

78 'Nietzsche as Forerunner in Psychoanalysis' in *Contemporary Studies by Charles Baudouin*, London, 1924. We can also see there the Jungian use of Nietzsche.

79 *Freud*, Ch. XIV. The rapprochement is made through the Overman; see below, pp 71 and 270.

80 *Correspondance de Sigmund Freud avec le pasteur Pfister*, letter dated 24 November 1927, p 169.

81 'La conception freudienne de l'homme à la lumière de l'anthropologie' in *Discour, parcours et Freud*, Gallimard, p 203. We note that it was Otto Binswanger, the uncle of the philosopher, who looked after Nietzsche in Jena.

82 Op cit., p 210, note 2.

83 *Freud, la philosophie et les philosophes*, p 181.

84 Beginning with *The Trauma of Birth*, Rank distances himself from Freud. We note that Freud again finds Nietzsche set before him as a referent in the disagreement, just as in the period of his controversies with Adler. See above, in this chapter, 'Nietzsche and the Attack on the Libido.'

85 Otto Gross, who participated in the analytic movement from the beginning, was at the time considered as original and held in defiance by Freud (cf. the correspondence with Jung). His avowed aim around 1913 was to combine Freudian techniques with Nietzschean concepts, conceived as support for a revolutionary and anarchist *Weltanschauung*, which led him in his writings to present Freudianism as the scientific application of Nietzschean institutions. Gross' theses were tested in relation to the astonishing anarchist philosophy of the 'cosmic Circle', a group of intellectuals in quest of a renovation of *Kultur* by women, and the 'Gruppe Tat' or 'Aktion Gruppe' of Schwabing, an activist movement. In his essays published in *Aktion*, Gross solidly presented Nietzschean thought and psychoanalysis as the principle of a philosophy of revolution. In his *Effets de la communauté sur l'individu*, Freud is presented as the authentic continuity of Nietzsche, the one and the other grasping through their theories the foundations of a conservative State. We thus find in Gross the tenet of a revolutionary anarchism that professes a Nietzscheo-Freudian credo. We can thus understand Freud's defiance before the Nietzschean Reich, presenting himself as the mediator in a marriage of psychoanalysis with Nietzsche (just as Reich entered psychoanalysis) and Marx, in order to engender a revolutionary vision of the world (on the homology of the mechanism, see our *Marx et la répétition historique*, p 174, note 3).

86 *Volonté et psychothérapie*, Payot, pp 21–6.

87 Op cit., p 27. See Nietzsche mentioned as an exception, p 28.

88 Op cit., p 30.

89 Op cit., p 139, note.

90 The original title was *Wahrheit und Wirklichkeit* (Truth and Reality), translated in French as *La volonté du bonheur*, Ed. Stock.

91 Op cit., p 17–18.

92 Op cit., p 18.

93 Op cit., p 20.

94 Op cit., p 21.

95 Op cit., p 43.

96 Nevertheless adding: 'Freud's theory is not a "repetition" of Schopenhauer's theory, although the parentage is close; my psychology of the Will is no more a repetition of Nietzsche's "Will to Power"' (pp 32–44).
97 Op cit., p 42.
98 Op cit., p 43.
99 Op cit., p 44.
100 Ibid.

Chapter 2 Nietzsche in Freudian discourse

1 See our analysis of Freud's general practice regarding philosophical references, of which Nietzsche is only a single case, in *Freud, la philosophie et les philosophes*, p 125f.
2 The collected references are analysed in this chapter. The principle references to correspondences are utilized in the course of this book.
3 See our *Introduction à l'épistémologie freudienne*, p 133f, and Part II, *passim*.
4 In question is the text where Freud recognized Schopenhauer's anticipation of repression. We have analysed this text in *Freud, la philosophie et les philosophes*, p 181f.
5 We can compare the present chapter with the fourth chapter of the second part of *Freud, la philosophie et les philosophes*, pp 177–205, 'Freud et Schopenhauer', in order to compare the physiognomy of the two referents in Freud's discourse, and to read there the correspondence between thematics and borrowings.
6 *GW*, X, 53.
7 See above, pp 7 and 11.
8 Schopenhauer is cited there in reference to the theories of sexuality and of repression.
9 *An Autobiographical Study*, *GW*, XIV, 86, .
10 The reference to Schopenhauer's theory of dreams, on the other hand, only figures as part of this history. *GW*, II–III, 39.
11 *GW*, II–III, 554.
12 *SW*, III, 25–6 ('The Logic of Dreams').
13 See below, Part II, Book 2, Ch. III, pp 191f.
14 *GW*, IV, 162, note 2.
15 *SW*, VII, 78.
16 See above, p 9.
17 *Notes Upon a Case of Obsessional Neurosis*, *GW*, VII, 407.
18 In fact, Lanzer had come to hear of Freud from *The Psychopathology of Everyday Life*, which was one of Freud's most widely read books.
19 Supplement to Ch. XXXII. See our study of the text in *Freud, la philosophie et les philosophes*, pp 186–8.
20 We know that, from October 1865 when Nietzsche found Schopenhauer's masterpiece at Rohn's second-hand bookshop in Leipzig, he became imbued with its ideas. Thus it is not surprising that Nietzsche should spontaneously reformulate one idea from a book with which he had become literally impregnated.
21 See below, Part 2, Book III, Ch. 1, 'The Theory and Pathology of Memory.'
22 *Psychoanalytic Notes on an Autobiographical Account of a Case of Paranoia (Dementia Paranoides)*, *GW*, VIII, 290.
23 *SW*, VI, 180–4, the fourth episode of the third part, 'Before Sunrise'.
24 *GW*, VIII, 290, note 2.
25 See above, 'Introduction,' note 59.
26 See below, Part II.
27 On the role of the 'fundamental biogenetic law' in Nietzsche and Freud, see below pp 122 and 157.
28 See below, Part II.
29 *Some Character-Types Met With in Psychoanalytic Work*, *GW*, X, 391.

30 *SW*, VI, 38–41. This text is analysed below, Part II, p 225.
31 See below, Part II.
32 *Group Psychology and the Analysis of the Ego*, *GW*, XIII, 138 (Ch. 10).
33 *On Narcissism, an Introduction GW*, X, 141.
34 See below, Part II.
35 In question is Manuscript N joined to letter 64 of 31 May 1897, in *La naissance de la psychanalyse* [*The Birth of Psychoanalysis*], 186.
36 See below, pp 159f.
37 A new occurrence of the word *Ubermenschliches* (1914) which indicates an inflection of Nietzsche's vocabulary, *The 'Moses' of Michelangelo*, *GW*, X, 198.
38 'I am not the Overman that you have represented in your imagination' wrote Freud to Ferenczi on 6 October 1910. At the very least, he did play the role of Father of the primitive horde for his first 'sons' (in the context of the early analytic movement).
39 *The Ego and the Id*, *GW*, XIII, 251.
40 *New Introductory Lecture*, *GW*, XV, 79 (No. III, 'The Dissection of the Psychical Personality').
41 Correspondence of Freud-Groddeck, in Georg Groddeck, *Ça et Moi*, Gallimard, p 94.
42 For example, to his brother Carl (op cit., p 135) or to the philosopher Vaihinger (see below, note 44).
43 Letter of 11 June, 1929 'to a medical patient', op cit., p 167.
44 See the interesting document that is Groddeck's response to Hans Vaihinger, author of *Nietzsche as Philosopher*, who had questioned Groddeck about the possible influence on Nietzsche of Groddeck's father, Carl Theodor, author of a doctoral dissertation entitled *The Democratic Illness, a New Type of Madness* (1850). Reproduced in *Ça et Moi*, p 170f. (letter of 8 May 1930).
45 'When in 1904, with Mme. Förster-Nietzsche, I visited Nietzsche's tomb, she told me that the night before, Gersdorff, a Friend of Nietzsche's, had come to see her and that he had spent three hours without interruption in the company of Mme Koberstein' (Groddeck's grandmother) (op cit., p 171). So there is a quasi-familial link between the two clans. Elisabeth reserved for friends the visits to Nietzsche's tomb in Röcken. With Groddeck, Freud fell once more into a living Nietzschean filiation, without really exploiting it.
46 See below, in Part Two, Book II, Ch. 2, 'The Id and the Self.'
47 Conforming to the approach announced above, p 15.

PART TWO: NIETZSCHE AND FREUD

Introduction

1 Our initial approach naturally remains the interpellation of the stakes from the privileged point of view of Freud, both because he comes *after* Nietzsche and because our inquiry is borne from the outset by a stake that interested Freud (see the conclusion, which is our own balance sheet). But we will not hesitate to reactive, *behind* Freud, Nietzsche's point of view as revealing something notably *unthought* in Freud in the course of his critique, which will fill a sort of perverse role in relation to the institution of the analytic law (see below, *passim*). This frees us to reactivate to a second degree an analytic interpretation of Nietzsche's declarations.
2 The structure of a level of analysis, or of a chapter, is thus the following: (A) the genesis of the Nietzschean problematic; (B) the genesis of Freud's problematic, on the same theme; (C) the state of the problem, both in the form of the position of the question and of the given response. This schema is complicated by the multiplication of sub-themes and by the necessity, in a given conext, of enticing a comparison with Freud, thus inverting the diachronic order according to our thematic requirements.

3 Note here the pitfalls of language, whereby such-and-such a *word* shared by Nietzsche and Freud reveals a considerable difference in both its context and the scope of that content. Likewise, an impressive analogy may be expressed by a very different terminology. That is why, if we must follow the analogies by their terminology, we must also demonstrate linkages where they are not explicitly indicated, given that the relationship between Nietzsche anmd Freud, in its most important respects, is revealed to be amorphous, that is to say it only appeats at a distance sufficient to overcome distortions.

4 Nietzsche, through his mode of aphoristic expression, destroys any illusion of a system. The clearest expression of this comes in *Twighlight of the Idols*. 'I distrust all systematizers (*Systematikern*) and I avoid them. The Will to a System indicates a lack of integrity' (*Rechtsschaffenheit*) ('Maxims and Sayings,' § 26, *SW*, VIII, 84). Already *Daybreak* had asserted 'Beware of systematizers!,' and denounced their 'comedy' (§ 318, *SW*, IV, 222). In another expression, Nietzsche declared 'puerile' the project of 'constructing systems' (*SW*, IV, 222). Freud would agree with Nietzsche's diagnosis of an 'illness of character' typical of philosophers (*SW*, X, 377) and their 'Will to Systems' (*Wille zum System*). For Freud, the 'system' is characteristic of a 'world-view' (*Weltanschauung*). To the extent that psychoanalysis is a science in becoming, it aspires neither to totalization, nor to systematization (see *Freud, la philosophie et les philosophes*, p 45f). 'What psychoanalysis carefully avoids being' is precisely 'a system' (*GW*, X, 96). For very different stakes, Nietzsche and Freud thus fundamentally refuse the etiquette of 'systems.' That is why we will (and must) compare two geneses.

5 Book I.

6 Book II.

7 Book III.

BOOK I: THE FOUNDATIONS

Chapter 1 Instict and Drive

1 We discuss the distinction between *Instinkt* and *Trieb* below: for Nietzsche, see this chapter; for Freud, see Ch. 2.

2 The word literally teems in Nietzsche, and occurs regularly in Freud when he demands its function. See below, on the significance of the semantic distinctions between these two approaches.

3 The development of the concept may be summarized by three regimes which correspond, for Nietzsche, to three chapters of Book I: Ch. 1, the period between 1869–76; Ch. 2, the years after 1878; Ch. 3, the period between 1883–8. For Freud, we can distinguish three parallel regimes: the period starting in 1895 (before the literary introduction of any drive terminology); the period beginning in 1905 with the introduction of the term; and the period between 1910–20, when Freud systematized the instinctual problematic, while developing the concept of the dual drives. This synchronicity makes possible a comparative study of the genesis of two instinctual problematics. It is another matter to define the *logical moments* which the chronology supports, but the chronology expresses the overall, general movement of Nietzschean thought and Freudian theoretical construction, for which instinct is a special revelation in itself.

4 *Homer and Classical Philology*, *SW*, I, 3–4. The lecture in question is the *Antrittsvorlesung* delivered in February, 1869, in Basel, when Nietzsche assumed the chair of Extraordinary Professor of classical philology.

5 *SW*, I, 5.

6 *SW*, I, 8.

7 See below, in Book I, Ch. 1, 'The Historical Paradigm of Nietzschean Instinct'.

8 *SW*, I, 3.

9 *SW*, I, 15–16.

10 *SW*, I, 22.

11 The 1795 *Prolegomena ad Homerum* of Friedrich August Wolf (1759–1824) established the paradigm in classical philology which was still dominant when the young Nietzsche came to the discipline.
12 *Homers Wettkampf.*
13 *SW*, I, 238–9.
14 *SW*, I, 241.
15 *SW*, I, 249 (Fragment 5).
16 *SW*, I, 250.
17 *SW*, I, 251.
18 *The Birth of Tragedy*, *SW*, I, 52.
19 *SW*, I, 53. The emphasis is Nietzsche's.
20 *SW*, I, 61.
21 *SW*, I, 47. This is the first phrase in *The Birth of Tragedy*. On the meaning of this text in Nietzsche's general conception of sexuality, see below, in Book II, Chapter 1, 'Eros and Dionysus.'.
22 *SW*, I, 116f. Socrates is defined as 'nature at once abnormal' (ibid., p 118) – a teratological vocabulary which confirms the naturalist acceptation. It is a question of a 'monstrosity by default', which imprints its 'natural force' on the 'greatest instinctive forces'.
23 *SW*, I, 182.
24 *SW*, I, 118.
25 Fragments dating from 1872, reproduced in the collection *Le livre du philosophe* and in *SW*, X, 29–91.
26 On Nietzsche's instinct of cognition, see below, in Book II, Chapter 1, 'Cognitive Instinct and Drive to Know,' for a comparison with Freudian homologies. We only mention it here as a moment from the first general period of the conceptualization of *Instinkt*.
27 We can see the schizogenetic process at work by listing the compound words that Nietzsche forms with *Trieb*. This survey will permit us to see and grasp the extent of this concept–inflection in Nietzsche's work – wissenschaftliche und ästhetisch *Triebe*; künstlerische Volks*triebe*; Kunst*trieb*; dionysische *Triebe*; politische *Triebe*; logische *Triebe*; metaphysische *Trieb*; Erkenntnis*trieb*; Wissens*trieb*; Welt*trieb*; Einheits*trieb*; Kultur*trieb*; *Trieb* nach Erkenntnis; Warheits*trieb*; agonale *Trieb*; *Trieb* der Weltbildung; Spiel*trieb*; Philosophische *Trieb*; *Trieb* zur Metapherbildung; Fundamentaltrieb; *Trieb* nach Glauben an die Warheit; höchste *Triebe*; *Trieb* zur Lüge; *Trieb* zur Wissenschaft; *Trieb* zur Gerechtlichkeit; analytische *Trieb*; Bautrieb; Massen*triebe*; Lebens*triebe*; *Trieb* zum klasichen Altertum; egotische *Triebe*; unegotische *Triebe*; Natur*trieb*; Nach*trieb*; Geselligkeits*trieb*; *Trieb* nach Ausziechnung; *Trieb* nach leben; *Trieb* nach Ruhe; *Trieb* nach Anhänglichkeit und Fürsorge; Grund*triebe*; Erb*triebe*; soziale *Triebe*; *Triebe* der Redlichkeit; *Trieb* der Alt-Erhaltung; Aneignungs*trieb*; Unterwerfungs*trieb*; kritische *Triebe*; intellektuelle *Trieb*; schlimme *Triebe*; *Trieb* zu strafen; *Trieb* zum Zwecke, zum Höheren, Ferneren, Vielfacheren; Selsterhaltungs*trieb*; *Trieb* des Geistes; Eigentumtrieb; Unberwältigungs*trieb*; anzweifelnde *Triebe*; verneinde *Trieb*; abwartende *Trieb*; sammelnde *Trieb*; auflösende *Trieb*. This list, by no means exhaustive, shows the prodigality with which Nietzsche created these instincts, by tieing *Trieb* to another term or inflecting it with an adjective. If these instincts share neither the same conceptual importance nor the same sense of dignity, they nonetheless all actualize the omnipotence of instinctuality, a common inexhaustible base from which each instinct departs by a sort of spontaneous generation. We cann appose them here with the rather small group of instincts with which Freud expresses his system of drives: Partial*trieb*; Selsterhaltungs*trieb*; Sexual*trieb*; Ich*trieb*; Todes*triebe*; Lebens*triebe*; Bemächtigungs*trieb*; Agressions*trieb*; Destruktions*trieb* (to which we could add some conjunctural uses). Freud then hierarchizes this group according to the explanatory levels where they intervene (see below, Chapters 2 and 3). Freud's employment of *Trieb*

is not without problems or confusions; for instance, he evokes the same Herden*trieb* (herd instinct), both to deny it (*Psychoanalysis and Theory of the Libido*, *GW*, XIII, 232) and to relativize it (*Group Psychology and the Analysis of the Ego*, *GW*, XIII, 129).

28 *SW*, X, 45.

29 *Le livre du philosophe*, p 94. An anthropomorphic illusion, in Nietzsche's diagnosis, causes man to 'take the effects of the most complicated mechanisms, those of the mind, for effects identical to the effects of the origin.'

30 *SW*, X, 64.

31 *SW*, II, 13, 'David Strauss, the Confessor and the Writer', § 2.

32 *SW*, II, 153. It is also the subject of the entire second of the *Untimely Meditations*, 'On the Uses and Disadvantages of History for Life'.

33 *SW*, II, 125.

34 *SW*, II, 190–1.

35 *SW*, II, 437 (Second Lecture).

36 *SW*, II, 462 (Third Lecture).

37 *SW*, II, 470–1.

38 See below, in Book I, Ch. 2, 'The Drive, Freud's Meta-Psychological Unity.'.

39 This text was recovered and reproduced, along with the Freud–Fleiss correspondence, in *La naissance de la psychoanalyse* [Paris], p 313f.

40 Op cit., p 315.

41 Op cit., p 317.

42 Op cit., p 3. Freud even distinguishes between two types of neurons respectively charged with exogenous and endogenous functions. He then designates more precisely this 'force ... derived from the instincts' which is 'the will'.

43 Op cit., p 336.

44 A position readily found in the *Three Essays on the Theory of Sexuality* (*GW*, V, 67); *Instincts and Their Vicissitudes* (*GW*, X, 214); *Outline of Psychoanalysis* (*GW*, XVIII, 70).

45 See below, p 80.

46 *Instincts and Their Vicissitudes*, *GW*, X, 214–15.

47 Since neither Nietzsche nor Freud invented the concept of instinct, but found it in the intellectual baggage of modern thought, we need to establish a genealogy of the term, by recalling the state of the concept up to the moment when Nietzsche and Freud adopted in the last quarter of the nineteenth century.

The term first arises in the first half of the eighteenth century; in fact, it is in the context of the old question of animals having souls that the thematic of instinct becomes possible. However, despite conscious reflection in Greek antiquity from Aristotle on, the question had never been formulated as such. Thus, it is informative, in order to grasp the significance of an instinctualist problematic, to understand how this question is opposed to individualization as well as to the very naming of a principle such as 'instinct'.

In the Aristotelian perspective, which lasted through Stoicism and Hippocraticism until the beginning of the Middle Ages, the difference in nature between human and animal souls was never problematized. Aristotle's trinary hierarchy of souls dispenses with the search for a binary principle of opposition which will later lead to the notions of intelligence and instinct. Interestingly, it was the Thomist scholastic, concerned to protect the dignity of the human soul by the screen of the difference-in-principle, and to assure himself of a nature that is distinctly correlative to immortality, who laboured to establish a hierarchy of the faculties. The Scholastic conception had inherited from the Aristotelian perspective an anthropomorphism based on a schema where animal souls exercised a type of judgement isomorphic to human judgement (even if in a distinct register). Beyond this, St Thomas assigned animals their own faculty and avoided the possible confusion between it and human judgement (he called it *estimative* judgement). Curiously, this animal faculty combines the intellectualist perspective of anthropomorphic judgement with the mystery of the future concept of instinct; in fact, it comes to fill the very place and function of the modern conception of instinct!

In this conception, Cartesian mechanism opposes the representation of an animal automatism. Having raised the idea of an animal soul to the rank of a fiction, the correlative idea of instinct is discredited. The configuration of bodies and movements rejects any notion of *impetus*. The opposition human/animal must become even more radical, but this duality no longer occurs through two types of judgement correlative to two types of souls; instead, it raises as a particular case the metaphysical duality of body and soul. The Cartesian duality does not abolish this oppositional representation, but rather marginalizes it. It will return to be invoked in animism and raised to the status of doctrine by neo-Hippocratic and Stahlian medicine.

Such was the general state of affairs at the moment when Buffon undertook to institutionalize the concept. Now, instinct comes to be thought of as the particular effect of one type of soul, and is rejected as a special motor. In both of these cases, it is denied as a *principle*. Here, the animistic and mechanistic conceptions reinforce each other, paradoxically in order to make economy the autogenetic principle. The decisive event that Buffon incarnates is *necessity*, finally shown to postulate a principle able to account for the 'economic animal'. It is precisely the discovery of this specific economy, as an order of reality generating an order of rationality – a science of animal nature – that calls for the individualization of a motor principle, which in turn demands to be *named*. *Instinct* thus ceases to be a useless fiction, as the Cartesians believed, as soon as the economic animal emerges as something other than an indifferent extension of matter (*la physique*); or, if there is an animal materiality (*une physique animal*), instinct is its new principle. But this is not purely and simply a reactivation of the old animism. Instinct is not an abstract principle, but is read in animal behaviour as the expression of its immanent teleology. Thus if animal instinct is required, it is in order to name that functional *telos* that Buffonian naturalism permits it to exhibit.

However, eighteenth-century naturalism also inherited from Cartesianism an irreducible suspicion. Everything proceeds as if instinct, already an annoyance that one must tolerate as the postulate of an animal economy, equally demanded that one signify the possibility of dismissing it. According to Réaumur, 'instinct' did not initially appear in his work on insects, in which he would finally impose the term. That is to say that we judge much of what happens *after the word appears*, even at the price of postulating a reality that corresponds to its *appearance*.

Those who turn away from the generalized use of the term *instinct*, consequently, can point to a fissure between human intelligence and animal instinct; sensualism, combined with intellectualism, combats this idea accredited by the term. So, if the word did make its way into an article in the *Encyclopedia*, its author, Leroy (also the author of a *Letter on Instinct*), also rejected the opposition (human/animal) that the word might accredit. Leroy is quick to denounce the polysemy of the word:

> This word is one of the most abused and one most often pronounced without being heard. Everyone wants to designate it as *the principle which directs the animals in their actions*, but each in his fashion determines the nature of or fixes the extent of this principle. We agree on the word, but the ideas attached to the word are essentially different.

This confusion nonetheless points out an alternative. Either instinct was a 'beginning of cognition', albeit one 'deprived of reflection' and acquired by reasoned experience, as Condillac in particular thought; or else it names a special principle that rivals intelligence. Out of this confusion over the term, there arose distinct uses of *instinct* in France, Britain and Germany.

We note a precocious tendency in Germany to hypostasize the concept in principle, and consequently to inflate the number of instincts. For example, H.S. Reimar, in his *Physical and Moral Observations on the Instincts of Animals* (1760), multiplies instincts out to infinity, instituting a primitive use of the concept without hesitating to posit as many instincts as there are activities or modes of behaviour. This temptation is part of the fate of the concept. But in France, such a temptation was provisionally squelched by the demands of the natural sciences, due largely to Cuvier's methodology. Cuvier had linked the proportional development of the two faculties intelligence/instinct to the taxonomic scale of living beings, based on their anatomical characteristics, and from this point on, the principal duality was fixed.

Curiously, the Cartesian tradition combined this acquired duality with a mechanical inspiration. According to Cuvier, instinct assimilates animals to 'sleepwalkers', but it remains a specific principle. The one who 'contributed more than any other to popularize this thematic in the Nineteenth century', Fluorens, a disciple of Cuvier and the one who 'contributed more than any other to popularize this thematic in the nineteenth century', commented in 1841 that we had arrived at the notion that 'the most absolute opposition separates instinct from intelligence. Everything in instinct is blind, necessary and invariable; everything in intelligence is elective, conditional and modifiable.' It is a clear enough expression that the instinctualist conception had resulted in an *established fixism.*

It is no accident if, within the framework of this transformist conception, Lamarck, at the beginning of the nineteenth century, no less firmly opposed the hypostasis of a principle called instinct. For him, the term constituted a dynamic phenomenon, the acquisition of a habit, by the emergence of new needs, themselves resulting from changes in circumstances. The opposition intelligence/instinct is again reduced, this time to the scale of living beings under the regime of an adaptive dynamic. Although this dispute did not affect the progress of the instinctual thematic, which flourished in the nineteenth century, it did point out a cleavage which threatened, in the last analysis, any theory of instinct that demonstrated a fixist temptation.

The Darwinian revolution, the final step in the complex genesis which guided the idea to the point where Nietzsche and Freud both take it up, modified finally and decisively the conceptual problematic where instinct is engaged. Precisely, Darwin indicated the manner of overcoming the antinomy between a fixist conception of instinct (in the lineage of thought extending from Cuvier) and a transformist conception without a theory of instinct(the lineage from Lamarck). Darwinian instinct appears as an activity that modifies itself under the influence of variations determined by natural selection. With Darwinism, the protean idea of instinct changes form for the last time, but it is in order to accede to the rank of aptitude, branched along an evolutionary dynamic.

We can see in this evocation of the genesis of the concept of instinct that several levels of meaning were successive deposited on the same term by the time that Nietzsche and Freud had begun to adopt it. Before being able to use it, though in a profoundly modified form with respect to the function that the word would perform in their respective conceptions, they must come to terms with this inherited confusion, the singular fact that these semantic levels have remained linked to a conceptual tool as traces of an ancient use. Now the purification of a conceptual tool is not a prerequisite to any new uses; on the contrary, the meaning of the concept is modified by those uses. But this inevitably acquits us of the debt we incur from the moment we adopt a concept already in use. To integrate the traces of prior usage into a new sense is the way that an intellectual heritage can acquit itself of the price of ideological succession.

For us, the double error would be to misrecognize the weight of this heritage on the one hand, while immediately assimilating every use of the thematic to its prior uses on the other. In other words, the central place of the notion of instinct in the Nietzschean and Freudian problematics authorizes no one to label them 'irrationalists'. This label does not force them to return *ipso facto* to the great family of instinct theories. Yet it remains no less true that, mobilizing this term, they situate themselves in relation to this problematic, constructed through philosophical thought, and their contribution can be measured only in relation to the genesis of the concept over the century and a half that preceded them.

We must preserve the balance sheet of this history of the word and idea *instinct*, in the end to begin to understand the heritage and the transgression, to see the emergence of a new function in the conceptual economy labelled elsewhere and before:

1 The problematic centred around the concept and connoted by the term *instinct* is constituted in the eighteenth century, in the discourse of the French naturalists, from the time of Buffon, and surmounted the double obstacle of anthropomorphic animism and Cartesian mechanics.
2 From the moment of its introduction, *instinct* is treated as a polysemy, by the diversity of its phonemes and semantic referents.
3 The conception which supports the instinctualist problematic long remained fixist. Evolutionism, in its attempt to dynamize the concept, encounters a fixist conception which resists the evolutionist appropriation.
4 Born from an integrated problematic in the natural sciences, *instinct* quickly tends to surpass its original framework, which had guaranteed a conscripted extension of the concept. It is the unrestrained process of metaphorization which diffuses the concept through the eccentric ideological spheres of the initial discourses of the naturalists, notably *ethics* and *aesthetics*.

48 See Pierre Grappin, *La théorie du génie dans la préclassicisme allemand* (Paris, 1952), especially Ch. III.
49 Op cit., p 119.
50 See Grappin, op cit., Ch. IV.
51 Charles Andler, *Nietzsche, sa vie et sa pensée*, t. 1, *Les précurseurs*, p 43.
52 We can grasp precisely the regime and function of the concept of Trieb in Schiller's *Letters on Aesthetic Education*. The word first appears in the fourth letter, where it is said that 'because no one can count on the moral conduct of man with as much certitude as with his physical effects, it is necessary that morality in itself become natural and that by his instincts man is already induced to act as only a moral character can do' (p 87). Instinct thus plays the role of a veritable *schema*, in that it endows moral character with sensibility. It is the remedy for *barbarism*, which consists in deriding nature and sacrificing the natural in oneself to the principles of art; but we must not start from the sacrifice of the principles of art to nature, which we might call *savagery*. Being civilized means being one who 'makes a friend of nature' by respecting its liberty; instinct thus constitutes the sacred knot of nature and morality. That is why, against both savagery and barbarism, the double symptom of modern decadence, aesthetic education depends on the instincts, at the same time that it *elevates* (*élève*) them, overcoming the informal (savage) state of the *blinder Triebe* (blind instincts)(p 123), which expresses 'the blind violence of nature'.

In the eighth letter, this role is further specified. Schiller underscores the fact that in order to fulfil its truth function, Reason must become Will, that is to say Force (*Kraft*), which implies that reason 'establishes an instinct to represent it in the domain of appearances', because the instincts, Schiller specifies, 'are the only motor forces in the sensible world' (p 129). This is Schiller's first true definition of instincts as *einzigen bewegenden Kräfte in der empfinden Welt*. We can therefore think of instincts as motor schemas.

At the beginning of the twelfth letter Schiller, introducing his famous distinction, produces the nominal definition. It is a question of forces (*Kräfte*) that, 'as they push us to realize their object, we find an adequate term in *instincts*' (p 167). A curious definition of an apparently impressionistic concept, the instincts are *die Kräfte die uns antrieben, ihr Objekt zu verwicklichen*. Combined with the preceding formula, we can say that it is a matter of an eruption which sets into motion human necessity whose aim is our becoming-actual, by acquiring objectivity through the bias of interior motors.

Schiller distinguishes two fundamental instincts, the instinct which tends to actualize the necessary by giving it a material sensibility (*Sachtrieb*), and the instinct which tends to submit to the necessary law (*Formtrieb*), which is outside of itself, by imposing it on the forms: *sensible* instinct and *formal* instinct.

This distinction allows us to grasp the essential criteria which serve to characterize the instincts as such-and-such. In the first place, there is the *source*, which consists in the *form* of existence, either physical or rational. The source is thus *Existenz*, the existential modality of human *Natur*. In the second place, there is the sphere of extension (*Gebiet*) – limits of finite bodies or infinity. Here it is a question of phenomenal extension, the sphere of the application of the aspect of human Nature concerned. In the third place is the role or the function – the insertion into matter or human liberation, which constitutes its teleology. Finally, there is the *object*, the one demanding that reality change, and the other demanding the immutability of form, one creating the discrete case (*Fälle*) and the other creating the laws (*Gesetze*).

Schiller postulates at the same time a distinction between these two types of instincts and a reciprocity (*Wechselwirkung*) of a type of activity (*Wirksamkeit)*. This makes both possible and necessary a third type of instinct, the instinct of play (*Spieltrieb*) (p 191), reciprocally limiting the two types of instincts which aspire respectively to the *receptivity* of the object and to its *production* (see the fourteenth letter). *Spieltrieb* is the supreme instinct because it combines, as two modalities of its reality, the aptitude for the enjoyment of the object as well as the awareness of one's independence from the object. The aesthetic aim of instinct is thus revealed; it functions to exhibit the possibility of the motive, as a synthesis between sensible determinism and moral liberty.

53 See Hölderlin's letter to his brother, dated June 4 1799.

54 Andler, op cit., p 69.

55 Ibid.

56 Op cit., p 340f.

57 The title of one of his essays.

58 A Newmanian expression, but inspired by Emerson, that designates the sensible and intuitive cognition of immediate reality.

59 Op cit., p 340.

60 Op cit., p 340.

61 Compare, for instance, the style of the *Untimely Meditations* with that of the *Characteristics* or *Signs of the Times*.

62 The encounter in question only took place in 1854. See E. Gans, *Richard Wagner et la pensée schopenhauerienne*, p 17f.

63 *Gesammelte Schriften und Dichtungen*, III, 68.

64 Op cit., p 36. See *Art and Revolution*: 'This nature had demonstrated how strong it is, how inexhaustible is its productive fecundity and its endless renewal . . .' (p 59 in the Opale French translation).

65 Op cit., p 31.

66 Op cit., III, pp 3–4, the introduction to the third and fourth volumes of the *Works*.

67 Jones, op cit., I, 31.

68 Jones, op cit., I, 45. From 1845, this is the objective of the *Berliner Physicalische Gesellschaft*.

69 See below, Ch. 3, p 134.

70 For an analysis of this model, please see our work *Introduction à l'épistémologie freudienne* (Paris: Ed. Payot). The contrast is struck precisely between the philosophical overdetermination of Nietzsche's concept of instinct, and its scientific neutralization by Freud – who does not raise himself above every overdetermination, but obliges us to arrive at a scientific plane, from Freud's perspective.

Chapter 2 Nietzschean Psychology, Freudian Psychoanalysis

1 This level thus corresponds to the second phase of the conceptualization of instinct (see above, Book I, Ch. 1, note 3), at the same time as the study of the form of knowledge which takes it into account.

2 *SW*, III, 15.
3 *SW*, III, 16.
4 *SW*, X, 56.
5 *SW*, XI, 107.
6 *SW*, XI, 280. (In *Systementwürfe und Pläne aus den Jahren*, 1882–8.), § 831.
7 *SW*, IX, 122.
8 *The Will to Power*, *SW*, IX, 425 (§ 630).
9 We know of Nietzsche's interest in the Dalmatian Jesuit physicist Roger Boscovitch (1711–87). See *Beyond Good and Evil*, *SW*, VII, 19 (§ 12).
10 These are the words used in *The Neuro-Psychoses of Defense* (1894).
11 *GW*, XII, 184.
12 On the epistemological foundation of this recourse to chemistry as an epistemic model for psychoanalysis, see our *Introduction à l'épistémologie freudienne* (Part I, Ch. II).
13 *GW*, XII, 185.
14 *GW*, XII, 186.
15 *GW*, X, 143–4. [Translator's note: from the perspective of the end of the twentieth century, in a climate of genome research and brain-chemistry therapeutic regimes like Prozac, this is an astonishing anticipation on Freud's part.]
16 *GW*, XIII, 229.
17 *GW*, XVII, 80.
18 *SW*, III, 2, 17 (aphorism 13).
19 *GW*, X, 320.
20 The expression is from *Ecce Homo*, *SW*, IX, 359.
21 *SW*, III, 49 (§ 35, 'The Advantages of Psychological Observation').
22 *SW*, III, 16, (§ 1).
23 *SW*, III, 17 (§ 2, 'The Common Failing among Philosophers').
24 Ibid., (§ 3, 'Estimation of Unpretentious Truths').
25 *SW*, III, 45 (§ 32, 'Injustice Necessary').
26 In *The Will to Power*, Autumn 1883 [In the Bianquis translation, I, p 125, § 265].
27 Op cit.
28 *SW*, III, 69 (§ 57).
29 *SW*, III, 87 (§ 98, 'Pleasure and Social Instinct').
30 *SW*, III, 88 (§ 99, 'The Innocence of So-called Evil Acts').
31 *The Voyager and His Shadow*, SW, III, 177 (§ 16, Where Indifference is Needed').
32 *The Voyager and His Shadow*, SW, III, 167 (§ 3, 'In the Beginning').
33 *SW*, III, 191 (the title of § 31).
34 An expression used in § 31, ibid.
35 It is remarkable that Nietzschean instinct inherits its characteristics of self-love or self-interest from La Rochefoucauld, starting with the emergence of the second model. After the Beyreuth rupture, the first model is abandoned. In this way the French moralists, beginning with La Rochefoucauld, furnish a new content adapted to the new function of the concept. Even if 'the influence of La Rochefoucauld on Nietzsche . . . had a very brief impact, but a decisive one', we can bring that impact back to life in the genesis of the idea (Andler, op cit., I, p 190).

The description of self-love that opens La Rochefoucauld's *Reflections, or Sentences and Moral Maxims* (1665) is remarkably characteristic of Nietzsche's *Trieb* and of its effects on morality, as we see for instance in *Reflection* I. It is the *primum movens* of all human reality, the principle of intimate identity that is simultaneously the principle of alienation. 'It renders men idolaters of themselves, and it renders them tyrants over others if chance gives them the means.' Not fortuitously, it is hypostasized as the *Id* or the 'It' which governs all human activity. The 'It' is invested with a virtual characterology. It is attributed to a febrile hyperactivity, a radical selfishness (*égoïsme*). 'It never rests outside of itself and only remains in other subjects as bees on flowers, in order to make them its own.'

Above all, it is assimilated to a Machiavellian potency that is forever masked. 'Nothing is so impetuous in its desires, nothing so hidden in its designs, nothing so clever in its drives.' The evocation of the multiplicity of self-love will pass literally into Nietzsche's *Trieb*. 'Its versatilities cannot be represented, its transformations go beyond metamorphoses, and its refinements transcend chemistry.' Neither can one fathom its depths, nor pierce its gloom or its abysses. There, it is hidden to the most penetrating of eyes, and it makes a thousand turns and returns.

By that we find evidence of the unconscious character of self-love, a fundamental instinct, founded on the misrecognition of the Self or on self-mystification. 'It is hidden to the most penetrating of eyes'. As a consequence, 'it is often invisible to itself; it conceives, nourishes and grows without itself knowing a great number of affections and hatreds; it forms such monstrosities that, when they see the light of day, it misrecognizes them, or cannot resolve itself to acknowledge them.' Self-love thus takes the place of the will-to-live in the function of a grand deceiver.

> From this night whose cover gives birth to the ridiculous persuasions that it has of itself; from whence come its errors, its ignorances, its crudities and its foolishnesses on the subject of itself; from whence come the belief that its sentiments are dead when they are really only sleeping; that it imagines that it no longer desires to move from where it lies, and that it thinks it has lost the tastes it has merely sated.

But self-love has, despite its blindness, the same infallible lucidity that *Trieb* has for Nietzsche:

> But this dense obscurity which conceals itself from itself does not occlude what it sees perfectly as outside itself, and in this it is similar to our own eyes, which discover everything but are only blind to themselves. In fact, in *Trieb*'s greatest interests and most important affairs, where the violence of its desires calls everything to its attention, it sees, feels, hears, imagines, suspects, penetrates, and divines all; so that one is tempted toward the belief that each of its passions has a magic all its own.

In self-love, viscosity combines with lability. 'Nothing is as intimate or as strong as its attachments, which try in vain to break off the vista of extreme misfortunes which threaten it. Meanwhile, it sometimes does, quickly and without any effort, what at other times it cannot do with all its might, over the course of several years'. This establishes the nexus of self-love, or of Instinct, with Desire.

> We might reasonably enough conclude that it is through itself that its desires are fired, rather than by the beauty or by the merit of its objects; that its own appetite is the prize which enhances them and the paint which embellishes them; that it chases after itself, and that it follows its own whim when it pursues something that catches its fancy.' In this way we find the enunciation of the fundamental narcissism of the instinct.

La Rochefoucauld achieves his description of self-love by evoking its turbulence. 'Self-love is only a great and long-lasting agitation', which, like the sea, 'finds in the ebb and flow of its continual waves a faithful expression of the turbulent succession of its thoughts and its eternal movements.' The key to this turbulence is the *coincidentia oppositorum*. 'It is all of the oppositions; it is imperious and obedient, sincere and dissimulating, merciful and cruel, timid and audacious'. That expresses an essential characteristic of the instinct, its aptitude to free itself from contradiction, by taking in all of the oppositions, as merely so many aspects of its protean reality. Here is also the source of its fundamental perversity. 'It is bizarre, inconsistently inconsistent', in finding the more pleasure in objects, the more unexpected the use. In other words, the principles of identity and of non-contradiction are natural strangers to the instinct. 'It is only concerned to be, and provided that it is, it only wants to be its own enemy'. It is the remarkable expression of the union of the forces of life and death operating in the *Trieb*.

The essential practical consequence of this characteristic is the a-sociality of the instinct. The Other is at once an obstacle and a means, but never an end.

36 See above, in Book I, Ch. 2, 'Freudian Drive: Origins of the Concept.'
37 *Instincts and Their Vicissitudes*, GW, V, 67.
38 *GW*, V, 33–4.
39 See above, in Book I, Ch. 2, 'Nietzschean Instinct: Origins of the Concept.'
40 *GW*, V, 67.
41 *GW*, V, 68. It is a quasi-anatomical idea, linked to the primacy of space.
42 For example, the musculature in the case of the gripping drive. See below, p 154f.
43 *GW*, V, 108.
44 *Die 'kulturelle' Sexualmoral und die moderne Nervosität*, *GW*, VII, 150.
45 *GW*, XI, 327.
46 *The Disposition to Obsessional Neurosis.*
47 *GW*, XIII, 220.
48 See above, in Book I, Ch. 2, 'The Historical Paradigm of Nietzschean Instinct,' and Book I, Ch. 1, note 47.
49 Text dating from 1872, in *Le livre du philosophe*, p 117.
50 *Instincts and Their Vicissitudes*, *GW*, X, 211.
51 *GW*, X, 214.
52 *GW*, V, 67.
53 *GW*, X, 214.
54 *Psycho-Analytic Notes on an Autobiographical Account of a Case of Paranoia (Dementia Paranoides)*, *GW*, VIII, 311.
55 *GW*, XVII, 70 (Ch. II).
56 *Why War?* (1932),*GW*, XVI, 22, See also the 32nd of the *New Introductory Lectures*, 'Anxiety and Instinctual Life', in (*GW*, XV, 101).
57 This is why Nietzsche begins with a hermeneutic of morality, while Freud undertakes a therapeutic science (see below).
58 That is also why Nietzschean psychology can give the impression of anticipating psychoanalysis.

Chapter 3 Principles of the Drive

1 We will begin this time with Freud in the order of confrontation, because for him the dualism of the drives is an explicit functional requirement.
2 *The Psycho-Analytic View of Psychogenic Disturbance of Vision*
3 *GW*, VIII, 97.
4 *GW*, VIII, 97–8.
5 Refer to Schiller's formula, in the poem on *The Sages* (*die Weltweisen*): 'In expecting the philosopher to support the edifice of the world, nature sustains motion by hunger and by love'.
6 See above, p 68.
7 On the question of sexuality, see the comparison below, Bk. II, Ch. I, note 1.
8 See Ch. 2.
9 *SW*, V, 247 (Book V, § 349).
10 *SW*, V, 247–8.
11 *SW*, V, 248.
12 *Streifzüge eines Unzeitgemässen*, § 14, *SW*, VIII, 139.
13 *SW*, VI, 221 (Book III, § 6, 'On Old and New Tablets'),
14 *SW*, VIII, 139 (§ 14, 'Skirmishes of an Untimely Man').
15 *SW*, XI, 109 (§ 291, 'Cognition, Nature, Humanity').

16 *SW*, XI, 437 (§ 652).
17 *SW*, IX, 437 (§ 652).
18 *SW*, IX, 436–7 (§ 651).
19 *SW*, IX, 437 (§ 652).
20 We need to compare this theory of hunger with Nietzsche's strange preoccupation with culinary questions, as expressed in the last months of his lucid life, notably the considerations in *Ecce Homo* on the art of eating well ('Why I am so clever', § 1, *SW*, VIII, 314–18). 'Another question that interests me even more (than the religious question), and the health of humanity depends on more than on some curiosity for the theologians, and that is the question of *nutrition*. One can pose it thus: "How must one nourish oneself, in order to attain a maximum of force, or virtue . . . ?"' Hildebrandt suspected a pathological prodrome in this preoccupation (see Podach's discussion, pp 37–9). We point out a fact that confirms the reports of Basel and Jena: Nietzsche's bulimic appetite in the first months of his illness, which 'reverts continually to eating' (p 119). 'Eat with a very strong appetite' (p 122); 'the sick often eat very quickly' (p 140). This form of maniacal exaltation can be linked to the stakes of Nietzsche's reflections on nutrition and power, by revealing so many recessive forms.
21 *Beyond the Pleasure Principle*, *GW*, XIII, 41.
22 *GW*, XIII, 66, n. 1.
23 *Outline of Psychoanalysis*, *GW*, XVII, 71.
24 *GW*, XIII, 69.
25 *SW*, II, 156 (§ 7).
26 *SW*, III, 4.
27 *SW*, III, 329.
28 *SW*, III, 266.
29 *Thus Spoke Zarathustra*, *SW*, VI, 116.
30 *Twilight of the Idols*, *SW*, VIII, 139.
31 *The Will to Power*, *SW*, IX, 37.
32 *SW*, IX, 339.
33 *SW*, IX, 396.
34 *SW*, IX, 433.
35 *SW*, IX, 419.
36 *SW*, VI, 124.
37 *SW*, VII, 20 and 200; IX, 46 and 184; XI, 307.
38 *SW*, IX, 432.
39 *SW*, IX, 467.
40 *SW*, IX, 468.
41 *SW*, IX, 476.
42 See in particular *Human, All Too Human*, II, 80; *The Voyager and His Shadow*, § 185.
43 *SW*, VI, 46.
44 *SW*, VI, 47.
45 *SW*, VI, 77.
46 *On the Genealogy of Morals*, *SW*, VII, 310 (second essay, § 12).
47 Under the influence of Jung. See *Psychoanalysis and Theory of the Libido*, *GW*, XIII, 230–1.
48 In a passage added in 1915, *GW*, V, 118.
49 *Group Psychology and the Analysis of the Ego*, *GW*, XIII, 98.
50 *GW*, V, 118.
51 *GW*, V, 118.
52 *GW*, V, 119.
53 *SW*, VII, 48.
54 *SW*, XI, 95 ('Cognition, Nature, Humanity', § 246).
55 *SW*, XI, 244.
56 *SW*, IX, 433.

57 *SW*, XI, 116.
58 *The Will to Power*, I, (§ 393).
59 *SW*, II, 102.
60 *SW*, II, 595.
61 *SW*, VIII, 192.
62 *SW*, VIII, 288.
63 *SW*, X, 243.
64 *SW*, IX, 302.
65 *SW*, XI, 242.
66 *Twilight of the Idols*, *SW*, VIII, 160 (§ 38, 'Untimely Points').

BOOK II: THE THEMES

1 The precursor thematic thus forms the *centrepiece* of the comparison, to the extent that it develops the most spectacular analogies retrospectively perceived between Freud and Nietzsche, but it also functions, in our overall inquiry, to assure the passage from the fundamental problematics (Book 1) to their applications (Book 3). That is to say that we will seek to clarify the content of the relation with the aim of dissipating the profound ambiguity of the very idea of a 'precursor' as well as of verifying the elements of this rapprochement. The examination of each theme demands that we consider the complete evolution of the ensemble of Nietzschean and Freudian problematics.

Chapter 1 Love and Sexuality

1 We have already shown the libido as the principle of the drive and the sexual drives as the fundamental drives (Book 1, Ch. 3), so we are relieved from having to treat that as a theme here: to be precise, from the Freudian perspective, libido is the drive, but for our comparison it is necessary to treat it as a 'theme'.
2 *SW*, I, 47 (§ 1)
3 *Le livre du philosophe*, p 40, § 20 (by analogy with the cognitive instinct).
4 *SW*, III, 87 (Ch. II, § 98, 'Pleasure and Social Instinct').
5 *SW*, IV, 66 (Book I, § 76)..
6 *SW*, X, 290.
7 *SW*, X, 294.
8 *SW*, X, 298.
9 *SW*, X, 304.
10 *SW*, VII, 79 (Ch. 4, § 75).
11 *SW*, XI, 49.
12 *Beyond Good and Evil*, *SW*, VII, 99 (Ch. V, § 189).
13 *SW*, VIII, 181 ('What I owe to the Ancients', § 4).
14 *SW*, VIII, 344 ('Why I Write Such Good Books', § 5).
15 Op cit., p 345.
16 *SW*, XI, 149.
17 *SW*, XI, 340.
18 *SW*, XI, 461.
19 *SW*, IX, 185 (§ 255).
20 *SW*, IX, 540 (§ 805).
21 *SW*, IX, 550 (§ 800).
22 *SW*, IX, 536 (§ 815).
23 *SW*, XI, 534 (§ 799).
24 Op cit., p 535.
25 Op cit., p 536.

26 Op cit., p 539.
27 We might note the curious influence on some of certain passages in *Thus Spoke Zarathustra* as a critique of sexual conformism. Ernst Thiel, future benefactor of the Nietzsche Archives, includes in the passages critical of children and marriage ('Of Old and New Tablets', Book III, § 24), a justification for breaking off conjugal relations (cf. Peters, op cit., pp 271–2). In general, we can feel the audacity of erotic resonances in *Zarathustra*. At the same time, we can connect to the elements of a psychoanalytic diagnostic (see above, in the 'Introduction,' '"Nietzsche" in the Wednesday Seminars (2)') traces of obsessional erotic elements in Nietzsche's delirium after his collapse. In his first report, Baumann de Turin notes that 'he never ceases asking for women' (Podach, op cit., p 119); in the journal from the Sanitarium in Jena, 2 December, 1889, 'he claims to have seen tonight young ladies completely mad' (Podach, p 140). See also the evocation of the daughters of the desert in the fourth part of *Thus Spoke Zarathustra*.
28 *GW*, V, 83.
29 See above, [in Book I, Ch. 2, 'The Drive, Freud's Meta-Psychological Unity.'.
30 The moment corresponding to the introduction of the concept of narcissism, in 1910–14.
31 This expansion was also recommended by Plato. See *Freud, la philosophie et les philosophes*, pp 146–50.
32 *Introductory Lectures on Psychoanalysis*, *GW*, XI, 331 (XX, 'The Sexual Life of Human Beings').
33 *Beyond the Pleasure Principle*, *GW*, XIII, 54.
34 There is a note dating from 1925 in *Traumdeutung* which articulates this equivalence by declaring that 'psychoanalysis now readily uses' the word 'sexual"in the sense of Eros' (*GW*, II–III, 167).
35 We call attention to the tone of *Group Psychology and the Analysis of the Ego* (Ch. 4) (1921), at the very moment when the terminology of Eros comes into use (*GW*, XIII, 99). There Freud suspects 'the most distinguished terms (*vornehmeren*) of Eros and the erotic' of compensating for the negative charge of sexuality as 'something which brings shame to human nature and humiliates it'. The equivalence of usage is thus tolerable, but as a rhetorical facility it is not innocent, because 'we begin by conceding the words and end by conceding the thing'. Now, *libido* designates more adequately *the thing*, whereas with *Eros* we risk having to pay the price for *the word*. It is a tone on the whole sublimely erotic, and can be understood in a certain sense similar to the Nietzschean conception.
36 We have already located this special instinct in the vast Nietzschean herd of instincts (see above, Book II, Ch. 1, note 27) and we have noted its role in the genesis of the concept (pp 90f). But here it appears with a privilege which allows us to establish its importance.
37 *SW*, I, 119.
38 *SW*, X, 45.
39 Ibid., pp 45–46.
40 *Le philosophe*, French translation, p 41; Beck, § 20.
41 *SW*, X, 47.
42 *SW*, X, 50 and 52.
43 *SW*, X, 53.
44 *SW*, X, 50.
45 *SW*, I, 265.
46 See below, Bk. III, Ch. 2.
47 *SW*, II, 156.
48 *SW*, III, 47 (I, § 34, 'In Mitigation').
49 *SW*, III, 207 (V, § 252, 'Pleasure in Knowledge').
50 *SW*, IV, 256 (Book V, § 429).
51 *SW*, V, 219 (Book IV, § 333).
52 *SW*, V, 247.
53 *SW*, XI, 165.

54 *SW*, VII, 12 (Ch. I, § 6).
55 *SW*, V, 288.
56 *GW*, V, 95 ('Infantile Sexuality').
57 *Notes on a Case of Obsessional Neurosis*, *GW*, VII, 460.
58 *GW*, XIII, 46.
59 *Leonardo Da Vinci and a Memory of His Childhood*, *GW*, VIII, 144.
60 *The Disposition to Obsessional Neurosis*, *GW*, VIII, 450 (see below pp 233f).

Chapter 2 The Unconscious and Consciousness

1 See above, in Book I, Ch. 2, 'Instinct and Psyche.'.
2 *SW*, I, 22.
3 On this point, see *Freud, la philosophie et les philosophes*, pp 189–90.
4 Op cit., p 219, note 1.
5 *SW*, I, 123 (§ 14).
6 *SW*, II, 105.
7 *SW*, II, 451.
8 *SW*, II, 69 (§ 57).
9 *SW*, II, 16 (§ 1).
10 This is the Nietzschean conception that Adler refers to in *Entlarvungspsychologie*. See above p 43.
11 Thus we christen the primacy accorded to the Conscious. For a Freudian homology, see *Freud, la philosophie et les philosophes,* p 23–44.
12 *Daybreak*, *SW*, IV, 46 (I, § 48).
13 *SW*, V, 42 (Book I, § 11).
14 An idea which coexists in Nietzsche along with an anti-Darwinianism that conceives of evolution as the disappearance of the best; this idea will attain its fullest form in the theory of *Will to Power*.
15 *The Gay Science*, *SW*, V, 42 (Book I, § 11).
16 Ibid.
17 Ibid.
18 In that, Nietzsche remarkably anticipates the reversal that Freud will express in presenting himself as the Copernicus of the psyche (see below, p 187).
19 *The Gay Science*, *SW*, V, 253 (Book V, § 354).
20 Op cit., p 254.
21 Op cit., p 255.
22 Op cit., p 256.
23 *Beyond Good and Evil*, *SW*, VII, 9 (Ch. I, § 3).
24 *On the Genealogy of Morals*, *SW*, VII, 380 (3rd essay, § 18).
25 *SW*, X, 270 ('Psychological Observations' § 732), from the period of *Human, All Too Human* and *Daybreak*.
26 *SW*, XI, 54 ('Cognition, Nature, Humanity,' § 115), from the period of *Daybreak*.
27 For example, in *Ecce Homo*, 'Why I am so clever', § 9 (*SW*, VIII, 331).
28 *The Will to Power*, *SW*, IX, 204 (Book II, § 289).
29 Op cit., *SW*, IX, 205 (Book II, § 291).
30 Op cit., *SW*, IX, 289 (Book II, § 291).
31 Op cit., *SW*, IX, 308 (Book II, § 440).
32 Op cit., *SW*, IX, 303 (Book II, § 434).
33 Op cit., *SW*, IX, 307–8 (Book II, § 439).
34 Op cit., *SW*, IX, 331 (Book II, § 472).
35 Op cit., *SW*, IX, 347 (Book II, § 505).
36 Op cit., *SW*, IX, 334 (Book II, § 478).
37 Op cit., *SW*, IX, 346 (Book II, § 504).

38 Op cit., *SW*, IX, 450 (Book II, § 674).
39 Op cit., *SW*, IX, 358 (Book II, § 523).
40 Ibid., § 524, p 359.
41 Ibid., p 360.
42 Ibid., § 524, p 361.
43 *SW*, IX, 452 (§ 676).
44 Ibid., p 451.
45 *SW*, XI, 98 (Cognition, Nature, Humanity, § 256).
46 Ibid., § 255, p 98.
47 Ibid., § 318, p 116.
48 Ibid., § 343, p 126.
49 *The Will to Power*, *SW*, IX, 477 (Book III, § 707).
50 *SW*, XI, 106, (§ 279).
51 *SW*, IX, 481, (§ 711).
52 *SW*, XI, 308. It is the topic of point 7 of an outline of *The Will to Power*, in 'Systemwürfe und Pläne' (§ 880).
53 This is the objective of the metapsychological essay on the Unconscious.
54 See below, Book III, Ch. I.
55 *Selbstdarstellung*, *GW*, XIV, 55 (Ch. III).
56 See above, in Book I, Ch. 2, 'Instinct and Psyche.'
57 See above, p 44f.
58 *SW*, VI, 35 ('On the Despisers of the Body').
59 *The Ego and the Id*, *GW*, XIII, 262 (§ III).
60 *GW*, XIII, 258 (§ III).
61 *GW*, XIII, 251; See above, p 44f. This definition equally applies to Nietzsche's *Selbst*.
62 *SW*, VI, 35.
63 *New Introductory Lectures*, *GW*, XV, 80 (no. XXXI, 'Dissection of the Personality').
64 Ibid.
65 *Assorted Opinions and Maxims*, *SW*, III, 154 (§ 366).
66 This is the formula which closes the 31st of the *New Introductory Lectures*, *GW*, XV, 86.
67 See below, on the theory of culture, p 158.
68 In the same text, Freud in fact assigns the transformation of the Ego's organization to the aims of the therapeutic effort, 'so that it may appropriate new portions of the Id', adding that 'that is a task which is incumbent on civilization, not unlike the draining of the Zeider Zee'.
69 *The Will to Power*, vol I, Book I, § 147.
70 Op cit.
71 See *Freud, la philosophie et les philosophes*, pp 23–44.
72 See above, pp 88f and p 93f.

Chapter 3 Dreams and Symbolism

1 *SW*, I, 48 (§ 48).
2 Ibid., p 49.
3 Ibid., p 50.
4 Ibid., p 48.
5 *SW*, I, 53 (§ 2).
6 *SW*, I, 89 (§ 8).
7 *SW*, I, 61 (§ 4).
8 Ibid., p 62.
9 *SW*, III, 19 (The title of § 5, Ch. I).
10 In 1872, Edward Burnett Tylor's work, *Primitive Culture: Researches into the Development of Mythology, Religion, Art and Custom* [London], appeared, supporting the animist thesis of the origin of religion, and launching an illustrious career for the

anthropologist. Tylor maintained that primitive religion was born out of the notion of a soul, and that humans are constituted by two types of biological facts, on the one by sleep, enchantment, sickness and death; on the other by dreams and visions, which led to a representation by a separate principle, distinct from the body. Dreams figure, as for Nietzsche, as an ethnological stake of a 'psychology of religious belief.'

11 *SW*, III, 23 (The title of § 12, Ch. I).
12 *SW*, III, 24 (The title of § 13, Ch. I).
12 On this law, see below, in Book III, Ch. 2, 'Instinct and Culture.'
14 *SW*, III, 23.
15 *SW*, III, 23–4.
16 A theme dear to the Romantic conception of the dream. See below.
17 *SW*, III, 24 (§ 13).
18 Ibid., p 25.
19 This conception bears strong affinities with Schopenhauer, especially in the curious study 'Essay on the apparitions of spirits' (in *Parerga et paralipomena*, vol IV, translated into French as *Memoires sur les sciences occultes*, 1912). There, Schopenhauer maintained that the principle of reason 'must also react to dreams in a certain manner, the manner in which they are produced' [p 125]. 'Necessarily, there must be a cause which provokes these forms of dreams' [p 128]. This argument is supported by the fact that

> the brain reacts with respect to all excitations which come to it, conforming to its proper function. This function consists first of all in projecting images into space ... it later consists in making these images move in time and following the thread of causality being equally the functions of the cerebral activity proper to it. The brain, in every period, must only speak its own language; it will translate, later on, into this same language, these feeble impressions which arrive from within the body during sleep, just as it acts toward strong and distinct impressions which arrive during a waking state, from the outside via a regulated path' [pp 134–5].

See also the essay on the principle of sufficient reason. On the influence of this conception on Freud, see *Freud, la philosophie et les philosophes*, pp 179–80.

20 Ibid., pp 25–6.
21 See above, in Part One, Ch. 2, '*Traumdeutung*: The Theory of Dreams.'.
22 Ibid., p 26.
23 Ibid., p 27.
24 *SW*, III/2, p 40 (§ 76, 'Interpreting by dreams').
25 *SW*, III/2, pp 266–7 (§ 194, 'The Dream').
26 *SW*, IV, 106, Book II (§ 119, 'Experience and Invention').
27 Ibid., p 107.
28 *SW*, IV, 111 (Book 2, § 128, 'Dream and Responsibility').
29 On the importance of the thematic of dreams among the Romantics, see Albert Béguin, *l'Ame romantique at le rêve* (1939). In particular, we know of Nietzsche's interest in Jean-Paul, for whom dreams are permanent experiences (see *Choix des rêves*, published in France in 1934). Nietzsche's discourse on dreams is remarkably close to that of the Romantics on the subject. On the moral stakes, see for example the author of *La symbolique du rêve*, G.H. Schubert:

> It is by no means the most brilliant part of ourselves which is harnessed to our flesh in the form of a vegetative soul, but rather the shameful part of our poor being in fragments. We only discover it too clearly when, even for brief moments, it is freed from its chains. I am terrified when sometimes I perceive in dreams this shadowy side of myself in its true aspect (cited in Béguin, p 116).

It is a question which tormented Jean-Paul. We note equally that Béguin wrote his work in part to oppose the psychoanalytic conception of dreams with a 'richer' conception inspired by the Romantics (see p xvi), indicating in the passage the diversity of conceptions. Nietzsche, in this sense, elaborates this opposition.

30 Associating dreams with Oedipus is literally a premonition . . . .
31 *SW*, V, 170 (Book 3, § 232)
32 *SW*, VI, 205 (Book 4, 'Noon')
33 *SW*, VI, 206 (Book 3, 'Of the three evils).
34 Ibid., p 207.
35 *SW*, VII, 103 (Ch. 5, § 193)
36 *SW*, IX, 335 (Book 3, § 479).
37 *SW*, IX, 534 (Book 3, § 798).
38 See above, in Part One, Ch. 2, '*Traumdeutung*: The Theory of Dreams.'.
39 The object of Ch. VI of *Traumdeutung*, *GW*, II–III.
40 This principle is formulated at the end of Ch. II and is developed in Ch. III of Traumdeutung.
41 See § 1–2 of Ch. VI.
42 See Ch. VI, § 9, of *Traumdeutung*.
43 More than in *Traumdeutung*, it is in *Remarks on the Theory and Practice of Dream-Interpretation* (1923) that Freud puts into evidence this idea. *GW*, XIII, 304. Even in a note in *Traumdeutung*, Freud warns us not to confuse dreams any more with latent thoughts than with manifest thoughts (*GW*, II–III, 585, note 1).
44 See § of Ch. VI, *Traumdeutung*. On the link with regression, see *GW*, II–III, 551–4.
45 See above, p 190.
46 *Traumdeutung*, *GW*, II–III, 571.

BOOK III: THE STAKES

Chapter 1 Neurosis and Morality

1 *SW*, III/1, 231 (Book 5, § 289, 'Value of Illness').
2 *SW*, III/1, 263 (Ch. VI, § 299, 'Advisor of an Invalid').
3 *Assorted Opinions and Maxims*, *SW*, III/2, 153 (§ 356, 'The Usefulness of Illness').
4 *SW*, III/2, 215 (§ 78, 'Faith in Sickness as a Sickness').
5 *The Voyager and His Shadow*, *SW*, III/2, 255 (§ 174, 'Entertainment for Invalids').
6 Op cit., *SW*, III/2, 319–20 (§ 314, 'Do Not Be Ill Too Long').
7 Op cit., *SW*, III/2, 323 (§ 325).
8 *SW*, IV, 49 (Book 1, § 54).
9 Daybreak, *SW*, IV, 207 (Book 4, § 269). See below, p 167f. A curious echo of the *Herzenelend* that Freud complains about.
10 Book 4, § 409.
11 The infirm are the creators of the nether-world, 'visionaries of the beyond' (*SW*, VI, 30), despisers of the body and of the earth, whom Zarathustra calls 'weary' (p 33). In the central passage of 'Of Old and New Tablets', illness is defined by an impotence with respect to creation.
12 On this point, see our 'Réflexions critiques sur le normal et le pathologique' in *Revue d'Anthopologie médicale*, Les Nouvelles Editions de l'Université, vol I, no. 1, 1978, pp 25–58, and especially pp 54–6.
13 Letter to Fliess, 25 May 1895, op cit., p 106.
14 *SW*, VII, 257 (I, § 6).
15 *SW*, VII, 263 (I, § 10).
16 *SW*, VII, 265.
17 *SW*, VII, 266.
18 *GW*, I, 84.

19 *GW*, I, 86.
20 *GW*, I, 87.
21 *GW*, I, 90.
22 *On the Genealogy of Morals*, *SW*, VII, 318 (II, § 16).
23 *SW*, VII, 319.
24 *SW*, VII, 321 (II, § 17).
25 *SW*, VII, 372 (III, § 15).
26 *Instincts and Their Vicissitudes*, *GW*, X, 219f.
27 *GW*, X, 220.
28 *GW*, X, 219.
29 *GW*, X, 220.
30 *SW*, XI, 11 (An aphorism from the period of *Daybreak*, § 23).
31 Ibid., *SW*, XI, 12 (§ 25).
32 *The Will to Power*, *SW*, IX, 346 (Book 3, § 502).
33 Ibid.
34 *SW*, XI, 111 (An aphorism from the period of *The Will to Power*, § 211),
35 *GW*, I, 292 (IV, 'The Psychotherapy of Hysteria', § 3).
36 *GW*, I, 293.
37 Letter no. 52, op cit., pp 153–4.
38 *GW*, II–III, 544–5 (Ch. VI).
39 *Beyond the Pleasure Principle*, *GW*, XIII, 25 (§ IV).
40 *Civilization and Its Discontents*, *GW*, XIV, 426–9 (§ 1).
41 *SW*, IV, 126 (Book 2, § 140, 'Praise and Blame').
42 *SW*, VI, 179 (3rd part, 'Before Sunrise').
43 *SW*, XI, 218 (§ 688).
44 *The Genealogy of Morals*, *SW*, VII, 294 (II, § 6).
45 Ibid., II, *SW*, VII, 300 (§ 8).
46 Ibid., *SW*, VII, 302 (II, § 9).
47 Ibid. p 314 (II, § 14).
48 Ibid., p 315.
49 Literally, 'to pay in return'.
50 Ibid., pp 323–4 (II, § 19).
51 Ibid., pp 327–8 (II, § 21).
52 Ibid., p 387 (III, § 20).
53 *SW*, VIII, 307 (§ 5, 'Why I Am So Wise').
54 Book 4, II, § 1021. It is the first of the 'five Nos' by which Nietzsche defines his project of transmutation.
55 *SW*, XI, 218 (An aphorism from the period of *The Will to Power*, § 687).
56 *Heredity and the Etiology of the Neuroses* (written in French), *GW*, I, 420–1.
57 See the following chapter, p 164f.
58 *GW*, X, 276 (§ III).
59 *An Introduction to Psychoanalysis*, *GW*, XI, 344 (21st part).
60 *The Economic Problem of Masochism*, *GW*, XIII, 379.
61 *A Child Is Being Beaten*, *GW*, XII, 215 (§ V).
62 Ch. V.
63 *GW*, XIII, 282.
64 *Civilization and Its Discontents*, *GW*, XIV, 495 (VIII).
65 Ibid., p 496.
66 *GW*, IX, 176.
67 *Civilization and Its Discontents*, *GW*, XIV, 496 § VIII).
68 See the narrative on debt which locates the great 'obsessional apprehension' in the history of illness. *GW*, VII, pp 390f. The impossible payment of a debt contracted *by* the real father and *towards* the symbolic Father.
69 *The Genealogy of Morals*, *SW*, VII, 292 (II, § 4).

70 It is one of the explicit references that Freud makes to Nietzsche found in the first part of *Thus Spoke Zarathustra*, *SW*, VI, 38–41. See above, in Part One, Ch. 2, 'Character-Types: Crime and Guilt.'
71 *SW*, VI, 40.
72 We should remember that the science of criminology was just being formed at the time of Nietzsche's writing.
73 *SW*, VI, 303 (Part Four, § 9, 'The Shadow').
74 *SW*, VI, 304.
75 *SW*, III, 72 (Ch. II, § 66, 'Punishable, Never Punished').
76 *SW*, III, 96 (Ch. II, § 107, 'Unaccountability and Innocence').
77 See above, p 128f.
78 *SW*, III/2, 261 (§ 186, 'Retrogressive').
79 *SW*, IV, 47 (I, § 50, 'Faith in Intoxication').
80 *SW*, IV, 154 (III, § 187, 'From a Possible Future').
81 *SW*, IV, 172 (III, § 202, 'For the Promotion of Health').
82 *SW*, IV, 170–1.
83 *Daybreak*, *SW*, IV, 237 (IV, § 366, 'The Affliction of the Criminal').
84 *SW*, VII, 83 (IV, § 109).
85 SW, VII, 83 (IV, § 110).
86 SW, VII, 112 (IV, § 201).
87 *SW*, VIII, 89 ('The Problem of Socrates', § 3).
88 *SW*, VIII, 167 ('The Criminal and Related Types', § 45, in 'Skirmishes of an Untimely Man').
89 *SW*, VIII, 167–8.
90 Ibid, p 166.
91 Ibid, p 167.
92 *SW*, IX, 496 (III, § 739).
93 *SW*, IX, 498 (III, § 740).
94 *GW*, XIII, 282. To compare this with Nietzsche's formulae, see above, in Book III, Ch. 1, 'Guilt and Debt.'
95 *GW*, X, 390. This is the third article of *Some Character-Types Met With in Psychoanalytic Work*, 'Criminals from a Sense of Guilt', which appeared in *Imago* (IV, 1915–16).
96 Ibid, p 391. In 1926, Freud had occasion to take part in the concrete question of punishment; Emile Desenheimer, a judge in the court of Assizes had asked him to take a position on the death penalty, along with other persons. We can find Freud's position expressed in his name by Theodor Reik, a specialist on this topic in the analytic movement, in *Freud's Point of View On the Death Penalty*, reproduced in Reik's *Le besoin d'avouer* (French translation 1973, pp 399–400).
97 *SW*, I, 213 (An aphorism from the period of *The Birth of Tragedy*).
98 *SW*, III, 58 (II, § 43, 'Cruel Men as Retarded Men').
99 *SW*, IV, 22 (I, § 18, 'The Morality of Voluntary Suffering').
100 *SW*, IV, 32 (I, § 30, 'Refined Cruelty as Virtue').
101 *SW*, V, 89 (II, § 73, 'Holy Cruelty').
102 *SW*, V, 176 (III, § 266, 'Where Cruelty is Needed').
103 *SW*, VI, 242 (3rd part, 'The Convalescent').
104 *SW*, VII, 155 (Ch. VII, § 229).
105 Ibid., p 156.
106 Ibid., p 158 (§ 230).
107 See especially the second thesis.
108 *SW*, X, 269 (An aphorism from the period of *Human, All Too Human* and *Daybreak*, § 726).
109 *SW*, X, 285 (An aphorism from the period of *Thus Spoke Zarathustra*, § 859).
110 Ibid. (§ 860).
111 Ibid. (§ 861).

112 Ibid. (§ 862).
113 *SW*, XI, 38 (An aphorism from the period of *The Gay Science*, § 89).
114 *SW*, XI, 199 (An Aphorism from the period of *Thus Spoke Zarathustra*, § 570).
115 *SW*, XI, 183 (An aphorism from the period of *Daybreak*, § 455).
116 Ibid., p 260 (§ 789).
117 *Human, All Too Human*, *SW*, III, 61 (II, § 47, 'Hypochondria').
118 *Thus Spoke Zarathustra*, *SW*, VI, 172 (Third part).
119 *The Antichrist*, *SW*, VIII, 195 (§ 7).
120 See the location of reactionary effects in Freud's clinical work.
121 *Three Essays On The Theory of Sexuality* (2nd Essay), *GW*, V, 92.
122 *GW*, V, 93–4.
123 *GW*, VIII, 448.
124 *GW*, XIII, 58.
125 Cited in a letter from Freud to Putnam, 8 July 1915.
126 Ibid., in *L'introduction de la psychoanalyse aux Etats-Unis* [Paris: Gallimard], pp 219–20.
127 *Our Attitude with regard to Death* (1915), *GW*, X, 350.
128 Freud often discussed morality with Pfister, a pastor, and Putnam, the son of a pastor.
129 Letter to Pfister, 24 February 1928 (*Correspondence*, pp 178–9).
130 *Civilization and its Discontents* qualifies the 'ethical differences' between 'good and evil' as 'undeniable' (§ VI, *GW*, XIV, 470). See also below p 158f.
131 *The Will to Power*, French translation vol I, Ch. III, § 224, p 112.
132 Ibid., § 231, p 115.
133 Ibid., § 270, p 126.

Chapter 2 Culture and Civilization

1 Nietzsche, who was a professor at Basel from 1869, became friends with the author of *Reflections of Universal History*, *Italian Renaissance Culture* (1860) and *Cicero* (1855). Nietzsche also attended Burckhardt's courses on 'Introduction to Historical Studies' and on Greek civilization. See Andler, op cit., vol 1, Book 3, pp 265f.
2 *SW*, II, 195 (II, § 10).
3 *SW*, IX, 88–9 (II, § 121).
4 This is found at the end of manuscript N, 31 May, 1897: 'Incest is an anti-social act which civilization has had to renounce bit by bit in order to exist'. There follows an allusion to Overman as an 'antinomy'.
5 *GW*, VII, 149.
6 *GW*, VII, 155.
7 *GW*, VII, 167.
8 *GW*, XIV, 446 (§ III). Paragraph VII of *Civilization and Its Discontents* constitutes in a way a Freudian 'genealogy of morals'.
9 *GW*, XIV, 448–9 (III).
10 Ibid., p 457.
11 *GW*, XIV, 328 (I).
12 For the most general debasements of amorous life, see *GW*, VIII, 89 (§ 3).
13 *GW*, VIII, 91.
14 *GW*, XIV, 501 (§ VIII).
15 Ibid., p 505 (The conclusion to § VIII).
16 *GW*, XIV, 500 (§ VIII).
17 Ibid., p 501.
18 *'Civilized' Sexual Morality and Modern Nervous Illness*, *GW*, VII, 150. See also the *New Introductory Lectures*, *GW*, XV, 103.
19 We should recall that in chemistry, sublimation refers to the direct transformation of a solid to a vapour without passing through a liquid state.

20 *Human, All Too Human*, *SW*, III, 15–16 (I, § 1).
21 *SW*, X, 331 (An aphorism from the period of *Human, All Too Human* and *Daybreak*, § 1048).
22 *SW*, VII, 155 (Ch. VII, § 229).
23 *SW*, IV, 147–8 (Ch. III, § 173, 'Those Who Commend Work').
24 *SW*, I, 209 (Writing from the period of *The Birth of Tragedy*).
25 *GW*, XIV, 438 (Ch. II, note 1).
26 For Freud's philosophy, see *Freud, la philosophie et les philosophes*, pp 91–108; for Nietzsche, see above, *passim*. It is the stake and the resultant of the entire double thematic, and thus of the present comparison – rather than any particular point.
27 *GW*, XIV, 453 (Ch. III).
28 *Science and Wisdom in Conflict*, *SW*, I, 355.
29 See above, Book One, Ch. I
30 *SW*, VIII, 295 (*Foreword*, § 4).
31 See above, Book III, Ch. 1.
32 *On the Genealogy of Morals*, *SW*, VII, 390 (III, § 21).
33 See also the declarations in *The Case of Wagner*.
34 *Ecce Homo*, *SW*, VIII, 369.
35 See the letter of 12 December 1897, op cit., p 210.
36 *GW*, IV, 288 (Ch. XII).
37 *GW*, VII, 138–9.
38 *GW*, IX, 39 (Ch. II, § 2).
39 *GW*, VIII, 195 (§ V).
40 *A Seventeenth-Century Demonological Neurosis* (1923).
41 *Totem and Taboo*.
42 *My Life and Psychoanalysis*.
43 *GW*, XIV, 342 (the conclusion of § III).
44 *GW*, XIV, 354.
45 *GW*, XIV, 352–3 (§ VI).
46 *Civilization and Its Discontents*, *GW*, XIV, 422 (§ I).
47 *GW*, XIV, 461 (§ IV).
48 *GW*, VIII, 236.
49 Especially in relation to science; see below, p 263.
50 *The Birth of Tragedy*, *SW*, I, 99 (§ 10).
51 See above, on the conception of instinct, Book One, Ch. I.
52 *Human, All Too Human*, *SW*, III, 180 (IV, § 222, 'What is Left of Art').
53 *The Genealogy of Morals*, *SW*, VII, 401 (III, § 25).
54 *GW*, VIII. See our translation, op cit., p 90, and our commentary, p 174f.
55 *GW*, XI, 390.
56 *GW*, VIII, 236.
57 *GW*, IX, 91. The word used is *Zerrbild* (caricature).
58 *GW*, IX, 111.
59 *GW*, XIV, 335.
60 *GW*, XIV, 433.
61 *GW*, XV, 173 (XXXV, 'A Weltanschauung?').
63 *The Will to Power*, *SW*, IX, 548 (Book Three, § 813).
63 Ibid., p 549.
64 *Essay on Self-criticism*, *SW*, I, 31 (§ 2).
65 *The Birth of Tragedy*, *SW*, I, 128 (§ 15).
66 *SW*, I, 127.
67 *SW*, II, 435.
68 *Human, All Too Human*, *SW*, III, 207 (V, § 252, 'Pleasure in Knowledge) .
69 *SW*, III, 208–9 (V, § 256, 'Science Furthers Ability, Not Knowledge').
70 *SW*, V, 66 (I, § 37).

71 *Thus Spoke Zarathustra, SW*, VI, 275 (4th part, 'The Leech').
72 *Thus Spoke Zarathustra, SW*, VI, 275 (4th part, 'On Science').
73 See above, Book I, Ch. I.
74 *On the Genealogy of Morals, SW*, VII, 395 (III, § 23).
75 Ibid., p 401 (III, § 25).
76 Ibid., p402.
77 Ibid., p403.
78 Lou Salomé, op cit., p 2.
79 *GW*, VIII, 236.
80 *GW*, XIV, 379 (§ X).
81 Ibid., p 380.
82 *A Special Type of Choice of Object Made By Men* (part of *Contributions to the Psychology of Love I*), *GW*, VIII, 67.

Chapter 3 Therapeutics

1 A pertinent metaphor that denotes the nutritive connotation of the theory of instincts (see above, p 87).
2 Aphorism 109, Book 2, entitled 'Self-Mastery and Moderation and Their Ultimate Motive.'
3 *SW*, IV, 89.
4 Ibid., p 90.
5 Ibid., p 91.
6 Ibid., p 92. Note especially for Nietzsche his mania for pharmacopoeiae.
7 See above, pp 9f.
8 If education for Nietzsche is personal, it is because it is first off a domination over the *body*. From the Wagner period up to the pedagogy of Will to Power, institutional therapy is assimilated into a 'gymnastic'. Zarathustra articulates this when he declares that 'there is more reason in your body than in your wisest sage'.
9 In *On Psychotherapy*, a conference held at the medical college in Vienna on 12 December 1904, *GW*, V, 25. Literally, *Nacherziehung* would have to be translated as 'post-education'.
10 Ibid., p 21.
11 See also *Freud's Psychoanalytic Method*, written by Freud himself in 1904 (*GW*, V, 9). On the ethical selectivity of the cure, see especially Freud's correspondence with Eduardo Weiss (*Letters on the Psychoanalytic Practice*).
12 See *Studies on Hysteria*, Ch. 4. 'We act, insofar as we can, as instructors where ignorance has provoked some fear, by representing a world that is free, enlightened, maturely reflected upon, finally as a confessor . . . .' (French translation, p 228).
13 *Lines of Advance in Psychoanalytic Therapy* (1918), *GW*, XII, 187. See the discussion with Ferenczi.
14 An expression from a letter to Oscar Pfister, 25 November 1928. 'I would like to assign him (the analyst) a status that does not yet exist, the status of priests of *secular* souls who would have neither the need to be physicians nor the right to be priests.' (*Correspondance*, p 183).
15 We might mention, in this perspective, the strange situation of Nietzsche actualizing in himself, in the framework of his impenitent self-analysis, a homology to resistance and transference, which is expressed by the alternation of periods of hostility towards himself with those of self-praise.
16 The first book of *The Will to Power* addresses this pathology.
17 *Thus Spoke Zarathustra*, *SW*, VI, 84 (First Part, 'On the Gift-Giving Virtue').
18 Op cit., p 70 (The Old and Young Woman).
19 Op cit., p 90 (2nd part: 'Upon the Blessed Isles').

21 Op cit., p 90 (Second part: 'The Priests').
20 Ibid.
22 *The Gay Science*, *SW*, V, 231 (Book IV, § 341, 'The Heaviest Weight').
23 *Thus Spoke Zarathustra*, *SW*, VI, 27 (1st part, 'Of the Three Metamorphoses).
24 *SW*, VI, 319, (4th part, 'Of the Superior Man').
25 *SW*, VII, 226, (Ch. 9, § 287).
26 The Ego–Ideal is not, properly speaking, an apparatus; Freud reserves this function first for the 'moral conscience', then for the 'Superego'.
27 *On Narcissism: An Introduction*, *GW*, X, 161 (III).
28 The gap from the Ego to the ideal Ego is experienced, in fact, as *shame*, so that the conflict between the Ego and the Superego is experienced as *guilt*.
29 Formulated contemporary with *The Ego and the Id* (1923).
30 *Group Psychology and the Analysis of the Ego*, *GW*, XIII, 147 (Ch. XI).
31 Festivity in the sense that we find in Nietzsche's maniacal explosion following his collapse in January, 1889 (see above, 'Introduction', note 54).
32 *SW*, V, 231 (4th part, § 341).
33 Ibid., pp 231–2.
34 *Remembering, Repeating, and Working-Through (Further Recommendations On the Technique of Psycho-Analysis II).*
35 *GW*, X, 129.
36 *GW*, XIII, 249.
37 *GW*, XIII, 251 (§ II).
38 We refer to the specific experience of illumination at Sils-Maria in August, 1881.
39 Alongside this concept, for Freud there is also, it is true, a metaphor of the eternal return, significantly linked to the theme of feminine and maternal immortality – see *Jensen's Gradiva* and the small work 'Great is Diane of Ephesia' (1911, *GW*, 360–1).
40 *SW*, VI, 217 (Book III, 'Of Old and New Tablets').
41 Op cit., p 222.
42 *Michelangelo's Moses*, *GW*, X, 175 (I).
43 Op cit., II, p 190.
44 Freud imagines in effect Moses hearing the rumours of the people adoring the Golden Calf, a report of perversion.

Conclusion

1 Nietzsche expresses the real, never-filled gap between these two identities with a delirious lucidity when he confides to Burckhardt (in his letter of 5 January 1889, an irrefutable document of his madness) that 'I would be, at base, much more willingly a professor at Basel than God, but I dare not press my own selfish ambitions (*égoïsme personnel*) far enough to abandon, because of it, the creation of the world' (cited by Podach, who gives this letter its full importance, op cit., p 107). Likewise, Overbeck notes that Nietzsche in 1890 endlessly recalled 'his old position at Basel'. 'This was for me' Overbeck adds, 'a particularly striking symptom of the derangement of his brain, because I recalled how for years, before his illness, he attached such importance to the fact of his being freed from that position!' (cited by Podach, p 151). It is precisely indicative of the profound duality between Nietzsche's vocation and his historical and social situation, never totally surmounted, and reactivated by his regression.

2 The gap remains just as wide for Freud, who never fully knew whether he had in fact created an 'ideal child' or a problem child – psychoanalysis or metapsychology – which he nevertheless fiercely protected against the powers of strangers – physicians and priests of every stripe – doomed to remain a stranger opposite his own product and indecisive with respect to its own epistemological identity, which he schematizes with the aid of language borrowed from its constituent sciences. See our *Introduction à l'épistémologie*

freudienne (Ed. Payot), where we seek to begin to unravel this shared identity that speaks the language of the science of his time.

3 This is Nietzsche's definition of true originality, *The Gay Science*, *SW*, V, 175–6 (III, § 261, 'Originality').

4 *The Gay Science*, *SW*, V, 1 ('Inscription above my door').

5 Letter to Jung, 30 November 1911 (*Correspondence*, Gallimard, vol II, p 230). On the sense of property combined with an overture to other sciences, we refer to our preface to *L'intérêt de la pyschanalyse* (Retz, 1980).

6 Note the formula by which Freud presents his discovery. 'I believe that it is a question of a capital revelation, something akin to the discovery of the sources of the Nile of psychopathology'. These are the terms with which he announces his discovery to the neuropsychology society in Vienna in 1896.

7 *Constructions in Analysis*, *GW*, XVI, 45.

8 See 'The Wolf Man' (*From the History of an Infantile Neurosis*), *GW*, XII, 137 (§ VIII, note 1).

9 The letter of 21 September 1897. See above, p 19.

10 See above, in the 'Introduction,' '"Nietzsche' in the Wednesday Seminars (2).' It is a question of the text of Freud's remarks on 28 October 1908.

11 In *Les premiers psychanalystes*, vol 2, p 36.

12 On this point, see our *Introduction à l'épistémologie freudienne*, Part One, Ch. 1.

13 *On the Genealogy of Morals*, *SW*, VII, 403 (III, § 25).

14 See the beginning of *European Nihilism* (the first part of *The Will to Power*), § 1, 5°, *SW*, IX, 8.

15 See *A Difficulty in the Path of Psychoanalysis*, *GW*, XII, 7. The idea is developed in a similar fashion in the last psychoanalytic lecture, 'Analytic Therapy' (3rd part, XVIII), *GW*, XI, 294–5.

16 It is in other respects a common trope of scientific discourse in this period. See in the epilogue to our *Introduction à l'épistémologie freudienne* the study of its source (Haeckel).

17 *GW*, XII, 9.

18 [Translator's note: In the 1980–2 edition, the subtitle read 'the material status (*le statut matérial*) of the drive, in lieu of 'subject.']

19 *Freud, la philosophie et les philosophes* (1976), *Marx et la répétition historique* (1978), *Freud et Nietzsche* (1980) mark out in effect a reflection that should be read as the history of a field under construction in the sense defined here.

20 [Translator's note: In the 1980–2 edition, the phrase read 'materialist theory' (*la théorie matérialiste*) in lieu of the 'theory of the subject' (*la théorie du sujet*).]

21 On the aporias of the dialectic and non-dialectic, we refer to our contribution to the CURSA colloquium, *Dialectique et métapsychologie* (papers given at the colloquium, Ed. Anthropos).

22 The concept of repetition is a privileged scheme in this comparison. We set out to compare the materialist status of repetition and its drive-related figures in Nietzsche and Freud.

23 [Translator's note: the 1980–2 text ends at this point.]

24 See our *Freud et Wittgenstein*, op. cit.

INDEX